The Fiction of Robin Jenkins

Scottish Cultural Review of Language and Literature

VOLUME 26

The titles published in this series are listed at *brill.com/scrl*

The Fiction of Robin Jenkins

Some Kind of Grace

Edited by

Douglas Gifford
Linden Bicket

BRILL
RODOPI

LEIDEN | BOSTON

Cover illustration: *Rainbow*, by Dan Ferguson RSW RGI. Copyright The Ferguson family.

The Library of Congress Cataloging-in-Publication Data is available online at http://catalog.loc.gov
LC record available at http://lccn.loc.gov/2017005282

Typeface for the Latin, Greek, and Cyrillic scripts: "Brill". See and download: brill.com/brill-typeface.

ISSN 1571-0734
ISBN 978-90-04-33704-6 (hardback)
ISBN 978-90-04-34249-1 (e-book)

Printed by Printforce, the Netherlands

Contents

Notes on Contributors

Ingibjörg Ágústsdóttir

Ingibjörg Ágústsdóttir is Senior Lecturer in British Literature at the University of Iceland. She holds a PhD in Scottish Literature from the University of Glasgow. Her main research interests are in the field of historical fiction and contemporary Scottish literature. She has published articles and book chapters on Charles Dickens's historical novels, the historical novelist Philippa Gregory, fictional representations of Mary Queen of Scots, and the novels of the Scottish writer Robin Jenkins.

Timothy C. Baker

Timothy C. Baker is Senior Lecturer in Scottish and Contemporary Literature at the University of Aberdeen. He is the author of *George Mackay Brown and the Philosophy of Community* and *Contemporary Scottish Gothic: Mourning, Authenticity, and Tradition,* and has published widely on Scottish fiction and poetry. Forthcoming projects include a monograph on the relation between animality, suffering, and language in contemporary fiction and another on gender and space in twentieth-century women's fiction.

Linden Bicket

Linden Bicket is a Teaching Fellow in Theology and Ethics in the School of Divinity at New College, University of Edinburgh. She is the author of *George Mackay Brown and the Scottish Catholic Imagination* (forthcoming in 2017). Her work focuses mainly on patterns of faith and scepticism in modern fiction and drama, but she has also published work on fiction for children and arts-based peacebuilding. She has published articles and book chapters on George Mackay Brown, Alice Thomas Ellis, Bruce Marshall, and George MacDonald.

Gerard Carruthers

Gerard Carruthers is Francis Hutcheson Professor at the University of Glasgow. Professor Carruthers is also Principal Investigator of the AHRC project, 'Editing Robert Burns for the 21st Century', which underpins the first phase of the new Oxford University Press edition of the Works of Robert Burns for which he is General Editor. He is author of *Scottish Literature, a Critical Guide* (2009), is Co-Editor (with Liam McIlvanney) of *The Cambridge Companion to Scottish Literature* (2012) and has published extensively on twentieth-century as well as eighteenth-century Scottish writers.

Cairns Craig

Cairns Craig is Glucksman Professor of Irish and Scottish Studies at the University of Aberdeen. He has published widely on Scottish and modernist literature, including *Yeats, Eliot, Pound and the Politics of Poetry* (1982), *Out of History: Narrative Paradigms in Scottish and English Culture* (1996) and *The Modern Scottish Novel* (1999). His most recent book is on Ian Banks's *Complicity* (2002). He was general editor of the four-volume *History of Scottish Literature* (1987–89) and general editor of the determinations series published by Edinburgh University Press from 1987–97.

Douglas Gifford

Douglas Gifford has been Emeritus Professor and Senior Research Fellow in the Department of Scottish Literature at the University of Glasgow since 2005. He was previously Chair and Head of the Department of Scottish Literature. His publications include the studies *James Hogg, Gunn and Gibbon, The History of Scottish Literature: Nineteenth Century* (ed.), *A History of Scottish Women's Writing* (ed., with Dorothy McMillan), and *Scottish Literature in English and Scots* (ed., with Dunnigan and McGillivray). From 1993 till 2015 he was Honorary Librarian, (for the Faculty of Advocates) of Walter Scott's Library at Abbotsford.

Michael Lamont

Michael Lamont is a lawyer and independent researcher.

Margery Palmer McCulloch

Margery Palmer McCulloch has published widely on twentieth-century Scottish literature. She was co-editor of *Scottish Literary Review* from 2005–2013 and is currently Honorary Senior Research Fellow at Glasgow University working on a joint biography of Edwin and Willa Muir, research which was funded by a Leverhulme Emerita Fellowship from 2013–15. In addition to earlier critical studies of Neil M. Gunn and Edwin Muir, her recent books include *Modernism and Nationalism* (2004), *Scottish Modernism and its Contexts* (2009), and the co-edited *Edinburgh Companion to Hugh MacDiarmid* and *Scottish and International Modernisms* (both 2011). She has contributed a chapter on Scottish Modernism to the recent *Oxford Handbook of Modernisms* (2010) and one on Hugh MacDiarmid to Wiley Blackwell's *A Companion to Modernist Poetry* (2014) as well as comprehensive bibliographical articles for MacDiarmid and Muir to Oxford University Press's online bibliography project (2012).

Isobel Murray

Isobel Murray is Emeritus Professor in English at the University of Aberdeen. Her work includes definitive editions of Wilde, a critical biography of Jessie Kesson (which won the Saltire Award) and three volumes of interviews, *Scottish Writers Talking*.

Glenda Norquay

Glenda Norquay is Professor of Scottish Literary Studies at Liverpool John Moores University. Her PhD thesis at the University of Edinburgh was on moral absolutism and realism in the novels of Robin Jenkins, Robert Louis Stevenson and Muriel Spark. Author of *Robert Louis Stevenson and Theories of Reading* (2007), she maintains her interest in Stevenson and is currently editing *St Ives* for the EUP edition of Stevenson's Collected Works. She has published widely on twentieth-century Scottish fiction and edited and contributed to *The Edinburgh Companion to Scottish Women's Writing* (2012).

Alan Riach

Alan Riach is Professor of Scottish Literature at the University of Glasgow. He is the General Editor of the multi-volume Carcanet Press *Collected Works of Hugh MacDiarmid*, including the *Selected Poems* (1994). He is the author of *Hugh MacDiarmid's Epic Poetry* (1991), *The Poetry of Hugh MacDiarmid* (1999) and the co-editor of *The Radical Imagination: Lectures and Talks by Wilson Harris* (1992), *Scotlands: Poets and the Nation* (2004), *The Edinburgh Companion to Twentieth-Century Scottish Literature* (2009), *Lion's Milk: Turkish Poems by Scottish Poets* (2012) and *The Smeddum Test: 21st-century Poems in Scots* (2013).

David S. Robb

David S. Robb is a Research Fellow in English at the University of Dundee, where he had been a Senior Lecturer. His work as both teacher and writer has been mainly concerned with Scottish writing of the nineteenth and twentieth centuries, and he is, in particular, the author of important studies of George MacDonald and of the twentieth century poet Alexander Scott. A book on Stevenson's fiction is due to be published shortly. He has been both Secretary and President of the Association for Scottish Literary Studies. He is currently a member of the Saltire Society's Literature Committee.

Stewart Sanderson

Stewart Sanderson recently completed a PhD in Scottish Literature at the University of Glasgow. Twice shortlisted for the Edwin Morgan Poetry Award, in 2015 he received an Eric Gregory Award.

Bernard Sellin

Bernard Sellin is Emeritus Professor at the University of Nantes. A former President of the French Society for Scottish Studies, he is the author of *The Life and Works of David Lindsay* (1981) and has published widely on twentieth-century Scottish fiction. He also edited *Voices from Modern Scotland: Janice Galloway, Alasdair Gray* (2007) and *Écosse: l'identité nationale en question* (2009).

In Memory of Gavin Wallace
(27 May 1959–4 February 2013)

This book was inspired and enthusiastically supported by Gavin Wallace, Literature Director of the then Scottish Arts Council and then as Portfolio Manager for Literature for Creative Scotland till his death in February 2013. Gavin was friend to and respected by innumerable Scottish writers whose work he had helped to publish and promote, and who miss hugely his literary judgement, as well as his humanity and humour. The author James Robertson wrote and delivered this poem at his funeral.

These Tall Trees

For Gavin Wallace (27 May 1959–4 February 2013)

When you lay down in the middle of the wood,
may there have been some closing peace.
May the storm have eased and the downpour ceased,
and if it was dead of night may these tall trees
have let some kind moonlight slip through
to comfort you.

Remember how once in a book there were men
who climbed such trees and gathered the cones
to save and sow?
They did their work, and look –
the forest has grown.

And you did yours, and we walk the paths
you made for us. It will soon be spring,
and the trees will be full of birds at song,
and the forest floor a riot of flowers.
You let them sing, you let them seed.
And although you have left us now
they will not go: we will not let them go.

So when we hear those gladdening songs
and see those bonnie blooms,
we'll know you too were here.

And maybe even, now and again,
we'll catch a glimpse of you, old friend,
moving with grace and ease, like a deer,
in your place, in the strong, quiet comfort
of these tall trees.

James Robertson

The Range and Achievement of Robin Jenkins: An Introductory Overview

Gavin Wallace and Douglas Gifford

Brief Biography

Little is known of the man behind the writer, Robin Jenkins.[1] He kept himself at a distance from publishers, journalists, other writers, and admirers. He was never anxious to appear at 'meet the author' sessions, although he would give interviews – on fiction, rarely on himself. Nor did he review other people's novels, on the ground that it was hard enough to write his own.

John Robin Jenkins was born on 11 September 1912 (intriguingly, the same birthdate and location as Gregor McLeod of *Childish Things* (2001)) in Flemington, a mining village between Cambuslang and Hamilton, where his father worked in the steel industry. Before the boy was two years old the Great War broke out and his father joined the army. Four years later he came back, but the trenches had ruined his health. He died of rheumatic fever at the age of thirty. By then his son was nearly seven, old enough to realise that 'the land fit for heroes' could conceal brutality and injustice, perhaps initiating a sense of the destructiveness in human life that was to pervade all of Jenkins's work.

His young mother was left on her own to bring up four children, working as a cook and housekeeper to look after her family. A scholarship enabled Jenkins in 1926 to attend prestigious Hamilton Academy. This is the matter of Jenkins's second novel, *Happy for the Child* (1953), dedicated to his own children. Arguably the main character, called John like the author, reflects Jenkins's early situation; a bright young boy, as clever at arithmetic as at football, but also of a sensitive and brooding nature, who resents the humiliation of poverty. The family did not attend church, though he described his grandfather as a 'Protestant freethinker', and a big influence. (Jenkins has also recorded that as a boy he went round various churches 'trying them all out' though 'I never tried the Catholics [...] Because the Catholics were a breed apart'.)[2]

---

1   The editors are grateful to Bernard Sellin for providing much of the biographical information.
2   Isobel Murray, ed., 'Robin Jenkins', in *Scottish Writers Talking 3* (Edinburgh: John Donald, 2006), pp. 101–146 (p. 105). See also Ingibjörg Ágústsdóttir's interview 'A Truthful Scot', in *Scotland 1* (Autumn 1999), pp. 13–22.

When asked by Murray regarding the influence and help of his schoolteachers, Jenkins sharply replied –'Absolutely none! The very opposite! My experience of teachers was discouragement upon discouragement!'[3] Yet childhood was also, in his own words, 'a time of wonder', of football and games, in spite of the effects of war and of the Great Depression. Flemington stayed with Jenkins for the rest of his life, suggesting why, in novels such as *Happy for The Child, The Changeling, Guests of War, A Love of Innocence, A Would-be Saint*, and *Fergus Lamont*, he has depicted childhood with such sensitivity, understanding – and affection. Like so many modern Scottish novelists Jenkins felt strong kinship with the working class, so that when dealing with aristocracy or even the middle classes, his treatments tend to be negative. 1926 was also the year of the General Strike. Although the Strike is rarely mentioned in his novels, this prolonged period of adversity further confirmed Jenkins's sense of the injustice of the social system and the need for ordinary workers to stick together in hard times. The violence associated with the Strike strengthened Jenkins's movement towards pacifism, and his later conscientious objection to war.

After completing secondary school, Jenkins went on to Glasgow University and Teacher Training College, a period he remembered with sardonic disappointment at what he saw as an overly rigidly academic educational system. 'I detested my university days. Disliked them tremendously!'[4] Yet he graduated as MA in English literature in 1936, going on to teach in schools in Glasgow's East End until the outbreak of war in 1939. By this time Jenkins was a committed pacifist. The growing pacifist Peace Pledge Union movement in Britain was strong in Scotland and Jenkins applied for registration as a conscientious objector. Since a common tribunal decision was to exempt the objector from military service on the condition that work of national importance was undertaken, from 1940 to 1946 Jenkins was to work for the Forestry Commission in Argyll, just south of Tarbert, Loch Fyne. (All this is echoed in the experience of Gavin Hamilton of *A Would-Be Saint*, while conscientious objection is a recurrent issue in his fiction from his very first book, *So Gaily Sings the Lark* in 1950 to *A Would-Be Saint* in 1978; it is the core of one of his greatest novels, *The Cone-Gatherers* (1955)). The work in Argyll, despite the consolations of working in one of the most beautiful areas of Scotland, was hard, planting trees and walking for miles in all weathers – yet years later, Jenkins told Isobel Murray

3 Murray, 'Robin Jenkins', p. 108.
4 Ibid., p. 109. Jenkins stresses his deep disappointment in his University of Glasgow education. (He also detested his Teacher Training College.) When asked by Murray regarding his outstanding memory of his Glasgow university days, he tells of running through the bitterly cold river Kelvin with the university's cross-country club! (pp. 114–115).

in her interview that that he had enjoyed working with forestry and forestry workers. This experience, and the beauty of the west of Scotland, pervades many of his Scottish novels.

In 1946 he returned to teaching in Riverside school in Glasgow's working class East End area where his teaching ability was severely put to the test. Yet this period produced his first five novels, culminating in *The Cone-Gatherers* (which won the Frederick Niven Literary Award in 1955) and *Guests of War* (1956). In 1955 he took up a post for two years in Dunoon Grammar School, in the Argyllshire which he had come to love during the war. One of his finest novels originates from this period; *The Changeling* of 1958 tells of a would-be idealistic school class teacher who takes a slum boy from the dirt and misery of his working class ghetto for a holiday near Dunoon from Glasgow and the corruption, with tragic results. *The Changeling* confirmed Jenkins's preoccupation in fiction with deprivation, particularly that of children.

Jenkins was by now established as one of the best novelists in Scotland and Britain. Up to this point he had insisted on writing about Scotland, arguing that he had to write about the people he knew best; yet, possibly through a disillusion and condemnation of aspects of Scottish society, reflected in novels like *The Thistle and the Grail* (1954) and *The Missionaries* (1957), he was now to make a complete break with Scotland. He taught in Kabul, Afghanistan, from 1957 to 1959; in Barcelona from 1959 to 1961, and finally in Sabah, formerly North Borneo from 1963 to 1968, the longest and the most enjoyable of his spells abroad.

The result was seven novels and a collection of short stories, all set abroad. Most of them have emigrant Scots or Englishmen as central figures, which gave Jenkins the opportunity to satirise his fellow expatriates and the vulgarity and pretensions of western culture when compared to these so-called 'backwater countries' – outstandingly in the Afghanistan of *Dust on the Paw* (1961), one of his most ambitious novels.

After his return in 1968 Jenkins taught for a further two years in Dunoon, living in his hillside house at Toward, next to the village of Innellan. He also returned to writing about Scotland (although many later novels had foreign settings). Among these later Scottish novels are the grimly satiric *A Very Scotch Affair* (1968), the partly autobiographical *A Would-Be Saint* (1978); and the ambitious, ambiguous and complex *Fergus Lamont* (1979). In 1988 Jenkins lost his wife May; her death led him to write poetry for the first time.[5] His son Colin died in 1992. Jenkins was awarded the OBE in 1999, while in 2002 he received the Andrew Fletcher of Saltoun Award for Lifetime Achievement from the

---

5   Jenkins's poetry is listed in the Further Reading section.

Saltire Society. He died aged ninety-two, in February 2005, leaving his two daughters Anne and Helen.

Jenkins and Scottish Fiction

Jenkins has gone on record to say that he does not acknowledge previous Scottish or English writers as influences, although he admires Scott and Stevenson.[6] (His courses in the thirties at Glasgow University would offer little Scottish literature).

At the beginning of the twentieth century there were two traditions in Scottish fiction. Jenkins would know and dislike the popular sentimental novels of the 'Kailyard' school – but he also knew George Douglas Brown's grimly negative *The House with the Green Shutters* (1901). This bleak view of Scottish community was continued in Patrick McGill's savage *Children of the Dead End* and *The Rat-Pit* (1914, 1915). This anti-Kailyard view reaches its height in Ian Niall's *The Wigtown Ploughman* (1939), with its presentation of the violent, drunken, unthinking wife-beater Galloway ploughman Andy Walker. However, the novel was also written specifically in savage contrast to and reversal of the values of the movement in literature of the 1920s and thirties calling itself the 'Scottish Renaissance'. 'Would you have me tell you a fairy tale', asks Niall (born John McNeillie) in his Preface to his grimly realistic novel.[7]

Briefly, the essence of this literary 'Renaissance' was a desire to rediscover an older and essentially rural Scottish identity. The work of poets and novelists like 'Hugh MacDiarmid', Neil Gunn, Lewis Grassic Gibbon, Eric Linklater, Sorley Mclean and many others sought to reawaken a sense of lost and 'essential' Scottish identity through reviving Scots languages, folk tradition and mythology in literature, and through emphasising enriching human communion with landscape.[8] (In these respects its ideology drew inspiration from Yeats and his

---

6   See the interview with Isobel Murray.

7   John McNeillie, *The Wigtown Ploughman* [1939] (Wigtown: G.C. Books Ltd, 1991), introductory p. 3. This preface anticipates the post-war challenge implicit in Jenkins's essay 'Why I decided Scotland must be seen through fresh and truthful eyes' which demonstrates a similar agenda, one which challenges the central and essentialist rural mythology of Gunn, Gibbon and Linklater and 'Renaissance' fiction. Robin Jenkins, 'Why I decided Scotland must be seen through fresh and truthful eyes', *Glasgow Herald*, 12 October 1982, p. 11.

8   For a fuller account of 'Scottish Renaissance' in literature, see: Douglas Gifford, 'Remapping Renaissance in Modern Scottish Literature' in Gerard Carruthers, David Goldie and Alastair Renfrew, eds., *Beyond Scotland: New Contexts for Twentieth Century Scottish Literature* (Amsterdam and New York: Rodopi, 2004), pp. 17–38; and relevant chapters in Douglas Gifford,

emphasis on 'the Great Memory' in the preceding Irish Literary Revival, as well as Carl Gustav Jung's concept of a collective unconscious). The 'Renaissance' believed that tradition, legend and myth, as expressed and carried in older language, could regenerate, enrich, and recover an older and essential Scottish identity for the future (thus tying in with the inter-war years of the movement in political Scottish nationalism).

The Second World War, together with Britain's post-war poverty, changed the Scottish literary scene drastically. Post-war 1950s writers, led by Jenkins, reacted strongly against what they saw as a 'Renaissance' preoccupation with Scotland's rural essentialism and past and its irrelevance to the harsh economic realities of post-war industrial economic recession. Jenkins was not alone in this deconstructive period; the fiction of James Kennaway (outstandingly *Tunes of Glory* in 1956), and Muriel Spark's *The Prime of Miss Jean Brodie* of 1961, share Jenkins's pervasive satire on Scottish iconography.

Indeed, Jenkins's writing from 1950 on can be seen as a response, if a negative one, to Scottish fiction (and literature generally) of the preceding half century, and in particular to the fiction of the so-called 'Renaissance' in poetry, fiction and drama running through the 'twenties', 'thirties', and 'forties'. It is this essentialist rural rather than urban ideology which would be dramatically challenged after 1950 by Jenkins and others.

The Early Novels; a Chronological Summary

It may be argued at this point that Jenkins frequently sets his fiction in rural settings. Yet these settings are almost invariably set against the city origins of their protagonists; and the contrast is always meant to satirise and dispel any illusions the reader may have regarding 'escape' to the conventional verities and consolations of countryside and nature, as in Jenkins's first novel.

So Gaily Sings the Lark (1950) is the story of David Sutherland, an industrial worker seeking escape from his Lanarkshire mine. It might at first seem to echo Neil Gunn's *Wild Geese Overhead* (1935), Gunn's account of a Glasgow journalist seeking escape from harsh slum realities. Jenkins's title, additionally, echoes, and then satirises the popular music hall song, 'The Uist Tramping Song', (with its chorus, 'So gaily sings the lark') and its hymn of release to

---

Sarah Dunnigan and Alan MacGillivray, eds., *Scottish Literature in English and Scots* (Edinburgh: Edinburgh University Press, 2002).

the country.[9] Yet where the song and Gunn's journalist finds rural redemption, Jenkins's miner, far from finding fulfilment in rural escape, finds instead that Argyllshire, despite its natural beauty, has just as much ugly complexity of human relations as anything in the industrial Lowlands.

This was followed by a much grimmer picture in *Happy for the Child* (1953). Its title mocks the Kailyard sentiment of the old folk-song refrain 'home then was home, happy for the child', presenting an unremittingly pessimistic account of Scottish urban poverty in its evocation of dreary lives – mainly those of two contrasting protagonists, the one a self-torturing but brilliant schoolboy, the other a crass guttersnipe. Between their extremes lie the many positions of self-deluding humanity which Jenkins will go on to anatomise even more perceptively. Parents and sisters, teachers and middle-class employers, are shown as victims of their prejudices and guilt, in a Lowland Scotland devoid of the consolations of landscape beauty or human grace – although, as always in this early fiction, glimmers of human goodness fitfully illuminate the moral twilight. *The Thistle and the Grail* (1954) was even more satirical about Lowland Scotland in its picture of Drumsagart, a blighted small industrial town (based on Rutherglen) and its investment of all its damaged hopes for the Scottish Cup final success of its football team – the 'Thistle' of the title, as Drumsagart Thistle strives for The Junior Scottish Cup, the town's holy grail. Two characteristics of modern Scotland are treated ironically here – economic depression and football worship; while the events are seen through the first of a recurrent figure in Jenkins's work, that of the team manager Rutherford, who can be read as either a suffering saint or a whining hypocrite – he may even be something of both.

This began a long series of complex and morally ambiguous novels, one of the greatest of which is *The Cone-Gatherers* (1955), the harrowing account of the hatred of a gamekeeper, Duror, for the two cone-gatherers posted on his estate during the war. The two are brothers, one a simpleton dwarf with a beautiful face and natural kindness towards all created things. In his trees, Calum the innocent is at one with birds, skies, nature – his deformity cancelled out as he climbs confidently to the highest places. Duror hates him because his own mind is by now poisoned by his own deformed life. The end, both tragic and hopeful, is typical of Jenkins's enigmatic juxtapositioning of despair and hope. The reader is left to wonder how Jenkins can produce such a hint of human grace from such bleak evidence – and to realise that virtually none of the perceptions or epiphanies of Jenkins's characters or endings can be taken at face

---

9   The popular music-hall song, 'The Uist Tramping Song', is clearly the origin for Jenkins's title, though Jenkins reverses the song's anticipation of a happy outcome for the journey.

value, but must instead be placed within the author's detached and ironic view of humanity as a spectrum of self-delusion, in an inscrutable universe, with Jenkins leaving only the faint glimmerings of the possibility of human grace as amelioration of human fallibility.

This was followed by *Guests of War* (1956), which perhaps of all Jenkins's novels most strongly repudiates previous 'Renaissance' fictions. Bell McShelvie is a middle-aged, country born woman who is evacuated with Glasgow school-children from the Gorbals district of Glasgow during the war. Jenkins makes the war the point of clarification for her and for us that older romantic ideologies are delusive anachronisms. Bell and her simple but innocent son Sammy go with eight hundred others to Langrigg, a town like Biggar or Peebles. There, Bell makes two discoveries; that her nostalgic memories of her original green places don't stand up to the actualities of Langrigg's snobberies, gossip and inability to cope; and that, in setting up a hostel, she has the qualities of leadership which town officials lack. The novel is one of Jenkins's richest in its varieties of character and moral perspective. No-one, not even Bell (or with the exception of tragic Sammy?) is clear-cut in goodness or badness. The novel's main candidate for hero, the enthusiastic and idealistic teacher Edgar Roy (disliked by Bell), who seems to work hard for the incoming children, if not revealed as having feet of clay, is shown to have mixed motives – to bomb German children or die? Jenkins mocks his romantic idealism, especially in his love affair with a local aristocrat – although, as so often with his would-be do-gooders, the reader is left torn between respect and suspicion, to wonder if the grace of true goodness can ever be found.

The novel constantly reverses 'Renaissance' conventions. Bell turns out to be no Chris Guthrie (the heroine of Gibbon's *A Scots Quair*, 1932–34) content beneath her standing stones; instead, Bell fails to climb the mountain, Brack Fell, which she has dreamed of, in a symbolic ending which implies that escape to Langrigg, the country, and landscape cannot be enough. Her innocent son Sammy is killed in this green place; her dreams fade; and she turns down the chance to stay on as warden of the hostel she has successfully piloted. In her climb down the darkening mountain, and her return to her husband in slum Glasgow, Jenkins embodies what he sees as the real choices to be made in his post-war Scotland.

These early novels continued to explore and satirise traditional Scottish beliefs and values in *The Missionaries* (1957), which mocks the secular 'missionaries', the officials who heavy-handedly try to evict the 'real' missionaries, a fanatical sect who are squatting in a holy Hebridean island. Who are most false? Or are there perhaps real miracles and grace to be found? And the darkest of Jenkins's novels so far comes with *The Changeling* (1958), with its account of well-intentioned but ill-thought-out idealism, in which a Glasgow schoolteacher takes a slum boy with his own family on holiday down the Clyde – only to find that naive goodness can end in horrible tragedy. Again Jenkins adapts traditional ideas, here that of the folk legend of the change-ling, from its traditional rural location as the substitution by the fairies of a fey weakling for a healthy human child, so that the sensitive slum boy Tom is twisted from innocence into a demonic intruder by the well-meaning but self-deluding teacher and family, failed Samaritans who show the boy prospects and beauty that can never be his, since he must return to his slum family. This first great period of creativity ended with an even more anguished novel, *Love is a Fervent Fire* (1959), where Jenkins examines a nasty Highland community given over to lechery, gossip, and yearning for lost innocence. Again the war marks the final decline; the protagonist is an incomer seeking to atone for his war actions, but marred by drink and disillusion, and hated by those he naively tries to help. As with *The Cone-Gatherers*, the abrupt shift from despair to hope may not convince all readers. In any event, the novel suggests an author who has himself come to a point of crisis.

The Middle Period: Exile and the 'Foreign' Novels

Given his disillusioned view of Scotland, it comes as no surprise to find Jenkins leaving Scotland in 1957, virtually until 1968, to teach in Afghanistan, Spain and Borneo. And while these new locations allowed Jenkins to encounter new cultures and to find release from Scottish restrictions, they did not eliminate Scotland from his fiction; instead, it helped him create a series of novels in which he explored his own perceptions of his native country through a series of protagonists – complex, well-meaning but damaged Scots who, like himself, are forced to make comparisons of their own and the very different cultures of these three locations. The confused nature of being Scottish is just as much at the forefront of these novels as the other great theme, that of the moral hypoc-risy and injustice of imperialism.

Some Kind of Grace (1960) fittingly opens the foreign quest. John McLeod hunts through the mountains of Afghanistan for the people he believes have murdered his compatriots Donald Kemp and Margaret Duncan. What he discovers overturns all his preconceptions; the Scots are not dead, but living through choice among the Afghans, and refusing to return, for religious rea-sons which he cannot understand. The Afghans and their leaders are no mur-derers; poor and backward, they show him a dignity and grace which shames him, and inspires him far more than his compatriots. This first 'foreign' novel exploited the thriller genre; the next, *Dust on the Paw* (1961) is one of Jenkins's most ambitious. Jenkins knew Afghanistan now, and its tensions arising from Russian-American imperialist ambitions. He mocks older British imperialism first. The perspective is initially that of the British embassy, viewing Afghan affairs with superiority and condescension. But Jenkins does not stereotype; as in so many of these novels, there are decent human beings associated with embassy, like Howard Moffat, deeply committed to the Afghans, angry at embassy prejudice. But he has a hypocritical secret in his deeply concealed racism, in his self-denied reason for not allowing his beautiful and utterly honest Chinese wife Lan to have children. Her grace is to know his real reasons and yet to forgive. Set against this relationship is that of another idealist, Afghan Abdul Wahab, and his English wife-to-be, the disabled Laura, which brings Moffat's hidden racism to the surface, as he attempts to blacken Wahab in the eyes of the authorities. He fails; the poisoner is himself poisoned, yet somehow, and convincingly, through his wife's immense love and grace, a charity all the more impressive because she herself has suffered more than any of them (losing her sister in the Chinese revolution), Moffat is redeemed. Lan becomes pregnant, with Moffat becoming Wahab's friend, and welcoming Laura – who shames the embassy with her quiet self-possession and dignity. And around this ironic pairing of opposites Jenkins places rich supporting patterns, with the embassy snobs contrasting to their discredit with natives; Oxford-educated, liberal and coolly effective Prince Naim, or local officials like the education minister and police chief. Does Jenkins symbolise the finding of grace and a kind of communal human transcendence in this novel with the final moment when the shaddry (the baggy purdah garment which conceals Muslim women) is abolished and the police chief's wife is revealed as a glorious beauty? Or, as Glenda Norquay will suggest later in this volume, might this moment also be read as less than liberating?

In Jenkins's work, communal affirmation is not often to be repeated. In *The Tiger of Gold* (1962) Sheila McNair journeys to self-discovery through India, following her love for Prince Chandra – who is, in his wealth and beauty and power, the tiger of the title – although the title carries other rich symbolic resonances. As India reveals its contrasting squalor, Sheila reveals to us her shame at her own superficial superiority; she finds humility, and reverses her estimates of those around her, rejecting Chandra, and finding decency and humanity in the apparently crude and materialist American family with whom she travels. And throughout, as in all these foreign novels, Jenkins manages to juxtapose Scottish and foreign experience in perceptive and liberating ways, finding both worth and defect in the national traditions and identities of Scotland, Afghanistan, India – and in his next novel, Spain. *The Sardana Dancers*

(1964) reflects Jenkins's two years spent there, and his comparison of the harsh treatment of the Catalans by central government with relations between Scotland and England at home. As with the previous novel, self-discovery does not go along with personal happiness and fulfilment. Jenkins contrasts two expatriate painters, one upper-class English and the other working-class Scottish, the first merely competent, the second a genius. Their relationship, and their relationships with Catalans and Scots, ultimately leads them both to varying degrees of self-knowledge and release – but hardly to happiness, since both are too much the victim of their national backgrounds.

After his return to Scotland in 1968, Jenkins continued to write 'foreign' fiction. (These later foreign novels and stories are mainly set in Borneo, and for continuity are discussed here, even though they post-date the 1968 return.) *The Holy Tree* (1969) is perhaps the novel most fiercely critical of Empire and its patronising yet ultimately dismissive treatment of native talent. Once again, the title symbolises ambivalently; the tree is at once the poisoned tree of Western learning and culture, and the Oxford scholarship which native Michael Eking yearns to attain, and the ambition which his imperial teachers betray; but it is also the very real and sacrificial holy tree of his people, beneath which he is killed – or sacrificed? – by them, for what they perceive as his betrayal of his roots and race – or, as a propitiation of their gods? Yet another innocent is sacrificed in *The Expatriates* (1971), because of the mixture of arrogance and guilt of expatriate businessman, Ronald McDonald, who has returned to Scotland, and who forces his former Malaysian housekeeper lover to give up their child to be brought up in Scotland with his new wife. In the suicide of the girl's mother Jenkins again controversially finds a kind of redemption and grace in the chastening of the McDonalds.

A Far Cry From Bowmore (1973) is Jenkins's first collection of short stories, the enigmatic title story itself exemplifying Jenkins's unique juxtapositioning of Scottish and Eastern values and settings, in a way which honours the foreign and satirises the Scottish. A pious and priggish Scot (of a kind traditional in Scottish fiction since Scott and Hogg) is persuaded to go up country in Borneo to visit a dying fellow Scot. The reader's expectations, implied in the title, of exile calling nostalgically to exile (Bowmore is a village on Islay), are typically turned around, as yet again a kind of grace is discovered by Hugh Macpherson as he discovers the immense dignity and love of his fellow Scot's Bornean wife; and, through fellow Scot MacArthur's dying words, MacPherson is enabled to see the worth of his own wife. There is unusual affirmation in this story, and a hint of the supernatural in the uncanny way the local people know that the man has died. Macpherson learns to allow Eastern religion its place, as he re-aligns his values, guided by the simplicity and vision of characters like Dr Lall and

MacArthur's wife, and, it must be conceded, the residual goodness of some fellow Scots. But it is the Scots who are mainly in need of such epiphany; and clearly Jenkins locates a higher worth in his East Asian characters, a location which separates him from so many of contemporary Western writers, and places his work well before the critical and moral revisions of the post-colonial movement. Equally clearly, the story juxtaposes the ridiculous with the profound, MacArthur's trivial last words with Macpherson's vision, in ways which allow the reader to keep the possibility of some final huge irony; is the far cry, which could be seen as that of Macpherson as well as MacArthur, for human spiritual redemption, indeed a far and lonely cry of humanity into the void? More simply and typically, another story here, 'Imelda and the Miserly Scot', reveals Jenkins's disgust with the egotism and dour rectitude of the Scot abroad, and – as Jenkins will increasingly show – the resilience and the drive of the Asian women who fascinate these Scots, and who represent the movement to independence of their colonised peoples. Andrew McAndrick from Paisley is the womanising dentist of Api in Borneo. The latest in his conquests, a beautiful Asian girl, rejects his condescending domination, and kills him – the blowpipe which she uses, and her reversion to her roots, symbolising the way in which the East will reject Western imperialism.

These recurrent themes and patterns in the foreign fiction are emphatically reiterated in two strikingly similar novels separated by twenty-one years, *A Figure of Fun* (1974) and *Leila* (1995). As always, they show Jenkins's hatred of British arrogance and complacency. The later novel is in some ways a rewrite of the earlier. Both are set in Borneo; both centre on a Scotsman with divided loyalties – a deputy director of education, a deputy principal of a training college – and a tendency to pomposity and an idealism laughed at by other expatriates. Both novels make their uncertain colonialist choose between fundamentally opposite women as wife; on one hand, a practical Scottish nurse, on the other, a beautiful and politically idealistic Bornean woman. The position of both Scotsmen is compromised by their high standing in expatriate society and their links through clubs, golf, yachting, and the like with the powerful Bornean leaders whom their Bornean lovers oppose. These similarities emphasise how deeply matters of moral choice pre-occupy Jenkins with an intensity beyond that of any other modern Scottish author. In a sense, the foreign settings of these novels merely emphasise and polarise moral issues which originate in Jenkins's Scottish experience. The basic questions are to do with whether one chooses to accept social hypocrisy, injustice and comfortable privilege, or whether one asserts fundamentals of Christian-rooted morality, but with the resultant price of being regarded as naive and untrusted and as a pretentious betrayer of Western values. As in so many novels, Jenkins leaves it to the reader to allocate praise or blame to his would-be idealists. His men and women of vision, for all their apparent humility and charity, may be self-deluding and self-justifying sinners, latter-day believers in modern versions of that older creed which so plagued earlier Scottish writers, the Doctrine of the Elect.

Return to Scotland: The Later Fiction

Whether set abroad or in Scotland, the work of Jenkins exemplifies the prevailing post-war mood of disillusion with the trite and conventional truisms of fundamentals of Scottish identity. Yet Jenkins had not turned his back on Scotland. Moreover, three novels, *A Love of Innocence* (1963), *A Very Scotch Affair* (1968), and *A Toast to the Lord* (1972), written during and just after the years of self-imposed exile, show that he had lost none of his sardonic and reductive attitude towards Lowland Scotland. The first, one of his most ambitious and moving novels, can be seen as a return to the themes of *Guests of War*; the theme of innocence at risk, revealed through displaced slum children at odds in a more privileged setting, allows Jenkins to achieve his finest effects, with a finely-crafted interweaving and contrasting of places and symbols. John Sneddon is one of Jenkins's most compelling innocents; he has seen his father murder his mother, and he and his wee brother Tom are taken from a Glasgow Orphanage to Calisay (a version of Colonsay?) for trial adoption. Around this simple situation Jenkins weaves one of the most complex of his patterns of idealism and betrayal, as the island, though transcendentally beautiful, is barren, in the sense that its womenfolk are childless, its economy failing. One of Jenkins's most challenging characters stands at its heart, a figure whose Viking stature and attractiveness to women seems to mark him as an archetype of West Highland manliness. But Angus McArthur hides a sinister and devious Celtic rottenness behind his apparent charm and good nature; like the later Agnes Tolmie (of *A Toast to the Lord*), *Fergus Lamont*, and the sinister adolescent Duffy, he believes himself to be one of God's Chosen (The Elect?) and therefore above moral law. This is arguably Jenkins's most affirmative novel, however, and for once the goodness of children and women is allowed to transfigure the disillusioned Glasgow officials and the God-fearing islanders. Even scheming Angus is allowed a second chance to transcend his bigamy and betrayal, and to find dignity in self-recognition.

This novel marks a significant change in Jenkins's fiction. With *A Very Scotch Affair* (1968) Jenkins began even more negative presentations, in a series of deeply questionable protagonists, at best ambiguous in their worth, more usually petty and egotistical in their holier-than-thou self-deception. Mungo

Niven (no saint) obviously represents a Scottish type, and his 'affair' is both a general comment on Scottish hypocrisy and his own local affair, as he abandons his dying wife and children in Glasgow for a brief Barcelona fling with a ruthless mistress who in turn leaves him. He is a moralising charlatan, a variant on Angus McArthur; and Jenkins's satire turns even nastier – and with a new touch of surrealism – in *A Toast to the Lord* (1972), with its Ardhallow (Dunoon) set next to the American nuclear base in the Clyde's Holy Loch. Agnes Tolmie is the modern equivalent of Hogg's justified sinner, Robert Wringhim. She too has a father who is a religious fanatic, who has poisoned her mind. She and her father bring blight and death to those around them – her mother, worn out with repression; the American sailor, Luke, whose shallow sensitivity and moral scruples she overcomes with guile and rape; and the by now familiar innocent scapegoat, Tommy Springburn, who will die horribly and alone in the wild. With echoes of Willa Muir's *Mrs Ritchie* (1933), this is a daring fusion of traditional satire on Scottish religiosity with a modern setting which includes weapons of mass destruction, thus adding an additional layer of irony to the moral confusions of Jenkins's townspeople.

A Would-Be Saint (1978) reverses the irony. Young charismatic Gavin Hamilton in Lanarkshire is apparently a model adolescent – a scholar and outstanding athlete – and more, in his shining goodness an impossibly Christ-like figure, but presenting the reader with the question – is he too good to be true? Gavin gives up a brilliant football career, since football has become Scotland's false religion; he gives up his beautiful girlfriend, instead giving shelter to a prostitute; and he becomes a conscientious objector. Jenkins is asking if genuine goodness can ever be accepted by fallen humanity. Gavin gains grudging respect, even from army officers, but he forfeits any place within ordinary community. The ending is as enigmatic as his life; the last traces of him are cycle tracks into a wintry and inhuman whiteness. Jenkins leaves the reader with the responsibility of deciding; is Gavin full of a grace which is too good for this world – or is he a self-destructive egotist?

In *Fergus Lamont* (1979) Jenkins next approaches a character of even deeper complexity from a different angle, but with the same ruthless aim of forcing us to reject conventional assessment and face the complexity of human motivation. More developed now is Jenkins's surrealism, which will appear again in *Just Duffy* (1988) and *Poverty Castle* (1991). In *Fergus Lamont* Jenkins for the first time adopts a first-person mode of narration, as in the sinner's account in Hogg's *The Justified Sinner*. Fergus tells his own story with apparent but deceptive candour. He is a child of the slums of Gantock (Greenock?). He learns that he is possibly the bastard son of a local Earl's son. The knowledge, together with hatred of his grandfather's unforgiving Calvinism and his wrongs towards Fergus's mother inspires (or corrupts?) him to manufacture himself an image – kilted, of noble bearing, eventually military – which will let him take his place (via the 1914–18 war) with aristocracy. He marries money in the wealthy and morally hypocritical authoress of pious sentimental novels, Betty Shiels. Yet underneath this obvious snobbery, which leads him to some ruthlessly selfish actions, is his secret and totally conflicting ambition, which only the reader knows – his (dubious) ambition to be the redeeming poet of the Gantock slums. Fergus looks back from embittered old age over the chapters of his life. His movement towards disillusioned self-knowledge takes Fergus from membership of the aristocracy and rejection by his wife and the society he has prized, to an apparent humility and genuine love in the Hebrides. But this ten-year idyll passes also; and the reader is left to decide whether Fergus has been the quintessential hypocritical and selfish Scottish social climber, denying his background; or whether he can be redeemed in reading by understanding his tormented background, and his strange, but just possibly genuine idealism. And the novel, like Fergus, operates on a deeper level still. Like Mungo in *A Very Scotch Affair*, Fergus is archetypally Scots, and the novel uses him as a way of satirising Scotland, and aspects of deforming religion, education, class prejudices and bigotry.

After *Fergus Lamont* in 1978, so complex and different from his previous novels, Jenkins was exhausted. *Fergus Lamont* showed that Jenkins was seeking to break new ground both formally and in terms of subject matter. This reorientation took some time. There followed an interval of seven years before *The Awakening of George Darroch* (1985), one of Jenkins's two historical novels, set at the time of the Disruption in the Church of Scotland in 1843.[10] Jenkins's analysis of the religious politics of the time is impressive. The evocations of Edinburgh, The Disruption and the Lanarkshire coalfields effectively emphasise the central questions of principle and privilege. The novel's subtle exploration of moral motivation focuses on the Reverend George Darroch, who seems blessed with good looks, charm, a handsome family, the prospect of a wealthy parish, and an apparently simple and pious worth which makes his fellows uneasy. But his wife is dying; he sleeps with (then dismisses) his housekeeper and he will shortly have to decide in the crucial vote of 1843 whether he will stay with or leave the Established Church on principle. Darroch's person and action is presented in terms which at times bring him close to the humbuggery of Fergus Lamont. He knows how his golden-haired appearance impresses his listeners, especially women, and his appeal for the church to extend its hand to

---

10   The other historical novel is the late *Lady Magdalen* of 2003. See the essay by David Robb, 'The Past is not a Foreign Country: Jenkins, Scotland and History', in this volume.

the new industrial workers, while at one level seeming authentic, is undercut by his vain self-awareness of virtue; his son James sees that, 'given the best opportunity of his life to show off, his father had not been able to resist it'.[11] Indeed, hardly anyone is left unquestioned in this novel about ministers as to their real aims; vanity, martyrdom, and self-interest are seen by Jenkins as being ubiquitous amongst clergymen. And when Darroch finally does choose to join the walkout of the Free Church, it is his son who judges that 'for the sake of a minute's vanity he had sentenced his family to years of poverty'.[12] Darroch is in fact not stupid, and has a fallback appointment; but Jenkins has successfully posed fundamental questions regarding the claims of religion, family and morality.

   Just Duffy (1988) returns to contemporary Scotland, and in ways reminiscent of the very similar plot and theme of George Friel's *The Boy Who Wanted Peace* (1964). Thomas Duffy – but just called Duffy – is an illegitimate and introverted adolescent in a small town outside Glasgow, with a bleak setting of urban decay. He is a kind of innocent – not simply so like Calum in *The Cone-Gatherers*, but rather a Holy Fool turned sinister, an innocent but dangerous idealist. Human evil perplexes Duffy. If people can be good, why are they not consistently so? Whereas in *A Would-be Saint* the thought of war led Gavin to pacifism, here it provides the justification for Duffy's holy war to 'save' society. But Duffy is corrupted by his own idealism. The motley assortment of people who comprise his army demand complicated moral responses with which his undiluted idealism cannot cope. He resorts to what he sees as justified murder, an act of treachery to his friends. His mind cannot cope with his conflicting moralities; he retreats into silence and the realisation that the world is unchanged. Jenkins's conclusion here is bleak; although goodness exists, the evil within us all inevitably overcomes it.

   The surrealist tinge to Jenkins's work which had appeared in fiction like *Fergus Lamont* makes *Just Duffy* particularly disturbing in its oscillation between realism and caricature. In a different blend of modes, *Poverty Castle* (1991) also disturbs the reader who seeks to find the meaning of the symbolism of the title. The novel plays new formal games, with fiction set within fiction. The first story is a fiction which tells of a novelist in his seventies (like Jenkins himself?) who wishes finally to write 'a celebration of goodness, without any need of irony'.[13] He will die, and his long-suffering wife will bury him in Kilmory in Argyllshire. This enclosing fiction is interspersed with his 'main' story, of

11   Robin Jenkins, *The Awakening of George Darroch* (Edinburgh: B & W, 1995), p. 266.
12   Ibid.
13   Robin Jenkins, *Poverty Castle* (Nairn: Balnain Books, 1991), p. 7.

how the (simple?) Sempills build their dream house, Poverty Castle, in Argyll. Like Gavin Hamilton of *A Would-Be Saint*, they seem too good to be true, with their disregard for title, their candour, their family beauty. Their neighbours, whether ordinary or aristocratic, are nonplussed and charmed, and their visitor, Peggy, the unglamorous but highly intelligent and critical Glasgow working-class university friend of Diana and the exceptionally lovely daughters and their too-good-to-be-true family, is unable to find the flaws she expects. Jenkins manages, however, to suggest that flaws there are, in hints of selfishness and complacency, in Diana's marrying into aristocracy, in Edward Sempill's lifelong but futile attempt to complete a great work on Sir Walter Scott, in his wife's self-destructive obsession with producing a male heir for Edward. Jenkins's final irony, the reader suspects, is that he is satirising himself in the novel's presentation of the fictional author, whose testy crankiness has tried his wife sorely.[14] And the urge to write fiction concerned with the question of 'goodness' emerges again in *Willie Hogg* (1993). This is the deceptively simple story of the hospital porter Willie Hogg, retired after an uneventful life. He has been well-liked; he is a decent, ordinary Glasgow man who lives up a close with his apparently simple wife Maggie. Maggie's sister Elspeth, who always despised Willie, is dying of cancer. She runs a mission for Navajo Indians in the Arizona desert. Willie and Maggie are violently wrenched out of their retired world, because a tabloid Glasgow newspaper takes up their plight as a human interest story, organising a fund and sending them from one world to another, utterly different. The strain of the situation reverses the relationship of Willie and Maggie. Hitherto Maggie has almost given the impression of being disabled; now she emerges as decisive, aware, alert on the flight to America and in the choices thereafter. Willie stays aware, but is surprised and increasingly confused. The bleakness of the desert, the run-down settlements and Indians, the greed of Elspeth's congregation who are there for the free handouts, the sheer shabbiness of the doomed Christian Mission, with its fragile distorted cross as symbol of religious failure – all these force recognition of the question which is present in all Jenkins's novels, but never more central than here. The question concerns God: is it all colossal irony in his part, a shabby mockery in which the good like Elspeth are left to die in agony, while the opportunists of the tabloids, the pompous of the town councils and the posh hotels, and the entire garish American way of life, roll on regardless? Even here, in the depths of tragedy, however, the humble Willie Hogg remains a symbol of residual human decency.

---

14   This takes on added poignancy, when the reader knows that in real life May, Jenkins's wife, died just before this novel appeared.

Lunderston Tales (1996) develops the theme of the preceding two books of hidden and surprising worth, focusing with a new charity, yet still enigmatically, on varieties of Scottish character. In thirteen stories unified by their location, a Clydeside town is created, as so often in Scottish fiction, from several originals. Lunderston fuses Largs, Gourock, Dunoon, and the American presence in the Clyde, holding them together under the name of the actual Arran-viewing bay. The device indicates the intention; which is to work through stereotypes of douce small-town Scotland to explore their deeper layers, their ambiguities, until essences of situation and character stand clear. The deceptive low-key simplicity of these stories of small hypocrisies and rebellions, of absurd sexual liaisons, of the parochial juxtaposed with the exotic, recalls that older historian of Clydeside manners, John Galt – the difference being that where Galt mocked the pretensions of his provosts and pompous townspeople, Jenkins manages simultaneously to reduce and ennoble his Lunderston worthies. Jenkins's Foreword – unusual practice for him – sees these stories as representative of a Scotland and Lion unrampant, 'happier on his belly, with his paws covering his eyes', given its political failures – yet 'paradoxically, its individual people [...] as interesting as any in America and Russia'.[15] His fiction usually divides its attention between novels about Scotland and novels set in far-off locations; but in these short stories, as in the previous collections like *A Far Cry From Bowmore*, Jenkins juxtaposes prosaic home and glamorous away so that both emerge as overrated in their romantic respects, but undervalued in their essential virtues. However, beyond the reductive evocation of the town and its characters, the rollickingly bawdy widows and the cowed menfolk who make love under wraps once every six months, the visitors from the big outside world who at once fascinate and annoy Lunderston, lies Jenkins's final insistence on some kind of grace – that redeeming moment which can emerge at the most unlikely time and in the most unlikely circumstances. The greengrocer who finds out the irrelevance of Family Respect; the young plumber who breaks through Lunderston primness to find grotesque and almost holy sexuality; the savage old lady who tempers her sarcasm to forgive badly written books and their readers at the last meeting of the Ladies Book Club; the tart who marries the American serviceman, only to find herself stranded with him in the loneliest of desert filling stations in the USA, who has the grace to laugh and endure – these and their modest epiphanies show that even at age 84 Jenkins seeks redeeming signs in a too-often sordid world.

Matthew and Sheila (1998) opens with typical ironic inscrutability in its reworking of self-justifying sin. 'Matthew was nine when he discovered, or more

---

15   Robin Jenkins, Foreword to *Lunderston Tales* (Edinburgh: Polygon, 1996), p. x.

accurately, decided that he was one of the Chosen, those favourites of God who could do no wrong, or rather who, if they did what in others would be called wrong, were immediately absolved and protected from punishment.'[16] All that consoles Matthew for his motherless, lonely, yet privileged childhood is his moment of epiphany in the Hebrides when he felt assured of this election; but this assurance is to be challenged by one of Jenkins's most striking creations. The almost childish ring to the novel's title belies the monstrous nature of Sheila, the angelic, talented schoolgirl who forces a horrific intimacy on Matthew – horrific because her ugly private face is utterly opposed to her public moral and physical beauty. Manipulating all around her, she succeeds in forcing herself as homeless into Matthew's house; and then he becomes her unwilling confidante, forced to keep silent about the unbelievably wicked things she claims to have done. Has she indeed murdered a baby, and then the simple slum boy Davy? Does she go on, as she tells Matthew she will, to drown her father, leaving her to grieve impressively amidst Lunderston's sympathy, but to boast to the bewildered boy of her joy in the deed? And, when Matthew's father does eventually return with a native South American wife, is it Sheila's sacrificial magic on a bleak bay in the Hebrides which kills her and her baby? This classic juxtapositioning of apparent Good and Evil is of course set up to be questioned. After all, Matthew's belief in his Chosen status as one of God's Elect leads him to see himself justified in seeking Sheila's aid in his desire to eliminate the only rival for his father's affections, his stepmother. It is Matthew who commits the final act of mimic ritual killing on the sand-statue which represents his stepmother? And if Matthew's sensitivity and quiet decency is undermined, Sheila's astonishing duplicity is rendered as tragic when Jenkins effectively suggests the terrible self-torment that this far-too-intelligent girl endures as she fails to find any decency, morality or God behind human hypocrisy. What remains enigmatic about the book is its genre. In its curious pseudo-simplicity, is it to be accepted as a return to dark moral fable, the territory of *The Cone-Gatherers* – or is Jenkins working deliberately with an apparent realism which gives way to surreal improbability? From *Fergus Lamont* on these later novels emphasise an uncertainty of genre and interpretation as in *Poor Angus* (2000), which slyly asks if the sins of Colonial exile return to exact retribution from the novel's typically self-deluding protagonist, while *Childish Things* (2001) is one of Jenkins's most devastating satires on a vain-glorious peacock of a retired teacher, who tries to find a comfortable eventide in the bed (and fortune) of an ageing Hollywood star. Where Fergus Lamont arguably believed his own self-justifications, his noble ends meant to justify his ignoble

---

16   Robin Jenkins, *Matthew and Sheila* (Edinburgh: Polygon, 1998), p. 3.

means, now Gregor McLeod consistently lies and pretends without scruple to a phoney middle class identity. As so often Jenkins leaves the reader to wonder whether, despite his lies, Gregor might yet find a kind of redemption. (This novel also leaves the reader with another unanswered question – why did Jenkins give Gregor the exact date and year of his own birthday and why the same industrial Lanarkshire origins?)

Jenkins could still surprise at ninety; in 2003 he produced his second historical novel in *Lady Magdalen*. As before, however, the history is a vehicle for a timeless sardonic comment on vanity and hypocrisy, as the novel sees the archetypal romance of James Graham, the Marquis of Montrose and Scottish icon, the covenanting-cavalier, cut down to lesser glory through the eyes of his saintly and long-suffering wife. At ninety-three, however, and with his last novel, Jenkins's deconstruction of human folly was partly relented. *The Pearl Fishers* (2007) combines satire on the way society's misfits, here the travelling gypsy pearlfishers, are treated by community with stupidity and bigotry, together with the abiding Jenkins fascination for the would-be saint who risks destroying himself and those he loves. Yet, as so often, despite scepticism, Jenkins finally allows a glimpse of the elusive grace which haunted all his fiction with the novel's last words regarding the possibility of a benign future for its lovers – 'It could all happen.'[17]

Tradition and Legacy?

This Overview has argued that Jenkins was followed by the reductive fictions of Spark and Kennaway (see also Spark's *The Ballad of Peckham Rye* (1960)) and James Kennaway's *Household Ghosts* (1961). Following them, a range of modern and contemporary writers continued to question traditional Scottish values in the later industrial and lowland realism of writers such George Friel, William McIlvanney, and contemporary novelists like Janice Galloway, Alison Kennedy, James Kelman, Alasdair Gray, and James Robertson. It can plausibly be asserted that Jenkins has been the beginning of this rich and diverse modern and contemporary fiction.

That said, Jenkins, however, in his obsessive moral questioning and constant ambiguities, is unique. Very broadly he can be seen as satirising Scotland in the way of Scott, Galt, Hogg, Stevenson and Douglas Brown. Yet while these novelists present broad divisions and ambiguities in religion and national loyalties, Jenkins takes these ambiguities and divisions to extremes. His work does

---

17   Robin Jenkins, *The Pearl Fishers* (Edinburgh, Polygon, 2007), p. 179.

re-present and satirise the unhappy doctrine of the Elect, and its consequent figure of the 'justified sinner' – but he secularises and complexifies this figure, allowing deeper insight and forgiveness for his self-justifying extremists, so that the reader eventually sees them, not as sinners, but as exemplars, of an essentially flawed humanity.

Yet for all Jenkins's repudiation of belonging to any school of fiction, Jenkins (and Spark in her Scottish fiction) arguably mark a continuation of the 'state of Scotland' tradition from Scott, Hogg and Stevenson to the later fiction of John Buchan and Neil Munro, which sought to satirise and expose what these writers saw as deeply negative aspects of Scottish history, character, and culture.[18] Additionally, in his portrayals of his many self-justifying protagonists whose twisted idealism lead them to appalling actions of cruelty and deceit, Jenkins initiates a tradition in Scottish fiction of Holy Fools, insufficient idealists, who, in the later work of writers like George Friel and Alasdair Gray, reveal an anomie, a personal and spiritual paralysis and confusion, at the heart of modern Scotland. The work of leading contemporary novelists since Jenkins continues to deconstruct this history and culture, with the empathetic anger of Kelman and Gray, and many others (like Tom Leonard in poetry) foregrounding those excluded by issues of privilege, class and voice, from value in British culture. Jenkins, however, remains a novelist who is unique in his desire to find grace even in the characters he would seem most to abhor.

Works Cited

Ágústsdóttir, Ingibjörg, 'A Truthful Scot' (interview), in *Scotland 1* (Autumn 1999), pp. 13–22.

Gifford, Douglas, 'Remapping Renaissance in Modern Scottish Literature' in Gerard Carruthers, David Goldie and Alastair Renfrew, eds., *Beyond Scotland: New Contexts for Twentieth Century Scottish Literature* (Amsterdam and New York: Rodopi, 2004), pp. 17–38.

Gifford, Douglas, Sarah Dunnigan and Alan MacGillivray, eds., *Scottish Literature in English and Scots* (Edinburgh: Edinburgh University Press, 2002).

Jenkins, Robin, *The Awakening of George Darroch* (Edinburgh: B & W, 1995).

Jenkins, Robin, *Lunderston Tales* (Edinburgh: Polygon, 1996).

---

18   For further discussion of the satirical 'State of Scotland' fiction, (including the fiction of John Buchan and Neil Munro), a tradition which has been described as 'positive negativism', see Douglas Gifford, 'Remapping Renaissance in Modern Scottish Literature', pp. 17–38.

Jenkins, Robin, *Matthew and Sheila* (Edinburgh: Polygon, 1998).

Jenkins, Robin, *The Pearl Fishers* (Edinburgh, Polygon, 2007).

Jenkins, Robin, *Poverty Castle* (Nairn: Balnain Books, 1991).

Jenkins, Robin, 'Why I decided Scotland must be seen through fresh and truthful eyes', *Glasgow Herald*, 12 October 1982, p. 11.

McNeillie, John, *The Wigtown Ploughman* [1939] (Wigtown: G.C. Books Ltd, 1991).

Murray, Isobel, ed., 'Robin Jenkins', in *Scottish Writers Talking 3* (Edinburgh: John Donald, 2006), pp. 101–146.

'Fresh and truthful eyes': Jenkins's Early Scottish Fiction (1950–1958)

Isobel Murray

Abstract

Jenkins's early fiction deals with poverty and aspirations towards escape. *The Thistle and the Grail* illustrates the poverty of a society where the 'religion' that unites it has dwindled to the desperation of a town concentrated on the misfortunes of a junior football club. Jenkins returns to the basic shape of *The Thistle and the Grail* for *Guests of War*, one of his finest books. *A Love of Innocence* deals with childless women and orphaned children on the small island of Calisay, doomed to depopulation in the modern world. The calm is jarred by the figure of Angus McArthur, whose manipulation of women's hopes, fears and money is undetected by most of his victims. If Charlie Forbes is perhaps the first Jenkins central humbug, Angus is a full-blown selfish one, in a line that will stretch through many variations, including possibly Gavin Hamilton and certainly Fergus Lamont.

Keywords

humbug – hypocrisy – poverty – community – evacuees – religion – World War

Robin Jenkins was never a novelist who sought publicity or popularity. Despite being a teacher of English for twenty-two years at home and abroad between 1957 and 1968, after a day in the classroom, he saw his job as writing novels. I learned a lot about him from an extended set of interviews in 1985, when he was in rare talkative vein, and by reviewing or writing about the books, and from the occasional helpful critic.[1] The most useful of these was Brian Morton's

---

1   Isobel Murray, 'Robin Jenkins', in *Scottish Writers Talking 3* (Edinburgh: John Donald, 2006), pp. 101–146. See also the fine extended discussion of these early novels in Francis Hart, *The Scottish Novel: A Critical Survey* (London: John Murray, 1978), pp. 272–276. The title 'Fresh and Truthful Eyes' is taken partly from the title of Jenkins's essay in the *Glasgow Herald*, 12 October 1982, p. 11.

'Goodness in a Fallen World: The fate of Robin Jenkins'.[2] Morton had what seems a unique advantage: he was a school pupil of Jenkins, and later his friend. He encouraged me generally to view Jenkins as a writer who never discussed a work in progress, who belonged to no kind of literary circle, and preferred to keep his writing very much to himself. After writing, he put a book away and started another: Morton confides that he did no re-reading until many years later. But he was by no means unsophisticated or unsubtle. Reviewers have praised brilliant dialogue – especially in Scots – and his handling of character and setting, comedy, and irony. It is always important to read Jenkins carefully, and to notice which character's views and perceptions are being presented: many characters are seen to lie to themselves, as well as others. Jenkins is of course a moralist, but one who leaves his reader to find the moral.

Jenkins wrote at first about the worlds he knew best – Glasgow, the industrial lowlands, and Argyllshire. *So Gaily Sings the Lark* (1950) begins in Glasgow, and then moves to Argyllshire where as a conscientious objector Jenkins had worked for six years in forestry during the war. *Happy for the Child* (1953) is even closer to home. It is based on Jenkins's own experiences as a child in very straitened circumstances in post-industrial Lanarkshire (who nevertheless as a bursary pupil attended Hamilton Academy, a prestigious fee-paying school). *The Thistle and the Grail* (1954) deals with Jenkins's ironic perception that football has become Scotland's religion. He examines a junior team in a small lowland industrial town (Rutherglen?) which he knew well, and with characters such as he knew and had himself played football with. *The Cone-Gatherers* (1955) again revisits his days in forestry for its setting, and *Guests of War* (1956) starts from his own experience, when he accompanied war-evacuated school children from Glasgow to Moffatt, while *The Changeling* (1958) exploits the two territories Jenkins knew best, Glasgow and Argyllshire. Only two novels from this early period move outside these settings; *The Missionaries* of 1957 (set in an invented Western island) and *Love is a Fervent Fire* of 1959 (set in Perthshire). These novels reveal that Jenkins is experimenting (with questionable success) with changes in location, style, subject matter, character and class. Is it significant that these generally dark novels, so critical of modern Scotland, were being written as Jenkins was deciding to leave Scotland for Afghanistan in 1958?

I propose to approach these early novels in conventional order: at this stage, there is no problem determining order of composition. *So Gaily Sings the Lark* is a straightforward first novel. The title is taken from the popular 'Uist tramping

---

2 Brian Morton, 'Goodness in a Fallen World: The Fate of Robin Jenkins', *Scottish Review of Books*, 1:3 (2005), p. 1.

song': 'Come along, come along,/Let us foot it out together.' The first line of the song, 'O gaily sings the lark', seems appropriate for David Sutherland, a Lanarkshire miner leaving closed pits and hoping to escape to the Highlands, perhaps to find work in forestry. (The contrast of dismal and dirty towns with a radiant vision of natural beauty will become a constant feature of Jenkins's writing.) He is introduced to Kilcalvonell by a fat and unpleasant local minister, Eric Kinross, and is put off by his conversation, 'a gangrene of discontent'.[3] He overhears himself spurned as guest by Kinross's sister Isobel. Almost immediately, he meets local Kirstie, very beautiful but reputed to be sexually generous. Here is the whole novel in little, with its main moral question: will Kirstie marry David, poor and careless of money, whom she finds very attractive, or the unpleasant and materialistic minister Kinross, who will move up and prosper?

The setting is already effective, but the characters less so. The two women are both rather caricatured, and David's inner life is not rendered with conviction. For a writer who confessed that he was no good at describing love affairs, this is unfortunate.[4] Other parts of the novel carry more conviction, since they are drawn from Jenkins's own Argyllshire years – David's conversation with an elderly roadman, or his experiences on the local bus or his interaction with other forestry workers, and his gradual assimilation into the neighbourhood. This promising first novel leaves the reader, as will be the case in so many Jenkins novels, with questions rather than answers regarding the future of David and Kirstie.[5]

After this, *Happy for the Child* (1953) is arguably the nearest Jenkins came to writing autobiography in fiction without losing necessary critical distance. John Stirling shares many of the circumstances of Jenkins's own early years in mining Flemington, at the heart of Scotland's industrial belt. Stirling's mother is a widow in very poor circumstances, who devotes her own life – and her daughter's – to caring for and promoting the future of her brilliant and sensitive son. Stirling's life is constantly compared and contrasted with that of Sam Gourlay, the crude, cruel and stupid product of a slum dwelling where his father is defeated, his mother poisonous and violent and his sister

---

3   Robin Jenkins, *So Gaily Sings the Lark* (Glasgow: William MacLellan, 1950), p. 17.

4   Jenkins says in our interview: 'I wasn't any good at describing love affairs [...] my son-in-law [...] accused me of never being able to describe love in my books. He probably meant love with sexuality in it, thought I was too much of a Calvinist'. Murray, 'Robin Jenkins', p. 140.

5   Francis Russell Hart finds the ending happy; although in fact (and typically) Jenkins leaves the reader unsure regarding Kirstie's decision, which she does not tell to Davis, who wonders, when she finally calls goodnight to him, whether she is glad or weeping. Hart, *The Scottish Novel: A Critical Survey*, p. 273.

miraculously good and loving, and ruthlessly cheated and bullied by him. The contrast of Stirling and Gourlay is central (though typically not in self-centred and hyper-sensitive Stirling's favour: slum Gourlay has qualities of spirit which Stirling lacks). Gourlay and his sinister manipulative friend Charlie Stirling torment Stirling, who in turn torments both himself and his self-denying mother. Jenkins shows (as so often in the main protagonists of later fiction) how he consciously indulges his hyper-sensitivity, deliberately making his endlessly sacrificing mother suffer. The complex nature of their relationship is introduced in the first chapter, where she has been to find a second-hand outfit for him to wear at the high school to which he has just won a bursary. He loves his mother, but is secretly (and to the reader offensively) ashamed of her since she is a charwoman. How to keep this hidden is John's greatest challenge when he goes to his new school. When she returns, inevitably and unhappily, with a non-uniform outfit, he punishes her unmercifully:

> She had been watching him anxiously in the hope that, with a little bravery, a little understanding, he would after a minute's forgivable disappointment, shrug his shoulders, laugh, and then blithely try on the new clothes, which, though not what he had wanted and she had promised were nevertheless better than any he had ever worn before. Now when he said so quietly they were of no use she knew he was going to give way to his weakness and torture himself and her. He was so sensitive it was like a disease.[6]

Jenkins makes it clear John feels love and pity for his mother, but here he walks out. Stirling is the first of many such self-centred protagonists in Jenkins's fiction.

This novel is unhappy for the child in the Stirling home, in the Gourlay slum, in the privileged school, but in the end Stirling is allowed the grace of some moral redemption. After driving his mother beyond despair, he manages at last to face the circumstance of his mother's charring being widely known and yet remain at school. This eventual transcendence is bitterly contrasted with the appalling end of his dubious friend Gourlay, alone in a derelict shelter in utter misery.

In these early Scottish novels, poverty is a central issue; poverty of mind and outlook, poverty of spirit – above all the simple physical poverty that Jenkins's

---

6   Robin Jenkins, *Happy for the Child* (London: John Lehmann, 1953; repr. Nairn: Balnain Books, 1992), pp. 14–15.

characters so often and so desperately try to escape. Escape is always an ambition; and dreaming of escape will become a recurrent motif throughout Jenkins's work. In or out of the ghetto, Jenkins's concern is with cruelty and its rarer opposite, kindness, and with love, in however mutilated a form, and with guilt and its nature and cause. Characteristically we are shown a character's meanness or evil, and are tempted to condemn him (as he sometimes does himself), but the picture is then complicated by the novelist's making us aware of other factors; unexpected generosities of spirit, recognition of damaged heredity, and the frightening regularity with which the sins of the fathers – and mothers – are visited on the children, the effects of religious or communal condemnation or narrowness, and the all-pervasive and harmful effects of class distinctions. Final moral judgment becomes impossibly difficult.

Happy for the Child was followed by a novel on a very different scale. *The Thistle and the Grail* (1954) is 'the football novel'. It is concerned to show that the Scottish traditional stays of religion and left wing politics have failed, and that the mass religion of football provides the only remaining hope. Jenkins wrote in 1955:

> It would be about a Junior team, because of the local patriotism displayed in Junior circles. It would include a picture of the whole village, with as many salty characters as one wished. And it would honestly try to recapture the pleasure, the atmosphere, and the camaraderie, of football. It would indeed have to suggest the desolation behind this passionate dependence upon football, and to draw comparisons between this new religion and the old.[7]

Jenkins presents a small Lanarkshire town, Drumsagart, arguably modelled on Rutherglen, with its hapless junior football team, Drumsagart Thistle (thus indicating that Drumsagart can stand for Lowland Scotland?). Drumsagart is described as a town that is rotting; its devotees of football are many, including a range of figures emblematising age and disease and infirmity; they show the state of the Scottish industrial central belt crumbling into desuetude. There is the hideously blind Harry Lynn, beggar and moral blackmailer; there is old Tinto Brown, unregenerate profligate, and his one-legged friend Crutch Brodie, and there are younger men in terminal despair, the dying miner Nat Stewart, and unemployed Jock Saunders, nonconformist in a town of football worship. And there is Rab Nuneaton, referred to above, whose malice is 'feared like a disease',

---

7   Robin Jenkins, 'Novelist in Scotland', *Saltire Review* 5 (1955), pp. 9–10.

who lives on the edge of terror and despair: terror that his wife may be pregnant yet again, despair at the death of his daughter, while he clings to football as his protection against madness.[8]

Thus the inhabitants of Drumsagart are shown as a wide circle of failure, their gossiping reminiscent of the 'bodies' of George Douglas Brown's dark novel of broken community, *The House with the Green Shutters* (1901) as they form a dramatic chorus surrounding the central figure of Andrew Rutherford, president of the football club, Sunday School teacher, and possessor of an uncomfortable conscience and an inability to be part of any community. He is unhappily married to a cold, conventionally respectable wife, whose well-off brother helps him to a reasonable business career. Hannah wants him to leave Drumsagart and move to a nicer house – and social circle – in Helensburgh. He despairs of being close to his son, and is at odds with his father, famously a highly principled socialist local councillor, who despises his son for what he sees as his feeble compromises.

A grey Calvinistic propriety is another element (which we might see as a Scottish middle-class alternative to football) that Andrew reacts against. It is another reason for his affection for his disreputable football worthies, who offer a more vivid and gutsy attitude to life than the 'better class' of townspeople. Yet he will finally leave the town and these worthies. On his father's death, he discovers that the saintly old socialist had a healthy bank book. This allows Andrew a chance to abandon some of his scrupulosity and relax; he can now move to douce Helensburgh with his wife and son. (Jenkins allows him a comfortable ending; but does the reader sense a gentle authorial irony in Rutherford's escape from poverty and moral decision?)

Football is important to everyone in Drumsagart, from the Rev Lockhart, who wants to address the blasphemous, drink-taken crowd at half time, about their bad language, to the same crowd, who live for it all week (though they cannot afford away games.) Six games occur during the novel, which takes the Drumsagart team from bottom of the League to the Scottish Cup, with dubious incidents along the way. The road to the Cup is not smooth, and Andrew has to involve himself in some morally questionable activity before his beaten team is restored to the fight, when its victorious rival is disqualified.

Jenkins here develops his comic and satiric talent for the first time, having begun to hone it (to my mind unsuccessfully) in *The Missionaries*. The novel's opening paragraph shows what he is capable of stylistically:

---

8 Robin Jenkins, *The Thistle and the Grail* (London: Macdonald & Co., 1954; repr. Edinburgh: Paul Harris, 1983), p. 9.

> A thousand martyrs were being persecuted. Their howls of anguish mingled in one enormous snarl of lamentation that fluttered even the hardened sparrows on roofs around and made the women shoppers in the adjacent main street pause a smiling moment in their gossip. Drumsagart Thistle Junior Football Club was again being defeated at home, for the ninth time in succession; and its devotees were on the rack.
>
> Defeat can be accidental, unlucky, honourable, – even, against impossible odds, ennobling; but in football seven goals to nil, at home, can never be anything but amaranthine humiliation.[9]

Overall, the use of a large range of characters, and the presentation of a different, solitary central protagonist was a success. Jenkins would return to it even more successfully in *Guests of War*, but first he would work with changes of genre, scale, and emotional involvement. Jenkins in our interview (perhaps encouraged by its popularity) declared *The Cone-Gatherers* of 1955 his favourite amongst his fictions. It is a novel in striking contrast to the crowded world of post-industrial, decaying Drumsagart in its movement to the Argyll forests (where Jenkins spent his own war). I find it a somewhat flawed masterpiece, a dark and elemental moral fable, astonishing in its ambivalent tree symbolism, in which the forest can be an almost holy place of green simplicity for the innocence of the cone-gatherers, but also a place of a primeval evil, depending on the moral perspectives of the forest inhabitants. It has few characters, movingly presented. Brothers Calum and Neil are simple and clearly presented. They are employed to gather cones during the war in order to reseed the estate later. Calum is beautiful in face and nature but twisted in body, and with no worldly understanding of a fallen, wicked world. Angry at unfairness, his brother has made it his vocation to protect and care for him. The lady of the house, Lady Runcie-Campbell, endeavours to keep the estate going while her husband is away at war, and finds it difficult to reconcile her Christian beliefs with her traditional aristocratic values. Ironically, her son Roderick displays a genuine Christianity which shows up the falseness and snobbery of her values. Other more humane viewpoints than hers are voiced by the doctor, and the forester Mr Tulloch. But Duror is the centre of it all, a man made monstrous by suffering. The reasons for his utter hatred of misshapen Calum are convincing and intense, and his eventual killing of Calum, the utterly innocent little cone gatherer, is made to seem inevitable.

---

9   Ibid., p. 5.

The flaw which mars the book is to do with its inappropriate ending, where Lady Runcie-Campbell reacts to the death of Calum and the unexpected rescue of her own son. In the final controversial page of the novel, she goes down on her knees amidst the blood and spilt cones; her heart fills with 'pity, and purified hope, and joy.'[10] Jenkins does not earn this quasi-religious epiphany. Douglas Gifford pointed this out in 1986:

> Anyone who can find the justification for Runcie-Campbell's 'purified hope' from the grisly events which have preceded it is piously ignoring the novel's overwhelming blood and pain, and I accuse Jenkins of ignoring it for the shocking uplift of an inappropriately religious and uplifting end.[11]

I agree with Gifford here, but I think it does not destroy the overall power of the book. Like some of the great ballads, it conveys a brooding evil. Duror's suffering and his tormented conscience, and his horror of misshapen creatures, including his obscenely fat bedridden wife, shows that he has become a diseased part of the wood itself, lending it a symbolically powerful horror. His name indicates his hardness and endurance, but also something more sinister, as his mind becomes fully poisoned against the cone-gatherers. Lady Runcie-Campbell begins to see this sinister change in Duror, a change which transforms the woods in the second half of the story to a place of evil. Young Roderick, seeking the cone-gatherers to restore his friendship with them, sees trees distorted into grotesque faces and monstrous shapes. He begins to sense Duror as an infection polluting the forest.

In these closing chapters, the wood itself becomes an episode from 'a macabre fairy-tale'. Trees are transformed into warty bushes swarming with worms. Images of rottenness and death emphasise how the territory has become that of grim fable. As Duror stalks off (to kill Calum), he is likened to a rotting tree which begins to move. He is clearly now seen in terms of decay and ordure. Jenkins's story has become a fusion of fiction and nightmare fable – and Lady Runcie-Campbell's controversial epiphany cannot mar the fable's nightmare intensity.

But this very intensity may well have sent Jenkins back to the larger scale he had mastered in *The Thistle and the Grail*, with one central and a

---

10   Robin Jenkins, *The Cone-Gatherers* (London: Macdonald, 1955; repr. Edinburgh: Paul Harris, 1980), p. 223.

11   Douglas Gifford, 'God's Colossal Irony', *Cencrastus* 24 (1986), 13–17 (p. 13).

credible range of minor characters. *Guests of War* (1956) is based on a situation in which the novelist found himself in real life: 'I did go with Strathclyde Primary School kids to Moffatt [sic], and quite a lot of the things that happen in the book did happen in real life. Pretty much as I describe it, too: It was hilarious!'[12] The novel is tragic-comedy, playing with the idea of very different kinds of war. Evacuation of city children to the country was one of the main preliminaries to the declaration of the Second World War, Glasgow being a major target for the Germans. (Evacuation petered out when the expected bombs failed to appear till later. In the novel, more than half of the evacuees have gone home before the end.) Behind the book's dark comedy is another kind of war, as the Gowburgh (Glasgow) teachers are reminded as they are about to leave for Langrigg (Moffat?), their Border sanctuary: 'Remember war is about to be waged, not between Great Britain and Germany, but between ourselves and the inhabitants of Langrigg's cottages, villas, mansions and miniature castles.'[13] The war closer to home in the novel is the class war between the slum-dwellers of Gowburgh and the well-off middle-class citizens of Langrigg, with the evacuees as the guests of war. Jenkins's achievement here is to turn his satiric attention on both sides, successfully, although the greater liveliness always belongs to the Gowburgh intruders. The book is full of comic set-pieces – bath night in Gowburgh before the exodus, the procession to the train, the chaotic scene of arrival at Langrigg, the utter shambles made out of the job of billeting; yet the humour can turn sharply satiric about class and privilege. The Langrigg Baillie's wife, against all the rules, arrives at the evacuees billeting site:

> 'I want two little girls [...] They must be clean, obedient, quiet, well-spoken, house and bed trained, and without a criminal pedigree [...] I happen to believe, however, that in a free country, which thank God ours still is' – here she gave Roy a look which asked more rudely than words why he was not being eviscerated somewhere to preserve that freedom – 'though not perhaps for much longer, I happen to believe that we are entitled to refuse to harbour scoundrels, actual or potential.'[14]

War is also Jenkins's central ironic metaphor for inner conflict, and here major characters often suffer inner wars – outstandingly Bell McShelvie, from Glasgow with the evacuated slum children, a middle-aged, ordinary-looking

---

12   'Robin Jenkins', in *Scottish Writers Talking 3*, p. 138.

13   Robin Jenkins, *Guests of War* (London: Macdonald, 1956), p. 18.

14   Ibid., pp. 88–89.

woman (who discovers that she has surprising administrative talents) who guiltily yearns to stay with the evacuees in the country as a permanent helper. She is another of Jenkins's many self-tormentors, always seeing her own actions in the worst possible light. She feels guilt about leaving her husband and Glasgow:

> Here indeed was her battlefield: the enemy she had to fight was despair at the ugliness shutting her in, at the inevitable coarseness and pitiable savagery of many of the people shut in with her, and above all at her inability to keep her own family healthy, sweet and intact. She was weary of fighting. Even soldiers in war were given relief [...] The battle was at its height [...] and she had made up her mind to desert.[15]

Bell is a very stern judge of herself. In her view, Langrigg is a test which she dismally fails, but the reader is unlikely to judge so harshly. She grows in stature when she is put in charge of the evacuee families in Cairnban (the huge house allocated to the Gowburgh evacuees). While she is briefly tempted to see herself as rather above the rest, her self-inflicted 'punishment' for this is out of all proportion – in the questionably accidental death of her son Sammy, whom Jenkins presents as simple, but having a special innocence, although neither clever nor handsome. Like so many of Jenkins's innocents, from the simplicity of Calum the cone-gatherer to the intelligent Tom Curdie in *The Changeling*, this kind of simple goodness lends grace and warmth to those close to them, as Sammy does with his mother, a city dweller in Glasgow sorely missing her country origins:

> Some said he was too soft in the head [...] and sniggered at his bespectacled simplicity; but most admitted the softness, and greenness, were in his heart. As a substitute for those meadows and hills, Sammy all his twelve years had sufficed.[16]

By the end Bell will have transcended her grief for Sammy, and moved to a mature and self-denying decision. It has been her Langrigg ambition to climb the local hill, Brack Fell. As she struggles in her ascent, she realises that her duty lies in returning to Glasgow and her husband, rather than taking the offer of remaining in Langrigg:

---

15   Ibid., pp. 11–12.
16   Ibid., p. 7.

Before it was too late, she must make amends to the folk she had betrayed. Returning to Gowburgh would do, but only if she returned cleansed and unresentful, prepared to create as much light there as she could, not only for herself and her family, but for her neighbours.[17]

She has to do more: she has to admit to herself that she cannot reach the summit in time to return safely. So she turns back, but not in symbolic defeat. In contrast with Fergus Lamont's self-dramatising notion of returning to the slums of Gantock with a redeeming love, his return seems highly suspect, where Bell's quiet and unobtrusive return to Glasgow is seen as heroic. She ends up on the road back to her friends: 'She no longer saw defeat or disappointment, but only a necessary resolution. As she plodded along the road her feet stung and her whole body ached, but she was smiling, with the tears running down her cheeks'; hardly a traditional happy ending, but an affirmative ending for this, one of Jenkins's finest novels.[18]

So, given that none of the major characters questions the necessity of the war, does Jenkins, the conscientious objector novelist, speak out in the book on the question of war and the justness of fighting? Yes; but not as we might have expected. Jenkins puts his denunciation of war in the mouth of a cynical, unlikeable older teacher who attacks the idealism of the young teacher Roy, who is only waiting in Langrigg for his call-up to the RAF. Campbelton has pretended for years that he has an honourable war wound from World War One, although it is only the result of falling over a bucket in a latrine. Yet, as so often in his fiction, Jenkins confuses the reader with his ambivalent presentation of moral truth. There is undoubted validity in what the older teacher says here, but his speech must be heard in the context of his selfish cynicism:

> 'We are about to enter a slavering, snottery, gnashing, bloody, excremental, universal madness, dear boy,' he said gently. 'I refer, of course, to war. It will not do to gird on your sword, like Sir Galahad, and rush off to slay the ogre responsible for it all. You will achieve your ambition, Edgar, and become the pilot of an aeroplane. You will cross to Germany with a load of bombs and drop them to the best of your ability upon some munition work, but really they will fall on tenements filled with women and children similar to those at present detained in the school [...] You will fight the good fight, in the twentieth-century style. You may become a hero,

---

17   Ibid., pp. 282–283.
18   Ibid., p. 286.

with medals. But, bless you, you will never be Sir Galahad, who slew only ogres, and on whose soul consequently there was not to be found one blemish.'[19]

Here, as with moral issues throughout his fiction, Jenkins constantly confuses his readers' responses by expressing judgements, through unreliable characters and situations, which may or may not be his own. (Jenkins will treat the subject of war and its effects in similarly disconcerting manner in novels such as *Love is a Fervent Fire* (1959) and outstandingly in the later *Fergus Lamont* (1979)).

The Missionaries (published in 1957, just before Jenkins departed for Afghanistan), returns to Jenkins's frequent contrast of idyllic natural setting and fallen humanity with its invention of the lovely island of Sollas and its unattractive inhabitants. Unfortunately, Jenkins uses ornately pretentious language and metaphor for a story which hovers unconvincingly between realism and supernatural myth. The main protagonist, the pretentious young graduate Andrew Doig ('unafraid of conceit') is an egotistical rebel who does not know himself or his aims – to be worldly successful or dramatic debunker of his family's conventional pieties? The novel is over ambitious; Jenkins has far too many characters representing far too many points of moral view, and too many bizarre situations which can be taken as supernatural or simply coincidental. There are two sets of missionaries; on one side the almost druidical and haunting figure of Donald McInver, who claims the island in the name of ancient holy Saint Solla for his unconvincing religious sectarian squatters; on the other, the forces of modern civilisation, represented by the Sheriff sent with policemen on the mission to clear them off the island. Andrew is caught between McInver's idealism and his worldly temptation by the island owner's daughter Marguerite, who at times seems to bewitch him. Jenkins overstretches himself with his bewildering variety of meanings and moralities, in a fable which leaves the reader confused by what appear to be moments of genuinely supernatural events. Jenkins himself admitted he had problems with this novel:

> *The Missionaries* is a peculiar book. I don't understand *The Missionaries* myself [...] You have to suspend your belief and I can't suspend it to that extent. Would you take *The Missionaries* seriously in the sense that it's a book worth reading? It's a book that I sort of nervously tiptoe away from.[20]

---

19   Ibid., p. 105.
20   Murray, 'Robin Jenkins', p. 144.

That said, just after *The Missionaries*, Jenkins returned, in one of his finest novels, to the worlds he knew well; slum Glasgow (and its schoolteachers) and Argyllshire, which he loved from his war years in forestry. *The Changeling* (1958) can be compared with *The Cone-Gatherers* in the shocking quality of its ending. The abrupt death of a vulnerable child is always shocking, and coming after *Guests of War* and its gentler closure, in this novel is doubly so. Its ending is much more genuinely tragic than that of *The Cone-Gatherers* in its inevitability, and the fact that Tom Curdie, the misunderstood, yet sensitive and talented slum boy, destroys himself rather than being destroyed, heightens the tragedy. In our interview, Jenkins told us the ending was so shocking that when a television film was made, the ending was changed, much to his annoyance: 'I think they tried to give it the kind of ending that you could assume it was going to be reasonably happy.'[21] (Elsewhere in this volume, Douglas Gifford discusses the novel more fully than is possible here; arguably, this is Jenkins's most concise and disturbing novel.)

In 1957, Jenkins moved to Afghanistan, which begins the period of teaching abroad which would produce his very different 'foreign' fiction. The separation of 'early' fiction from later is conjectural, since *Love is a Fervent Fire* (as with *The Changeling*) may also have been conceived and started before the 1957 departure. It is an 'early' novel, just as his third period, back in Scotland after 1968, produced 'foreign' novels. If *The Changeling* played to Jenkins's strengths in terms of its portrayal of the two worlds he knew best, *The Missionaries* (published just after Jenkins's 1958 departure for Afghanistan) and *Love is a Fervent Fire* (published in 1961, but perhaps written well before?) seem to show Jenkins experimenting (with questionable success) with new settings and characters. *Love is a Fervent Fire* (surely written prior to the 1957 departure from Scotland) is a novel which is deeply negative about twentieth-century Scotland. Its protagonist is Hugh Carstares, wounded (physically and mentally) in the war. He is an incomer, as Forestry District Officer, to Kinlochgarvie, a nasty Highland community given over to lechery, gossip, and malice. Jenkins's portrayal of this war hero, who seeks to atone for what he sees as the evils of war, is unconvincing, as indeed is much of the story. The portrayal of his drunken efforts to express this atonement in his ludicrously rough wooing of impoverished aristocrat Constance Kilgour meet with contempt. Constance has had a child with her wartime lover (who has abandoned her, to be killed in the war shortly after.) This has caused her to withdraw with her daughter into a sustained coldness, while gossiping Kinlochgarvie thinks that Carstares is the father of

---

21   Ibid., p. 142.

her child. Carstares has in fact only just met her and her daughter; and on the basis of having driven her home, she unsurprisingly rebuffs him. All this and the predictable coming together of aristocrat and war hero (and child) is implausible and contrived, as are most of the supporting characters, like Helen Carmichael the sexually frustrated schoolteacher, who is falling into madness and a 'sexual brainstorm', and Margaret Kirn, the mature hotel keeper, who is 'saved' from frustration and aridity by her barman Jock only just in time, but who then wants him also to save Helen Carmichael from her sexual frustration by servicing Helen too! This novel, arguably the last of the early novels, is marred by such overall improbability and by its bizarre treatment of sexuality which goes so far as to suggest that any woman who has not been awakened into full bloom by a sexually potent man is bound to wither on the bough. Beyond this, in its surprisingly unconvincing background of its forestry setting and tree symbolism, the overall effect is to suggest disillusionment, despite its improbably happy ending. *The Missionaries* and *Love is a Fervent Fire*, in their portrayal of characters who mar the beauty of their natural setting with their ungraceful humanity, suggest an author whose experimentations have lost their way, and who has become deeply negative about his countryfolk. Did Jenkins now realise it was time to break and begin again?[22]

Works Cited

Abrams, Lynn, *The Orphan Country: Children of Scotland's Broken Homes from 1845 to the Present Day* (Edinburgh: John Donald, 1998).
Gifford, Douglas, 'God's Colossal Irony', *Cencrastus* 24 (1986), 13–17.
Hart, Francis Russell, *The Scottish Novel: A Critical Survey* (London: John Murray, 1978).
Jenkins, Robin, *The Cone-Gatherers* (London: Macdonald, 1955; repr. Edinburgh: Paul Harris, 1980).

---

22 There are two novels set in Scotland which, published while Jenkins was teaching abroad (1957–68), lie outside the 'early' category, and are thus dealt with elsewhere in this volume. *A Love of Innocence* (1963) chose (as in *The Missionaries*) to invent an island in order to emphasize the moral dilemmas of his characters; while *A Very Scotch Affair* (1968) focused on a Glasgow philanderer trying to escape his Glasgow family. In a way the separation of 'early' Jenkins fiction from later is artificial, since while abroad Jenkins wrote 'Scottish' novels after 1958, just as in his third period, back in Scotland after 1968, he drew on his earlier experience abroad to produce 'foreign' fiction; the short stories of *A Far Cry from Bowmore* (1973), *A Figure of Fun* (1974) and *Leila* (1995). After the return to Scotland in 1968, two novels, *The Expatriates* (1971) and *Poor Angus* (2000), combine both overseas and Scottish experience.

Jenkins, Robin, *Guests of War* (London: Macdonald, 1956).

Jenkins, Robin, *Happy for the Child* (London: John Lehmann, 1953; repr. Nairn: Balnain Books, 1992).

Jenkins, Robin, 'Novelist in Scotland', *Saltire Review*, 5 (1955), 7–10.

Jenkins, Robin, *So Gaily Sings the Lark* (Glasgow: William MacLellan, 1950).

Jenkins, Robin, *The Thistle and the Grail* (London: Macdonald & Co., 1954; repr. Edinburgh: Paul Harris, 1983).

Jenkins, Robin, 'Why I decided Scotland must be seen through fresh and truthful eyes', *Glasgow Herald*, 12 October 1982, p. 11

Morton, Brian, 'Goodness in a Fallen World: The Fate of Robin Jenkins', *Scottish Review of Books*, 1 (2005), p. 1.

Murray, Isobel, 'Robin Jenkins', in *Scottish Writers Talking 3* (Edinburgh: John Donald, 2006), pp. 101–146.

Ironic Mythology: Reading the Fictiveness of *The Cone-Gatherers*

Gerard Carruthers

Abstract

The Cone-Gatherers (1955) is a text of large symbolic import featuring an Edenic Argyllshire landscape. Into this setting pollution is poured in the form of an incipient evil agency which might either affirm the Calvinist world-view, or alternatively, could be its bleak, morbid, self-prophesying result. A wider than Scottish (Calvinist) context also pertains, the novel clearly riffing upon John Steinbeck's *Of Mice and Men* (1937), with writ-large allusions to folk legend (especially the Green Man), the life of Francis of Assisi, and classical theories of western tragedy as well as the Bible. In retrospect the alert reader might see this inter-textual exchange as proof of the profound fictiveness, the suspicious heaping up of symbolism and story, in Jenkins's novel, something that this essay will principally elaborate upon.

Keywords

Inter-textuality – Fictiveness – Calvinism – Good & Evil Intertwined – Classical Tragedy

The first sentence of *The Cone-Gatherers* features a spare, Genesis-like opening: 'It was a good tree by the sea-loch, with many cones and much sunshine'.[1] This biblically-resonant opening sets up a central terrain in the novel, moral 'good' and its correlative, 'evil' and it does so with a realistic clarity of vision that might lead the reader to expect a story where the discernment of these things is relatively straightforward. Iain Crichton Smith has rightly observed that Jenkins's text 'appear[s] like a fable'.[2] Fables do not necessarily represent an obvious reading process, but by the end their 'moral' should be more or less clear, or at least decodable. Another of the questions that this essay will explore is what is the moral of *The Cone-Gatherers*, granted that there is one in

---

1 Robin Jenkins, *The Cone-Gatherers* (London: Macdonald, 1955; repr. Edinburgh: Canongate, 2012), p. 1.
2 Iain Crichton Smith, *Robin Jenkins's The Cone-Gatherers* (Aberdeen: Association for Scottish Literary Studies, 1995), p. 36.

© KONINKLIJKE BRILL NV, LEIDEN, 2017 | DOI 10.1163/9789004342491_004

the novel, and, indeed, is there any decoding (as we might do with a fable) to be done? The setting of the book, a wood in Argyllshire deliberately draws us into a primal place where we might expect a clear or at least natural vision. However, we should notice the novel's large contextual inversion. Around its plot's local action swirls the Second World War, secure now as in the 1950s, in its popular and historical account as a struggle against Nazi evil. It might be suggested that, implicitly, Jenkins's book ironicises this conception. The war against evil (or terror) is a rather pointless war, since it can never be won. Evil does not reside in only one place or regime, but, if it is a concept with any deep and meaningful traction, must be present or at least possible within the human moral condition however that is defined. Somewhat evasive about values (and, indeed, about his own biography generally), Jenkins himself took an ethical stance in deciding during World War II to be a conscientious objector, something that informs the fabric of his novel, albeit in minor key. The main protagonists as 'cone-gatherers', Calum and his brother Neil, are not themselves conscientious objectors but they work alongside 'cos' in this work towards improving Britain's forestry provision. The cos are glimpsed as a benign, mildly outsider presence, men, implicitly, of some moral complexity on whom the bitter game-keeper, Duror ought, perhaps, more reasonably than the educationally sub-normal, Calum, to turn his ire. However, it is precisely this moral complexity that Duror eschews, opting instead to despise that which is most obviously 'despicable', Calum's simple-minded, physically misshapen being.

There are two other places where the war impacts on the action: the absent, aristocratic estate owner Runcie-Campbell serving as an officer in the British army and in the estate's loss through war of the tolerant woodsman, Tulloch, whose brother has been killed at Dunkirk. All of this 'off-stage' placement of the war counterpoints the fact that another war in its own way terrible and visceral is occurring in the quiet woods.

Jenkins's achievement in *The Cone-Gatherers* is not simply to show that the battle between good and evil is as local as it is global, but to present a local struggle that is seemingly much more difficult ethically to discern than the world-wide conflagration swirling around it. It may be that Duror reflects a Nazi-like attitude in wanting to purge the imperfection that is Calum, but his motivations are at least as primally ancient, perhaps Freudian, as anything in the ideas and attitudes of Hitler and, arguably, he stands for something much more enduringly ancient. At one level Duror can be read as the European-wide folk-type, the Green Man. Often seen as more explicitly present in English than in Scottish culture, the Green Man is one of the sub-texts of George Douglas Brown's *The House with the Green Shutters* (1901), from which Jenkins may also have borrowed its strongly signalled context of classical tragedy. Brown's

physically-imposing John Gourlay is an alpha-male life-force ever more driven
to dominate his vicinity as his own family succumbs increasingly to both physical and mental illness. The trajectory of Duror's all-consuming tendency to
domineer has a similarity to Gourlay's in that both have a critically ill wife,
driving the former like the latter to give weakness no quarter. Brown's novel
has a more understated green man theme, though the folk-type is signalled in
his domestic setting (the *green* shutters). In Jenkins's text, the Green Man conclusion is even more compelling as Duror the stalker of the woods, becomes
more and more dishevelled or 'natural' and seeks, as a principle of seemingly
healthy, brutal nature, to purge from his perfect, arboreal habitat the imperfection that is Calum. Is this, then, what the novel is about? Is Jenkins reflecting
on the Nazi ideologies of strength and race and telling us that such attitudes
are not peculiar to the Germans? Is he essaying Darwinian biology and pointing out that 'survival of the fittest' is simply the way it is in a Godless universe?
Certainly, Jenkins possesses no Christian (or any other religious) faith and in
the 1950s might well be working in the post-Auschwitz mood. That is to say,
Hitler and his allies may in the end have lost the war and the world may well
have been fully appalled by the revelation of the Holocaust, but in a sense the
Nazis (crudely in tune with the twentieth-century's increasing apprehension
of a post-Darwinian, Godless 'nature') were part of (indeed largely set) the
agenda for a post-Modern condition that emphasised selfish, primitive motivations and paid no deference to older Western narratives about a moral universe with its various sub-narratives in both religion and philosophy about the
universal sanctity of human life. We might see this playing out of history even
in the post-World War II establishment of 'human rights', where the formal
codification of such a set of rights implicitly acknowledged a new world mindset where such things could no longer be taken for granted (as these had been,
at least theoretically, previously in the spheres of civil society, philosophy, religion and so on). Does *The Cone-Gatherers*, then, simply acknowledge that
there is a struggle within human life (perhaps within nature, more generally)
that is not so much to do with good and evil but is more to do with contest-
ing egos, wills and power generally? Such a bleak idea would ironically counterpoint much of the novel's narrative surface (including its play on the word
'good' in the opening sentence). It would also shift Iain Crichton Smith's idea
of the possible fabulistic fabric of the novel in an unconventional direction,
towards a fictional pattern that says the 'moral' is that there are no 'morals',
because human behaviour is differently constituted and motivated from the
idea of moral agency. Related to this proposition is the potential suggestion
within the text that our beliefs in progress (the ideas that the human species
has moved beyond primal motivation and continues in enlightened fashion to

progress) are suspect. Whether or not the book is taken finally to make such claims, it at least raises this scenario as a distinct possibility.

As well as being constructed along the lines of the Green Man, Duror is an even more recognisable type within Scottish Literature, that of the 'justified sinner'. In fiction, the archetype, a Calvinist individual vouchsafed his predestined salvation and so not subject to the normal moral code is found in James Hogg's *Private Memoirs and Confessions of a Justified Sinner* (1824). Although the character-type is somewhat reprised in Robert Louis Stevenson's novella, *The Strange Case of Dr Jekyll and Mr Hyde* (1886) and in James Bridie's drama, *The Anatomist* (1931), the 'justified sinner' has most direct purchase in twentieth-century Scottish fiction. As well as Jenkins in *The Cone-Gatherers*, Muriel Spark draws on the type in *The Prime of Miss Jean Brodie* (1961) and, somewhat later, we have another version of the character in James Robertson's *The Testament of Gideon Mack* (2006).[3] In *The Cone-Gatherers*, the malevolent Duror in his novel believes himself justified in purging his beautiful woods of the deformity that Calum represents. At the same time, Duror is a Green man presence, a stalker in the woods (ambiguously standing both for life and for death) and carries an obvious Book of Genesis allusion in being somewhat a serpent in paradise (and so again his own darker, unjustified nature is signalled).

For all Hogg's influence on the text as it deals with conjoined good and evil within the human frame, *The Cone-Gatherers* is very different in tone. F.R. Hart describes its 'ritualistic intensity', something too that distinguishes it from its most apparent model, *Of Mice and Men*.[4] Jenkins's novel here belongs to some extent alongside a new anthropological emphasis in British fiction, exemplified most clearly by William Golding's *Lord of the Flies* (1954) and *The Inheritors* (1955). At the same time, however, as wielding a primal realistic action that is related to Golding's text, the 'ritualistic intensity' which Cairns Craig identifies in *The Cone-Gatherers* owes a debt in the long term to J.G. Frazer's *The Golden Bough* (published from 1890 onwards). Craig describes Frazer's guide to the myths underlying the western mindset 'that shape human culture [as] a revelation of what modern humanity has discovered about the primitive [and]

---

3   It is no accident that this later twentieth century reception of the 'justified sinner' occurs, as for most of the nineteenth-century Hogg's profoundly dark and ambiguous novel had languished in obscurity. Its eventual fame across the western world arrived after André Gide edited the novel for publication in 1947. Gide recognised Hogg's fiction as, precisely, a study of fanaticism that had great pertinence following the Nazi death camps.

4   Francis Russell Hart, *The Scottish Novel: From Smollett to Spark* (Cambridge, MA: Harvard University Press, 1978), p. 275.

also what it has repressed in order to believe in the benign force of history'.[5] Jenkins's compendious novel of allusions, mythic and inter-textual, recreates, among so many large cultural echoes, Frazer's 'sacred grove' in the Argyllshire woods. However, this is not necessarily, as in Frazer, a special place in the community mind. Indeed, a propos the war effort and the gathering of cones, it is a functional locality, for Lady Runcie Campbell it is part of the aristocratic family's patrimony (and so precisely non-communal), and it is only for Duror that the woods represent some kind of pure space. We learn eventually why this might be psychologically, since his game-keeping beat is an alternative to his domestic life where he has to care for a sickly, bed-ridden wife. This personal mindset of Duror's is arguably why the symbolic shapes within the novel, its mythic and fictional allusions, become as it were larger than life. And the same possibility arises in relation to other characters: that their perceptions, rather than an omniscient and objective narrator are creating the metaphoric texture of the novel. *The Cone-Gatherers*, for all its surfeit of reference and allusion, indeed because of this, leads us to the possibility that the novel is largely about how human beings subjectively construct for themselves symbolic shape that they take to be objective, but which is not. It is in this large postulation, arguably, that Jenkins's novel most inhabits the mode of Hogg's 'justified sinner'.

Also related to *Confessions of a Justified Sinner* is a demonic texture. This has to do with a crucial Gospel text underlying the uncertain personality of Hogg's central character, Robert Wringhim. In the three synoptic gospels we are told the story of Christ driving the demon into the Gadarene swine. Before doing so, Christ interrogates this demon within a possessed man as to its identity, the reply being given, 'My name is Legion for we are many.' This is the sub-text to the slippery, uncertain multi-voiced narrative of Hogg's book. We see a similar demonic texture in *The Cone-Gatherers*, not only in the excess of allusion, but in a more particular ambiguity of perspective in the novel. For instance, if we return to the opening sentence, 'It was a good tree by the sea-loch, with many cones and much sunshine [...]' we realise, as we 're-read' the novel and given what has just been said about Duror's desire for his pure, sacred space, that this sentence might, in fact be focalised through, or represent the perspective of the game-keeper. Indeed, in its initial, spare simplicity, what we perhaps have is the beginnings of a trajectory. What we have represented, it can be suggested, is Duror's healthy outlook prior to his moral and mental decline, or his primeval nature at least before this becomes polluted. At the same time, and here is where we find exactly the slippery, double-tonged, demonic textual embedding, the opening

---

5   Cairns Craig, *The Modern Scottish Novel: Narrative and the National Imagination* (Edinburgh: Edinburgh University Press, 1998), p. 146.

sentence might as equally channel the apprehension of Duror's arch-enemy, Calum. For all its echoes of *Genesis*, the phraseology is exactly appropriate to the 'simple-minded', straightforwardly responsive character of the cone-gatherer. We might especially think that it is Calum's viewpoint that is being reflected when we take the sentence in its entirety: 'It was a good tree by the sea-loch, with many cones and much sunshine; it was homely too, with rests among its topmost branches as comfortable as chairs.' The physical facility of the treetops, among which Calum is agile and graceful in contrast to his more cumbersome physicality on the ground, is registered in their being 'as comfortable as chairs' and here as elsewhere in the opening the language is both allusive, metaphorical, and, at the same time, not particularly so, in its plain speaking.

We can see slipperiness in the text again, indeed something akin to demonic shape-changing both in Duror's descent into a more slovenly, unshaven appearance, and also in the toll taken likewise amid the action on Calum's brother, Neil. Tulloch, the good overseer of the cone-gatherers observes Neil:

> He turned round and saw, with a shock he did not show, how stooped and contorted Neil was then, by rheumatism and despair: it was as if, in some terrible penance, he was striving to become in shape like his brother.[6]

Here, for all that Tulloch is the most reasonable character in the novel, the reader ought to wonder is this truly, entirely what he sees, or is this Tulloch's projection? We might wonder this especially as underpinning Tulloch's thought is another clear Gospel reference, 'am I my brother's keeper?' (Genesis 4: 9). Precisely because Tulloch is also the most consciously good character in *The Cone-Gatherers*, we have to ask is he seeing events within an imaginative shaping (Christian) which is for him formative, or received? Is *The Cone-Gatherers* a novel that ultimately says that we are all conditioned to see things not originally but in prefabricated, culturally conditioned fashion? If it is, we might see the text as a very modern one, indeed looking towards the post-modern condition, where our truth claims do not exist independently of our culture. Such a reading would also lead us to the view that the novel is a sceptical, unromantic product setting up a large mythic, symbolic terrain but ultimately contradicting the perspicacity of this symbolism and allusiveness. Historically, after the death-camps and with the new anthropological turn taken in the western novel, as signalled by Golding, this would make sense. It would make sense too in the specifically Scottish context, as Scottish writers of the 'second generation' of the twentieth-century 'Scottish Renaissance', among which Jenkins is

---

6   Jenkins, *The Cone-Gatherers*, p. 164.

often identified, turn away from the large symbolically replete, 'condition of Scotland' texts of the pre-World War II first 'Scottish Renaissance' generation. Jenkins is at odds with that previous generation of Scottish writers in being much more sceptical 'of received notions of community in Scotland'.[7]

However, as well as potentially relating *The Cone-Gatherers* in these ways to the primal ambiguities of the late twentieth-century novel, generally, we might also repatriate the text within a specifically Scottish canon by arguing that the demonic texture can be seen as a channelling of the Calvinist outlook. Classically, this is seen as mistrusting the world (after the Fall it is the devil's place). It is a place with nothing good in it, including no good stories or narratives since the one sure support in this Puritanical stance is the Bible, all other (man-made) expression being, exactly, profane. Duror's increasingly diseased apprehension of the landscape might corroborate such a Calvinist perspective, as might the slipperiness of the text in refusing to yield up any univocal reality or 'truth'. In such a reading the narrator is complicit with Duror as he (Jenkins?) affirms this unpleasant earthly mutability. Beyond any complicities of the narrator, we might ask is this also the controlling author, Jenkins's, view? Not an orthodox Calvinist himself, Jenkins perhaps sardonically mocks this world-view, relishing the instability of his subject-matter and the reading experience he provides. *The Cone-Gatherers* is perhaps a satire on Calvinism as it turns over one of its central precepts: that the post-lapsarian world is the playground of Satan. Here, though we ought to bring into consideration two more explicit sites of Christian reference, the first of these surrounding the hunchback simpleton, Calum. Calum in his closeness to nature and love of animals fairly obviously references St Francis of Assisi, a real-life exemplar of goodness (cheerfully embracing poverty, part of the logic for which is that the only material necessary to man is the natural world). Like Francis, Calum talks to the birds and even the dogs in the street and has next to no material wants, loving nature and the simple family companionship of his brother, Neil. Calum might be read, then, as primeval innocence or goodness, ironically destroyed in the novel's denouement by Duror who deplores the hunchback's imperfection. *The Cone-Gatherers* might be taken as saying that this is the eternally recurring story of human history. As the Home-front functions in the novel, the conventional view of which is healthy, communitarian sacrifice towards the ends of defeating an evil foe, here in the most intimate space of that Home-front, urges and actions unfold as rebarbative as Hitler's scape-goating of the Jews. It may

---

7   Gerard Carruthers, 'Fictions of Belonging: National Identity and the Novel in Ireland and Scotland' in Brian W. Shaffer, ed., *A Companion to the British and Irish Novel, 1945–2000* (Oxford: Blackwell Publishing, 2005), pp. 112–127 (p. 120).

be that here we glimpse something of Jenkins's own Home-front history as a 'CO', refusing to take part in a war because he does not believe in a just or good war, or one that can really triumph over badness. If we do see something here of Jenkins's own moral compass, it is one that might be read variably as profound or defeatist. It may even be charged with containing a Calvinist tincture, pessimistic and revolted by the world.

The second manifestly Christian co-ordinate in the novel is the young cadet of the Runcie-Campbell family, Roderick. Like Duror, the boy has a strong discernment of evil, in this case, Duror himself. With some understandable misgiving as he, like others, has witnessed the sullen, unfriendly aspect of the gamekeeper as the action unfolds, he sees Duror loitering among the trees:

> When he realised that the motionless figure under the cypress was Duror, he crept in dismay into a cave of yew. It was his first retreat, and it was cowardly. Yet he could not force himself to complete the pilgrimage and knock on the door. Duror was a barrier he could not pass.[8]

With a young boy's intelligence as well as instinct, Roderick rightly discerns Duror's growing malevolence towards Neil and Calum, indeed, has the apprehension that the gamekeeper is 'stalking' the pair as though they were animals. On one level, the writing in the passage just quoted reports with accuracy on this state of affairs, applies to it a suitable metaphoric elevation that is not melodramatic. In so far as the symbolism of the passage *is* overwrought, this is so precisely because it conveys to the reader the magnitude of a small boy feeling himself in conflict with a powerful adult. The quasi-supernatural or at least primitive world, where the cypress stands both for ancient endurance and an omen of foreboding (in longstanding western mythology) sums up accurately the atmosphere surrounding and giving rise to Roderick's emotions. At this point, we must think, the heavily redolent style of *The Cone-Gatherers* is being sympathetically rather than ironically deployed. The narrator here is in league with the character, as he focalises his *mentalité*, in straightforward sympathy.

At the same time, as Roderick the Christian 'pilgrim' registers also uncertainty within himself (this can also be read as part of the orthodox psyche in the Christian outlook). As he watches the sinister watcher, Duror, Roderick feels himself somewhat contaminated by this feral contact:

> As he crouched in the earthy darkness *like an animal*, [my emphasis] he wondered what Duror's purpose could be in lurking there. [...] Was he now spying on them in the hope that that he would find them engaged

8   Jenkins, *The Cone-Gatherers*, pp. 144–145.

in some wrong-doing, such as working today, which was Sunday? [...] But Duror himself shot deer on Sundays; he did not often go to church, and when he did he sat with his arms folded and a smile of misery on his lips. Why then did he hate the cone-gatherers and wish to drive them away? Was it because they represented goodness and himself evil? Coached by his grandfather, Roderick knew that the struggle between good and evil never rested: in the world, and it in every human being, it went on.[9]

The protean (or slippery or diabolic) nature of characters already observed in the novel is here again evident. Calum has been established variously as deformity and innocence, Roderick is both creature spiritual and creature animal and, yet again reiterated by the boy's perception, Duror is both upholder of Christian regulation and its transgressor. At first, Roderick reaches for a straightforward symbolism of good (cone-gatherers) and evil (gamekeeper) that is consonant with a very basic moral reading of the novel's main scenario. Although, he then rejects this simple binary for something more complex and protracted: good and evil are wrapped around one another in the world and in the individual, not so easily to be disaggregated. Profoundly, Roderick (having been mentored by a philosophically-Christian grandparent), realises that judgement must never be so sharp (otherwise one runs the danger of believing oneself saved or one of the elect as Robert Wringhim does). He gleans that human judgement must always be somewhat provisional or uncertain since good and evil abound closely together. Essentially, this reflects the doctrine of Original Sin, that while on earth the human cannot totally evade the evil that is in his makeup alongside the God-given goodness or innocence that equally resides therein. Does the slippery, provisional texture of *The Cone-Gatherers*, then, point us to a generally Christian, rather than specifically Calvinist view of the world? It can certainly be read in this way, most especially if we contrast the 'Christian' outlook of Roderick's mother, Lady Runcie-Campbell. Sincere in her way as a disciple of Christ, her actions at the end of the novel are simultaneously shocking and in keeping with the primal mythology and theoretical classical tragedy of the action. Lady Runcie-Campbell shares with the other characters, obviously enough, a strong sense of the striking Argyllshire countryside in which she lives. A strange moment of communing with nature occurs amid a situation of great panic. Duror is on the rampage, Calum is in great danger and Roderick too might be in peril, either from Duror or from Roderick's attempts to negotiate the branches of the high trees as he attempts to follow the path of Calum. As she and her employee Baird try to discover exactly what is going on and to intervene, Lady Runcie Campbell has an epiphany:

9   Ibid., p. 145.

> From a bank of whins and bracken she looked down on the promontory. Never had the loch been so potently beautiful: it was vast, bright, and de-tailed as in a dream; and there seemed to be a wonderful interpretation, if it could only be known. A warship steamed down the loch. So intimate a part of the dream was it, she seemed, during those few moments of sus-pense upon the bank, to know all its crew and what was to be each man's fate in the sea towards which it was bound. There, too, dreamlike, were the pines, her favourite trees, marking against sea and sky what had al-ways struck her as Scottish gestures, recalling the eerie tormented tragic grandeur of the old native ballads. Gulls, as prodigal of time and sky as she must be parsimonious, flew and shrieked high over them.[10]

Like her son Roderick or Duror, Lady Runcie-Campbell attempts to read the world or rather impose her own prior 'reading', a 'wonderful interpretation', lurking vacuously behind the situation she is actually amidst and the beautiful but ultimately uncaring landscape. This 'interpretation' never actually decoded is actually mood music taken from her 'dreams' or 'old native ballads'. *The Cone-Gatherers* is, on one level, about the human aesthetic urge. Lady Runcie Campbell is only one among a number of characters who practise pathetic fal-lacy. However, as a proper reading of the novel makes clear, it is human beings who create signification and not the landscape. In the passage just cited we have empty symbolism (never actually unpacked by Lady Runcie-Campbell) pointing to the fact that this is how human beings project stories – often meaningless, not to be decoded, onto the physical world. In other words, and in Formalist conception, the 'narrative constitution' of human beings becomes apparent.

We see Lady Runcie-Campbell's function as an artistic ordering outlook in the denouement of the novel. Calum has been shot by Duror who has commit-ted suicide and Roderick is safe. Neil frantically seeks to reach his brother slain in the branches of the tree into which he has attempted to escape:

> First she said, 'Help him, Baird.' Then she went down on her knees, near the blood and the spilt cones. She could not pray, but she could weep; and as she wept pity, and purified hope, and joy, welled up in her heart.[11]

Here we have catharsis in the definition of tragic art as called for in a long line of theorists from Aristotle to A.C. Bradley. Lady Runcie-Campbell's emotions are

---

10   Ibid., p. 218.
11   Ibid., p. 220.

cleansed as the badness has happened, passed away and can now be lamented, supposedly to the observer's moral gratification. Lady Runcie-Campbell a sincere Christian, consciously not so sure her faith is as full or robust as those of Roderick or his grandfather, 'could not pray'. Here it is as though an evasion is taking place by Lady Runcie-Campbell. Instead of seeking religious solace, or perhaps praying for the dead (albeit something a little theologically uncertain within the Episcopalian communion to which she belongs), she reaches for art. She turns the situation into a dramatic tableau, as she gives free vent to her emotions. True, the weeping denotes a dropping of the usual aristocratic sang-froid, a phrase that might be quite pointedly here used. It is not the 'cold blood' but the hot spilled blood of Calum that allows her relief to come (her tears of joy more than of pity). Her actions are deliberately described within the context of catharsis, and there is a strong symbolic undertone too clearly of the Christ-sacrifice. But both of tragedy and Christ-sacrifice are brought to the scene prefabricated by Lady Runcie-Campbell. Her actions shock Baird, 'even there amidst these shocking sights'.[12] Some kind of artistic satisfaction is derived by Lady Runcie-Campbell, which is related to her understandable pleasure that Roderick is safe, and also to a darker, more selfish feeling, perhaps: that the problem of Duror and Calum has solved itself. This impaired catharsis at the end of the novel continues the theme prosecuted throughout the text that says human life projects grand, delusional narratives onto events that are much more naturally visceral and without symbolic meaning and which are devoid of interpretative depth. Unlike the final blood-letting of a Shakespearean tragedy, then, there is no release, but instead a continuation of *The Cone-Gatherer's* claustrophobic look at or conception of human life, within the confines of a dense wood and of continual story-telling from which there seems to be no way out.

Having dealt with occlusive themes of artistic patterning/story-telling/dramatisation within the novel, we might attach to that reading at least one other prime consideration. The modern critical preoccupation of 'masculinity' is unmistakeable to early twenty-first century eyes. Duror's sexuality as a powerful driver of the plot is to the fore, including where he seeks to hope that Calum might be some kind of sexual deviant. Insofar as the reader might extend some sympathy to the gamekeeper, Duror is obviously suffering from a sense of emasculation. A possible extramarital affair cannot be properly entered into, not owing to his moral sense, but because his back-history long years tending to an ill, disabled wife has unmanned him, we might infer. However, there is

---

12   Ibid.

a complication here in that his problem with imperfection (and so impotency) is of longer standing even than his marital experience:

> Since childhood Duror had been repelled by anything living that had an imperfection or deformity or lack: a cat with three legs had roused pity in others, in him an ungovernable disgust. Other boys had stripped the wings off flies, he had been compelled to squash the desecrated remnants: often he had been struck for what was considered interference or conceited pity. Nobody had guessed he had been under a compulsion inexplicable then, and now in manhood, after the silent tribulation of the past twenty years, an accumulated horror, which the arrival of these cone-gatherers seemed at last about to set loose.[13]

The psychology suggested here is that Duror has himself long been perceived as weak (both his 'interference or conceited pity' read by the other boys), and has been on the receiving end of beatings for his actual over-sensitivity of sorts. Again we can read the heightened drama or 'literary-ness' of *The Cone-Gatherers* as index of this hyper-sensitivity. In 'manhood' his sterile marriage confirms his feelings of inadequacy, and the fertility of the woods, indeed, of the very pointed symbolism of the cone-gathering (to seed new forestation) both combine to exacerbate his frustrated male-ness. Of course, Duror's hatred and destruction of Calum argues, in his warped mentality, an actual identification with the hunchback, whose 'deformity' is more obvious than his own. The combined deaths of Duror and Calum at the end of the novel are read by Lady Runcie-Campbell in her 'catharsis' as the end of a struggle between good and evil. However, the gamekeeper and his human quarry, in the eyes of the former and also in one possible reading of what Jenkins's text is saying is that here, in fact, a non-moral, Darwinian conclusion is reached. Both the 'weaklings' Duror and Calum are expunged in a predatory fashion that is commonplace in nature. Good characters, such as Neil (whose love for his brother is real and absolute, if not always entirely courageous), Tulloch and perhaps Roderick are powerless in the face of the naked exercise of predatory, natural power. The only alternative, which is little effective alternative at all, to the feral male power that provides the main narrative arc of the novel, is a refusal to behave with that mentality. This is true for Neil's attempt to keep his and Calum's heads down through much of the action of the novel, and for Roderick's romantic and ultimately less than muscular Christianity (his mother fears that he is not

---

13   Ibid., p. 13.

masculine enough for the world) and for Tulloch's patent kindness both to the two beset brothers and also to the conscientious objectors, against whom he has no grudge even though he could opt for a lazy logic of bitter connection, given that his brother has been lost at Dunkirk.

This reading of the novel, drawing on an actual scepticism about the reality of moral agency in the world, and instead drawing upon Darwinian and essentially Freudian well-springs of anti-rationality, maleness, selfishness and survival of the fittest contradicts the overactive 'story-telling' and symbolic shaping of their world by the main characters. However, the caveat must be added this extends potentially also to Duror's own Darwinian outlook (if that is what it is) in his persecution of Calum and his desire for self-extinction. What we perhaps see in the end with *The Cone-Gatherers* is a thorough scepticism about how humans (through their fictions, religions and philosophies) see and present the world to themselves and others. Power will be exerted in the death camps and in the forests of Argyll, or anywhere really in the human world against weaker elements, and this is the unchanging story of the world of *homo sapiens*. Our myths of progress do not supplant older, more unchanging, primal myths, which are so obviously part of the symbolic currency of *The Cone-Gatherers*. Published on the cusp of a new literary age when subjective Modernism gives way to an even more sceptical Post-Modernism, Robin Jenkins's novel in its large symbolism and labyrinthine literary playfulness, as argued for in this essay, is truly a post-Auschwitz work that offers much poignant observation but no answers to the human condition. At the same time, as alluded to earlier, there is a weakness of good, or a kind of (quiet, undramatic) quietism that might allow *The Cone-Gatherers* (whatever its author might believe, though perhaps like his characters constrained within the mindsets in which he has been culturally conditioned) as a Christian novel. This pertaining ambiguity, whether the novel is to be read as affirming nature red in tooth and claw or a Christian view of sorts, perhaps confirms how consistently well designed *The Cone-Gatherers* is as an unsettling and unsettled reading experience.

Works Cited

Carruthers, Gerard, 'Fictions of Belonging: National Identity and the Novel in Ireland and Scotland' in Brian W. Shaffer, ed., *A Companion to the British and Irish Novel, 1945–2000* (Oxford: Blackwell Publishing, 2005), pp. 112–127.

Craig, Cairns, *The Modern Scottish Novel: Narrative and the National Imagination* (Edinburgh: Edinburgh University Press, 1999).

Hart, Francis Russell, *The Scottish Novel: From Smollett to Spark* (Cambridge, MA: Harvard University Press, 1978).

Jenkins, Robin, *The Cone-Gatherers* (London: Macdonald, 1955; repr. Edinburgh: Canongate, 2012).

Smith, Iain Crichton, *Robin Jenkins's The Cone-Gatherers* (Aberdeen: Association for Scottish Literary Studies, 1995).

'To Bring Profoundest Sympathy': Jenkins and Community

Timothy C. Baker

Abstract

Over the course of his career, Robin Jenkins repeatedly returned to the theme of community. In many of his novels he juxtaposes a placed, and often utopian, community with an individual protagonist in some form of exile. In *The Missionaries* (1957), *Some Kind of Grace* (1960), and *Willie Hogg* (1993) he depicts geographically and intellectually permeable utopias. In *The Thistle and the Grail* (1954) and *A Would-Be Saint* (1978), Jenkins examines the relation between active communal experience, specifically football, and traditional community structures. Reading these texts in relation to both sociohistorical accounts of secular community and contemporary philosophical perspectives reveals the extent to which Jenkins ultimately locates the importance of community not in a particular place, but in time: utopian or shared communal experience leads to a vision of a personal future. Jenkins's discussions of community ultimately lead to an ethics of individual action that is consistent throughout his work.

Keywords

community – religion – secularism – utopia – death – football

Over the course of his career, Robin Jenkins repeatedly returned to the theme of community. The catalyst for many of his novels is the intrusion of an outsider into a pre-existing, geographically-determined community, while other novels concern the conflict between different communities, or even different ideas of community. Far more than many of his contemporaries, however, Jenkins is interested not only in community as 'a real society in a real world', in Iain Crichton Smith's formulation, but in its utopian possibilities.[1] This focus arguably arises from Jenkins's oft-noted preoccupation with questions of good and

---

1 Iain Crichton Smith, *Towards the Human: Selected Essays* (Edinburgh: MacDonald, 1986), p. 46.

evil, as well as innocence. In his aligning of moral questions with notions of social responsibility, Jenkins considers what it is to have one's knowledge of good and evil come from individual encounters with a particular collective, as well as geographic, experience. In this he is aligned with contemporary thinkers such as Jacques Ranciére, who argues that '[t]here is no longer any need to be summoned to the desert to know good and evil. It is only a matter of walking and looking. Truth is not in some distance that the voice or the sign could point out, at the risk of betraying them.'[2] For Jenkins, likewise, knowledge of good and evil is based not in received precepts or inherited religion, but in walking and looking, or in the specifics of individual experience. Utopian communities are not located elsewhere, but are frequently permeable, such that anyone can enter them. At the same time, many of Jenkins's novels are also concerned with the desire for a communal experience based on retreat; many of his characters respond to the ethical ambiguities and difficulties of contemporary life by founding a world away from the world, or by leaving community entirely. This utopian impulse, and its eventual failure, occupies a number of Jenkins's texts. In this, he again calls to mind Ranciére, who argues that utopia is not a place that exists nowhere, removed wholly from society, but rather 'the ability of overlapping between a discursive space; the identification of a perpetual space that one discovers while walking within the *topos* of the community'.[3] The founding of such a discursive space is one of the central concerns of all Jenkins's work. Throughout his fiction he examines not only the constitution of community, but also the perpetual desire for it. In both novels set in Scotland and more far-flung locations, and in texts focused on both the sacred and the secular, Jenkins always returns to the question of the innate human need for community, and the impossibility of any community to cohere.

As numerous critics have noted, community is a central topic in much Scottish fiction. For Francis Russell Hart, the 'the moral primacy of community' is one of the most noteworthy features of Scottish fiction, while Cairns Craig argues that one of the central conflicts in many Scottish novels is between the 'fierce communal ethic of the repressive forms of Calvinism' and the isolated, and hence 'fearful', individual.[4] Smith's story 'The Existence of the

2   Jacques Ranciére, *The Flesh of Words: The Politics of Writing* [1998], trans. by Charlotte Mandell (Stanford: Stanford University Press, 2004), p. 17.

3   Ibid., p. 19.

4   Francis Russell Hart, *The Scottish Novel: A Critical Survey* (London: John Murray, 1978), p. 401; Cairns Craig, *The Modern Scottish Novel: Narrative and the National Imagination* (Edinburgh: Edinburgh University Press, 1999), p. 38.

Hermit', for instance, presents a community disturbed by the appearance of a hermit; arguing in a collective voice that 'the very fact of his existence was a kind of insult to us all'. As the community explains: 'human beings are made in such a way that anyone who lives differently from themselves, even though he does not seek to influence them in any way, is a challenge and a cross'.[5] The community is a moral as well as geographic centre and consequently, in Smith's works, often hostile to change. In contemporary works by authors such as George Mackay Brown and Muriel Spark, however, community is predicated on a recognition of individual difference; community is not so much an organic whole as an intentional combination of individuals whose unique identity is made apparent only as they are seen in relation to the community. Jenkins's work falls between these two contemporary positions. Like Smith and Brown, he focuses on communities that are unified by place, most often the West of Scotland, as well as in many cases religion, class, and politics. As in Brown and Spark, the community highlights, rather than diminishes, individual difference. In many of Jenkins's novels the sheer number of names and identities can be overwhelming: what is initially presented as a unified identity is gradually revealed to be made of a multitude of individuals. More than for many of his contemporaries, for Jenkins community is not only a setting but an explicit theme. In both his localised novels of Glasgow and its surroundings and his more utopian fiction, Jenkins constantly foregrounds the interrelation between lived experience of community and its more abstract or ideal state. As Edwin Morgan notes, 'however much local detail and dialect may be employed', Jenkins's novels 'do sometimes present an extremely peculiar world [...] in part symbolic and fabulous'.[6] This is rarely more evident than in his portrayal of community, which always exists as both a tangible reality and an abstract ideal; the difficulty of navigating between these positions occupies many of his best novels.

The Thistle and the Grail is focused on one of the most stable communities in Jenkins's oeuvre. Drumsagart, a small mining town, is familiar from much twentieth-century Scottish writing; the novel's portrait of the ostracisation of a powerful man from his community, predicated in part on the gossip of his neighbours, is also reminiscent of George Douglas Brown's *The House with the Green Shutters*, among other texts. The explicit theme of the novel is the way secularisation changes conceptions of community; in this case,

---

5 Iain Crichton Smith, *The Red Door: The Complete English Stories 1949–76*, ed. by Kevin Mac-Neil (Edinburgh: Birlinn, 2001), p. 440.

6 Edwin Morgan, *Essays* (Cheadle: Carcanet, 1974), pp. 242–245 (p. 242).

the community is centred around football rather than religious practice. Football, as the minister simply says, 'is their religion now'.[7] As T.C. Smout notes, this transition was endemic in mid-twentieth-century Scotland: with the diminishment of church attendance, 'pubs, music halls, and football grounds provided the meeting places and the common experience that previously only the church had provided'.[8] Callum G. Brown has more recently argued that the period saw a decrease in all voluntary communal activity, whether religious or secular, in favour of a 'sense of ethnic community, family activity and the isolation of the individual'.[9] The difference between these perspectives illuminates the central discursive space of the novel: at the same time that certain characters bemoan the replacement of religion with football, others note the more widespread failure of community feeling on any basis. Andrew Rutherford, the novel's protagonist, initially sees football as 'the quintessence of Drumsagart, his native place'; the importance of the team is not found simply in the games themselves, but in the knowledge that '[w]orthies long since dead had forgathered there, to argue, laugh, cheer, boo, and discuss the history of the town'.[10] Football is the locus of collective memory; as each game is played the discussions surrounding it effectively renew the town's sense of itself. Rutherford also laments the secularisation entailed in this activity, however:

> We are a dreich, miserable, back-biting, self-tormenting, haunted, self-pitying crew, he thought. This sunshine is as bright as any on earth, these moors are splendid: why are not the brightness and splendour in our lives? Seeking them, here we are speeding at fifty miles an hour to see what – a football match, a game invented for exercise and recreation, but now our only substitute for a faith and purpose.[11]

If football can function as a central discursive space for the foundation of community, it also potentially reveals the extent to which any sense of community is arbitrary. Similarly, the dismissal of football by certain inhabitants of the town represents their disillusion with any sense of collective identity. Football spectatorship is itself presented as exclusionary: it is entirely homosocial,

---

7   Robin Jenkins, *The Thistle and the Grail* (London: Macdonald, 1954; repr. Edinburgh: Polygon, 2005), p. 42.

8   T.C. Smout, *A Century of the Scottish People: 1830–1950* (London: Fontana, 1987), p. 203.

9   Callum G. Brown, *Religion and Society in Twentieth-Century Britain* (Harlow: Pearson, 2006), p. 12.

10   Jenkins, *Thistle and the Grail*, p. 132.

11   Ibid., p. 166.

while away games can only be attended by the better-off residents. For many
of the town's inhabitants, then, especially its women, football fandom is simply
an imposed identity.

Although *The Thistle and the Grail* begins with the assertion that 'love of
their native place and its team' are virtually synonymous for the men of Drumsagart, it ends with an idea of community predicated on individual empathy
in the face of death.[12] Early in the novel the town's graveyard is described as
wholly neglected: 'Nobody was sure who lay buried there; not a name was to
be made out on the smooth slabs; but most people supposed they had ancestors under that hallowed grass.'[13] The remnants of religion, and the lives of
the town's former inhabitants, pale in comparison with the excitements of
football. At the novel's close however, as the town celebrates a football victory, Rutherford, now exiled from the town, returns to visit another equally-
deserted cemetery, sanctuary only for birds. In his loneliness he finds 'a rest, a
recuperation, a breathing space'.[14] The cemetery is a place where the collective
and individual merge; the idea of community can no longer be contested, but
is stabilised in the memory of individuals. Rutherford visits the recent grave
of Tinto Brown, an irascible, drunken and lecherous pauper at the centre of
the town's circle of gossips, who has been quickly forgotten after his death.
Rutherford encounters another of the town's lonely old men, Crutch Brodie,
who informs him that Brown always thought well of him. The sense of community and shared experience is momentary – Rutherford and Brodie do not
even leave the cemetery together, as they walk at different speeds – but the
two share an immediate recognition of the 'ultimate, irremediable loneliness
of every human being, which might bring regret and sorrow but which also
ought to bring profoundest sympathy, as it did here'.[15] True community, Jenkins
suggests, can be found not in the passing joys and pains of voluntary association, as with the collective appreciation of football, nor in the vanished world
of religious experience, but only in the mutual recognition of loneliness and
isolation. It is only on the physical outskirts of the town, amongst those it has
rejected, that true community can be known. Here Jenkins approaches Sarah
Kofman's influential formulation that 'the strongest community [is] the community (of those) without community'.[16] Community is best understood, and

---

12   Ibid., p. 11.
13   Ibid., p. 33.
14   Ibid., p. 293.
15   Ibid., p. 296.
16   Sarah Kofman, *Smothered Words* [1987], trans. by Madeleine Dobie (Evanston, IL: North-
      western University Press, 1998), p. 70.

perhaps best experienced, from a position of exile, and it is to this idea of exile that Jenkins returns over many of his subsequent novels.

Like *The Thistle and the Grail*, *A Would-Be Saint* is centred on a small mining town unified by football. Auchengillan is perhaps the closest Jenkins comes to a portrayal of an idealised community; Gavin Hamilton, the titular protagonist, initially finds that although it is 'too small for a town and too scattered for a village', it nevertheless is capable of constituting 'his world'.[17] Although class disparities are certainly prevalent, in Auchengillan, like the larger town of Lendrick, the 'wise-like folk' believe that as 'far as goodness went everybody, apart from known rogues, was pretty much alike'.[18] Both communities are relatively insular, despite the loss of many of their men to the First World War early in the novel. As Jenkins explains:

> This apparent indifference to the events and the men shaping the history of the twentieth century was not the result of small-mindedness or ignorance. It was simply felt that people known personally were more interesting and sustaining topics of conversation.[19]

Like Dalmailing in John Galt's *Annals of the Parish*, world-historical events are always related back to the local. Unlike many of Jenkins's other novels set during the Second World War, such as *The Cone-Gatherers* and *Guests of War*, the war is almost entirely separated from everyday experience, and only impinges briefly. The concerns of the given community are always paramount.

This isolation is called into question when Hamilton, a gifted footballer who bemoans the substitution of football for religion in Scottish society, abandons the game after an outbreak of violence on the pitch. When war breaks out, just a page later, he adheres to the same principles, and registers as a conscientious objector. While Rutherford in *The Thistle and the Grail* argues that religion and football both spring from an innate need for violence, Hamilton opposes religion to both. Yet Hamilton's religious fervour often appears as self-righteousness, and earns him the simultaneous respect and derision of his peers. This is especially evident when Hamilton moves from the organic community of Auchengillan to the more artificial community of conscientious objectors at Creag, where '[t]here seemed little spirit of community'.[20] While

---

17   Robin Jenkins, *A Would-Be Saint* (London: Gollancz, 1978; repr. Edinburgh: B&W, 1994), p. 3, p. 6.
18   Ibid., p. 59.
19   Ibid., p. 101.
20   Ibid., p. 136.

Hamilton sees his exile as an opportunity to negotiate his understanding of community and to consider the limits of his faith, his compatriots view their time in Creag simply as an interruption in the course of their regular lives. As Hamilton gradually disappears from the narrative towards the novel's end, however, his very existence becomes the centre around which a new community can form. One of the objectors refers to Hamilton as 'blossoms, sunshine, and hope', and believes his companions feel likewise.[21] The novel thus moves from an idealised portrait of community to an idealised portrait of an individual who operates as the foundation of community. If in *The Thistle and the Grail* Jenkins suggests that exile and isolation are necessary for the consideration of community, here he frames those attributes more positively: exile becomes the foundation for a new type of community that can exist in parallel to the more traditional community of Auchengillan. Jenkins here suggests the possibility of a community grounded in individual difference. Such a community can be considered in terms of what Jean-Luc Nancy calls a 'rupture' or 'gap'; for Nancy such a rupture is not the opening of a 'possible world', a potentially utopian alternative to experience, but rather invites a formulation of the world based on an adoration of the opening itself. Viewing the world as opening avoids the totalising impulse of many utopian ideals; rather than the utopian desire to see the world as it should be, Nancy consistently advocates seeing the world as it is, as fragmented and individuated. As he writes: 'Rupture opens identity by way of difference'; adoration consists in embracing this difference, rather than looking for a singular 'something' at the heart of experience.[22] Hamilton is himself such a rupture: by loving the world and being loved by it, yet also remaining apart from it, he is able to suggest the possibility of a new form of community predicated on difference.

While the two forms of community presented in *A Would-Be Saint* are given equal prominence, Jenkins is often more concerned with the attraction and failure of 'possible worlds'. *Guests of War* concerns the meeting of two distinct organic communities, when the impoverished urban population of Gowburgh is migrated to the more idyllic rural town of Langrigg at the outbreak of the war. Although Jenkins admits that it would be 'sentimental to hope that the fields and hills of Langrigg would purify what the streets and backcourts of Gowburgh had helped to pollute', nevertheless the novel begins with the potential argument that environment is central to character, and that the effects

---

21   Ibid., p. 212.
22   Jean-Luc Nancy, *Adoration: The Deconstruction of Christianity II* [2010], trans. by John McKeane (New York: Fordham University Press, 2013), p. 15.

of urban squalor can be lessened by exposure to a rural landscape.[23] Langrigg is 'the land of fairytale', a pastoral utopia untouched by war, despoiled by vulgar 'invaders'.[24] Similarly, the remote isle of Calisay in *A Love of Innocence* is called by its inhabitants 'a good place, [...] a beautiful place, there is none fairer'; its small community is disrupted when two orphans from Glasgow are placed in a foster home there in order to recover from early trauma.[25] Unlike the similar setting of Auchengillan, Langrigg and Calisay are disrupted by external pressures. Crucially, the primary representatives of Gowburgh and Glasgow, Bell Aldersyde and Tom and John Sneddon, respectively, are eager to be assimilated into their new community. In both cases, however, their acceptance in that community is first retarded by administrative procedures, and then by the community's distrust of outsiders. The community of Calisay cannot accept the Sneddon brothers not because of their potential 'danger [...] to every living soul on the island', as many believe is occasioned by their early exposure to familial violence, but because of what Angus MacArthur terms 'the inescapability from self'.[26] It is not the poverty and violence of the city dwellers that makes any negotiation of community impossible, but rather the insularity of each member of the community that reveals that community itself is impossible. The presence of an outsider reveals the utopian, organic community to be a falsehood; rather than founding a community based on difference, as Hamilton does in *A Would-Be Saint*, difference is shown to be insurmountable and an end in itself.

Bell Aldersyde ends *Guests of War* looking at the two communities from a mountaintop, finding them 'the most poignant sight she had ever seen'. From her distance, she is able to appreciate both the 'simple and courageous faith' of Langrigg and the 'vulnerability' of Gowburgh.[27] Yet this appreciation is possible only from a point of remove; utopia can only be realised by 'walking and looking', not by finding a place within another community. Here, like Rutherford in *The Thistle and the Grail*, she approaches Roberto Esposito's challenging negation of community. Life, according to Esposito, 'is nothing other than the desire (for community), but the desire (for community) is necessarily configured

---

23   Robin Jenkins, *Guests of War* (London: Macdonald, 1956; repr. Edinburgh: B&W, 1997), p. 35.

24   Ibid., p. 42, p. 53.

25   Robin Jenkins, *A Love of Innocence* (London: Cape, 1963; repr. Edinburgh: B&W, 1994), p. 49.

26   Ibid., p. 102, p. 314.

27   Jenkins, *Guests of War*, p. 292.

as the negation of life'.[28] Both Rutherford and Aldersyde are only able to confront their own desire for community when alone, and when thinking of the
recent dead; it is only in the absence of community that community can be
known. Community, Esposito argues, is known only in its withdrawal; it is best
formulated not as a 'thing', an independent and cohesive entity, but precisely
as a 'no-thing', a lack of identity. While Rutherford and Aldersyde certainly still
look to real, placed communities, their absence from their community combined with a longing for it suggests that it is precisely a lack of community that
enables understanding. Both novels, as well as *A Love of Innocence*, suggest that
life is predicated on a desire for community that must nevertheless accept its
failure. Only Hamilton, in *A Would-Be Saint*, is able to escape this paradox, simply because he appears wholly uninterested in community, and adheres to his
own sense of self. At the close of the novel Hamilton sets 'forth on his long hard
perilous journey that had brought him to a loneliness few people could have
endured, and a spiritual fullness'.[29] He is, as one character notes, like the 'holy
men so disgusted with the degenerate ways of their fellows that they hiked off
into the desert'.[30] Hamilton leaves behind him a community, but only because
he has no apparent need for it.

Hamilton's departure from community is reframed in two of Jenkins's novels
that deal more explicitly with utopian imaginings, *The Missionaries* and *Some
Kind of Grace*. Both novels focus on the insularity of the utopian mindset, and
the extent to which a utopian desire closes off the rest of the world. The young
protagonist of *The Missionaries*, Andrew Doig, has his intellectual approach to
religion and ethics tested when he encounters a small community who believe
they have been directly called by God to inhabit the island of Sollas and found
an intentional, and arguably utopian, community there. The community's
right to inhabit the island is framed as a legal question: in the absence of a
verifiable, manifest God who can support their claims of his intervention, they
are trespassers. As Doig struggles to understand the motivations behind the
community's actions, he feels 'not like a modern man at all seeking a buttress
for faith, but like the adventurer of fable who needed and obtained the help
of the gods in a world where rocks could speak, birds were wise men translated, out of the waves came green monsters to devour, and a beautiful woman

---

28   Roberto Esposito, *Communitas: The Origin and Destiny of Community* [1998], trans. by
      Timothy Campbell (Stanford: Stanford University Press, 2010), p. 121.

29   Jenkins, *Would-Be Saint*, p. 212.

30   Ibid., p. 226.

was a witch and a murderess.'[31] While in the novels above the central conflict is between urban and rural communities, here the utopian community is almost completely fabular. Yet Sollas is not a utopian paradise: its inhabitants are revealed to be just as petty, and its leader arguably as misguided, as those in mainland communities. Instead, Doig's own renunciation of society is framed as a more properly utopian ideal. In the final moments of the novel Doig leaves his possessions in a pool 'where crabs and prawns lived' so that he can be 'free to explore the infinities of life'.[32] Like Rutherford and Aldersyde, any sense of community can be found only in isolation; here, however, Doig constructs his idea of community not in relation to death, but through embracing the fullness of nature and abandoning all models of civilisation. What remains at the end of the novel is not a utopian community, but the utopian individual: while the inhabitants of Sollas might be flawed in their vision, the possibility of such a vision still serves as a basis for individual thought and development.

The Missionaries posits an elsewhere that allows for a radical rethinking of the relationship between the individual and the community. That the community is in many ways deluded is not, perhaps, as important as it might at first appear: certainly Doig is no less deluded himself, if in more familiar ways. The question of delusion, and its relation to an innate desire for community, reappears in *Some Kind of Grace*, where the choice is not between two kinds of faith so much as between faith and political awareness. Like Andrew Doig, the novel's protagonist John McLeod is an apparently rational figure searching for people whose ideas he fundamentally does not understand. Unlike *The Missionaries*, however, the representatives of spiritual enlightenment or delusion are not a community, but rather two people, Donald Kemp and Margaret Duncan, who may or may not be married. Kemp, the reader learns early on, thinks of himself as emulating Christ while Margaret, McLeod thinks, represents '[t]hat piety so like humbug: put your hand in God's and He will lead you into the enclosure marked: For the Saved Only.'[33] What separates Kemp and Duncan from Donald McInver, the leader of the Sollas community, is that while all three characters believe themselves to be doing God's will, the former have no supporting community. Instead they journey, as does McLeod, through a variety of isolated, if potentially utopian, communities that they reject in order to find their own individual salvation. On McLeod's journey to a valley prohibited

---

31   Robin Jenkins, *The Missionaries* (London: Macdonald, 1957; repr. Edinburgh: Polygon, 2005), p. 115.
32   Ibid., p. 229.
33   Robin Jenkins, *Some Kind of Grace* (London: Macdonald, 1960; repr. Edinburgh: Polygon, 2004), p. 188.

to foreigners where Kemp and Duncan may reside, he describes several utopian spheres. There is an embassy in Kabul where, as one character says, '[o]utside, above the spacious, silent gardens, the moon shines on the white walls, balconies, and flowered terraces of the Residence. Here God lives.'[34] If this is a secular joke, it repeats the notion found throughout the book that Afghanistan is a land shaped by God. After seeing the famous Buddhas at Kalak, McLeod finds himself in Faizabad:

> Suddenly, in a land as arid as the moon, there they were, blue and suavely green, set in deep canyons of red cliffs. [...] Along the cliff edges the ground was so dry it would have seemed nothing could ever grow and live in it; yet hundreds of prickly plants grew in the dust, with flowers and leaves of strange shapes and colours, and myriads of grasshoppers as big as dragonflies kept leaping as high as a man's hand in a constant chirp and dance. [...] Little wonder that a shrine containing the bones of a holy man had been built on the shore of the large blue lake.[35]

McLeod, like Doig, sees the possibility of holiness in the immanent and the natural. Moreover, the landscape of Afghanistan is repeatedly compared to Scotland. In this respect, *Some Kind of Grace* can be seen as a refashioning of John Buchan's final novel, *Sick Heart River*, where the divine is looked for in the solitude of foreign landscapes, yet the protagonists see only Scotland.

Yet communities, in *Some Kind of Grace*, are far from utopian. McLeod discovers that Duncan and Kemp have stopped into the small village of Haimir, an impoverished community where he sees only filth and disease. Despite McLeod's revulsion for Haimir, he is revolted when he discovers that the local authorities have done great violence to the townspeople, believing that they may be responsible for Duncan and Kemp's rumoured death. Although McLeod has earlier argued that the entire community should be punished for the deeds of anyone within that community, he is horrified when this plan is carried out. What is clear here is that the Scots cannot enter into the local community, nor understand the life there. This is more than a cultural or religious difference: community, in this novel, is hostile to the sort of thinking that the Western characters indulge in. It might be that utopia is possible in Afghanistan, but none of the Western characters know how to look for it. Instead, after Kemp's death, Duncan creates a utopian community of one. In Duncan's final

---

34   Ibid., p. 48.
35   Ibid., p. 121.

letter, she writes of her life in the valley community in the north, where she has been, if not welcomed by any means, not completely dismissed:

> I find I have no wish to return to what is called the world. [...] I have discovered that the attachment of these people to their Moslem faith is not nearly as strong as I supposed. What is strong is their love of God, and their determination to lead godly lives. It would seem to me that, if I show patience and, above all, a good example, I may succeed in interesting some of them in Christ. One or two – I shall mention no names – are already almost converts. This is a great comfort and encouragement to me.[36]

This letter ends the novel, and neither McLeod nor the reader is able entirely to decipher Duncan's motives, or indeed her sanity. What remains apparent, though, is that she has not chosen a utopian place where she is in full concord with the people around her; indeed, given all that has come before, it seems unlikely that she will convert any of her neighbours.

As in the novels discussed above, in both *The Missionaries* and *Some Kind of Grace* characters seek for a sense of community in its traditional geographic and organic formulation, but find an understanding of community only in isolation. Utopian communities are not ultimately possible as places set apart, but exist in the discourse surrounding independent thinking. While Jenkins does not negate the importance of the communitarian impulse, he suggests that it must radically be rethought. His approach to community is most fully realised in the late novel *Willie Hogg*. The novel combines each of the themes discussed above, most notably in its juxtaposition of the local community found in Glasgow with a potentially utopian community in Arizona. Hogg's initial community is located in the pub *The Airlie Arms*, and consists of four or five men who meet twice weekly to play dominoes and discuss 'the affairs of the world', eking out their pints over two hours.[37] This is perhaps the smallest and most intentional community in Jenkins's novels, but it is one of care and compassion. The community is enlarged when Hogg and his wife Maggie learn of the illness of her sister Elspeth, who has served as a missionary among the Navajo and is days from death. With the help of local journalists who pick up the story, a public subscription is formed; the story catches the public

36   Ibid., pp. 226–227.
37   Robin Jenkins, *Willie Hogg* (Edinburgh: Polygon, 1993; repr. Edinburgh: Polygon, 1996), p. 4.

imagination and the fund raises enough for first-class travel to America. When Hogg is questioned about the expense, he responds with the voice of the city:

> They would say, we're sorry for Maggie's sister, a Glasgow woman, dying thoosands o' miles frae hame, but here's money for you baith to go and see her before she dees and maybe comfort her. Tell her all Glasgow wishes her well. We ken, Willie, it's nae pleasure trip but make it as easy on your-selves as you can. Remember you represent us. We've got a reputation in the world for decency and generosity. Don't let us doon.[38]

As much as this might appear self-serving, Hogg's conception of his commu-nity is largely accurate, as is seen in the immense turnout for Maggie's funeral after she dies unexpectedly in America. The communities of *The Airlie Arms* and Glasgow are presented in unified, even idealised, but they also benefit the individual.

Like the final community in which Duncan finds herself in *Some Kind of Grace*, the Navajo community in Arizona offers the potential of utopia, but is instead mired in poverty and distrust. Hogg finds that there is no place for the Red Bluffs Apostolic Mission in the romanticised vision of Native Ameri-can life; the Navajo, meanwhile, have little use for the Christianity Elspeth preaches. Precisely because the community has been politically forced into a geographic and ethnic unity, it does not cohere, but is a place of often indis-tinguishable individuals. While, as in *Some Kind of Grace*, the use of Navajo and Afghanistani characters as undifferentiated others against which Scottish characters can define themselves is undoubtedly problematic, the Hoggs' im-mersion in this failed community does enable them better to understand each other as individuals. It is only in Arizona, where they have no supportive net-work, that they are able to realise their love for each other, as well as the ways in which they have failed each other. Here they can speak 'as one Glaswegian to another': both individual and communal identities are reinforced from a position of remove.[39]

While this might suggest a new form of utopia based on love, the deaths of Maggie and Elspeth leave Willie Hogg alone. Like Rutherford, he ends the novel in a cemetery; he reads a poem at Maggie's funeral about how in losing her he has lost the world, and he resists the consolations of the larger Glasgow com-munity. Unlike Rutherford, he does not end the novel in complete isolation.

---

38   Ibid., p. 35.
39   Ibid., p. 118.

Rather, in understanding his own experience of loneliness and isolation, he is better able to empathise with his original community of pub companions. The novel concludes:

> Charlie patted him on the knee. 'You'll get ower it, Willie.'
> But Charlie, after fifty years, have you got over it?
> 'You did very well, Willie,' said Alec.
> They were now out of the cemetery and heading, no longer at a funereal pace, towards the *Auld Hoose*.[40]

In its brevity and subtlety, this is one of Jenkins's clearest statements on the nature of community. Alec and Charlie offer general words of sympathy that might amount only to truism or cliché. Yet in Willie's unspoken response the degree of his empathy is clear. Community consists not simply in recognising one's own loneliness, but the loneliness of others, and from that recognition being able still to see oneself as part of a collective. Community is formed at the point of absolute distance and remove, and yet still exists in a unified, placed experience. Community, here, arises not from shared experience, but an individual experience of death that can exist in tandem with other individual experiences.

Jenkins's writing on community continually privileges isolation rather than immersion. Yet in each of the novels discussed above, isolation is not an endpoint in itself, but reveals the nature of the relation between the individual and the community. As suggested above, Jenkins's portrayal of community often resembles Esposito's claim that community can only be defined in relation to 'the lack from which it derives'; Jenkins does not negate the idea of community, but rather places greater emphasis on it by showing how it originates in absence rather than presence.[41] If Jenkins might not align himself with the various theoretical approaches discussed above, he nevertheless is engaged in a similar rethinking of the value of community and the utopian impulse. The focus on the isolated individual found at the conclusion of many of his novels suggests a new possibility for community, one based not in space but in time. As Alexandre Franco de Sá argues, the modern utopia must be thought of as 'a space without a place, a space that is nonetheless possible and whose existence does not essentially contradict nature': a space that is made possible by

---

40   Ibid., p. 167.
41   Esposito, *Communitas*, p. 42.

putting utopia in the dimension of the future.[42] Utopia cannot be found in the here and now, nor in traditional models of community, but remains possible in the individual's duty to the future. Community, in Jenkins's novels, is always yet to come: its possibility is predicated on realising that the origin of community is not in place, tradition, or belief, but in the isolated individual's capacity for empathy. This somewhat surprising turn allows Jenkins to make a unique argument for the place of community in Scotland, and in Scottish literature, while simultaneously working within a longstanding thematic and formal tradition. His novels demonstrate the continued importance of the form as a vehicle for thinking about community, while the consistency of his approach suggests the often overlooked philosophical rigour of his writing.

Works Cited

Brown, Callum G., *Religion and Society in Twentieth-Century Britain* (Harlow: Pearson, 2006).

Craig, Cairns, *The Modern Scottish Novel: Narrative and the National Imagination* (Edinburgh: Edinburgh University Press, 1999).

Esposito, Roberto, *Communitas: The Origin and Destiny of Community* [1998], trans. by Timothy Campbell (Stanford: Stanford University Press, 2010).

Franco de Sá, Alexandre, 'From Modern Utopias to Contemporary Uchronia', in Patricia Vieira and Michael Marder, eds., *Existential Utopia: New Perspectives on Utopian Thought* (New York and London: Continuum, 2012), pp. 23–34.

Hart, Francis Russell, *The Scottish Novel: A Critical Survey* (London: John Murray, 1978).

Jenkins, Robin, *Guests of War* (London: Macdonald, 1956; repr. Edinburgh: B&W, 1997).

Jenkins, Robin, *A Love of Innocence* (London: Cape, 1963; repr. Edinburgh: B&W, 1994).

Jenkins, Robin, *The Missionaries* (London: Macdonald, 1957; repr. Edinburgh: Polygon, 2005).

Jenkins, Robin, *Some Kind of Grace* (London: Macdonald, 1960; repr. Edinburgh: Polygon, 2004).

Jenkins, Robin, *The Thistle and the Grail* (London: Macdonald, 1954; repr. Edinburgh: Polygon, 2005).

Jenkins, Robin, *Willie Hogg* (Edinburgh: Polygon, 1993; repr. Edinburgh: Polygon, 1996).

---

42   Alexandre Franco de Sá, 'From Modern Utopias to Contemporary Uchronia', in Patricia Vieira and Michael Marder, eds., *Existential Utopia: New Perspectives on Utopian Thought* (New York and London: Continuum, 2012), pp. 23–34 (p. 27).

Jenkins, Robin, *A Would-Be Saint* (London: Gollancz, 1978; repr. Edinburgh: B&W, 1994).

Kofman, Sarah, *Smothered Words* [1987], trans. by Madeleine Dobie (Evanston, IL: Northwestern University Press, 1998).

Morgan, Edwin, *Essays* (Cheadle: Carcanet, 1974).

Nancy, Jean-Luc, *Adoration: The Deconstruction of Christianity II* [2010], trans. by John McKeane (New York: Fordham University Press, 2013).

Ranciére, Jacques, *The Flesh of Words: The Politics of Writing* [1998], trans. by Charlotte Mandell (Stanford: Stanford University Press, 2004).

Smith, Iain Crichton, *The Red Door: The Complete English Stories 1949–76*, ed. by Kevin MacNeil (Edinburgh: Birlinn, 2001).

Smith, Iain Crichton, *Towards the Human: Selected Essays* (Edinburgh: MacDonald, 1986).

Smout, T.C., *A Century of the Scottish People: 1830–1950* (London: Fontana, 1987).

The Art of Uncertainty: Forms of Omniscience in the Novels of Robin Jenkins

Cairns Craig

Abstract

Jenkins's narrative technique might seem to be aligned with that return to 'realism' and rejection of modernist experiment which characterised many of the major novelists from the 1930s to the 1950s. But this adoption of an apparently straightforward third-person omniscient narration is continually undermined by an alternative perspective which emphasises the relativity of the judgments by which events are constructed. Such internal conflict within the texts produces formal structures which are much closer to the experiments of the modernists and the postmodernists than they are to the neo-realism of the 1930s, 40s and 50s. At a formal level, Jenkins's novels re-enact Nietzsche's dialectical conception of the birth of tragedy and, at the same time, sceptically negate the significance which Nietzsche still attributed to tragedy: Jenkins's novels represent a dialectic which has no resolution but produces instead an endless and mutual undermining of all possible human values.

Keywords

Modernism – Postmodernism – Nietzche – romance – realism – narrative voice

Robin Jenkins published his first novel, *So Gaily Sings the Lark*, in 1950, the year from which Rubin Rabinovitz dates the rejection, by British novelists, of the experimental treatment of narrative by the writers we have come to describe as 'modernist', from Henry James and Joseph Conrad to James Joyce and Virginia Woolf.[1] As Randall Stevenson has noted, the writers of the period after the Second World War returned to the manner of 'early twentieth-century writers whom modernism had rejected', such as Arnold Bennett, the massed particulars of whose realism apparently offered a better model for novelists engaged

---

1   Rubin Rabinowitz, *The Reaction against Experiment in the English Novel 1950–1960* (New York: Columbia University Press, 1967).

primarily in charting social change.[2] Thus far typical of his literary generation, Jenkins's early fiction shows no sign of an author who had grown up through or been influenced by the period of high modernism: rather it reveals an author determined to resist the illusions of romance with which nineteenth-century Scottish fiction was associated. Thus *Happy for the Child* opens with the shock of the child protagonist's ejection from the world of Robert Louis Stevenson's fiction into a degraded and degrading reality that Jenkins's novel will relentlessly document:

> Pages 256 and 257 were missing. Shocked, the boy slowly and in fear became aware that the book in his hands was merely a destructible contrivance of gum and paper, and that in spite of it, round him in the little kitchen crowded the familiar baleful furniture. The tall forests dwindled to the oilclothed table with the mended leg, the blue seas faded into the gray linoleum, and the voices of macaws and adventurers became the gabble of women outside hanging up washed towels and shirts and babies' napkins in the sooty sunshine.[3]

Desire for and ejection from the conventions of a romance narrative was to remain the persistent theme of Jenkins's fiction, often associated with the desire for wealth as an escape from poverty, a theme most ironically played out in the career of Fergus Lamont, who enjoys great wealth through the romantic fiction produced by his wife Betty:

> I felt sure that women who worked long hours at dreary jobs in bleak chilly factories would see through her as a fraud or at any rate a hypocrite. She came to them so fresh, so blooming, so fragrant, so expensively and warmly dressed. She spoke to them as though they were semi-imbecilic. She read out passages from her novels that might as well have been about cannibals with bones through their noses for all the relevance they had to working-class women worried about their men at war and their children sleeping three in a bed in a room-and-kitchen. Yet, to my astonishment, they listened to her with rapture on their haggard faces, showed their bad

---

2   Randall Stevenson, *The Last of England: The Oxford English Literary History, Volume 12, 1960–2000* (Oxford: Oxford University Press, 2004), p. 405.

3   Robin Jenkins, *Happy for the Child* (London: Lehmann, 1953; repr. Nairn: Balnain Books, 1992), p. 9.

teeth in smiles of delight, and clapped their work-worn and lumpy hands in delicate applause.[4]

Like Fergus, Jenkins's fiction lives check by jowl with romance, both tempted by it and resistant to it. As Gregor McLeod says of himself in *Childish Things*, 'I couldn't bear to quit dreamland and return to reality', and the journey towards or away from dreamland is one that many of Jenkins's characters are forced to undertake.[5]

It is a pattern established in Jenkins's first novel, *So Gaily Sings the Lark*, which follows an unemployed miner on a journey from the desolation of modern Scotland's industrial heartland to the Highlands, the heartland of the country's romantic past. The book opens with his arrival at Loch Lomond, on the edge of enchantment:

> For half an hour he rested there, enjoying the warmth, allowing himself to be hypnotised by the glitter on the famous and fabled loch, and seeing like a mirage the Lanarkshire coal-fields from which he had come. Those huge sooty sheds of corrugated iron, the blank claustrophobic houses, everywhere the earth disenchanted by stale use into dirt, yonder was his home where he had been born, brought up and conditioned. Surely he could not, without deceiving himself, claim this spacious beauty as his birthright? Who, nowadays in Scotland could?[6]

Jenkins's focus on his central character's working-class background, and the several chapters which detail his work planting trees, makes *So Gaily Sings the Lark* a prefiguration of British novelists' concern in the 1950s and 1960s to document, in novels such as Alan Sillitoe's *Saturday Night and Sunday Morning* or David Storey's *This Sporting Life*, the gritty reality of modern working-class experience, even in the world of the welfare state. But for Jenkins's character, David, the lure of this 'fabled' world draws him not towards a modern urban environment but into a version of Scotland that would have been perfectly recognisable to any late nineteenth-century Scottish author – a Scotland in which the minister is central both to the social world and to the narrative, and in which the Highlands are the setting for a choice between two women, one of them the repressed inhabitant of her brother's Manse, the other an apparently

---

4   Robin Jenkins, *Fergus Lamont* (Edinburgh: Canongate, 1979), p. 118.
5   Robin Jenkins, *Childish Things* (Edinburgh: Canongate, 2001), p. 235.
6   Robin Jenkins, *So Gaily Sings the Lark* (Glasgow: William MacLellan, 1950; repr. Bath: Cedric Chivers, 1971), p. 1.

wild free spirit who looks to David, 'as beautiful as he could have wished', the embodiment of the 'exaltation and the tantalising unattainableness of that lucid land'.[7]

This is a land recognisably shaped by the conflict between romantic and realistic conceptions of the purposes of fiction that had formed a central strand of Scottish narrative from Walter Scott's *Waverley* in 1814 to J.M. Barrie's *Farewell Miss Julie Logan* in 1931: David travels towards that land of romance and the woman who embodies it, while she, Kirstie, is intent on travelling away from it, knowing its irrelevance to the modern world: 'She recognised the innocence and dignity of that old life, and even its desirableness; but at the same time she knew with a disappointment that must at all costs be concealed, that it was past forever.'[8] Both, however, are rendered in a narrative medium which would be recognisable to any of the writers in that nineteenth-century Scottish tradition: a linear plot, third person narration and each brief chapter focused on an individual incident that is announced by its chapter title – 'Visit to Kiltartin', 'Death of an Old Atheist'. As Francis Russell Hart suggests, 'The narrative is a simple episodic sequence of local places, events, character types variously illustrative of natural and religious attitudes'.[9] Indeed, in terms of narrative style, *So Gaily Sings the Lark* is closer to the popular fiction that Fergus Lamont's wife writes than to the explorations in the rendering of subjectivity that characterise mainstream modernism, or the experiments with vernacular made by the writers of the Scottish Renaissance movement. Indeed, there are occasions in Jenkins's later career when he seems, like some L.S. Lowry of literature, to adopt a deliberately naïve narrative style, uninformed by any awareness of the history of the genre. So, for instance, in *Willie Hogg*, despite the possible literary allusion of its central character's name, we are introduced to the friends of its eponymous hero with the cursoriness of a newspaper report: 'The three other regulars besides Willie himself were Charlie McCann, seventy-six, Alex Struan, seventy-two, and Angus McPhie, seventy.'[10] There then follow three paragraphs giving us thumbnail sketches of the three regulars, of which this is typical:

> Angus McPhie was small and fat. He had been born on the island of Barra and brought to Glasgow by his parents when he was a baby. He tried to

7   Ibid., p. 21, p. 111.

8   *So Gaily Sings the Lark*, p. 114.

9   Francis Russell Hart, *The Scottish Novel: A Critical Survey* (London: John Murray, 1978), p. 273.

10   Robin Jenkins, *Willie Hogg* (Edinburgh: Polygon, 1993), p. 5.

speak with a Hebridean lilt and liked to stick in a Gaelic word or two. He had been brought up a Catholic and still considered himself one though he seldom attended chapel. This was because Nellie his Protestant wife protested when he did, but also because, so he said earnestly, he was allergic to the smell of candles. He did not like jokes about the Pope except those he told himself. He had worked for the gas company.[11]

The abrupt casualness of that final sentence and the simple repetitions of syntax – 'He had been...He had been' – suggest an author fulfilling to the minimum the 'solidity of specification' that Henry James suggested was necessary to the novel. There is no sign here of a novelist who has accepted that his characters must 'show' themselves rather than have him 'tell' us about them.[12]

As a result, Bernard Sellin has judged that Jenkins's approach to fiction 'is definitely traditional, avoiding narrative disruptions, complex time patterns or narratorial inventiveness'.[13] This is true if we are comparing Jenkins to modernist or postmodernist experiments, but this does not mean that Jenkins simply replicates the same traditional mode of narration in every novel. Jenkins's novels experiment continually with what Jean Paul Sartre identified as the key issue for the contemporary novel in the late 1940s – the role of the narrator. Sartre castigates François Mauriac for his failure to acknowledge that there could be no place for God-like omniscience in a modern novel, since it implies a world overseen by a single divine creator rather than the relativity with which modern human beings have had to learn to live:

> Like most of our writers, he has tried to ignore the fact that the theory of relativity applies in full to the universe of fiction, that there is no more place for a privileged observer in a real novel than in the world of Einstein...M. Mauriac has put himself first. He has chosen divine omniscience and omnipotence. But novels are written *by* men and *for* men.

---

11   Ibid., p. 6.

12   The distinction between 'showing' and 'telling' was central to one of the earliest theoretical accounts of the novel, Percy Lubbock's *The Craft of Fiction* (London: Jonathan Cape, 1921): 'the art of fiction does not begin until the novelist thinks of his story as a matter to be shown, to be so exhibited that it will tell itself', p. 62.

13   Bernard Sellin, 'Robin Jenkins and Janice Galloway', in *The Edinburgh History of Scottish Literature, Volume 3*, ed. by Ian Brown (Edinburgh: Edinburgh University Press, 2007), pp. 231–236 (p. 233).

In the eyes of God, Who cuts through appearances and goes beyond them, there is no novel, no art, for art thrives on appearances.[14]

It would be easy for a Sartrean critic to show how Jenkins commits the same sins as Mauriac. In *The Changeling*, for instance, the teacher and his wife who have taken a boy from the slums on holiday with them silently communicate their reaction to the experience:

> Charlie and Mary exchanged glances, hers proud and content, his sombre; but each glance admitted the same thing, that their own son, if he had been taken from them at birth and brought up in Donaldson's Court, would have turned out to be no more honest than Tom and Peerie.[15]

The narrator's summation of their unspoken conclusion renders it a 'truth' of omniscience rather than simply a judgment of personal experience, with all the hazards of relativity that that might imply: readers, whatever their own views, have to acknowledge this 'truth' within the novel because it is given validation by its omniscient narrator. Rather than simply observing and recording the events of the narrative in the style which Ian Watt, in *The Rise of the Novel* (1957), described as 'formal realism', and to which he ascribed the rise of the novel as a form, Jenkins's narrator effectively intervenes in the narrative to indicate which views held by his characters are 'true' and which false.[16]

Such moments when omniscience *descends* to validate particular points of view among its characters, are balanced by moments when characters seem to be vouchsafed entry into the perspective of the omniscient. Thus in *So Gaily Sings the Lark* the free-spirited Kirstie whom David courts is also wooed by the minister, who tries to press her to a commitment:

> 'I'll want my answer soon, Kirstie.'
>   'You'll get it.'
>   He felt glad again, for it seemed clear enough what her answer would be.
>   'Here's that squirrel again,' he said. 'It's still not very sure of us, Kirstie.'

14 Jean Paul Sartre, *What is Literature?*, trans. by Bernard Frechtman (London: Methuen, 1950), p. 23.

15 Robin Jenkins, *The Changeling* (London: Macdonald, 1958; repr. Edinburgh: Canongate, 1989), p. 143.

16 Ian Watt, *The Rise of the Novel* [1957] (Harmondsworth: Peregrine, 1963), p. 33.

She stared at the small red creature and smiled. It struck him as a memorable smile. If she went with him, after twenty years of more or less successful living together he would remember that smile of hers to the squirrel; and it would torment him with a feeling of eternal exclusion and make his very soul squirm with hopeless longing.[17]

The narration is focalised from the minister's point of view, thereby ensuring the reader does not know which choice Kirstie is going to make – but the final sentence, although apparently continuing the minister's reflections, seems to have joined itself to an omniscience that reaches beyond the character to a certain foreknowledge of the future. As what is 'memorable' in the present becomes a 'memory' in a distant future, it seems as though the character has suddenly acquired access to the narrator's omniscient overview of all the possible outcomes of the narrative. Omniscience, it appears, has made itself available to the character it is presenting, as though the predestination implied by the minister's religion has become a reality of the character's experience.

Such moments when the omniscience of the narrator and relativity of the character are suddenly fused are crucial to certain of Jenkins's narratives. In *Guests of War*, for instance, the narrator seems to adopt a distant and ironic view of his characters, setting them in a historical context of which they are unaware but which allows readers to envisage the events described in a long historical sequence:

It was not the first time the people of Langrigg had made ready to receive invaders. Almost two thousand years ago they had skulked in their hills and woods to watch the Roman legionaries burn down their huts of clay and wattle. No doubt when darkness fell they had sneaked down for a rash and impudent blow at the masters of the world. Later came the English on their revengeful incursions: in a fit of imperial pique during their retreat from Bannockburn they had destroyed the Abbey.[18]

The ironic juxtaposition of far distant military invasions with the 'invasion' of mothers and children evacuated from the city at the outbreak of the Second World War underlines how ambiguous is the moral environment in which the characters have to act and the shifting points of view from which their actions will be evaluated. At the centre of the novel, however, is Bell McShelvie, its

---

17   Jenkins, *So Gaily Sings the Lark*, pp. 251–252.
18   Robin Jenkins, *Guests of War* (London: Macdonald, 1956; repr. Edinburgh: Scottish Academic Press, 1988), p. 57.

proletarian protagonist who, as seen through the eyes of a middle-class teacher, 'represented, in a baleful fashion, the realism of grey-haired, poverty-stricken, harassed maternity': her limited 'realism', however, is to become the vehicle of a spiritual vision which mere 'realism' would have denied was possible to her:

> Lifting her eyes, she gazed beyond the town to the north where, nearly a hundred miles away, lay Gowburgh back to which she must soon go. With its hunger, blacker smoke, its many emptier kirks, its thousands of tall chimneys, and its million people, it could not be in her vision as peaceful, innocent, or full of faith; but for that reason, because somehow of its vulnerability, it seemed to her even more dear. She did not forget how in its mixture of wealth and squalor it represented mankind's greed and brutal indifference to what was beautiful; and how it contained so many streets like her own, where human beings had to live their only lives in a sordid confinement. There on that hill, with space so vast and radiant around her, she withdrew nothing of her condemnation of Nan Ross's city; but over it nevertheless she wished most profoundly to cast whatever protection her blessing offered.[19]

Bell's consciousness merges with that of her narrator to realise the possibility of a city, even a city of proletarian poverty, redeemed by suffering and by the commitments of ordinary working-class people. The language of this passage is not the kind of language in which Bell speaks: narrator and character have become one, she sharing in her narrator's language, the narrator allowed, by her life of poverty and suffering, to claim a history which makes her spiritual vision no mere escapism. The God-of-narration can descend, dove-like (or Mauriac-like), to inhabit and validate the world of His creation, or can allow the novel's characters a moment of transcendence when they share in the omniscience of their narrator.

In other novels the possibility of such a coincidence of perspectives is held sceptically at bay. Thus in *A Would-be Saint* the narrative voice inhabits equally the consciousness of the central character, Gavin Hamilton –

> In the pocket of his jacket was his copy of the New Testament. He did not intend to read out of it at the Griersons' but he liked to feel that it was always there if he needed it, like a wildwest sheriff his gun. They did not know that he often made fun of himself.[20]

---

19   Jenkins, *Guests of War*, p. 133, p. 285.
20   Jenkins, *A Would-be Saint* (London: Gollancz, 1978; repr. Edinburgh: B&W, 1994), p. 70.

– and, with equal facility, the consciousnesses of the local community:

> Who the hell did Gavin Hamilton think he was? Jesus Christ? Better men
> than he would ever be had tossed bottles at referees. Did he think, be-
> cause his father had been killed in the Great War, that he had some spe-
> cial right to be shocked by a bit of violence?[21]

At crucial moments, however, the choice of the consciousness through which
events are narrated produces an uncertainty that undermines omniscience itself. When his form teacher tells the young Gavin that his mother is dead it is
through her perspective that we have to interpret his reaction:

> As his form teacher, Miss Fordyce knew of his intention to become a min-
> ister. She had never heard him talking about religion and had supposed
> that his interest in it was sensible and level-headed, like her own indeed.
> Therefore she was quite shocked to find him doing, or at any rate trying to
> do, what all Christians ought to do, she knew, but thank God seldom did,
> that was, when confronted by the death of someone loved, reject human
> grief and find too immediate consolation in thoughts of eternal glory.
> Surely he was too young, too sensitive, and too honest for that. Yet how
> else to interpret this would-be beatific smile and these dry eyes?[22]

Is her interpretation correct? She immediately offers another – 'His father had
been killed in the war. It could be that all his grief had been exhausted' – but
omniscience offers support to neither.[23] As readers we are left in an uncertainty
which is matched by the nature of the narrative we are reading – is Gavin's refusal to have any involvement in the war the fulfilment of his Christian belief,
and therefore evidence of its possible truth, or is it simply the misplaced fanaticism of someone who has not come to terms with the fact that in a universe
'extended for unimaginable millions of black empty miles'[24] there is no omniscience to appeal to? The novel, apparently presented from the perspective
of an omniscient third-person narrator, actually puts in doubt that narrator's
willingness to provide certainty about his own narrative:

---

21   Ibid., p. 106.
22   Ibid., p. 45.
23   Ibid.
24   Ibid., p. 215.

They did not envy Gavin. They would never have changed places with
him. They would have argued that by accepting the world with all its imperfections they were acting more sanely and compassionately than he.
[...] Yet their eagerness to speak to him or just to stand in his presence put
a beauty into their faces that had not been there before.

   Or so at any rate it seemed to McMillan.[25]

The apparent certainty of third person testimony – 'put a beauty into their
faces that had not been there before' – dissolves into being nothing but the
personal and provisional interpretation of one of the characters in the novel.
Omniscience turns into nescience, a term put into intellectual debates in the
nineteenth century by Sir William Hamilton in what became a famous essay
on 'The Philosophy of the Unconditioned': Gavin Hamilton in his effort to be
'unconditioned' by the war going on around him might be acting out the terms
of the essay by an author whose surname he shares.[26]

   Hamilton's concept was at the core of debates about the implications of
Darwinism in the late nineteenth century, and used both by agnostics and be-
lievers when dealing with that, seemed to be humanity's ignorance of God and
His purposes:

> Loth to admit that our science is at best the reflection of a reality we can
> not know, we strive to penetrate to existence in itself; and what we have
> laboured intensely to attain, we at last fondly believe we have accom-
> plished. But, like Ixion, we embrace a cloud for a divinity. Conscious only
> of, – conscious only in and through, limitation, we think to comprehend
> the Infinite; and dream even of establishing the science – the *nescience*
> of man, on an identity with the omniscience of God. It is this powerful
> tendency of the most vigorous minds to transcend the sphere of our fac-
> ulties, which makes a 'learned ignorance' the most difficult acquirement,
> perhaps, indeed, the consummation of knowledge.[27]

The desire to escape the limitations of our nescience necessarily invokes the
notion of omniscience but it is a notion which has only a logical justification – it

---

25   Ibid., p. 214.

26   Sir William Hamilton, *Philosophy of the Unconditioned* (Edinburgh Review, Volume 41,
      October 1829).

27   Sir William Hamilton, 'The Philosophy of the Unconditioned', *Discussions on Philosophy
      and Literature, Education and University Reform* [1829] (Edinburgh and London: William
      Blackwood, 1853), p. 43.

is everything that nescience is not – but precisely because of our nescience we can give no proper content to it. It is an illusion, a dream, a temptation – or, as the opponents of Darwinism claimed, an offer of or opportunity for faith:

> We are thus taught the salutary lesson, that the capacity of thought is not to be constituted into the measure of existence; and are warned from recognising the domain of our knowledge as necessarily co-extensive with the horizon of our faith. And by a wonderful revelation, we are thus, in the very consciousness of our inability to conceive ought above the relative and finite, inspired with a belief in the existence of something unconditioned beyond the sphere of all comprehensible reality.[28]

If nescience applies only to the activity of reason we are therefore allowed to give greater weight, many were to argue, to the significance of faith. At the level of plot, Jenkins's novels juxtapose different nescient value systems each of which claims to have divine or transcendent validity, or, at least to be grounded in some absolute necessity: the conflict of these different value systems produces an uncertainty which may be an opening for the perception of a still higher set of values or, simply, a chasm of doubt from which there is no escape.

Thus in *Guests of War*, the schoolteacher Mr Roy crosses the street to speak to mother-of-six Mrs Ross, who had just been rejected by another household that had been asked to give shelter to her brood. Roy would normally have avoided her but stops to sympathise with her plight:

> '... Cheerio, and the best of luck.'
> Luck?' she repeated, pausing. 'My man says there's nae such thing. He says, whit's for you will no' go by you; he says it was a' planned oot before the start o' time.'
> Thus with absolute humility claiming her present situation to have been the occasion of God's special foresight and wisdom before the evolution of the stars, she set out along the main street, followed by her flotilla. Gazing after her, Roy had in his vision too the large red-sandstone West Kirk, with its fine steeple; but it was she and her children who brought the awe into his mind. Humanity, he had always known, was many sided; it was comic, sad, wise, foolish, chaste, lustful, generous, greedy, sincere, hypocritical, and so on to the exhaustion of his vocabulary; but there was another element, not so easily named, there all the time possibly but seen

---

28   Ibid., p. 15.

only in glimpses, and when seen, as now in Mrs Ross, making the vastness of churches intelligible.[29]

She is the unlikely channel of an omniscient certainty which makes the uncertainties of their situation bearable, even if the religion on which it is based is, in Roy's eyes, groundless.

Similarly, *Dust on the Paw* traces the impact on an expatriate community in Afghanistan of the unsettling arrival of an English woman who intends to marry a local Afghani school-teacher: the conflicts of race, religion and ethical beliefs which such a marriage threatens disrupts the certainties on which each community's and each individual life has been built. Wahab, the schoolteacher, goes to tell his family about his English bride's arrival; they expect to profit from the relationship:

> Everyone in Kabul knew that perquisites were better than salaries, and the higher the post the greater the perquisites. That was as much a fact of life as eating or excreting. There was no reason to be shocked. Those who suffered from the swindles were the first to grant the swindler his right to perpetrate them, provided he did it discreetly. After all, had they been lucky enough to be in his place they would have done the same. They were too mature in the world's ways to expect a man to stay poor if he had the chance of becoming rich.
>
> 'It should be easy for you in a short time to afford two houses,' said his mother.
>
> 'Are you suggesting I betray my pupils?'
>
> 'What do you mean?'
>
> 'If I make use of my position, and of my friendship with men like Prince Naim and Dr Habbibullah simply to enrich myself, then I betray not only my pupils but every child in the country.'
>
> 'What nonsense, my son!' cried his mother. 'If you become rich and powerful, your pupils will be very proud. They will say afterwards, Abdul Wahab used to be our Principal.'
>
> 'No. My students are too intelligent for that. It is no doubt true that they expect to be betrayed, because always in the past betrayal has taken place; but there is always hope in their hearts that some day someone, some Afghan who has the opportunity to enrich himself by betraying them, will refuse to take that opportunity.'[30]

---

29   Jenkins, *Guests of War*, p. 104.
30   Jenkins, *Dust on the Paw*, p. 307.

For Wahab his family's attitude was 'ratified, if not sanctified, by thousands of years of social relationship, whereas his was that of the bleating lamb deserving to be devoured'.[31] His idealism and his individualism have no place in their ethical system and would seem to commit him to the Western scepticism implicit in the science which he teaches, but the nescience that follows from his education is haunted by an omniscience towards which the novel itself strives in its effort to portray the minds and actions of individuals from so many different communities and traditions:

> Behind him the music and laughter grew more faint, and soon, coming to a bundle of rags against a wall where some homeless old man tried to sleep, he had a feeling that, dead, he had been banished from paradise and sent for the purification of his soul among the damned. This was the first of many he would see. It was therefore with a kind of defiance of God Himself that he cautiously crossed the ditch, and crouching, sought for the creature's hand to place in it a couple of coins that would buy at least a slab of *nan* in the morning.
>
> As he went on again he heard the murmurs of surprise and gratitude behind him, and tears came to his eyes. Why do we hate one another? He wondered. Why do we take pride and pleasure in it? You, Mojedaji, with your gold ring and secret brotherhood; you, Harold Moffatt, with your poetry and your lies; you, Mrs Moffatt, with your strange beauty and mysterious mind; and you, Mr Gillie, with your big, red face and redder rose: all of you, please remember good or bad, are in the eyes of God no better than that abandoned old man, even if for purposes of His own He has decided to allow you houses and money and good clothes and always plenty to eat, while he sleeps cold and hungry against a wall pissed against in daylight by dogs and little boys. How do you know, indeed, that the old man is not God Himself?[32]

Omniscience may be outcast, like the old homeless man, but it continues to haunt the consciousness even of those who have dismissed it – just as it haunts the structures of Jenkins's novels.

The dialectic of omniscience and nescience is fundamental to Jenkins's narrative strategies and to his experiments in how to organise narrative point of view. Omniscience implies prescience – a knowledge of the future that is as certain as the knowledge of the past – and Jenkins uses prescience as a

---

31   Ibid., p. 307.
32   Jenkins, *Guests of War*, pp. 177–178.

self-conscious artifice in his omniscient narration. Thus in *So Gaily Sings the Lark* prescience is implied in relation to the death of Kirstie's father who has become an atheist after the death of his wife in a lightning strike. As Dugald, the church bell-ringer, tells David, 'I've read my Bible and nobody's going to tell me that the Lord's so fed-up after all the centuries that He's going to let a man off for saying what Duncan Hamilton has against him'.[33] When David first catches sight of Duncan he sees him as defying a narrative greater and more powerful than himself:

> 'He's an atheist,' said McDougall.
> 'So I've heard.'
> It seemed a reckless thing to be, under that overwhelming arrogance of light. The old man left the trees and shoogled across the field. He looked puny and absurd, and though the burning passion of repudiation in him might be greater than his physical self, still how small a flame it must be compared with the splendour above him. Yet as he went on, comically but steadfastly, and with patience climbed the dyke, it seemed somehow that the heavens for all their glory and puissance were being defied and were not able to prevent him. He had a glory of his own.[34]

Duncan, however, will in the end have to submit to that greater narrative, but in an accident whose cause is ambiguously distributed between David himself, the natural world and an omnipotent deity. Watching Duncan scramble up among rocks on the hillside above his house, David has a vision of Kirstie among the woods, 'their trunks so presbyterianly grey and their leaves so paganly green':[35]

> So moved was he by that vision, and so grateful for it, that he lifted the spade and pressed it against him. The movement seemed to have an instant consequence on the hill. There was a rumbling, and as he searched for its cause he saw that from the face of the cliffs a piece of rock had broken away. It seemed to fall slowly, and break into fragments that looked curiously inconsiderable. Down they bounced, like children's balls, fell on boulders, shot up into the air with a long singing crack, and came on again in that rather inconsequential descent [...] the old man scurried for the shelter of a big stone. He fell, scrambled along on his knees for a yard

---

33   Jenkins, *So Gaily Sings the Lark*, p. 44.
34   Ibid., p. 138.
35   Ibid., p. 176.

or two so frantic was he to escape, struggled to his feet, ran, fell again, and was fallen, with his arms covering his head, when the shower of rocks dropping as casually as hail reached him, struck him, and bounced playfully on.[36]

Is it David's vision which has set off the rock fall, as though his love for Kirstie's requires her father's death? Is it an accident of the kind which killed Duncan's wife – the random play of forces beyond humanity's control? Or is it omnipotence taking revenge? When David tries to call a doctor he is told he is in the local hotel:

> ...at that moment the doctor was probably hurrying not to find his bag with equipment and his car but to gulp down another couple of whiskies. If he did come he would be too tipsy to drive well and might run into a ditch or against a tree. It looked as if the vengeance on Duncan Hamilton was continuing. Providence that had found centuries-old rocks easy instruments to use, would hardly find a crapulous man difficult.[37]

The novel's uncertainty about which force sends Duncan to his death is, of course, ironic, since it is the novelist-God of this narrative who has determined in advance that Duncan will lose his wife, defy omnipotence and die. In its form the novel mimics Calvinist notions of predestination and of an omniscient God who knows in advance all that is to take place, but the narrative itself emphasises how its characters exist in a continuous state of uncertainty about which order of causation they inhabit, their moments of apparent entry into the perspective of omniscience only underlining their lack of any real understanding of the shape of their own life's story: as Dugald expresses it,

> I canna get rid of the fear that something unchancy's going to happen. What's the explanation of that? Whiles I think myself that it's just the unbalance of things. A man kens in his heart that this is an unfinished sort of place, not perfect like heaven; and when he sees something that he thinks is complete he looks roond, without meaning to, for the disappointment. And he always finds it.[38]

---

36 Ibid., p. 177.
37 Ibid., p. 186.
38 Ibid., p. 43.

In this dialectic between the certainty of omniscience, played out in the third person narrative, and the uncertainty of individual human experience, trapped in nescience, lies the explanation of many of Jenkins's narrative strategies: those apparently unsophisticated, third person summations of character point precisely to how gratuitously impertinent is the novelist's assumption of omniscience, and how the characters are limited by his rather than their choices.

In *The Awakening of George Darroch*, for instance, the narrative mode is that of a formal omniscience, in which, in the opening chapter, the narrator roams Darroch's manse from the attic where his daughters have their rooms to the kitchen where his servants are discussing his wife's many pregnancies, and confidently summarises his family's and his community's evaluation of him:

> He was considered timorous, by his sons, by his brother-in-law Robert, by his brother Henry the sea-captain, by Sir James Loudon, chief heritor of the parish, and by most men in his congregation; and perhaps so he was in many things; but for the beatific joy of lying in Eleanor Jarvie's arms he would, he thought, give up not only kirk and manse but wife and children too.[39]

As the novel proceeds, however, the omniscient narrator who seems to be there simply to provide that 'full and authentic report of human experience' described by Watt, is provoked into judgmental interjections: so, when a Mr Saunders states of a woman who has attempted suicide in prison that 'if she is already suffering the torments of Hell here on earth, Mr Darroch, it is only what she deserves', the narrator responds: 'Thus spoke one who might well become Darroch's comrade in the new Free Church. Alas, there would be more like him'.[40] The 'alas' turns omniscient expectation into retrospective judgment. But as omniscience ceases to be objective and becomes ethically implicated in the events it also declines into nescience, increasingly concluding scenes in rhetorical questions to which an omniscient narrator ought to be able to provide an answer. After the fulfilment of the Disruption of the Church of Scotland, in which Darroch has played a leading role, we are told that 'the divinity students were gleefully congratulating one another', a documentary assertion which is followed by an unanswered question: 'Was it because they loved spiritual independence or because a large number of comfortable livings

---

39   Robin Jenkins, *The Awakening of George Darroch* (Edinburgh: Harris, 1985; repr. Harmondsworth: Penguin, 1987), pp. 9–10.

40   Watt, *The Rise of the Novel*, p. 33. Jenkins, *The Awakening of George Darroch*, p. 167.

had suddenly come on the market?' It is a question that may, in terms of the narrative, have formed in the mind of Darroch's son James, who has been attending the session of the Church Assembly in which the decision to quit the Church is taken, and for whom, truly, there might be no clear answer, but it is a question which is left hanging at the conclusion of a chapter as though James's lack of ability to form an answer is shared by the narrator. The narrator has, effectively, been displaced from his position of omniscience by his character: it is Darroch himself who has come to be in control of the narrative and who sees all of its characters and their interactions as though from a point of omniscience: 'Darroch saw into all their minds with inspired insight'.[41] Darroch has become the author of his own narrative, organising the characters around him to fulfil his own ambitions, with the result that the displaced narrator is as baffled by Darroch's actions as are his sons: 'Arthur realised how unfathomable his father was, or rather had become'.[42] *The Awakening of George Darroch* is a novel which dramatises the failure of omniscience: a religion which believes in omniscience and in predestination produces a schism which emphasises how little either side in the debate were able to foresee the consequences of their actions, but which both sides had to present as the fulfilment of God's intentions for the nation of the Scotland. As the conflict reaches its predestined conclusion – predestined, from our point of view, because that was how the history happened, but predestined from the point of view of those involved in it because of their belief in predestination – the narrator of *The Awakening of George Darroch* is increasingly limited and confined by the apparent omniscience of his central character. Darroch is the 'first of the unknowns' – i.e. 'the lowly and obscure' – to follow the leaders in exiting the Church assembly, but 'unknowns' has, in this context a double significance: what could have inspired them to such an act, to such defiance, to such self-sacrifice is unknowable, defeating every expectation of normal behaviour: 'it was one thing to make exalted vaunts about upholding the Crown Rights of Christ the King, it was quite another to face the prospect of being evicted from your comfortable manse, you and your large family'.[43] Their confidence in omniscience makes them, to us, 'unknown' and 'unknowable', thereby underlining the nescience in which we are trapped.

The displacement of omniscience in *The Awakening of George Darroch* is reversed in *Willie Hogg*, a novel in which the narrator gradually acquires an omniscience that transforms our understanding of the characters. The novel

---

41   Ibid., p. 241.
42   Ibid., p. 206.
43   Jenkins, *The Awakening of George Darroch*, 'Foreword', n.p.

begins in the confident third-person mode of a *faux naïf* narration which claims to be able to summarise everything we need to know about its characters:

> After the War he had no difficulty in regaining his old job as a porter in the Glasgow Royal Infirmary where everybody, from patients to consultants, soon discovered that his usefulness did not end with his ordinary tasks like helping to life heavy patients or wheeling corpses to the mortuary. His very presence at a scene of crisis had a calming effect. His was one of those fortunate natures that steady the world. He never grumbled or looked for someone to blame. Duties outside the scope of his contract were undertaken with a meekness that mesmerised the most militant of trade unionists: whatever Willie was he was no scab or boss's toady. Indeed, he was a zealous union man himself, paying his dues on time and attending all the meetings, though he spoke at none.[44]

This succinct omniscient summation of Willie's character is matched by the account of his marriage:

> He had married Maggie when he was twenty-three and she twenty-one. Faithful to his Socialist Sunday school principles he could not have a minister of the gospel at his wedding. Besides, in spite of his pug nose, he was a romantic at heart and wanted to be married according to the old Scottish custom of declaration. Maggie had raised no objection, though for years afterwards she was still puzzled that there had been no one in a dog collar present or anyone holding a Bible. For it has to be said that if Willie at school had been thought a slow learner Maggie's teachers had despaired of ever teaching her anything at all. At first they had been impressed by her continual expression of rapt attention until they discovered that she was really in a day-dream or dwam [...] It was agreed that the poor girl wasn't all there, but where she was remained a mystery.[45]

We are being introduced to two characters about whom there can be little more to know: we will, however, follow them on a journey to North America that changes them both but changes them by revealing what omniscience did not think it important to reveal to us about them at the beginning – who would have thought, for instance, that the hospital porter was an art critic: 'A favourite refuge of his at home was the Glasgow Art Galleries which he often visited to

---

44   Jenkins, *Willie Hogg*, pp. 1–2.

45   Ibid., p. 2.

refresh his spirit'; or that his favourite painter was Rembrandt, whose self-portrait in old age might be an image of Willie himself; or that one of his 'heroes was David Hume, the Edinburgh philosopher, who at the age of twenty-seven had written a famous book *A Treatise of Human Nature*'.[46] The narrative reveals Willie to have qualities that were invisible to omniscience at the beginning of the novel, and does so precisely by sympathising with and yet challenging the belief in an omniscient God that is represented by his wife's sister, a missionary to Native Americans on a desert reservation:

> She closed her eyes. 'Would you believe me, William, if I was to tell you this pain has become a comfort to me, even when I have felt I could bear it no longer?'
>
> Aye, Elspeth, I could believe you and I've got enough imagination to know what you mean.
>
> 'It is not for His creatures to question God's purpose,' she said.
>
> That was something often discussed in the *Airlie Arms*: God's purpose; with as much pertinence and a lot more wit than in a theological college. He himself had pointed out how the human mind was slippery with – what was the word? – casuistry. (They had teased him for it.) It could escape from any philosophical impasse with the ease of a Houdini. God's purpose could be found in everything, from AIDS to the deaths by starvation of thousands of black children. In the one case it was to punish homosexuals, and in the other to test the compassion of Christians.[47]

As Willie and Maggie are revealed to us as much more complex human beings than the initial third-person summation implied, so omniscience is subverted, revealing the nescience which it is designed to conceal.

These are not novels with so-called 'unreliable narrators' – narrators who are, in effect, characters within the story they are telling. Jenkins's narrators are apparently omniscient and outside of the narrative they recount, but the nature of their knowledge, which at first appears to be complete is increasingly called into question; as the narrative proceeds the characters escape from the summary judgements and expectations of a narrator who is learning from his characters the limitedness of the perspective in which he initially understood them: omniscience, like Darroch's church, is disrupted by characters who change in ways that the narrator was apparently unable to foresee. Without prescience, omniscience is revealed as nescience in disguise.

---

46   Ibid., p. 110, p. 111, p. 115.
47   Ibid., p. 109.

The strategic importance of the intersection of omniscience and nescience in Jenkins's novels is underlined by his first person narratives, for what his first person narrators seek is precisely the controlling power of omniscience in the representation of themselves in their own narratives. Gregor McLeod in *Childish Things* has remade the narrative of his childhood by 'reconstructing the past as it should have been', and is trying to order his future as though he is the omniscient author of his own existence.[48] 'The hardest thing in the world is to tell the truth about oneself', he tells Linda, the rich widow whom he hopes will provide him with a lifestyle of which he could only ever have dreamed –

> No one's brave enough or rash enough. Not even you, my dear. Evasions, distortions, omission, embellishments are inevitable. We're human be-ing, not gods. There are so many things we don't know, even about ourselves.[49]

This assertion of nescience, however, is carried out only to conceal the certainty to which omniscience aspires: 'No one could have told her for no one knew, not even Madge. My lies were buried too deep. If I kept my nerve and went on practising Ulyssean guile, I could bring it off'.[50] The reference to Ulysses takes us back, of course, to the very beginnings of narrative realism and omniscient narration, a literary context reinforced by the fact that when Linda asks for a great book to read Gregor suggests *Middlemarch*, that master work of Victorian omniscience, and ends up performing the part of Casaubon to Linda's Doro-thea in a mock marriage-night encounter:

> Whether as Casaubon or Gregor McLeod, I was in need of stimulation. Casaubon would never have sought it from Dorothea, and Gregor could not expect it from Linda.
>
>   Whose hand then, Linda's or Dorothea's, that pulled up the nightshirt – whose nightshirt? – and took hold of – Casaubon was it? Or Gregor?[51]

Linda's adoption of the role of Dorothea puts Gregor in the control of a nar-rator more practised than himself in omniscience – 'I expected her to shout, "Cut!" and push me out of the bed' – and so it will prove when she hires private detectives to track down his true origins and reveal the real narrative of his

---

48   Jenkins, *Childish Things*, p. 217.
49   Ibid., p. 172.
50   Ibid.
51   Ibid., p. 134.

life – or the narrative of his real life.[52] Gregor's desire for an omniscient control over how everyone will view his character, and therefore over how he can chart his future, is one of life's *Childish Things* – like novels themselves.

Fergus Lamont too, in the novel named after him, invents an alternative identity for himself on the presumption that he is the bastard child of an aristocrat – 'my main concern was to turn myself into a gentleman, as the first stage of my campaign to be accepted, one day, in Corse Castle, as one of the family' – and so becomes, in effect, the omniscient narrator of his own life, a life led according to the dictates of his imaginary identity:

> I had been given a bedroom once slept in by Sir Walter Scott. A portrait
> of him hung in it. I studied this for some time, for he was a Scotsman who
> had done with success what it was my ambition to do: that was, write
> about common people and assort with nobility.[53]

The effect on the reader is to cast doubt on whether the narrative has any truth, or whether it is simply the fantasy of an old man who wishes, retrospectively, to give his life a significance denied to those working-class people with whom he grew up and with whom, at the end, he remains: 'When I went back to my native town therefore it must be, not just as hero, aristocrat, and poet, but as absolver and redeemer'.[54] Fergus is the salvational son of his own omnipotent God, his nescience continually transcended by an ever more challenging omniscience which redeems his actions in terms of an ultimate purpose he could not have been aware of at the time of its happening: 'It could well be that my experience in East Gerinish, taken all together, but particularly my love for Kirstie and hers for me, had made me, unknown to myself, a good man'.[55] Because of the novel's interpellation of events from late in his life at a time when he is writing his 'memoirs', we, as readers, know the outcome of events in advance of their happening in the narrative itself, a prescience which gives us access to an apparent omniscience, but one which also underlines that the narrative is itself Fergus's reconstruction of his past, a past over which writing has given him an omniscient control that conceals the nescience in which he has actually lived.[56] His exile to the Western Isles and his encounter with a Celtic amazon called Kirstie replicates the journey that David had made in *So*

---

52   Ibid.
53   Jenkins, *Fergus Lamont*, p. 56, p. 90.
54   Ibid., p. 117.
55   Ibid., p. 275.
56   Ibid., p. 108.

Gaily Sings the Lark and David's encounter with a woman of the same name – it is as though, when Fergus's own plot is defeated by his monstrous wife and her much more successful career as a writer, he re-enacts the narrative of one of Jenkins's earlier novels but with a control over it that the protagonist of the earlier novel could never achieve. Nescience becomes a fraudulent omniscience, casting doubt on the omniscience of the author who has, beyond the bounds of the narrative, created Fergus Lamont and his world.

Fergus Lamont may be, as Bernard Sellin suggests, the *most* innovative work that Jenkins produced, but its narrative methods can be found across the range of Jenkins's writing, suggesting that he was far from being as 'traditional' and 'anti-experimental' as his critics – and indeed he himself – have suggested.[57]

Works Cited

Hamilton, Sir William, 'The Philosophy of the Unconditioned', in *Discussions on Philosophy and Literature, Education and University Reform* [1829] (Edinburgh and London: William Blackwood, 1853).

Hart, Francis Russell, *The Scottish Novel: A Critical Survey* (London: John Murray, 1978).

Jenkins, Robin, *The Awakening of George Darroch* (Edinburgh: Harris, 1985; repr. Harmondsworth: Penguin, 1987).

Jenkins, Robin, *The Changeling* (London: Macdonald, 1958; repr. Edinburgh: Canongate, 1989).

Jenkins, Robin, *Childish Things* (Edinburgh: Canongate, 2001).

Jenkins, Robin, *Fergus Lamont* (Edinburgh: Canongate, 1979).

Jenkins, Robin, *Guests of War* (London: Macdonald, 1956; repr. Edinburgh: Scottish Academic Press, 1988).

Jenkins, Robin, *Happy for the Child* (London: Lehmann, 1953; repr. Nairn: Balnain Books, 1992).

Jenkins, Robin, *So Gaily Sings the Lark* (Glasgow: William MacLellan, 1950; repr. Bath: Cedric Chivers, 1971).

Jenkins, Robin, *Willie Hogg* (Edinburgh: Polygon, 1993).

Jenkins, Robin, *A Would-be Saint* (London: Gollancz, 1978; repr. Edinburgh: B&W, 1994).

Lubbock, Percy, *The Craft of Fiction* (London: Jonathan Cape, 1921).

Rabinowitz, Rubin, *The Reaction against Experiment in the English Novel 1950–1960* (New York: Columbia University Press, 1967).

Sartre, Jean Paul, *What is Literature?*, trans. by Bernard Frechtman (London: Methuen, 1950).

---

57   Bernard Sellin, 'Robin Jenkins and Janice Galloway', p. 233.

Sellin, Bernard, 'Robin Jenkins and Janice Galloway', in *The Edinburgh History of Scottish Literature, Volume 3*, ed. by Ian Brown (Edinburgh: Edinburgh University Press, 2007), pp. 231–236.

Stevenson, Randall, *The Last of England: The Oxford English Literary History, Volume 12, 1960–2000* (Oxford: Oxford University Press, 2004).

Watt, Ian, *The Rise of the Novel* [1957] (Harmondsworth: Peregrine, 1963).

Realism, Symbolism, and Authorial Manipulation in *The Changeling*

Douglas Gifford

Abstract

The Changeling is Jenkins's most focused psychological novel, with its dramatic contrast and ruthless anatomisation of its two protagonists, the slum boy who has created a protective shell around himself as his defence against poverty and contempt, and the would-be Samaritan, the idealistic teacher who fails to understand the boy behind the shell. By placing these protagonists in the contrasting worlds of slum Glasgow and rural Scotland, and by emphasising the beauty of Argyll, it enables Jenkins to make – with devastating effect – satirical comment not only on the failures of Glasgow, the educational system, and class division, but also on the earlier 'Scottish Renaissance' fictions of Neil Gunn and Lewis Grassic Gibbon, with what Jenkins sees as their unsustainable assertion of the redemptive power of rural landscape and cultural tradition and myth. This novel is arguably the most tragic of all Jenkins's fiction, with – unusually – no redeeming grace to be found.

Keywords

humbug – Scottish education – 'Scottish Renaissance' – folk tradition – Gaelic song – city and country

The Changeling (1958) can claim to be one of the greatest of the twenty-nine novels of Robin Jenkins. It is concise and persuasive in its inexorable movement toward tragedy, spare, yet consistently rich in metaphor and symbol, savage in its realism of description of slum Glasgow, yet with echoes of an older, pre-industrial Scotland, and – this from a teacher of huge experience – condemnatory of shabby expediency in education and society generally. All this is interwoven with recurrent black humour; yet in contrast to the ambivalent endings of many of Jenkins's novels from *The Cone-Gatherers* (1955) to *Fergus Lamont* (1979), the novel leaves no doubt as to the terrible tragedy of its climax and its implications. It is also Jenkins's most focused psychological novel, with its anatomisation of its two protagonists, teacher and pupil; the idealistic teacher, deceptively decent in his plan of taking the slum boy with his family on their annual Clyde coast holiday.

More clearly here than in any of his novels, Jenkins polarises his extreme evaluations of humanity. On one hand, he presents humanity, particularly as represented by the world of teachers and the complex figure of the would-be Samaritan, Charlie Forbes, and his all-too-human family, with scepticism, even cynicism; and on the other, Jenkins creates innocence and indeed a kind of grace, in his unlikely slum boy Tom Curdie. And by placing all this in the two contrasting worlds of city and rural Scotland, and emphasising the beauty of Argyll, it enables Jenkins to make his recurrent comment on the contrast between natural beauty and human failing. As in so many of his novels, there is a fundamental dualism in the way Jenkins sees Scotland – or two Scotlands. His childhood was spent in recession coalmining Lanarkshire, and his earlier teaching in Glasgow's deprived East End, in striking contrast to his war years as a conscientious objector, spent in Argyllshire, which he loved. He returned to teach in Dunoon, living in a house on the hill above Toward, the location of *The Changeling*.

As with so many of his novels, *The Changeling* reflects Jenkins's mutually exclusive perspectives on his native country. On one hand it reveals his disgust at Glasgow's cynical acceptance of slums and deprivation, while on the other there is no mistaking his profound love and idealisation of Scotland's natural beauty. The novel opens in a tough East-End Glasgow. Thus Jenkins engages with very real issues of Scotland industrial and rural. This novel has its roots in his disillusionment with post war Scotland, and its social and educational failures. Yet, in keeping with so many of Jenkins's novels, this effect of the horror of reality conceals complex and frequently contradictory strategies Jenkins had been developing from the beginning of his fiction with *So Gaily Sings the Lark* in 1950.[1] At one level Jenkins can be seen as a social and psychological realist, but this realism is manipulated through authorial shifts of perspective and complex symbolism so that in the end a kind of metaphoric surrealism surrounds his denouements, emphasising that it is the permanent human condition, in all its bizarre contrariness, rather than immediate social conditions, which concern him most deeply.

From the outset the reader has to be on guard against Jenkins's subtle and authorial strategies. He so often seems to be empathising with whichever character he's presently treating, but – and it is crucial to recognise this – swiftly changing this empathy, so that he then seems to empathise with his next character, thus allowing us to compare (for example) the self-image of Forbes as the idealistic teacher from his colleagues', his wife's, or Tom's perspective. This constant alteration of character and moral perspective is what makes all Jenkins's

---

1   See the discussion of Jenkins's reaction against the 'The Scottish Renaissance' in the Overview.

novels elusive in terms of ever finding a moral resting-place or conclusion. For Jenkins there is none, since we are all trapped within our particular and limited perspective of right and wrong (and Jenkins continually destabilises these terms). In this novel no-one is to be finally condemned, not Charlie, not his apparently cynical fellow teachers, not even the snobbish and materialistic Mrs Storrocks.[2] Yet clearly, behind his shifting moral perspectives, Jenkins as author has ideals; compassion, hatred of poverty and hypocrisy, a yearning for the world to show some grace and common humanity.[3] This yearning is however continually undercut by his deep scepticism regarding the possibility that humanity can ever find this grace. Yet in all his fiction, the elusive possibility of finding some kind of grace or redemption in fallen humanity persists.

To a greater degree than most of Jenkins's novels, these authorial contradictions of scepticism and grace are embodied in the two principal protagonists, Charlie Forbes and Tom Curdie. Despite Jenkins giving moral significance to other characters (especially Forbes's daughter Gillian), they structure the novel as a comparison and confrontation of archetypal moral opposites. Additionally, the novel is broadly two halves; moving from qualified optimism regarding the holiday possibilities through darkening complexities of the relationship of teacher and pupil to the final tragedy. At the core of this novel is a thematic issue of the difficulties in human communication, embodied in the tragic failures of the teacher (particularly the teacher) and pupil to understand and communicate with each other. The responsibility for this failure of communication with and understanding of a deeply damaged yet essentially decent child is essentially that of Forbes and his family. It is with them I deal first.

Chapters 1–10: Forbes, Family and Colleagues – and Tom Curdie

The Forbes family are a typical lower-middle class unit. Forbes may be the wage earner, but his pretty wife Mary is the unifying force. Sometimes ashamed of her clumsy, often pompous husband, she is fiercely loyal. Gillian, her daughter

---

2   Even Mrs Storrocks, for all her narrow and conventional ethical rigidity, is allowed by Jenkins her moment of 'grim charity', when, struck by Tom's intelligence and decency, admits that 'that boy, given a chance, could take his place in any company'. This is before she is told of his thefts, whereupon her plans to aid his advancement vanish – 'I'd help a thief only as far as the jail'. Robin Jenkins, *The Changeling* (London: Macdonald, 1958; repr. Edinburgh: Canongate, 1989), p. 151, p. 160.

3   The term 'grace' as deployed by Jenkins in his fiction is elusive; if not exactly *Christian* grace, it implies a possibility of spiritual worth and unusual goodness.

of 13 and Alistair, 10, and the snobbish and critical Mary's mother, make up the holiday family, on their way to their annual Clyde coast cottage (which belongs to Mrs Storrocks). Yet it is this ordinary seeming group which will destroy Tom Curdie; and it is Jenkins's achievement to show us how their prejudices and inability to empathise with the boy's appalling background and his strategies for coping lead to tragedy – for them as well as Tom, for this is a novel leaving the reader with a terrible sense of the family having utterly destroyed itself.

But it is Charlie Forbes and no-one else who initiates the tragedy. Yet from the novel's opening sentence he is explicitly linked with biblical idealism ('no one would belittle the benevolence of the Good Samaritan' – although this link is immediately qualified by an ironic authorial warning regarding 'the folly of interference').[4] Against all warnings from hard-bitten and cynically realistic teacher colleagues (whose 'realism' simply sees the boy as a hopeless victim and thief, and fail to see that under the mask the boy is intelligent and acutely sensitive, stealing only to survive), Charlie insists that the boy come with his family on annual holiday to Dunroth and Towellan.[5] Charlie's wife Mary hates the idea, but gives in. The family (with Mrs Storrocks, who only approves taking the slum boy since it should be good for Charlie's career) – travel optimistically enough, and the first half of the novel leaves the possibility that Tom will please them with his quiet intelligence and sensitivity. Yet the reader must be on guard. Forbes's defects are highlighted in the opening chapters, with the sly authorial undermining of Forbes's idealism with his 'lugubrious' baggy eyes, his pink plumpness, his platitudes and righteous homilies, and his 'leer' of sympathy. Yet (typically and unsettlingly for the reader) Jenkins then transforms these unflattering perspectives on Forbes. Forbes's belief in Curdie is now seen as credible and moving; even his headmaster admits that Charlie has a generous impulse, and by portraying Mr Fisher and his colleagues by their own admission as 'coarse and selfish and brutal' in their cynicism, Jenkins allows a glimpse of authorial disgust regarding his own profession's worldliness.[6] They sum up Forbes as 'a nice enough fellow', if also 'an awful humbug'.[7] Even Mary, Forbes's wife, for all her genuine love of her family, recognises the contradictions of decency and fecklessness in her husband, with his clumsy pomposity

---

4 Jenkins, *The Changeling*, p. 2.
5 Jenkins plays with place names; Dunroth seems to conflate Dunoon and Rothesay (although Rothesay *is* Rothesay in chapter 17). Towallan combines Toward and Inellan, its neighbour village.
6 Jenkins, *The Changeling*, p. 8.
7 Ibid.

and 'his martyr's face'.[8] With affection qualified by ominous reservations, she nevertheless agrees to taking the boy on the holiday trip.

In Chapter 7 Jenkins presents the outset optimistically, with Forbes viewed as endearingly ushering his family and Tom away from Glasgow down the Clyde on trains and boats. Forbes takes simple pleasure in his annual pilgrimage of renewal. By now, however, the reader must be aware of Jenkins's constant ambivalence in presenting Forbes's moral judgements. To add complexity, it could almost seem that Jenkins at times intrudes a personal instability of his own values, moral and aesthetic. This intrusion betrays itself when the author tells us what Forbes 'should' have cried to Tom about the magnificent landscape of loch and mountain unfolding as they pass The Holy Loch. Whose voice – author or Forbes? – wishes that this paean of praise to Scotland's beauty could have been spoken?

> 'Here it is', he should have been able to cry, 'our heritage, Tom, yours and mine, because we are Scottish; and what we see now is only the promise of vaster riches. In no other country in the world, not even fabled Greece, is there such loveliness in so small a space. Here is the antidote to Donaldson's Court; here is the guarantee of that splendid and courageous manhood to which every Scots boy is entitled by birth'. All this he should have spoken [...] But a voice, like Todd's most kept shouting: 'Guff, Charlie; admit it's a lot of guff.'[9]

Jenkins for a time allows the reader to enjoy the spectacle of a bickering but happy family, despite occasional reservations from Forbes and his wife regarding Tom, shy and hovering around their close family unit. As always, however, there are ominously discordant notes. Forbes has already 'at the very back of his mind' begun to admit 'that his befriending of the slum delinquent child might reach the ears of authority' and is already preparing false modesty for a promotional interview.[10] Yet tellingly, already he intuits the potential for his undoing (as well as foreseeing Tom as scapegoat);

> The danger lay in falling into resentment against Tom Curdie, in seeing the boy's admirable reticence as some kind of sinister senile composure, such as was shown by the changeling of Highland legend, that creature

---

8   Ibid., p. 15.
9   Ibid.,, p. 51.
10   Ibid., p. 50.

introduced by the malevolent folk of the otherworld into a man's home, to pollute the joy and faith of family.[11]

(The percipient reader may well already think that Forbes, if not malevolent, has himself introduced Tom to his family; and that any 'pollution' lies at his door.)

For all this disturbing early projection of 'changeling' on Tom, Jenkins clearly means the reader to join Forbes in his delight at Arran's mountains. Indeed, at times Jenkins comes close to endorsing a view of land and seascape familiar from 'Scottish Renaissance' fiction, with its belief in the possibility of ideal unity of humans in a redemptive natural setting. (Although, while Forbes insists that Tom should 'cherish that vision' of Arran's sleeping warrior; Jenkins acidly has Forbes add that 'it will sustain you in times of trouble', which will gain a terrible irony by the end). Indeed, Jenkins slyly qualifies all Forbes's glorying in natural beauty. 'Never [to Forbes] had the Firth looked so beautiful. The roadsides were gardens of honeysuckle and wild white roses. So simple those wild roses, so spare, so austere [...] their thorns as sharp as a wild cat's claws'. They symbolise for Forbes his country's 'sad harsh history, enacted against a background of magnificent loveliness'.[12] Forbes allocates the wild white rose of Scotland to Tom as his badge. (Here again Jenkins plays with 'Renaissance' symbolism, in appropriating for his own ironic and ominous purpose MacDiarmid's famous 'haiku' of the rose of Scotland which smells so sharp and sweet and 'breaks the heart').[13] And despite the ostensible happiness of the early holiday, Jenkins yet again undermines its positivity by emphasising the brash materialism of the tourist trip, the pier loudspeakers 'blaring' out 'Ye Banks and Braes o' bonnie Doon' and 'bawling' 'The Road to the Isles'.

And such oscillation between positivity and negativity is sustained throughout the novel's first half, as Forbes's black mood regarding materialistic tourists

---

11   Ibid., p. 51.

12   Ibid., p. 60.

13   Hugh MacDiarmid, 'The Little White Rose', *Complete Poems 1920–1976*, ed. by Michael Grieve and W.R. Aitken (London: Martin Brian & O'Keeffe, 1978), p. 461. Again Jenkins implies knowledge of the 'Scottish Renaissance'; by echoing, and then manipulating a famous short poem of 'Hugh MacDiarmid', usually accepted as the driving force behind the literature revival of the 1920s and 30s. Jenkins slyly deploys the poem, 'The Little White Rose', for his own sceptical ends, in that he exploits MacDiarmid's sense of Scotland's historical sadness. The white rose is seen by Forbes in his early self-indulgent magnanimity as Tom's 'badge'; but the poem's bitter sweet haiku carries an ominous anticipation of Tom's broken heart and suicide. (Like Jenkins, Forbes is an English teacher, and in the 'fifties would be likely to know of MacDiarmid's work).

changes to exultation. 'Like an exile returning', he sees the hills of Arran. Ignoring the pierman's prognostications about terrible clegs and diseased rabbits, his holiday mood reveals that he has an endearing side, especially impressive to Tom, as he takes up the holiday coachman's top hat and trumpet and shocks his family by loudly sounding his arrival 'in his kingdom, where regret, humiliation, and failure, did not exist'.[14] Jenkins leaves it (for now) open to the reader to view this annual holiday as genuine spiritual renewal for Forbes. On arrival at their holiday cottage Forbes betrays a disarming, if naive, Wordsworthian belief in the healing power of landscape; 'he breathed "thank God"'.[15]

There is a kind of innocence in this clumsy misfit; and for the first time we see Tom responding with wonder and affection; 'that blowing of the trumpet had opened the first small window'.[16] This affirmative side of Forbes is further testified to by the anecdote of Eddie Tulloch, the old roadman described as having 'an awfu sweet nature for a man'; the tale reveals that this undoubted community innocent never forgot Forbes's spontaneous kindness of eight years before, when Forbes welcomed the roadman to his family picnic.[17]

Chapter 8 presents Forbes and the Toward countryside in their most attractive light, despite Gillian's scepticism, and Chapter 9 continues to allow the reader to respond favourably to Forbes. On the second day of the holiday, Charlie sets out early to a favourite beach to collect spoutfish; his simplicity – and his very clumsiness – are now seen as almost delightful, as he imagines himself in turn as Crusoe, an ancient Caledonian, and a fighter against redcoats. His delight is terminated when he slips and drenches himself. His struggle to rise is 'far less graceful than Aphrodite's', yet there is no doubt that the reader is meant to empathise with his sense of fun and delight.[18]

These events are immediately qualified by his realisation that Tom Curdie has come to the beach also, and is watching him. Instead, however, of the moment allowing communication between teacher and boy, Charlie criticises Tom for his failing to laugh – the first of a series of Forbes's insensitivities to what is in fact Tom's genuine wonder and growing admiration of his holiday teacher. Tom follows Forbes home with 'a quiet, almost happy determination'; this is arguably the high point of their relationship. Yet it is at this point that, ominously, Charlie begins to have reservations about his 'squire'.[19]

---

14   Jenkins, *The Changeling*, p. 61.
15   Ibid.
16   Ibid., p. 58.
17   Ibid., p. 60.
18   Ibid., p. 64.
19   Ibid., p. 66.

This 'first long halcyon morning' is followed by Charlie taking the three children to the local castle ruins.[20] Hitherto an uneasy acceptance of Tom by Mary and Mrs Storrocks has held; now the threat is from an unexpected quarter, Gillian. With fine psychological insight, Jenkins delineates the Forbes family tensions and the jealousy of teenage Gillian as she watches Tom follow her father and mistakes his quiet reticence for contemptuous ingratiation. Her 'spying' will become the turning point of the novel. Each of the family now sees Tom in the light of their individual prejudices, Mary beginning to resent the boy for his disruptive effect on her family, Mrs Storrocks with her narrow conventional materialism, suspicious Gillian, thinking to protect her family, so turning spy on Tom – and Forbes slowly but surely resenting Tom's self-protective reticence. The castle visit sees Jenkins darken any optimism of the holiday spirit, and demonstrates Jenkins's ability to mock human pathetic fallacy in glorifying countryside with historical association ('Robert the Bruce once visited Towellan castle' Charlie tells the unresponsive children; 'he must have walked through these woods').[21] Any possibility of Forbes conveying his enriching pathetic fallacy to them is destroyed by ants, sheep dung, human excrement and clegs; and his enthusiasm about the perfect campsite for stargazing is utterly abolished by the appearance of the monstrously diseased rabbit, in the last stages of myxomatosis. Charlie cannot mercy kill the beast; it is Tom who efficiently does so, which Charlie's hyper-sensitivity abhors.

Thus, Jenkins presents Forbes on one hand sympathetically as a complex and all too human being, and on the other as a dangerously inconstant and self-deluding moral agent who wilfully plays with his own emotions and allegiances. He creates the Tom Curdie he needs to satisfy his desire for self and social approval – but will also make him scapegoat for his own and his family's failings.

Forbes's fickleness of projection is demonstrated in one of the most poignant moments of the novel, following the castle outing. Now, as Forbes and Tom go fishing in the evening, holiday optimism turns towards darkness (and literal darkness). A moment now occurs when Forbes might have understood Tom's buried sensitivity. Their fishing is finished as night falls:

> Suddenly Charlie's peevishness broke out. 'You've got to give us a chance, Tom [...] you never seem to let us know what you're thinking [...] And I haven't heard you laughing yet. You must let your heart thaw, Tom, if we're going to be able to help you.' In the darkness could not see that the

20   Ibid., p. 66.
21   Ibid., p. 68.

> boy was trembling and biting his lips. If it had been daylight and he could
> have seen those signs of physical distress, he would not have known what
> caused them. Tom knew very well [...] what was meant by letting his
> heart thaw because it was beginning [...][22]

Blaming Tom for the discord within his family (and failing to recognise his
family's faults), he is now seeing Tom as the family's disruptive 'changeling'.
In a diametrically opposed sense, Tom *is* changing, and does deeply appreciate the Clyde sea and landscape, Charlie's jokes and stories, – but secretively,
concealing this self-endangering change behind a carefully built shell of
self-protection.

   Yet overall, the first half of the novel overall allows the deceptive possibility
of the Forbes-Tom relationship as affirmative, with the first Go-as-you-please
competition in Dunroth. Tom's singing of 'Ho ro Mhairi dhu' (a favourite of
Forbes) at the Go-as-you-please is for Forbes the high point of his holiday
relationship with the boy. This crucial episode shows both how Forbes plays
with his own emotions, wildly changing from depression to elation (and vice
versa), and how Jenkins plays with his readers' changing responses, as he allows
both Forbes and the hitherto vulgar audience (and the reader?) to recognise
something genuinely moving from what Jenkins implies as more traditional
Scottish culture. Forbes has been disgusted with the cheap tawdriness of the
Go-as-you-please; now, for Forbes, the audience is transformed, as Tom movingly sings his all too sad (and prophetic) traditional lament.

> Charlie wanted to shout out how he loved them all [...] they were not
> cultural degenerates, they were not mercenary pleasure seekers, they
> were not litter louts, they were human beings, lovable, mortal and sus-
> ceptible to true sorrow. While he thought thus his hands banged like
> carpet-beaters.[23]

This is Jenkins at his ambivalent and manipulative best. We share Charlie's
affirmative delight, but recognise his unreliable emotional volatility; we recognise in Tom a rare natural taste and potential, while seeing also his terrible
vulnerability and potential for tragedy. The reductive simile of 'carpet-beaters'
somewhat deflates Forbes's discovery of grace in singer and audience, since
any grace exists mainly in Forbes's projection. For all the undoubtedly worthy
aspects of Forbes, we remember Jenkins's earlier caveats, that he is a dubious

---

22   Ibid., pp. 73–74.
23   Ibid., p. 83.

Samaritan, 'a crusader without a sword'; a timewasting teacher who moralises with rambling pomposity.[24] And while he can seem to utter tersely valid satiric comments regarding 'gluttonous sun-eaters' or 'is affection like money in a bank?'[25] Jenkins always places these in the context of a subtle and continuous undermining via denigratory description. Thus Jenkins plays out his dark oxymoronic game, shifting perspective between negative and positive so that the reader holds out hope that Forbes's instinctive (if naïve) goodness will yet prevail.

Tom Curdie – Changeling or Scapegoat?

It is appropriate at this midway point to consider Jenkins's complex deployment of the dominant changeling metaphor, which would appear at first to be appropriately best linked to Tom Curdie. Jenkins runs the idea of the changeling throughout the novel, twice giving explicitly folk-grounded descriptions. His usage raises more questions than answers, however, since we quickly recognise the term as metaphor, and its significance as unreliable and highly changeable.

Why did Jenkins choose such a folk-traditional title and image? As our overview suggested, Jenkins's fiction recurrently subverts the values and presentation of 'Scottish Renaissance' fiction such as Gibbon's *Sunset Song* (1932) or Gunn's *Highland River* (1937), where these authors insisted on a deep spiritual bond between their protagonists and their landscapes, with their ancient history, legends and myths. Jenkins regularly insisted that he wanted to see Scotland truthfully, and his truth is not theirs.[26]

Arguably through the idea of the changeling he repudiates his predecessors and their use of supernatural lore. Any credibility for the reader for the idea that Tom is presented as unnatural and sinister, rather than an intelligent and unfortunate boy, is quickly seen as unsustainable. Jenkins cleverly repudiates the Scottish Renaissance exploitation of folk and supernatural symbolism here, since rather than using it for Renaissance affirmative purposes,

---

24   Ibid., p. 36.
25   Ibid., p. 151, p. 76.
26   Jenkins regularly spoke of his desire to see Scotland through truthful eyes, underlying his awareness of contrasting ways of reading the nation. For example, see 'A Truthful Scot: Inga Ágústsdóttir talks to Robin Jenkins', *In Scotland* 1 (Autumn 1999), 13–22, and the interview by Isobel Murray (ed.) in *Scottish Writers Talking* (Edinburgh: John Donald, 2006), pp. 101–146.

he turns it into a corrosive metaphor for moral deceit and human betrayal. He also tricks us, since we come to realise that it is certainly not Tom who fulfils the folk-terms of the changeling. He changes, but simply in terms of psychological disintegration, brought about through the actions of Charlie and others who are far more changeable than him, their changing revealing the shifting hypocrisies and unstable moralities of 'normal' society. This is the definition Tom Curdie reads in the Dunroth library:

> Changeling: a creature, in animal or human form, supposed to be left by the fairies or "other folk" in place of one they had stolen: often applied to a dwarfish, ill-favoured person or animal, spreading an evil influence.[27]

It has been preceded by many explicit or subtle references. Early in the novel, Tom has soothed his baby sister to sleep, 'humming a song about a baby stolen by fairies in the Highlands'.[28] (The lullaby, unnamed, is clearly the traditional Gaelic 'Ho-van, ho-van, Gorry og O', which tells of how a mother's baby was stolen by the little people, thus echoing and anticipating Tom's spiritual abandonment).

Tom's innocent evocation of the changeling can be contrasted with Forbes's early inkling of the danger of falling into resentment against Tom's reticence, and then imagining him as the creature of Highland legend, polluting the joy and faith of family. This early thought will increasingly darken as Forbes changes his many differing perspectives on the boy, to the point where he explicitly identifies Tom as changeling. The earlier Gaelic song is echoed when Tom in Dunroth movingly sings 'Ho ro Mhairi dhu', the song echoing his loneliness and spiritual homelessness, and anticipating his tragedy as he sings 'mine but the lonely grave'.[29] Any perception by Forbes of grace in Tom's singing is shattered by his realisation that Tom is indeed a thief, caught in the act by Gillian. Ignoring his wife's realistic recognition that Tom 'is what he is' (just as he ignored his cynical colleagues), he is devastated. Where Tom, despite all warnings, had existed in Forbes's mind as suffering innocence, he now

---

27   Jenkins, *The Changeling*, p. 110.
28   Ibid., p. 28.
29   Ibid., p. 83. Intriguingly, Tom's singing of the Gaelic lullaby of the mother who loses her child to the fairies may suggest that Jenkins has read more 'Renaissance' fiction than he acknowledges. Neil Gunn brings his epic novel *The Silver Darlings* to a triumphant close with his young Finn singing the same song. Finn's singing pulls his past life together, but here, in contrast, Jenkins anticipates tragedy. Neil Gunn, *The Silver Darlings* (London: Faber and Faber, 1941), pp. 544–545.

becomes the scapegoat for the failings of Forbes and his family. Forbes fails to see the real Tom, who is indeed talented, but who has his own unconventional moral code which paradoxically co-exists with his thieving, lies and deception. It is Forbes, far more than Tom, who constantly changes, both in his own mind as regards Tom, and also in the reader's view, as the implications of his naïve views of Tom (and indeed the world) are exposed as dangerous games which grow into an appalling and irredeemable web of family tensions and jealousies. Forbes, the 'Samaritan without a sword', becomes the polluter of 'the joy and faith of family'.[30] That said, his family members change their view of Tom dramatically too, and they too are guilty of condescension, lack of patience and understanding for the slum boy (who sleeps, not in the family cottage, but in a shed outside).

The biblical scapegoat was literally a sacrificial goat sent by a priest into the wilderness to atone symbolically for the sins of the priest's people. The novel runs a satirical religious motif throughout (discussed below); Jenkins was no doubt aware of the original meaning of the scapegoat, but how does he use the term in relation to Tom? The answer, I believe, lies in the way that Forbes moves from his slow realisation of his self-deceptions to transfer his shamed awareness of his shortcomings on to Tom, who arguably becomes the Forbes family's sacrificial victim, the scapegoat of atonement for what are essentially Forbes's 'sins'.

If Tom Curdie is no changeling, what does Jenkins mean us to make of him? Early on, headmaster Mr Fisher indicates the danger implicit in the slum boy ('Pity is what he should get, but who would risk giving it to him?').[31] Fisher also recognises that Tom is outstandingly intelligent, and in Chapter 4 Jenkins takes great care to establish Tom's principles. This intelligent, sensitive boy, condemned to a disgusting slum and family, has had to build a shell around his vulnerability if he is to survive.

> Never to whine: to accept what came to wait for better: to take what you could: to let no one, not even yourself, know how near to giving in you were: these were his principles by which he lived [...][32]

Even Tom's thefts are for survival – and indeed, for others, since he hopes to pay for a holiday for his slum friends, Peerie and Chick.

---

30   Jenkins, *The Changeling*, p. 51.
31   Ibid., p. 5.
32   Ibid., p. 18.

Tom is portrayed throughout as a psychologically damaged boy trying to survive in a world of complexity he did not choose. Further, Jenkins means us to realise that this damaged child-thief has astonishing potential. Given reliable mentors and proper care, (as opposed to Forbes's cosmetic self-indulgence) he could flourish. Instead, Forbes totally fails to realise Tom's defensive reticence, and, caught up in his fantasies, fails to interpret the signs of Tom's growing desire to belong to a proper family (as for examples, his hugging of Charlie's coat in a 'sudden surge of love', or his Freudian slip in answering the telephone as 'Tom Forbes'). The inevitable price of Tom's letting go of his defence system is his recognition that he cannot ever go back to his family and Donaldson's Court ('I'm never going back to them', to Peerie), and finally, in the appalling mess of the Canada Hill trip: 'I cannae go there', both intimations, if we understand Tom, of his impossible dilemma, and anticipating his ultimate self-destruction.[33] Chapter 18 reveals the full extent of Forbes's change and betrayal, as he begins to think of transferring Tom to the non-academic junior secondary school at Brian Street, which would destroy any academic future for the boy. At this point the reader may question the credibility of the long-suffering boy, who is emerging as almost saint-like, the very opposite of the traditional changeling, in contrast to the pretentious failings of Forbes and human idealism generally. Does Jenkins wish us to read him as a self-camouflaged and – compared to Forbes – as a genuine example of grace and innocence, forced into disguise by society's inequality and injustice, not so much a would-be saint as a maladjusted and unrecognised martyr to failed humanity? Arguably Jenkins (deliberately) strains our credibility in this picture of suffering sensitivity, moving from psychological realism towards an almost surreal symbolism. Indeed, throughout his fiction Jenkins manipulates many of his initially 'real' characters, like Fergus Lamont or the would-be saint Gavin Hamilton or Lady Magdalen, to the point where they work as symbols for a kind of martyrdom and Jenkins's complex and often ambivalent ideas and ideals.[34] It is the outstanding paradox of this novel that the child thief and liar is by the end seen

---

33   Ibid., p. 119, pp. 153–154.
34   It is worth pausing to consider the eerie significance of Tom's singing of the Gaelic song, for the developing tragedy, with its implication that the cruel sea is more of a home for the moaning bird, compared to Tom, who is now beginning to realise that he is homeless:
"Hushed by thy moaning, lone bird of the sea,
Thy home on the rocks is a shelter to thee,
Thy home but the angry wave,
Mine but the lonely grave,
Ho ro Mhairi dhu, turn ye to me." (Ibid., p. 83.)

as 'a young prince', with 'eerie distinction', and by the reader as the principal example of the only kind of integrity and grace to be found in a fallen world.[35]

Chapters 12–22

The second half of the novel turns swiftly to nightmare. Jenkins makes the moment of complete change of direction from hope to tragedy depend on the apparently trivial matter of chapter eleven when Gillian saw Tom shoplift a tin opener and ointment in Woolworth's.[36] Forbes's and the family's unwillingness to believe Gillian now throws the family into mutual distrust and dislike, and finally to revulsion against Tom. As Forbes is persuaded by Mary of the boy's guilt ('you're making him out to be a veritable little monster, Mary; worse even than my changeling') we see, despite his apparent charity, how limited and shallow his understanding and empathy for the boy's appalling upbringing really are, as his approval swings violently and melodramatically to its opposite.[37]

The pattern and structure of the novel begins to change; Forbes now turns against Tom, while Gillian has, in her moment of triumph over the boy, begun to realise his stoic worth and dignity. Slowly – and strangely – Gillian will emerge as Tom's only ally. By the time of the second Go-as-you-please, where Forbes and Tom were in allegiance against the suspicions and doubts of Mary, Gillian and Mrs Storrocks, now, self-indulgent in his disillusionment, Forbes now mocks Tom's song, and his own exultation at the time of Tom's singing, 'Forbes sneered and quoted "Thy home is the angry wave, Mine but the lonely grave. You may go and sing. My rudder is broken"'.[38] From this point on the full egocentricity of Forbes emerges. Yet even now Jenkins allows him some slight redemption in his increasing perceptions of his self-delusion, though even this modest self-perception is vitiated as he tries to console himself and his wife by seeing Tom as 'a failed experiment', and with the hope that by sending Tom back to Donaldson's Court his family will heal itself.[39] They know their self-deception, however; they can see their failure, if not the tragedy which must follow. Chapter sixteen ends with their ominous recognition 'that love

---

35   Ibid., p. 176.
36   Ibid., p. 86.
37   Ibid., p. 96.
38   Ibid., p. 107.
39   Ibid., p. 139.

had failed amongst them, and for the rest of their lives they, and their children, must live in the shadow of that failure'.[40]

The family has poisoned itself. Forbes may not fully believe Gillian's accusation of Tom's thefts (while Mary certainly does); but the final damage to the family is yet to come, with Gillian's false retraction of her accusation. It is important to recognise that two distinct transformations are working in Forbes; firstly, that he is realising the implications for his family in having brought Tom on holiday, and secondly, in realising what was his real motivation, as the very sea seems to repeat, 'with subtle insistent variations, Todd's word: "Humbug"':

> He could no longer deny that his finding consolation in the loveliness of Nature, and his championing of the meek and oppressed against such as Todd had been insincere. The sight of the Sleeping Warrior [...] had certainly never compensated for his lack of professional success; and his Samaritan succouring of Tom Curdie had been motivated by an intricacy of selfish hopes.[41]

Yet while finally 'seeing himself clearly, unobscured by self pity', as a moral humbug, he does not extend this clarity towards Tom Curdie – rather the opposite, as Tom becomes scapegoat for his deficiencies; 'he began to give way to the feeling that he was in the grip of inimical non-human forces, whose instrument was indeed Tom Curdie' – and Mary, who knows her husband inside out, suspects his new meekness as 'some kind of new strategy'.[42]

From Chapter 13 until the final tragedy the atmosphere of nightmare grows steadily – not just in Tom's mind, but in the way Jenkins manipulates images and situations. Chapter thirteen has introduced what becomes a subplot. Tom has planned to help his slum friends Chick and Peerie to share his holiday (the Forbes family know nothing of this). The appearance of the two friends opens up a richly grotesque and at times surreal sequence of events. Chick, the sordid and genuine thief, even becomes in Tom's eyes, the likeness of the changeling of which he had read in the Dunroth library. Now, in revulsion against his former life and friends, Tom runs from them. He does return, taking them to camp in a derelict house 'like an enormous sinister trap'; the vulnerable Peerie feels ghosts all around, while grotesque Chick, in his colours becomes 'uncanny', with his bizarre American clothes and his sexual innuendoes, and his thievery will become for Tom the nightmare reminders of the world to which he

---

40   Ibid.
41   Ibid., p. 98.
42   Ibid., p. 101.

realises now he can never return.[43] Chapter 18 reveals the full extent of Forbes's betrayal, as he begins to think of transferring Tom from secondary school to the junior secondary school which will destroy any chance of his escaping his background. And when Tom finally admits to stealing Todd's school money, by this point Jenkins has altered our moral perspectives so radically that we deeply pity the socially deprived child (with 'that small remote indecipherable face'), and remember his real reasons. Forbes, however, glares in dislike; he now explicitly refers to Tom twice as 'Changeling'.[44]

Indeed, the final family sailing to Rothesay's Canada Hill, an annual pilgrimage for Forbes, becomes complete surreal nightmare. The trip begins with a temporary renewal of Forbes's holiday optimism as he wonders at the beauty of Arran and Rothesay's Canada Hill – but Jenkins typically destroys his pathetic fallacy with the sordid realism of pathetic Peerie, 'the poor idiot in the coloured jockey cap' shadowing Tom and the family as they climb the hill, only to find the hill's 'gluttonous sun-eaters', with their 'public lust', and a contraceptive hanging on a bush 'like an obscene fruit' – and always, the red-blue-green-white cap of the half-wit pursuing them, Peerie a reminder that for all the island's beauty there is another and darker Scotland.[45] As if to expose the illusory nature of Forbes's dream of beauty, Jenkins describes how Alastair, Forbes's son blows rainbow coloured bubbles around the cairn, their brief glory fading, as will Forbes's visions. The trip ends with Forbes telling Tom he must go home mid-holiday, since (he lies pathetically) the holiday hut is needed, and, after all, Tom has had the best weather!

If the subplot of Chick and Peerie had brought the Glasgow slums to holiday beauty, then the Glasgow slums enter again with a vengeance with the unwelcome visit of Tom's drunken bloated mother and Tom's brother, together with her deformed paramour, Shoogle, the cripple father of Tom's infant half-sister Molly. Their ingratiation and their insinuations of homosexuality in Forbes's relationship with Tom are presented by Jenkins as disgusting contrast with the Forbes family Tom now yearns for. Yet even now, when the reader feels that Forbes has finally realised his self deceptions, even as Forbes judges the drunken pair as 'unwholesome human rubbish', he can envisage a chance for rebutting Todd's 'guff' with 'a grand Samaritan gesture' by taking them in for the night 'while he and his family slept on chairs or floor'.[46] Mary finds the grotesque visit weirdly awful yet laughs, thinking that when Tom and family

---

43   Ibid., p. 116.
44   Ibid., p. 178.
45   Ibid., p. 151, p. 151, p. 152.
46   Ibid., p. 169, p. 168.

have left, 'the fun of this evening would be remembered for years'.[47] She fails to recognise that Tom is utterly appalled, and visibly in nervous breakdown.

Amidst this scene of embarrassing degradation, Jenkins once more presents another of his surprising shifts of judgement, as Tom's apparently obnoxious mother is allowed a moment of humane perception denied to her so-called betters. She alone sees Tom's disintegration:

> Whit it is that's broken his he'rt, I cannae say. Maybe ye'd think it was haeing me for his mither, and poor Shoogle for his faither. But it's no that, either, for he's never complained aboot us. You expect a wean to be greedy: but never him. Whit there was for eating, he ate; whit there was for wearing, he wore; whit was missing, he did without; and never once did he complain. But a' the time his he'rt's been breaking.[48]

One again, as so often, Jenkins finds dignity in degradation. Hearing this, Mrs Storrocks is 'astonished and displeased; she had not credited this hag with such eloquent sorrow'.[49]

Tom's spirit and his protective shell have been broken as well as his heart. Only Gillian now begins to understand the horror of his situation, trapped between the home he wants but can never have, and the home he now hates. The inevitable price of Tom's letting go of his defence system and having seen a proper family and another landscape from his slum, is his recognition that he cannot ever go back to Donaldson's court, and finally, in the appalling mess of the Canada Hill trip: 'I cannae go there', both intimations, if we understand Tom, of his impossible dilemma, and his ultimate self-destruction.[50] There is no possibility of redemption for him; and unlike the ambivalent ending of *The Cone-Gatherers*, with Lady Runcie Campbell's 'tears of holy joy' amidst the death of the innocents and his killer, there is here only the darkest of tragedy and not just for Tom, but for the entire Forbes Family, as the reader contemplates the implications of Tom's suicide.

Yet Jenkins, despite his tragic outcome, leaves the reader with a glimpse of the possibility of Innocence and Grace in poor Tom – and in Gillian, hitherto in her suspicion and spying the reverse of Good Samaritan. Now, in typical Jenkins paradox, it is Gillian who is allowed a kind of grace. Her belated gradual epiphanies entirely reverse her view of Tom, and she too late reaches out

---

47   Ibid., p. 171.
48   Ibid., p. 176.
49   Ibid., p. 176.
50   Ibid., pp. 153–154.

with love, with inexplicable complicity with him, 'a brightness about her, like sunshine through rain'.[51] Her efforts are unavailing; but she is witness to Tom's true nature, which marks her out as the one member of her family who may learn from the tragedy in an ending which carries far more conviction than that of *The Cone-Gatherers*.

Ambiguities of Morality – and Scotland?

If the novel centres around the idea of the changeling, then when we review the recurrent reverses of moral judgement with which the author has manipulated his readers, it is possible to extend this to see the idea of shifting and changing moralities and perspectives as central also, with Jenkins himself as the arch-changer, in terms of continually subverting and changing his presentation of his characters – as well as their territorial and national context. What are we to conclude from this continual changing?

Arguably, for Jenkins, Forbes, his family, including Storrocks, Forbes's fellow teachers, are simply fallen humanity, more to be understood and pitied than condemned, as virtually all Jenkins protagonists. The reader is left unsure how to judge them finally – and by this time we may suspect that ambiguities of moral judgement exist not just for the reader, but for Jenkins himself, who manages both to satirise his cynical teachers and yet to manage to present them as human and real. It is Todd the arch-cynic who flogs children for forgetting their bible, but gives money, when Forbes does not, to the beggar in the street. In the end we are left to wonder if he is such a failure, or, rather, if Jenkins means Forbes to be a representative of the failures – and virtues, however slight – of Everyman, no worse, and perhaps even better, than average humanity.

A Tale of Two Scotlands?

Throughout there has been an underlying commentary and reference to Scotland as a place of the broken extremes and contrasts of history and landscape. Forbes contrasts his country's sad harsh history and its background of magnificent loveliness. There is another tilt at Renaissance values in Jenkins's exploitation of the poet MacDiarmid's symbol of the little white rose, which

---

51   Ibid., p. 184.

Forbes sees as Tom's badge; 'it symbolized for Charlie his country's sad harsh history, enacted against a background of magnificent loveliness'.[52]

Read at a symbolic level, the entire novel embodies national duality. This is begun in terms of place – the opening scenes set Glasgow and slum Donaldson's Court set against the glories of the Firth of Clyde and Arran. As the novel develops it become clear that Jenkins's recurrent method is that of grotesque juxtapositioning, with on one hand Charlie's self-indulgent visions of Scotland's historical and topographical superiority as 'the antidote to Donaldson's Court', and also his romanticising reflections on Scotland's history, from the Covenanters to Robert the Bruce.[53] Forbes will incongruously link that most romantic of Scottish icons, Mary Queen of Scots, with a diseased rabbit, sharing their moments of execution, suggesting that he knows subconsciously that his romantic icons are deeply suspect.[54]

These incongruities multiply in the second half, again revealing the dualities of Scotland, for example in its songs and legends. Indeed, the Changeling legend itself reflects this duality, in the sense that (metaphorically) Jenkins implies a sinister side to Scotland; the traditional Gaelic lullaby 'Hovan, Hovan' which Tom sings to his wee sister early in the novel has also reminded us of the dark aspect of the Changeling legend ('a song about a baby stolen by fairies in the Highlands').[55] The Highland lament 'Ho ro Mhairi dhu' sung so movingly by Tom in Dunroth shares this reference to a dark side to Scotland in its prediction.[56] Jenkins suggests that these songs carry uncanny traditional race memories, as opposed to the superficial glib American imitations of the other precocious child singers and their pop gyrations. Significantly, it is Jenkins, not Forbes, who deplores the Clyde steamer's kitsch 'blaring' and 'bawling' of Scottish songs. There is a tension here and throughout Jenkins's work between what he regards as genuine, and *kitsch* Scottish history and culture, a tension between possible authentic value and dignity, and what Jenkins sees as contemporary impoverished vulgarity and cheapness.

This story is a tale of two Scotlands, and deeply revealing of Jenkins's own ambivalent response throughout all his fiction to his native country. The reader of Jenkins's novels cannot fail to be moved by the beauty of his descriptions of his Western Highland territory, in which he chose to spend the latter half of his

---

52   Ibid., p. 60.
53   Ibid., p. 51.
54   Ibid., p. 71.
55   Ibid., p. 28.
56   Ibid., p. 83.

life; but this must be set against his own early avowal that he would see Scotland through truthful eyes.

Certainly Jenkins uses a ferocious reductive symbolism throughout to emphasise another Scotland from that of Forbes's idealisation of his annual 'pilgrimage' to the beauty of the Clyde estuary. The foul degradation of slum Donaldson's court, with its squalid, urine soaked tenement closes, with their diseased cats, and denizens and Tom's utter poverty, is savagely contrasted with Jenkins's profound shift of perspective as Tom and the Forbes family leave Glasgow for the 'magnificent loveliness' as we see through Forbes's eyes (and Jenkins's?) of the Clyde estuary. From the beginning Jenkins emphasises the underlying ugliness of Glasgow so that we cannot forget that other Scotland. As they sail, Forbes, beginning to doubt his own holiday motives, focuses on the skeleton of a great ship, in a breaker's yard, rather than the spacious firth; and passing the Holy Loch we are reminded that it derives its name from the ship which carried earth from the Holy land to Scotland – but which wrecked in the loch.[57] Indeed, from the novel's beginning the dark side has been present – through Forbes's nightmare and prescient dreams, especially that of chapter nine, when nearing the turning point of the novel, Forbes dreams that 'while fishing in a boat with the whole family beside him, all strangely still and dumb like corpses, he pulled up his line and found hooked to it the rabbit that had been killed at the castle'.[58] Throughout Jenkins continually qualifies any scenes of natural beauty with insistently reductive detail, such as the seagull which dropped its dirt upon the hat of a small, shrill, large-nosed woman; just as images of ragged tinkers, midges and clegs, human excrement, used contraceptives, or diseased rabbits abound.[59] As noted above, Forbes's annual pilgrimage to Rothesay's beauty spot, Canada Hill, is the climax of this insistent reduction, with the grotesquerie of the almost bestial Chick and pathetic Peerie, endlessly calling, mocking any pretensions of the scene like Shakespeare's fool, juxtaposing Glasgow degradation with Forbes's annual pilgrimage to what he yearns for, a better Scotland. The final scenes of tragedy are filled with negative images of black peat hags, dead flies, skulls of sheep, with fleeing Tom – with a grotesque parody of Christian birth in a manger. Tom, his face already a skull, meets his death in the dark desolation of a shabby shepherd's hut. The tragic symbolism becomes clear: Tom, one of the only characters we have met to suggest elusive human grace, has been martyred, even crucified, by a fallen Scotland. We realise that the novel has been a bleak inversion of Christian parable.

---

57   Ibid., pp. 51–52.
58   Ibid., p. 77.
59   Ibid., p. 78.

From the beginning of the motif which ironically links Charlie with the biblical Good Samaritan, there has run with it a dark parodic Christian motif which emphasises again the disparity between Scotland's religious ideals and Scotland's hypocrisies. This shows itself in colloquial, humorous and yet satiric exchanges, as when Shoogle, Mrs Curdie's paramour, discusses Forbes's motives in taking Tom on holiday with Tom's mother. 'We've got to be careful, Queenie. This man Forbes might be a genuine Christian', to which she replies 'I thought they were extinct, like giraffes'.[60] Jenkins manages thus to convey her deprivation, at the same time allow that Forbes's motives may be good – but such is their deprivation that they have been conditioned to be suspicious, even of Christians.[61] When Forbes hears first from Mary of Tom's thefts of tin opener and ointment, he wails 'what in Christ's name would he want these for?' Mary has called him 'a damned fool'. Tom tells Forbes that he cannot go home: 'where in God's name can you go [...] if you don't go home?' Forbes asks the boy.[62] Gillian, not yet empathising with Tom, goads him with being a traitor to his slum friends. 'For Christ's sake...leave me alane' he whispers, twice, in mental agony. Tom's mother tells Mary Forbes 'the Christ's truth' that she has never understood her son.[63] What does Jenkins imply with these recurrent Christian colloquialisms? An answer could be that they tend to emphasise the irrelevance of religion in this contemporary world, and Jenkins underscores his tragedy, here as elsewhere through his fiction, by showing how trivial and precarious belief has become.

Thus the novel subverts religious parable, from its ambivalent use of the recurrent motifs of the Samaritan (with its dry opening warning of 'the folly of interference'). We noted the ambivalent reference to the Holy Loch, where the ship signifying holy commitment was wrecked – Scotland's failed Christian project?[64] With one authorial hand Jenkins mocks Forbes throughout as a dubious pilgrim and martyr; with another, he makes Tom, paradoxically, to have the greatest grace and integrity of the novel, and as 'a young prince', (with 'eerie distinction') to be martyr and scapegoat.[65] What then of the ending, with Gillian – arguably the reverse of Samaritan until allowed a kind of grace? In her sudden final epiphany which leads her to see sees Tom, bleeding like martyr, it is she who finally becomes unavailing witness to Tom's grace and

---

60   Ibid., p. 24.
61   Ibid.
62   Ibid., p. 154.
63   Ibid., p. 173.
64   Ibid., p. 51.
65   Ibid., p. 176.

tragedy. Jenkins suggests that she alone, 'very sure where she was going', will have the final integrity and honesty to face the appalling years for the Forbes family which lie ahead.[66] It is an ending which, with its simultaneous recognition of human failure, tragedy and grace carries far more conviction for this reader than that of *The Cone-Gatherers.*

Works Cited

Ágústsdóttir, Ingibjörg, 'A Truthful Scot: Inga Ágústsdóttir talks to Robin Jenkins', *In Scotland* 1 (Autumn 1999), 13–22.

Gunn, Neil, *The Silver Darlings* (London: Faber and Faber, 1941).

Jenkins, Robin, *The Changeling* (London: Macdonald, 1958; repr. Edinburgh: Canongate, 1989).

Jenkins, Robin, *The Cone-Gatherers* (London: Macdonald & Co., 1955).

MacDiarmid, Hugh, 'The Little White Rose', *Complete Poems 1920–1976*, ed. by Michael Grieve and W.R. Aitken (London: Martin Brian & O'Keeffe, 1978), p. 461.

Murray, Isobel, ed., 'Robin Jenkins', in *Scottish Writers Talking* (Edinburgh: John Donald, 2006), pp. 101–146.

---

66   Ibid., p. 184.

Robin Jenkins: Perspectives on the Postcolonial

Glenda Norquay

Abstract

The chapter considers Jenkins's colonial fiction from the perspective of his own experiences of colonialism and through the lens of postcolonial theory. It outlines the ways in which teaching in Afghanistan and in Malaysia extended Jenkins's interest in social and moral conflicts to issues of ethnicity. It examines *Dust on the Paw* (1961) as a striking engagement with difficult issues around interracial marriage and a bold confrontation of the political configurations of Afghan society. Jenkins's interest in uncomfortable clashes makes his analysis of colonialism particularly effective but also problematic in its handling of gender and race. *Dust on the Paw*, and later novels *The Tiger of Gold* (1962) and *The Holy Tree* (1969) are considered in the context of debates within postcolonial theory and other critical readings of Jenkins. Finally, the essay assesses Jenkins's own understanding of imperial contexts and their relevance to Scottish identities through discussion of his late novel *Leila* (1995).

Keywords

otherness – identity – class – gender – postcolonialism – ethnicity – alterity – orientialism – Scotland – Afghanistan – Malaysia

Robin Jenkins's engagement with 'postcolonialism' can be understood in two ways, both stemming from personal experience. First, the fiction based upon his early years working as a teacher abroad, in Afghanistan and in Sabah (then part of North Borneo), directly addresses the contexts in which western powers maintained power bases, examines the last days of imperialist attitudes and explores the spectrum of complex ethnic tensions which these produced. Secondly he drew upon those experiences to develop understanding of the ways in which Scotland itself can be understood in terms of both a colonised country and a colonising power. In both instances Jenkins's characteristically interrogative and scrutinising focus is used to ask difficult questions and make his readers appreciate the absence of easy answers.

Jenkins taught in Afghanistan (Ghazi School, Kabul, 1957–9), Spain (British Institute, Barcelona, 1959–61) and in Malaysia at Gaya College, Sabah, North

Borneo (1961–65), before returning to teach in Dunoon Grammar School in 1968. In the novels written about these experiences his consistent interest in complex moral questions is sustained but invigorated by an increasingly diverse range of characters and plot possibilities; it is also sharpened through appreciation of the tense political implications of human weaknesses when played across a global stage. Jenkins was in Afghanistan during a period in which Russian and U.S. powers were vying for control; the *burqa* was made optional rather than compulsory there in 1959; Sabah, where he worked, gained independence by becoming, as North Borneo, part of the new state of Malaysia in 1963. Fiction by Jenkins at this period is therefore best understood as written at a historical moment, the movement into 'post' colonialism, rather than knowingly informed by what we might now understand as the perspectives of postcolonial theory, however problematic these may have become. 'Difference' had real and dramatic dimensions in the contexts in which he lived and worked: that intensity informs the fiction he produced from them. But, as Michael Gardiner has noted, the term 'postcolonialism' 'does not just designate a country detaching chronologically after decolonisation; it is also more fundamentally a critique working within various forms of empire.'[1] Jenkins certainly offers 'critique' in his fiction but, as always in his writing, that critique is complicated, challenges easy categorisation and, as this essay suggests, produces its own problematics.

In one of his most powerful novels, *Dust on the Paw*, written on his return from teaching in Afghanistan, two moments exemplify the author's complicated engagement with postcolonial cultures.[2] The first is typical of Jenkins in its sense of irony: when the British residence gives its annual Birthday Garden Party the Ambassador is dismayed at the tattered state of the Union Jack flag. The mice had eaten large holes in it and 'parts of the Empire were missing'. Ransacking the embassy's resources to find replacement material of the right red colour they realise that 'by far the best match turned out to be an old pair of the Consul's underpants, which his wife, anxious to redeem him in his master's eyes, offered without his consent'.[3] Writing at a time when the power of the British Empire was itself becoming increasingly ragged, the unsavoury and ridiculous object holding the flag together embodies the parodic understanding of colonial performance which Jenkins sees in the English abroad,

1 Michael Gardiner, Introduction, M. Gardiner, G. Macdonald & N. O'Gallagher, eds., *Scottish Literature and Postcolonial Literature* (Edinburgh: Edinburgh University Press, 2011), p. 1.
2 Robin Jenkins, *Dust on the Paw* (London: Macdonald & Co., 1961).
3 Ibid., p. 240.

while also suggesting an insalubrious pragmatism in their attempts to retain the façade of authority. The fact that duplicity is forced on to individuals and is enacted through gender divisions and amidst a troubling marriage is also highly characteristic of the novel and of Jenkins's interest in configuring the politics of difference at domestic, national and international levels.

A second passage which demonstrates both the complex perspective of the author on such issues and his characteristic mode of blending narrative simplicity with the provocation of ambiguous responses comes late in the novel. Abdul Wahab, a Nuranian trained in England and wanting to marry the woman he met in Manchester, a man caught up by both accident and design in the unstable politics of his native land, takes a taxi journey to meet with the local potentate, uncertain both of his forthcoming marriage and his professional career:

> All the way to the heart of the city these human contrasts or contradictions rather kept leaping to his notice. For instance, the taxi-driver had pasted up on the cracked windscreen the coloured picture of an Indian actress, with breasts like melons about to roll out of a purple bag; yet the driver himself was thin and quite ugly, with a half-healed boil on the back of his neck. Then there were two donkeys making their water copiously under one of the triumphal arches. Along the streets decorated to celebrate freedom, brutal-faced policemen scowled and strutted. A large pink Buick car [...] crept behind a camel cart in which were crouched a nomad family with all their belongings [...].
>
> Yet the strange thing was that [...] Wahab did not feel cowed or depressed; on the contrary, he was elated with a sense of illimitable possibilities. All his sentimental hopes were surely realisable in a world of such shocking variety; his tears, in fact, were pearls.[4]

Key to Jenkins's engagement with postcolonialist contexts is this sensitivity to contrast and contradiction. The focus on contrast in some ways appears a typically orientalist perspective, reinforcing that emphasis which can be used, as Edward Said suggests, to 'Other' the East by stressing its distinctiveness from the West as exotic, different, plural and the unstable: the 'Oriental is irrational, depraved (fallen), childlike, "different"'.[5] In this passage from *Dust on the*

---

4   Ibid., pp. 353–354.

5   Edward W. Said, *Orientalism* (London: Routledge & Kegan Paul, 1978), p. 40.

Paw the world depicted brings together different phases of social and cultural development in 'shocking variety'. But Jenkins simultaneously deploys this idea of contradiction as a scalpel through which to incise facile notions of difference. Wahab is both a figure who challenges the dominant local power structures and the values of the expatriate community while at the same time embodying perspectives produced by colonial oppression. While Orientalism 'is premised upon exteriority', Wahab is at the same time a product and evaluator of the culture being categorised.[6]

The distinctions Wahab both criticises and embodies are produced by ethnic and cultural difference. He is consistently alert to the dynamics of skin colour: 'Was not the fat, fair-haired Englishmen married to a woman whose skin was yellow and whose eyes were narrower than a Mongol's? (At this point Wahab turned so that the sunlight shone on his hand; once again he saw that his skin could easily be taken for that of a European, nicely sunburned. [...]')[7] And later: 'Now, as he stared at the almost black Maftoon, he remembered how he himself in that very room had admired the paleness of his own hand.'[8] As if to exemplify Franz Fanon's psychoanalytic theories of the colonialist construction of dependency and inferiority set out in *Black Skin, White Masks* (first appearing in French in 1952, although only gaining international acclaim in the 1980s), Jenkins creates in Wahab a character who sees with the eyes of the dominant culture at the same time as he is presenting a serious challenge to its hierarchies: 'The black man stops behaving as an *actional* person. The goal of his behaviour will be The Other (in the guise of the white man), for The Other alone can give him worth.'[9]

The complexity of response this evokes in the reader is reinforced by that reluctance to settle on or in a single perspective which is so characteristic of Jenkins; his deployment of multiple points of views intensifies our consciousness of different ways of seeing and of different value systems, moral, social and cultural, which clash in uncomfortable ways. In *Dust on the Paw* this emphasis on a range of characters and their perspectives, however dissonant that assemblage may be, is one of the novel's strengths, making it a significant advancement on *Some Kind of Grace*, published in the previous year and again dealing with postcolonial contexts but through the perspective

---

6   Said, *Orientalism*, p. 20.

7   Jenkins, *Dust on the Paw*, p. 117.

8   Ibid., p. 233.

9   Franz Fanon, *Black Skin, White Masks* [Editions de Seuil, 1952], trans. by Charles Lan Markmann (London: Grove Press, 1967; Pluto Press, 1986), p. 154.

of one (albeit conflicted) man.[10] *Some Kind of Grace* adopts a genre closer to action adventure that most of Jenkins's fiction in its plot structured around John McLeod's quest to find out the fate of his friend Donald Kemp and his partner, Margaret, who appear to have been murdered in the mountains to the north of Kabul. It confines itself to his perspective, even if that is a self-questioning and shifting one. While the novel is consistent with much of Jenkins's fiction in its nagging exploration of the boundaries between extreme goodness and madness, focused on Kemp and Margaret, it insistently examines McLeod's own attitudes, shaped through the articulation of prejudices which he himself is forced to re-evaluate. So, his response to the villagers of Haimir, suspected of the Westerners' murders, embodies a construction of primitivism – 'these people had not reached the stage of morality; baboons he had thought of, baboons he thought of again' – that later changes to a recognition of their dignity and communality.[11] Other modes of behaviour, such as those of the wild hill-men who capture him and engage in bloody battle with each other, are not redeemed: 'the sight and feel and even the smell of all that blood could not so easily be washed away.'[12] In terms of morality, *Some Kind of Grace* retains its doubts and ambiguities until the end: in their adherence to different models of religion which, when realised in practice, are both damaging and inspiring, both colonisers and colonised appear to collude in networks of necessary lies.

Some Kind of Grace also deploys, more consistently than later novels, Scotland as a frame of reference. Kemp and McLeod share a background of Scottish university days and Scottish mountaineering expeditions, which McLeod draws on to familiarise and ground his experiences. There are frequent references to similarities in the landscape – 'he might have been a climber coming down from Rothiemurchus', listening to sheep he 'felt he might have been back in Wester Ross', a fort reminds him of 'Edinburgh Castle'.[13] James Meek suggests that further parallels can be found between McLeod's emotional movement from 'contempt through an unpleasant disgust to admiration, almost an implied envy' and 'the emotions expressed by English and Lowland visitors to the remote glens and islands of Scotland hundreds of years ago'.[14] Certainly

---

10   Robin Jenkins, *Some Kind of Grace* (London: Macdonald & Co., 1960; Edinburgh: Polygon, 2004).
11   Ibid., p. 113.
12   Ibid., p. 105.
13   Ibid., p. 136, p. 144, p. 39.
14   James Meek, Introduction, *Some Kind of Grace* (2004), p. viii.

that interest in notions of primitivism, translated from Scotland to different contexts, is one Jenkins shared with a key influence, R.L. Stevenson. But McLeod's discomfort with Kemp's suddenly talking to him in Gaelic suggests not only that he is 'troubled by the Gaelic words and associations of home' but also that the novel is pushing for a more sceptical attitude to such easy analogies.[15] The conclusion of *Some Kind of Grace* also serves as a stern reminder of the very different economic contexts in which different countries operate. The motivation behind much of the plot transpires to be commercial and political, as both Russia and America seek to exploit Afghanistan's unmined wealth in its natural resources.

Scotland may, as Meek implies, have been exploited and provoked but it has also participated and benefitted from these processes of exploitation. As Gardiner notes:

> Scottish literature as a counter-discipline [...] has rather frequently acted as a set of political interventions against the idea that literary value arises from a single pre-given cultural source, a stance which aligns it closely with the postcolonial. Nevertheless, the relationship between Scotland and ex-colonies or neo-colonies remains one of simultaneous solidarity and conflict.[16]

In his short stories, such as the title story in *A Far Cry from Bowmore*, Jenkins draws the reader's attention to such parallels between Scotland and the countries he lived in while also interrogating them. In the short story 'Siddiq', for example, the assertion made by a Scot to the Afghani central character – 'We're a highland race, like you. We're poor like you too' – both establishes a connection and calls into question exactly what is meant by 'poverty' in these very different contexts.[17]

Writing from the perspective of the coloniser, albeit an uncomfortable one, allows such contradictions and inconsistencies to be explored: Jenkins was clearly attracted to this as a device. *The Tiger of Gold* (1962) written from the point of view of Sheila McNair, a young woman working in 'Nurania' who falls in love with a young Indian man, adopts this formula of an external perspective on colonised people and colonial cultures.[18] *The Expatriates* (1972) also

---

15   Jenkins, *Some Kind of Grace*, p. 170.

16   Gardiner, *Scottish Literature and Postcolonial Literature*, p. 5.

17   Robin Jenkins, 'Siddiq', *A Far Cry From Bowmore* (London: Victor Gollancz, 1973), p. 99.

18   Robin Jenkins, *The Tiger of Gold* (London: Macdonald & Co., 1962).

focuses on the relationships across a racial divide, but opens in Scotland as Ronald McDonald confesses to his fiancée Margaret Ormiston that he has had a child while in Malaysia.[19] The novel then follows their journey, accompanied by his mother, to find and reclaim that child. This novel therefore situates itself explicitly in the intersections of Scotland and the 'Other', not just by the fact that it opens in a Scottish-village setting which could almost be that of a Kailyard novel, thereby creating a literary frame of reference and expectation shortly to be disrupted, but also because it sustains a discursive Scottish presence: Margaret, for instance, is 'firmly placed within a Covenanting Christian tradition'; McDonald lives at 'Martyrs Brae' and one of the characters remarks: 'As colonialists we never get ourselves disliked like the sassenachs'. But the dynamic (reiterated in *Some Kind of Grace*) also alerts the reader to the problematic understanding of the 'native' as pertaining to Scotland and the colonial context. Margaret, for example, seeks to keep those connections distant: she 'would never forgive anyone who forced her into recognising her own primitiveness.'[20] These novels therefore compel us into awareness, although not endorsement, of western perspectives and Scotland's ambiguous relationship to them.

Each of Jenkins's novels set in the lands he lived in creates a vivid depiction of colonial power in its latter days: the fact that characters from novels are transposed – Bob Gillie and Alan Wint appear in several as British officials – indicates both the wealth of material for his critique of the hypocrisy and hierarchies of that world, its internal politics and problems, and the confidence with which he addressed it. Bernard Sellin suggests that:

> Most of his foreign books give a harsh, sardonic view of the expatriate community where gin and lechery lead to sordid adventures and where gossip, jealousy and stupidity are the norms. Even those who mean well often find themselves trapped in their own contradictions or carried away by decisions which they can no longer control.

Sellin argues that a 'satirical excess' can inflect such engagements.[21] While Jenkins asserted that it was the duty of the Scottish novelist 'to write about what he knows best', his novels set in foreign territories are, as Sellin argues, more

---

19   Robin Jenkins, *The Expatriates* (London: Victor Gollancz, 1972).
20   Ibid., p. 20.
21   Bernard Sellin 'Exile and Expatriates in Robin Jenkins's Novels', *Études Écossaises* 13 (2010) 'Exil et Retour', 129–138 (p. 134).

interested in cultural confrontation than the behavior of Scots aboard.[22] Certainly the idea of the challenges produced by clashing values and expectations continued to preoccupy him.

The relatively late novel *Leila* (1995) returns to the theme of interracial relationships.[23] Here too, in the narrative of middle-aged and hitherto self-centred Scottish teacher, Andrew Sandiland, falling in love with and marrying the politically active, intelligent and beautiful lawyer, Leila Azaharri, the consciousness of the Scottish role in maintaining imperialism is articulated, most explicitly when a rebellion led by Leila is quashed by soldiers of the British army who turn out to be Scottish: 'Scottish troops had often been used by the English to build up their Empire and then defend it.'[24] Focusing on the expatriate's viewpoint allows Jenkins to analyse again that uncomfortable duality of position between oppressed and, arguably, exploited colonial oppressors.

Two of Jenkins's novels, however, move significantly beyond the perspective of the coloniser, producing powerful indictments of imperial power and some of his most nuanced writing, while also presenting their own challenges. *Dust on the Paw* and *The Holy Tree* (1969), with their multiplicity of perspectives, including those of central characters native to the country described, present the richest exploration of such conflicts. In *Dust on the Paw* much of the novel offers the point of view of Abdul Wahab, impoverished science schoolteacher who met the resilient Laura Johnstone while studying in Manchester and is bringing her to his country to experience it before they are married. The novel sees this interracial relationship through a series of different eyes – some sympathetic, some hostile. The imminent arrival of 'Miss Johnstone' throws the expatriate community into turmoil, forcing those who have their own 'mixed' marriages to reassess the dynamics. Harold Moffatt, lecturer in English at the local university, is forced to confront the abyss between his own supposedly liberal views and the inner tensions of own marriage to Lan, who is Chinese: 'by gibing so bitterly against racial prejudice, Moffatt more than helped to keep it in existence, he also kept himself infected with it'.[25] Contextualising these small-scale conflicts is the larger awareness that the country may be on the verge of abolishing the shaddry, the all-enveloping robes worn by Nuranian women. As Ingibjörg Ágústsdóttir has argued, the operation of power through hierarchies of gender and ethnicity represent the novel's most challenging

22   Sellin, ibid., citing Robin Jenkins, 'Novelist in Scotland', *Saltire Review*, 2: 5 (1955), p. 7, p. 130.
23   Robin Jenkins, *Leila* (Edinburgh: Polygon, 1995).
24   Ibid., p. 236.
25   Jenkins, *Dust on the Paw*, p. 33.

discourses. Ágústsdóttir reads Jenkins's texts as asserting that association of feminist and postcolonial thinking which emphasises parallels between them: both 'seek to reinstate the marginalised in the face of the dominant' and understand the relationship between Empire and patriarchy in terms of 'double colonisation' for women.[26] Certainly the plot structure of *Dust on the Paw*, in which both Wahab and Laura simultaneously occupy positions of victim and rebel, would appear to reinforce such a structural reading. Its narrative fluidity however, shifting from one character's interiority to another's, complicates such an interpretation.

The Holy Tree also challenges obvious interpretation. It takes as its focaliser Michael Eking, another young man with educational and social aspirations to move far beyond the position normally allocated to his race. Through a series of morally ambiguous actions and the misadventure of circumstance, Eking is propelled into controversial public success. As with Wahab, but to an even greater extent, the reader both sees his viewpoint and is distanced from it. While Eking can be understood as excluded from education by the dominant culture, its ethnic hierarchies and economic restrictions, his own perspective on race and gender is not presented in sympathetic terms: 'Though her body had excited him he was not pleased by the public impudence of the woman towards her husband. When the whites were gone, or rather when they gave up control of the country, care would have to be taken that such follies as the equality of women were not allowed to corrupt Kalimantan's way of life.'[27] While such a perspective may reinforce awareness of the double oppression of women and depict attitudes produced by the processes of inferiorisation, it also challenges the reader by preventing any simple notion of victimhood.

In both novels Jenkins is drawn to the creation of characters that embody aspiration and naivety and who, through their assimilation of dominant values while occupying positions of exclusion, become both foolish and inspirational, emblematic of the conflicting investments of western and national powers at work in their countries. Such characters are very familiar from other novels by Jenkins: from Calum in the early *The Cone-Gatherers* (1955) through Mungo Niven in *A Very Scotch Affair* (1968) and Gavin Hamilton in *A Would-be Saint* (1978) the idea of the 'holy fool' is key to Jenkins's challenge to glib moralities and social hypocrisies. Eking and Wahab are also endowed with the

---

26 Ingibjörg Ágústsdóttir, 'Surrender and Sacrifice: Imperial Subjugation and the Coloured Mistress in Robin Jenkins *The Expatriates* and "Imelda and the Miserly Scot"', Milli Mála-Tímarit um erlend tungumál og menningu, No: 5 (2013), 127–146, citing Ashcroft *et al.*, *The Empire Writes Back* (1989), pp. 174–175 (p. 132).
27 Jenkins, *The Holy Tree* (London: Gollancz, 1969), p. 20.

complexity of these other characters. Reading these novels in the context of postcolonial theory however, this 'holy fool' construction can cause a certain unease: while the 'subaltern' is allowed to speak, making the subaltern occupy that role of innocent comes curiously close to an infantalising which stresses 'the primitive' or childlike quality of the local people, characterised by Said as a key element within Orientalist definitions.[28] The correlation between dominant perceptions of 'innocent' natives and these central characters can make them appear more representative, less of a challenge to conventional modes of thought, than a similar figure in a Scottish context. The uncomfortable reading positions offered by such characterisation is further complicated in those instances where Jenkins adds his own sardonic emphasis. As with the leading character in the short story 'Siddiq', where we have to situate ourselves in relation to descriptions of 'His fluency in English, his handsome appearance, his knowledge of the city and its nefarious ways, and his flair for original and undetectable dishonesty', the characterisations of Wahab and Eking prove challenging.[29]

The second problematic issue for readers approaching Jenkins through the frame of postcolonial or feminist theory is the role of gender in his fiction. Jenkins is acutely aware that he is dealing not just with clashes of cultures but with cultural determinants of the body: skin and blood. As a result miscegenation becomes the focus for the most uncomfortable confrontations with the tensions of ethnicity. Yet this also means that much of the focus is upon, rather than from, the perspective of female sexuality. The moment in *Dust on the Paw* when the shaddry is removed is triumphant but also celebratory of dominant and exoticising images of female sexuality which now read as rather less than liberating. When the Minister of Justice's wife removes the silk veils covering her, British official Alan Wint is dismayed by feeling excited and by the comparison with his own wife:

> She was an excitingly beautiful, exquisitely groomed, superbly dignified woman [...] Paula – and he thanked God for it – was domestic in comparison: she was home to him, as a lush green field with cows in it was home; her loveliness was as English as buttercups or honeysuckle.

---

28   Said, *Orientalism* p. 39. For the 'subaltern' see Gayatri Chakravorty Spivak, 'Can the Subaltern Speak', from L. Grossberg and C. Nelson, eds., *Marxism and the Interpretation of Culture* (Urbana: University of Illinois Press; Basingstoke: Macmillan,1988), in Rosalind C. Morris *Reflections on the History of an Idea: Can the Subaltern Speak?* (New York: Columbia U.P. 2010), 237–291.

29   Jenkins, 'Siddiq', *A Far Cry From Bowmore*, p. 96.

Mrs Habbibullah, on the other hand, was remote and predatory; but he
would not, for the rest of his life, forget her as he now saw her [...] smiling
and representing not only the dignity and courage, but also the mystery
and menace of her sex.[30]

The case can be made (as Ágústsdóttir does) that Jenkins demonstrates how
'women share with colonised races and peoples an intimate experience of the
politics of oppression and repression, and like them have been forced to articulate their experiences in the language of the oppressors.'[31] In defence of Jenkins she employs Kanneh (1995) who argues that the 'feminising of colonised
territory is a trope in colonial thought.'[32]

Certainly to focus, as Jenkins does at various points, on the idea and fear of
miscegenation, goes to the heart of any critique of colonialism and he is highly alert to the body itself. In *The Holy Tree* we find 'dour and bony Scot', John
Melrose, the Chief of Police musing on how a friend had recognised that Melrose's mistress: 'Monica had a beautiful body, one of the very few rice-coloured
to compare with the slim golden ones of the young Chinese women'.[33] By
depicting the perspective of one of the colonisers in this way Jenkins demonstrate the intertwining of biology, ethnicity, sexuality and aesthetics in the
perceptions of the colonial oppressors and the resultant production of difference. Such distinctions are, in turn, adopted by colonial subjects. So Eking,
fascinated with the red lipsticks and breasts of Mrs Reynolds, is dismissive of
another teacher: 'an Indian, wearing a green sari, and with the black glossy hair
in a thick plait down past her waist. She too has big breasts but they would be
as dark as her face, and he had seen enough dark breasts before.'[34] This obsession with bodily difference is played out in relation to Eking himself: the eyes
of others and his own are frequently drawn to the (potentially) syphilitic sores
on his leg and the troubling tightness of his shorts, which embody a characteristically orientalist perception of manhood. By highlighting the importance of
bodily markers in sexualising otherness and othering sexuality Jenkins's novels
begin to suggest the kind of critique that is articulated by later theorists such as

---

30   Jenkins, *Dust on the Paw*, p. 383.
31   Ágústsdóttir, 'Surrender and Sacrifice', citing Ashcroft *et al.*, *The Empire Writes Back* (Lon-
      don and New York: Routlegde, 1989), 174–175 (p. 132).
32   Ágústsdóttir, 'Surrender and Sacrifice', citing Kadiatu Kanneh, 'Feminism and the Colo-
      nial Body' Ashcroft *et al.*, *The Post-colonial Studies Reader* (London: New York, Routledge
      1995), p. 346, p. 132.
33   Jenkins, *The Holy Tree*, p. 104.
34   Ibid., p. 63.

Anne McClintock in *Imperial Leather*.[35] He also demonstrates – in fiction such as *Leila* and 'Imelda and the Miserly Scot' – the ways in which non-white female bodies 'were associated with primitiveness, savagery and sexual deviancy, inviting to "both sexual and colonial conquest"'.[36]

What makes such readings of Jenkins rather problematic, in terms of a more explicitly feminist critique, is that Jenkins goes to some lengths to present white women as either sexually over-exuberant and therefore repulsive – as in *The Expatriates* with the image of Flo Bennett attracting mosquitoes 'with her fat arms and legs naked, and most of her chest, made a succulent pasture for them, if that was, they did not balk at sweat scented with gin, huge varicose veins, drenched hairy armpits, and at least four chins' – or 'unnaturally repressed' and again repulsive.[37] Margaret Ormiston in *The Expatriates* repels her husband on the first night of their marriage:

> He could not disguise his astonishment and dismay at the immaturity of what she was offering. Her breasts were only slight swellings on her chest; he had to look twice to see any nipples [...] Very soon he found himself not so much making love as establishing her as a woman, to her own satisfaction anyway [...] Once that was done, at her snarled but loving behests, he was allowed to find what pleasure he could in impregnating her. He did not find much.[38]

Likewise in *Dust on the Paw* the 'brazen bitch', Helga Larsen, is contrasted with Wahab's fiancée, seen from his point of view after their first love making: 'When, afterwards, he turned his head to look first at her naked but parsimonious breasts, and then further up her face twisted unrecognisably, he could not help considering the excellent reasons for not marrying her.'[39] Such passages could, of course, be read as Jenkins's interrogation of dominant models of both Western and Eastern sexuality, their interactions and the associated body images. However, the absences of alternative models of positive female sexuality – from any of the women whatever their background – in his novels

---

35   Anne McClintock, *Imperial Leather: Race, Gender and Sexuality in the colonial contest* (London: Routledge, 1995).

36   Maria Isabel Romero Ruiz, Introduction, *Women's Identities and Bodies in Colonial and Postcolonial History and Literature* (Cambridge: Cambridge Scholars Publishing, 2012), p. 3, quoting Janell Hobson, *Venus in the Dark* (London Routledge, 2005), p. 26.

37   Jenkins, *The Expatriates*, p. 122.

38   Ibid., p. 65.

39   Jenkins, *Dust on the Paw*, p. 294.

makes this a difficult argument to sustain. If Western women are seen to embody cultural deformity in terms of their sexuality, the more 'natural' sexual appeal of women in the East produces in itself a familiar and mystificatory racial stereotype.

Leila presents a late but key example of this problematic. While the novel is critical of the views of the expatriate community which 'exoticises' Leila, the novel itself establishes a comparison between her and Sandiland's Scottish lover, Jean Hislop, who is both sexually explicit or 'coarse' as the narrative describes her but also repressed: 'though she would parade naked in front of him she nevertheless had a curious shyness in relation to sex. She tried disguise it with obscene words and gestures.'[40] This kind of language appears to reinforce a very familiar opposition. The novel both sets up and interrogates Leila as a metonym of the colonised other and directly discussing her as territory: 'She was no simple soul. In her there were many intrepid discoveries too be made. It might take a more intrepid explorer than he.'[41] By presenting such a viewpoint as coming from Sandiland's consciousness creates further ambiguities and he struggles with his own ambivalences:

> She seemed to be carrying herself with exaggerated elegance, as if to emphasise how untouchable she was. He was being made to look crude and unworthy. Was that her intention? Did she suspect, from giveaway signs that he himself had not been aware of, that he had an instinctive or instilled prejudice against coloured skins and was challenging him? No, that was absurd.[42]

Yet while this delineation of conflicting emotions and dissection of prejudice is a nuanced one, there is no counter to it in the novel. Leila is viewed from the point of view of Andrew, or the expatriate community: she is given no interiority herself, which almost inevitably reinforces the construction of her as exotic cipher.

Such a construction could, however, be seen as a knowing one. A similar dynamic is evident in 'Imelda and the Miserly Scot', a short story about Andrew McAndrick, a mean-spirited Scot who negotiates and exploits the 'worth' of his 'native' mistress, in which those passages that might seem to reinforce racial and feminised stereotypes are contextualised by the understanding that

---

40   Jenkins, *Leila*, p. 52.
41   Ibid., p. 37.
42   Ibid., p. 95.

they articulate the views of certain groups. So when Imelda is first represented the language appears to reinforce both racial and gender stereotypes: 'All the most entrancing qualities of Asian women were assembled in her: the carriage of an Indian, the dignity of a Chinese, the golden colour of a Filipino with Spanish, and the sweet mouth of a Dusun, though not the thick lips.'[43] These lines are, however, are preceded by a sentence which suggests this might be the view of McAndrick's male friends: 'McAndrick's sari'd companion was passing close enough for them to get a good look at her, and none of them had ever seen a more beautiful woman.' Furthermore, Jenkins's narrator perhaps comes closest to acknowledging the central issue of the 'subaltern' by stating 'What Imelda herself thought of all the comments on her appearance on the course no one ever knew, for no one ever asked her; and she never offered opinions.'[44] Both novel and short story illustrate the structures of feminisation in colonial thinking – thus arguably acknowledging Gayatri Chakravorty Spivak's point that 'if, in the context of colonial production, the subaltern has no history and cannot speak, the subaltern as female is even more deeply in its shadow'.[45] Indeed both *Leila* and the short story struggle to find a specific narrative alternative, resorting instead to the 'speech' of violence. In the case of Imelda, this is the murder of her husband with a native blowpipe, witnessed by his female servant – 'showing her black stumps of teeth in a horror that had, he noticed, with his last flicker of intelligence, savage triumph in it.'; in that of Leila a decision to sacrifice herself in bloody revolution.[46] As Spivak later argued of women in certain colonial contexts: 'in attempting to make her body speak, even unto death' becomes 'a way of bringing subalternity to crisis.'[47]

Through his fiction Jenkins is interested in challenging the limits of human understanding, and in questioning – without dismissing – the possibility of empathy; this is most obviously true of his postcolonial writing. In this context his sense that in order to convey such social and moral complexities conventions of the realist novel itself might have to be challenged is also evident. There is a revealing moment in *Leila* where there is an uncharacteristically metafictional acknowledgement of literary tradition. Teaching his students literature Sandiland is puzzled by their responses to Jane Austen: 'they had baffled him

---

43   Jenkins, 'Imedla and the Miserly Scot', *A Far Cry from Bowmore*, p. 29.
44   Ibid., p. 50.
45   Spivak, 'Can the Subaltern Speak' in Rosalind C. Morris *Reflections on the History of an Idea?*, p. 257.
46   Jenkins, 'Imedla and the Miserly Scot', *A Far Cry from Bowmore* p. 64.
47   Spivak, 'In Response: Looking Back, Looking Forward', in Morris, *Reflections on the History of an Idea?*, 227–236, p. 229.

by not finding Mr Collins the figure of fun that Jane Austen had intended. On the contrary, all of the, Malays and Chinese, males and females, had made it clear they sympathised with the pompous parson [...] This was how a prudent man would act. [...] For them meek Mr Collins was really the hero of the novel, not the haughty D'Arcy.'[48] By alerting his readership to a different interpretation of the conventions of romantic fiction and the moral values of the English social comedy, Jenkins also highlights and draws into question dominant paradigms of the English novel form in terms of its capacity to delineate fully the challenging play of positions produced by imperialism and postcolonialism.

Jenkins continued to find his experiences working in other countries a fruitful source for his fiction. *A Far Cry from Bowmore* (1973) includes stories from both Afghanistan and North Borneo; from this collection 'Bonny Chung' and 'Imelda and the Miserly Scot' have been singled out for critical attention.[49] He drew on his time spent in Spain, as in *The Sardana Dancers* (1964) and in that country too noted similarities between the Scots and Catalans.[50] But his experiences abroad also fed into his writing about home: 'I would need as wide a perspective as possible if I was to go home and see Scotland truthfully.'[51] This is significant not only in terms of his deepening understanding of Scotland's colonial past or of an individual's positioning within clashing cultures and value systems. Rather in his 'postcolonial' fiction he was forced to engage with young countries and cultures forging – or attempting to forge – their own political destinies, challenging the histories that had been written for them by western powers. His increasingly sophisticated political awareness and analytic awareness of national identities, the aspirations and confusions created by mixed cultural messages – as explored in 'Bonny Chung' – is brought back to a Scottish setting in novels such as *A Very Scotch* Affair (1968), *Fergus Lamont* (1979) and *The Awakening of George Darroch* (1985). Marina Mackay, for example, argues that '*Fergus Lamont* is about the problems of how a national history can be told and passed on without the numerous forms of falsification and wishful

---

48   Jenkins, *Leila*, p. 15.
49   See Ágústsdóttir; Sellin.
50   'When I was in Spain I saw some links between the Scots and the Catalans, but they were much more fervent.' Glenda Norquay, personal interview, PhD thesis, 'Moral Absolutism in the Novels of Robert Louis Stevenson, Robin Jenkins and Muriel Spark' (University of Edinburgh, 1985) p. 438.
51   Ingibjörg Ágústsdóttir, PhD thesis, 'Pilgrims of Conscience: Quests for Morality and Self-Knowledge in the Fiction of Robin Jenkins' (University of Glasgow, 2001), quoting from Robin Jenkins, 'Why I decided Scotland must be seen through fresh and truthful eyes', *Glasgow Herald 12* October 1982: 11, p. 119.

thinking that tempt its literary hero'.[52] If, as he complained in 1983, 'Scotland is now a small nation which is only too willing to recognise its smallness and cringe submissively', his experiences in Afghanistan and Malaysia encouraged Jenkins to find a voice and means of dissecting and questioning that sense of restriction.[53]

Increasingly, of course, Scotland has turned to other 'small nations' to understand its own place in the dynamics of colonialism. The extent to which parallels can be traced between Scotland and colonised countries is much debated. Ágústsdóttir suggests that Berthold Schoene, who was one of the first critics to apply postcolonial perspectives to the Scottish context,

> fails to acknowledge that the role of the Scots themselves in the imperial mission complicates things considerably, despite the seeming parallels between Scotland and the colonies. According to Richard Finlay, the Scots 'prided themselves on being a race of empire builders' in the nineteenth and early twentieth centuries and for them, the British Empire 'was as much a Scottish creation as an English one'.[54]

Moreover, as Stefanie Lehner argues:

> not only does any claim for Scottish postcoloniality, which designates the country as an English colony, remain highly contentious [...], but postcolonial criticism within a Scottish context is almost inevitably prone to prioritising issues of nationhood and nationalism over other important categorical concerns of individual and communal identity such as class and gender.[55]

In the same critical vein Liam Connell has suggested: 'The designation of Scotland as an English colony is highly controversial and displays a dazzling

---

52   Marina Mackay, 'Rewriting and the Politics of Inheritance in Robin Jenkins and Jean Rhys', in Gardiner (eds), *Scottish Literature and Postcolonial Literature*, pp. 158–169 (p. 168).

53   Glenda Norquay, personal interview, PhD thesis, 'Moral Absolutism in the Novels of Robert Louis Stevenson, Robin Jenkins and Muriel Spark', p. 437.

54   Ingibjörg Ágústsdóttir, PhD thesis, 'Pilgrims of Conscience', p. 122.

55   Stefanie Lehner, 'Subaltern Scotland: Devolution and Postcoloniality', in B. Schoene (ed.), *The Edinburgh Companion to Contemporary Scottish Literature* (Edinburgh: Edinburgh University Press, 2007), pp. 292–300 (p. 292).

confusion of textual and social forms of exclusion.[56] Connell focuses in particular on the confusion of colonisation and imperialism, conflating political and economic agendas. Jenkins's fiction can be read as an embodiment of such debates. While scornful of literary theory himself, his fiction plays out the challenges to paradigms and contextualisation which these critics argue over. Jenkins was not someone who embraced literary theory: he would, however, have relished the lively debates over postcolonial contexts and Scotland's place within them. As if in anticipation of such controversy, his fiction set outside Scotland forces its readers into uncomfortable confrontations with cultural difference and refuses reconciliation or resolution.

Works Cited

Ágústsdóttir, Ingibjörg, 'Pilgrims of Conscience: Quests for Morality and Self-Knowledge in the Fiction of Robin Jenkins' (PhD thesis, University of Glasgow, 2001).

Ágústsdóttir, Ingibjörg, 'Surrender and Sacrifice: Imperial Subjugation and the Coloured Mistress in Robin Jenkins *The Expatriates* and "Imelda and the Miserly Scot"', *Milli Mála-Tímarit um erlend tungumál og menningu*, No: 5 (2013), 127–146.

Connell, Liam, 'Modes of Marginality: Scottish Literature and the Uses of Postcolonial Theory', *Comparative Studies of South Asia, Africa and the Middle East*, XXIII: No. 1 (2003), 3–18.

Fanon, Franz, *Black Skin, White Masks* [Editions de Seuil, 1952], trans. by Charles Lan Markmann (London: Grove Press, 1967; Pluto Press, 1986).

Gardiner, Michael, G. Macdonald & N. O'Gallagher, eds., *Scottish Literature and Postcolonial Literature* (Edinburgh: Edinburgh University Press, 2011).

Jenkins, Robin, *Dust on the Paw* (London: Macdonald and Co., 1961).

Jenkins, Robin, *The Expatriates* (London: Victor Gollancz, 1972).

Jenkins, Robin, *A Far Cry from Bowmore* (London: Victor Gollancz, 1973).

Jenkins, Robin, *The Holy Tree* (London: Gollancz, 1969).

Jenkins, Robin, *Leila* (Edinburgh: Polygon, 1995).

Jenkins, Robin, *Some Kind of Grace* (London: Macdonald and Co., 1960; Edinburgh: Polygon, 2004).

Jenkins, Robin, *The Tiger of Gold* (London: Macdonald and Co., 1962).

---

56   Liam Connell, 'Modes of Marginality: Scottish Literature and the Uses of Postcolonial Theory', *Comparative Studies of South Asia, Africa and the Middle East*, XXIII: No. 1 (2003), 3–18 (p. 4).

Lehner, Stefanie, 'Subaltern Scotland: Devolution and Postcoloniality', in B. Schoene (ed.), *The Edinburgh Companion to Contemporary Scottish Literature* (Edinburgh: Edinburgh University Press, 2007), pp. 292–300.

Mackay, Marina, 'Rewriting and the Politics of Inheritance in Robin Jenkins and Jean Rhys', in Michael Gardiner, Graham Macdonald and Niall O'Gallagher, eds., *Scottish literature and postcolonial literature: comparative texts and critical perspectives* (Edinburgh: Edinburgh University Press, 2011), pp. 158–169.

McClintock, Anne, *Imperial Leather: Race, Gender and Sexuality in the Colonial Contest* (London: Routledge, 1995).

Morris, Rosalind C., *Reflections on the History of an Idea: Can the Subaltern Speak?* (New York: Columbia U.P. 2010).

Norquay, Glenda, 'Moral Absolutism in the Novels of Robert Louis Stevenson, Robin Jenkins and Moral Spark' (PhD thesis, University of Edinburgh, 1985).

Ruiz, Maria Isabel Romero, Introduction, *Women's Identities and Bodies in Colonial and Postcolonial History and Literature* (Cambridge: Cambridge Scholars Publishing, 2012).

Said, Edward W., *Orientalism* (London: Routledge & Kegan Paul, 1978).

Schoene, Berthold (ed.), *The Edinburgh Companion to Contemporary Scottish Literature* (Edinburgh: Edinburgh University Press, 2007).

Sellin, Bernard, 'Exile and Expatriates in Robin Jenkins's Novels', *Études Écossaises* 13 (2010) 'Exil et Retour', 129–138.

Robin Jenkins: The Short Stories

Alan Riach

Abstract

Robin Jenkins's short stories are collected in two books: *A Far Cry from Bowmore* (1973), and *Lunderston Tales* (1996). This chapter discusses ideas of distance and proximity in Jenkins's writing, showing how stylistically he brings together apparently 'objective' prose describing events 'externally' with more insidious and sly representations of 'subjective' or 'internally'-realised intimations of characters' motives, prejudices and dispositions. The chapter goes through each of the stories in both books, and considers one further story published independently, chronologically between each of the books' publication dates. The developing argument centres on the relation between 'realism' and the sense Jenkins's writing delivers that realism is not all there is. The unexpected twists in the narratives, the moral ambiguities and unreliable co-ordinate points experienced by many of the characters, the recurrence of the inexplicable, make Jenkins's writing uniquely challenging and compelling in modern Scottish literature, and nowhere more evidently than in his short stories.

Keywords

Short stories – realism – irony – satire – morality

The short stories of Robin Jenkins are collected in two books of great contrast: *A Far Cry from Bowmore* (1973), set in apparently exotic locations such as Borneo, Afghanistan and Malaysia, but often with immediately recognisable characters drawing on familiar Scottish 'types', and *Lunderston Tales* (1996), set in the implicitly familiar location of a small Scottish seaside town on the west coast, yet populated by a sometimes surprising cast of characters, who do unpredicted things.

They may be read as counterpoints, both typifying the ironies, reductive humour, sympathetic insight, and satirical disdain of Jenkins at his best, and both delivering a characteristic combination of intimate understanding and high, sometimes ambivalent, moral judgement. The stories in both books present domestic closeness and haughty objectivity, extremes between which Jenkins's writing veers and shifts with exhilarating command and consistently sharp focus.

© KONINKLIJKE BRILL NV, LEIDEN, 2017 | DOI 10.1163/9789004342491_009

These qualities of intimacy and distance are essential to his work and key elements in each of the stories. They involve engagement, sympathy and suspension of moral judgement, and then they demand equally a removal from close identification with individual characters, and the intrusion of ferocious objectivity and the capacity to make – or at least consider – absolute moral judgements. They are therefore poised, or rather negotiating, between conventions of nineteenth-century realism and twentieth-century, modernist forensic detachment. In this they have much in common with early post-colonial or commonwealth fiction by, for example, Chinua Achebe and Ngugi wa Thiong'o. Arguably, this arises in part from Jenkins's early experience of Scotland, then from 1957 to 1968 as a teacher in Afghanistan, Spain and Borneo, and then of Scotland once again. Distance from, then reappraisal of, the familiar practice of English-language writing might help defamiliarise, and then reapply, linguistic conventions in that language, and deepen understanding of how it relates to literary and oral expression in other languages, whether Scots, Gaelic, Igbo or Kikuyu. There are therefore multiple contexts here in which the stories may be read: those of Scottish literature, of modernism, and of post-colonialism, and of the generic short story form.

Some qualities of narrative and idiom are dictated by the form itself. At the risk of stating the obvious, there are two essential qualities for any short story: it must be short, and it must be a story. To go a little further though, the classic examination of the form is in Walter Benjamin's essay, 'The Storyteller' (1936), which gives us two crucial, double distinctions: that between the story and the novel, and that between the storyteller who stays at home and gets to know everything about the locality he or she lives in, and the storyteller who travels the world and gets to know everything about other places and can compare and contrast them with the conventions and mores of home.[1] Jenkins partakes of each of these qualities. So does Lewis Grassic Gibbon. R.B. Cunninghame Grahame before them would better exemplify the latter kind of storyteller and George Mackay Brown after them would exemplify the former kind.

As Benjamin reminds us, storytellers predate print, and stories predate novels, but one critical distinction of the Scottish tradition in fiction is one that the greatest nineteenth-century Scottish novelists, Hogg, Scott, Galt and Stevenson, were keenly aware of – and to some extent simultaneously engaged with – both the oral as well as the print-bred literary arts of storytelling – and this legacy comes to Jenkins in particular ways. Indeed, there is a peculiar affinity in the unresolved ambiguities of the explanations of events suggested in

---

1   Walter Benjamin, 'The Storyteller', in *Illuminations*, ed. by Hannah Arendt, trans. by Harry Zorn (London: Pimlico, 1999), pp. 83–107.

Hogg's *Confessions of a Justified Sinner* (1824) with those suggested in Jenkins's 'A Far Cry from Bowmore', as we shall see. This might be described as 'a sense of supernatural or mystical grace' that may be a form of redemption, or may be a psychological self-deception, a source of fatal delusion. More generally, the ambiguous narrative, like the unreliable narrator, is familiar in Scottish fiction into the twenty-first century: Iain Banks's quasi-science fiction, quasi-realist novel, *Transition* (2009) begins with this sentence: 'Apparently, I am what is known as an Unreliable Narrator, though of course if you believe everything you're told you deserve whatever you get.'[2] The tone of that sentence is close to Jenkins in its relish of the act of vengeance upon the too-susceptible reader, the over-sympathetic engagement with characters whose come-uppance will be shocking, but leave you wondering how far your sympathy may have been warranted, and how much your judgement should have already been cutting in on your empathy.

There is a singular edge in Jenkins's style, honed over decades of writing and habitually resumed angles of approach, evident in both books of short stories: how the artifice of writing cuts deeply into the assumptions of reading along with, or seeing through the eyes of, his characters. We are always kept on this rather discomforting edge, our natural sympathies balanced against the blade of Jenkins's scorn, his satiric disdain, his critical decisiveness. Again and again, he holds in close reserve his chosen moment of revelation.

In modern writing, this edge is what Hugh Kenner described as the 'Uncle Charles principle' in *Joyce's Voices* (1978). Kenner draws a crucial distinction between Charles Dickens and James Joyce. Kenner describes Dickens's writing in *Oliver Twist* (1838) as 'perpetually *judging*'.[3] When Oliver says he wants more gruel, the master is described: 'a fat, healthy man' who 'turned very pale' and 'gazed in stupefied astonishment on the small rebel for some seconds, and then clung for support to the copper.' After exclaiming, 'What!' in a faint voice, he aims a blow at Oliver's head with the ladle. As we read we are chiefly aware of what Dickens is doing: 'ensuring by his sarcasms that no reader will miss the frigid hypocrisy of beadle and board, or the mad conviction of officialdom that a law of nature has been violated.'[4] In *Madame Bovary* (1852), Gustave Flaubert achieves different effects. When the boy Charles Bovary is described being humiliated in a classroom when he drops his cap, he is described through the eyes of his fellow pupils, and later Mademoiselle Rouault is described through the eyes of Charles, who, Kenner says, 'as usual does not know what is happening

---

2 Iain Banks, *Transition* (London: Little, Brown, 2009), p. 1.
3 Hugh Kenner, *Joyce's Voices* (London: Faber and Faber, 1978), p. 7.
4 Ibid.

to him.'⁵ This technique carries through to Joyce. The opening sentence of 'The Dead', from *Dubliners* (1914), is: 'Lily, the caretaker's daughter, was literally run off her feet.' The word 'literally' is inaccurately used (it should be 'figuratively') but it is idiomatically accurate to Lily. This is what she would say, not the objective narrator's description of her. Kenner's comment is: 'Description without knowledge is always potentially comic. It fails of intimacy with what is described. Being outside, it enacts a certain bafflement, as though it were a periphrasis for the intimate identifying word, such as Watch.'⁶ The 'Uncle Charles principle' for Kenner is that style which utilises the viewpoint and language of the character to create an intimacy from which the reader and author remain both aware and distanced, sympathetic and critical. The result may be both (or either) comic and (or) tragic. What determines that result lies mainly in the balance of sympathy or disdain. Jenkins manages this balance with sustained and often brilliant verve and *élan*.

When we come to Jenkins, then, the flat descriptions are in contrast with the nuance of sympathy, the precision of representation is given a tension and an urgency because of the imminence of judgement. And judgement, when it comes, can be fearfully fast and fatal. This is most poignantly expressed in the stories collected in *A Far Cry from Bowmore*.

The collection begins with 'Christian Justice' (first published in *The Penguin Book of Scottish Short Stories*, 1970). The title indicates clearly the irony that leans in on all the characters, as we accompany a married couple, teachers, Mr and Mrs Kishan, who take particular offence against a fellow-teacher, Mrs Kumar, and pursue their own prejudice to absurdly higher levels of authority and higher courts of appeal, to no avail. By the end of the story they are writing letters of complaint to the Prime Minister, to central government in Kuala Lumpur, and finally to the House of Lords in London. Mr Kishan tells his wife:

> 'That institution, you understand, is still the highest court of appeal in the Commonwealth.'
>   'Yes, my husband,' she said, quietly and proudly.⁷

This ever-aspiring list of courts of appeal mirror the quest at the heart of Jenkins's work, an aspiration towards sympathy that is grounded in an eternal, unbreakable connection between the failings and foibles of common humanity and our common human potential. There is no secure promise of fulfilment or

---

5   Ibid., p. 8.
6   Ibid., p. 30.
7   Robin Jenkins, *A Far Cry from Bowmore* (London: Victor Gollancz, 1973), p. 25.

appeasement because every promise can only be made in the understanding that the potential for fulfilment is common to humanity but without guarantee about what it may lead to. Every court of appeal has its own human failings. There is no assurance of ultimate justice in the human universe.

At the end of 'Imelda and the Miserly Scot' in *A Far Cry from Bowmore*, there is a stunning example of this. The story delivers a brilliant anatomisation of the miserly Scot, blatantly named Andrew McAndrick, a self-righteous, hypo-critical, lascivious dentist in the Borneo town of Api (the word means 'fire'), who acquires the native Imelda as his mistress. 'Thrifty men are always devious of bargains' Jenkins warns us, but when Andrew sees 'this jewel of a woman among the frangipani blossoms' he snatches her up, having 'spiered, as they said in his native Scotland, and found that though they were all tormented by her beauty and her bedworthiness none had tasted her.'[8] The emphatic use of the Scots word, the deployment of pomposities appropriate to McAndrick, the depiction of his lust and determination, all mingle apparent objectivities with descriptions of people and priorities from the point of view and in the language of the protagonist. We learn about Imelda's character from glimpses, mainly from McAndrick's perspective. We sense the threat she poses to him, while he remains in a state of acquisitive lust, psychological and cultural incomprehen-sion, and we sense that he is fatally undervaluing her difference and potential threat. Jenkins implies there is danger in what she might do. The scrupulous delineation of McAndrick's preferences, habits, limited points of view, self-delusions, gives us just enough of Imelda for us, reading, to understand more than the central character. We know what McAndrick only nervously suspects: that he is in a place of increasing threatening violence. Our sympathies are tainted. We feel outrage at the way he treats her; yet we feel fearful for what she will do to him. We know that he deserves comeuppance, even retribution, but we sympathise with him precisely because he cannot comprehend his own predicament. We know it will end badly, and it does, when she spears him with a blowpipe, after running across the bedroom 'with a strange bounding action no doubt inherited from her ancestors used to hopping over logs and roots,' driving 'the sharp point past his Api Yacht Club tie, gold sails on a black ground, through his white shirt of finest Hong Kong cotton, and into his belly made, thirty-six years ago, in far-off Scotland.'[9] The exaggerated patrician con-descension in the observation McAndrick is apparently making about Imelda's ancestors is countered by the violence of her action. Even here, however, we need to judge carefully the balance between, or measured blend of, realism

---

8   Ibid., p. 32.
9   Ibid., p. 64.

and design, sympathy and detachment, irony and despair. This story gives us a reality in two quite different but overlapping spheres of action. It is structured not only in a moral, social, cultural, or religious schema, but balanced on the edge of quality in the writing itself. This is a kind of realism, but it is not only that.

As Cairns Craig puts it, 'for Jenkins realism is what is left when ultimate meaning has been withdrawn from the world: it is the tragic stylistic condition which the modern novelist must both accept and resist at one and the same moment.'[10] Craig argues that Jenkins is not part of a Scottish realist tradition: 'rather, he is, like Muriel Spark, a novelist of absolutes which defy the secular realities of the modern world.'[11] Where Spark found faith in Catholicism, Jenkins finds 'in belief itself only another potential hypocrisy.'[12] For both, though, Craig says, fiction is a medium through which it is possible (in Spark's words) to see 'another world than this'.[13] Jenkins's 'stylistic condition' allows him to describe 'the real Scotland' (or 'real' and recognisable Scots outwith Scotland) but in testaments that show how insignificant 'the merely real' continues to be.

The title-character in 'Jeeva' is the daughter of a Professor of History at a college in Indonesia. She insists on giving alms to the city's beggars but at seventeen, with the imminent prospect of an arranged marriage, she is pressurised to end this practice of charity. She must swallow her pride and button down her independent spirit. The stage is set for a confrontation, a predictable rebellion of youth against convention but Jenkins pulls that expectation away dextrously, and ends the story with Jeeva looking forward to a marriage that 'might be a challenge, not a whimpering, sweet-eating surrender.'[14] Throughout, shifting perspectives, as we are made to look on people and events from the viewpoints of Jeeva, her father, mother, bridegroom-to-be and others, keep us unsettled. Similarly, the central character in 'Siddiq' finds himself pushed towards a destiny he had not wished for but discovers new ways of enacting revenge and reconciling himself to events. The story ends: 'As Siddiq rode off towards the heart of the city, not really knowing where there was for him to go to, he felt that fate, like the radio, could not be controlled, however much you turned this knob or that.'[15]

---

10   Cairns Craig, 'Robin Jenkins – A Would-Be Realist?' *Edinburgh Review*, 106 (2001), 12–22 (p. 22).

11   Ibid.

12   Ibid.

13   Ibid.

14   Jenkins, *A Far Cry from Bowmore*, p. 94.

15   Ibid., p. 133.

'A Far Cry from Bowmore' is the central story in the collection and the most memorable. It begins as another pious, pompous, self-righteous Scot, Hugh Macpherson, sitting in an airport seeing off a church minister, gets a message from a passing doctor just arrived from the interior. Dr Willard tells Macpherson that far in the interior, another Scot named McArthur has asked to see Macpherson, as a last favour, as he is dying of cancer. Macpherson's wife Mary and the minister Dougary, both Scots, urge him to go, but he is reluctant, not only because of the effort involved but because he is told McArthur has a native wife and two children: he does not approve of mixed marriage. The 'fair-haired' Mary asks him to go more than once ('he's one of us, Hugh, a Scotsman' she says, and that 'makes him closer to us'). Only when his engineering work prompts his journey part-way towards the dying man, and a further meeting with McArthur's doctor, Dr Lall, does he consent to travel to see him. Dr Lall beseeches Macpherson when at first he refuses, calling him 'a man without vision': "'If you do not go to hold that dying man's hand, do you know what you will have done? You will have stopped the stars in their courses.'"[16] Macpherson relents, and the encounter that brings the story to a culmination brings a multitude of contradictions together in a haunting and finally unresolved sense of mystery. When Macpherson meets Mrs McArthur and is shown the hospitality of their house, he is impressed by what seems a happy, domestic and balanced world. They must have been happy together, and this prompts reflection on his own marriage, his ideas about sexuality and the relation between individual self-determination and the laws of Christianity as he understands them. He finally meets the dying man, who, with his last words, says: "'Your... wife's... a... bonny... woman.'"[17]

What does this mean? It has been established that McArthur was from Islay and the Macphersons from Skye, and that they had met once, but only briefly. And it has been suggested that the McArthur house centres on a 'great round room, like a church, panelled and floored with exotic woods'.[18] This seems reminiscent of the round church in Bowmore in Islay, said to be built round so that there were no corners for the devil to hide in. In the McArthurs' house, there are carvings, dancing figures, 'each with a severed head clutched to his breast' and yet it is lit by electricity and far from simply a pagan shrine. The crucial sentence of the story comes in Macpherson's realisation: 'Dimly he perceived that there were aspects and areas of faith that he had not known existed.'[19]

---

16   Ibid., p. 153.
17   Ibid., p. 165.
18   Ibid., p. 160.
19   Ibid., p. 162.

Macpherson finally acknowledges the support and affinity between the pagan shrieks and gongs filling the air outside with their noise to keep evil spirits away, and the New Testament in his own pocket and his understanding of the relation between the spiritual and the physical, the value of sympathy, the physical cost it comes at, and what is at stake, which is more than many other characters do, in Jenkins's fiction. As the story ends, McArthur dies, and the beating gongs outside suddenly become louder, leaving Macpherson bewildered: 'how had those beating the gongs known that McArthur was dead?' He touches his New Testament, 'not to counteract the pagan shrieks and gongs, but to assist them.' There is, it would seem, hope for us yet.[20]

The last story in the book, 'Bonny Chung', set in Malaysia, returns us to a world similar to that of 'Imelda and the Miserly Scot', as a lascivious young teacher pursues various women, one of whom finally commits suicide and leaves him piously convincing himself of ways he might get over the situation and indeed turn it to his advantage in the future. Humanity is not redeemed, nothing is hopeful, the mix of cultures, appetites and aspirations promises nothing secure or restorative. A bleak vision closes the book, but the mystery enacted at the end of the title-story remains in the memory, understated, without emphasis, beautifully rendered in Jenkins's idiosyncratic and inimitable style.

One other story published mid-way between the two collections and set in Spain, Jenkins's other familiar locale in his novels, sums up key aspects of what we have been considering and should be noted: 'Exile', in *Modern Scottish Short Stories*, is a mere five pages long.[21] A retired teacher, Miss Struthers, waits for the postman to bring letters from Scotland, sips sherry, remembers her neighbours and pupils back in Scotland, and has invited one of her former friends to visit for Easter. In the event, the letters delivered are from former pupils, remembering her affectionately, though not always in perfect grammatical sentences. There are more than twenty letters. 'Reading them, and re-reading them, would make exile no matter how long not only worth-while but also far easier to thole.' The story ends with that last, Scots, word, as if bearing the burden of her condition in the sherry-sipping Spanish sunshine might be both truly a loss, but also, not so unbearable after all. The balance between or subtle blend of pathos and comedy is clear, beneath the lucid surface of the prose.

Lunderston Tales begins with a 'Foreword' that tells of a Scottish novelist's complaint that one of the disadvantages of living in Scotland was that 'nothing ever happened in it spectacular or exciting enough to be of interest to the rest

20   Jenkins, *A Far Cry from Bowmore*, p. 166.

21   Robin Jenkins, 'Exile', in *Modern Scottish Short Stories*, ed. by Fred Urquhart and Giles Gordon (London: Hamish Hamilton, 1978), pp. 140–144.

of the world.'[22] Referring to the sad result of the 1979 devolution referendum and the monotonous regularity of Scottish patriotism being only in evidence in the football stadiums, Jenkins says that nevertheless individual people are as interesting in Scotland as anywhere, and among the people of the small town he is introducing, there were 'individuals whose lives touched upon the great issues of our times and who represented the twentieth century as much as any inhabitants of New York or Moscow.'[23] This is a repudiation of parochialism. It is also an indication of how these tales will counterpoint those of the more exotic locations of his previous stories. Yet, empowered with the experience of life in other places, reading the local lives of Lunderston might exoticise them, not sensationalising but defamiliarising what otherwise might have seemed merely conventional. The irony and shrewd evaluations Jenkins brings to his writing, his characters and the favoured place, is an antidote to the habits of familiarity and comfort enacted in traditional 'kailyard' stories. There are no reliable, benevolent co-ordinate figures of minister or dominie. Nothing here can be taken for granted.

The very title of 'The Greengrocer and the Hero' juxtaposes the everyday smalltown shopkeeper and a mythic context. As with Joyce's Leopold Bloom, the opportunities are rich for both the reductive comedy of bathos and the understanding that heroism occurs in everyday, domestic circumstances. The story appears to be about a question of acknowledged paternity. When the Greengrocer's daughter Sadie has a son, the father, the feckless Gary, takes off for South Africa and becomes a mercenary; Sadie marries Rab Fairlie and they have five children as the years go by, while Gary's mother becomes a recluse. When Gary returns and meets the morally upright Greengrocer and town councillor, he refuses to accept any responsibility. The moral world described up to this point would seem to emphasise the hypocrisy of the 'hero' and the fortitude of Sadie's father, Jack Rankin, but when Jack confronts Gary's mother, he is shocked by her response:

> 'I'm Councillor Rankin, [...] Sadie's father. I've come to ask your son if he would like to meet his son, towards whose keep you have been contributing for the past eleven years. It may be his sense of humour or it could be that his recent experiences have deranged him, but he has denied paternity.'
>
>   'Does it matter,' she asked contemptuously, 'who your father is?'[24]

---

22   Robin Jenkins, *Lunderston Tales* (Edinburgh: Polygon, 1996), p. ix.
23   Ibid.
24   Ibid., p. 24.

And she turns and closes the door on him. He is left to ponder the question. All his assumptions about family, responsibility and social life are shocked by the question. He has failed in his mission to bring Gary back to a sense of conventional moral duty and his wife, daughter and grandson might complain about this, in one way or another: 'Nevertheless he felt that he had succeeded in a way that he could never explain to anyone. He had been let into a secret.'[25] The shock of this rejection of familiar social morality is in itself exotic and forceful, and the unexpectedness of this new sense of uncertainty shocks not only Jack in the story but literary conventions of realism as well. The story enacts and delivers an unpredicted judgement. This is arguably the main stylistic technique and the major theme running through all Jenkins's stories, and the novels as well. As Sadie's mother, Annie, tells her: 'Life's like that [...] We want to gang doon one road, it sends us doon another.'[26]

'The Provost and the Queen' exemplifies this as it looks over the entire career of John Golspie, the most notorious Provost in Lunderston's history, who invited the Queen to open a new conference hall. The reactions of various conservative, nervous, superior, self-deprecating, arrogant or hostile characters are considered sweepingly before the visit of the reigning royals is described and Golspie's transgression noted. He asks the monarch to sign two visitors' books. When the townsfolk are disdainful and disparage him, he paints his house bright pink, but after his death, when the town's relics are gathered in the burgh hall museum, the most revered item is Provost Golspie's autograph album. The vicissitudes of public opinion, the power of office and the Provost's strength of character are represented almost without comment. Jenkins's attitude to the whole saga seems magisterial, reserved, neither amused nor indignant, but simply acknowledging how people are, what absurdities folk are capable of.

'Don't You Agree, Baby?' addresses racism, hypocrisy and polite social manners, ending like 'Jeeva' not with a predictable confrontation but rather with an acceptance of challenge that might take the main characters beyond the confines of Lunderston. Different characters from different parts of the world at large come into Lunderston, and may leave it. Having dealt with racism, 'The Merry Widow and the Elder' introduces characters whose sexuality and appetite for the unpredicted demonstrate their willingness to engage each other in relationships at various levels of uncertainty. Sexuality in Lunderston, where the churches are 'numerous and solid' and worshippers 'sedate and

---

25   Ibid.
26   Ibid., p. 14.

respectable', is, despite appearances, 'libertarian'.[27] The comic undertone is beautifully sly: 'As for orthodox sex, the sort that most Lunderstonians practise, it is often indulged in for motives more subtle and human than the mere gratification of appetite.' The 'Merry Widow' might bring the 'Elder' to realise his sexual potential, and thus she might gain something she would be glad 'to thank the Lord' for, praying for so long that 'her knees began to ache, in spite of the thick carpet.'[28]

Even less predictable shenanigans tale place between the main characters in 'Doreen and the Village Plumber'. Doreen's husband arrives unexpectedly home and interrupts Doreen and Simon in bed together.[29] The juxtaposition of their behaviour with that of Simon is dry humour at its most arid, yet yields a final redemption: Simon 'had been made man. He wouldn't tell his friends about it, not just because his mother might get to know, but also because it was the kind of treasure you could keep to yourself without feeling selfish.'[30]

'The Locked Lavatories' uses the narrative device of letters to the Editor of the *Lunderston Gazette* in an epistolary short story, so the questions of who the narrator is and how realism is maintained and of how judgements are delivered in the commentary that contextualises them are balanced and highlighted from the start. Similarly, restraint characterises 'The Book Club'. Judgement is held back to the point of ambiguity. There is no Grand Guignol or melodramatic intervention but as the central character, Isabel, acknowledges in charity that poorly written books are not unforgivable, she maintains her dignity by refusing to behave like a character in one of them. Another subtle story of social subversion, 'The Ladies' Section' charts the infiltration of women into the hitherto male preserve of the golf club. 'The Consultant' and 'The Cabinet Minister and the Garbage Collector' both probe around in questions of social class and the assumptions of superiority and inferiorism.

'With a Tinge of Yellow' mercilessly takes us with Robert Nairn, as he travels to America to see his daughter Cathie, now married to a black American sailor, with whom she has had a daughter. Nairn's lustful racist thoughts about Cathie's mother-in-law are repulsive, comic, but finally hopeless as he leaves them, pocketing a cheque to help with his own travel expenses. In the closing paragraphs, the 'tinge of yellow' might refer not to anyone's skin colour but to the cowardice and abject motives of the story's main character, which

---

27   Ibid., p. 50.
28   Ibid., p. 70.
29   Ibid., p. 83.
30   Ibid., p. 85.

paradoxically yields a sense of pity, if not sympathy. Jenkins is marvellously deft in balancing and blending these aspects of the reader's emotional engagement.

'Goodbye, Phoenix Arizona' takes us with Bella and Annie on an adventure from Lunderston to Las Vegas, and a marriage proposed and avoided in an instant cut of a deck of cards. 'She Had to Laugh' takes us with a young woman, a prostitute, into an arranged marriage and another far distant location, this time in California, as if to drive home the point that however much Lunderston might seem like the back of beyond, there are always other places even more so. Beyond the limitations of place, however, the resources of individual characters are where redemption, if at all possible, might arise. Just as individuals are the sources of their own failings and unpredicted fate, so their capacities for devising new ways forward are celebrated, in Jenkins's work. At the end of the story, Tessa, the woman who has followed her road to the loneliest of American deserts and a world apparently bereft of the kind human company assured by at least some of Lunderston's folk, considers her own predicament: 'She went round to the back of the store, leaned against it, lit another cigarette, shivered a little, shaded her eyes against the brilliant sun, and laughed.'[31]

The journey Tessa makes universalises or internationalises the human story in Jenkins's work. It is Scottish writing but intrinsic to it are qualities of irony and understanding which locate it in a tradition of prose fiction which carries us from Hogg, Scott and Stevenson to Gray, Kelman and Kennedy, as much as from Dickens to Flaubert to Joyce, and in a way which sees it moving from the governing criteria of realism to a world of contingency and always only partial fulfilment.

Both Tessa's shivering and her laughter are essential responses to the world in Robin Jenkins's short stories, and his writing puts his characters, measuring scorn and compassion, under the most brilliant light, for both our moral judgement and our human sympathy.

Works Cited

Banks, Iain, *Transition* (London: Little, Brown, 2009).

Benjamin, Walter, 'The Storyteller' (1936); in *Illuminations*, ed. by Hannah Arendt, trans. by Harry Zorn (London: Pimlico, 1999), pp. 83–107.

Craig, Cairns, 'Robin Jenkins – A Would-Be Realist?', in *Edinburgh Review*, 106 (2001), 12–22.

---

31   Ibid., p. 214.

Jenkins, Robin, 'Exile', in *Modern Scottish Short Stories*, ed. by Fred Urquhart and Giles Gordon (London: Hamish Hamilton, 1978), pp. 140–144.

Jenkins, Robin, *A Far Cry from Bowmore* (London: Victor Gollancz, 1973).

Jenkins, Robin, *Lunderston Tales* (Edinburgh: Polygon, 1996).

Kenner, Hugh, *Joyce's Voices* (London: Faber and Faber, 1978).

'Pilgrims of Conscience' in the Fiction of Robin Jenkins

Ingibjörg Ágústsdóttir

Abstract

A central aspect of Robin Jenkins's fiction is his exploration of human fallibility and the ambiguous nature of goodness through a portrayal of central characters whose experiences bring them towards self-knowledge and love of their fellow humans. Through these aspects of his characters' development, Jenkins consistently emphasises the essentially flawed nature of humanity and thereby the near impossibility of achieving moral perfection. These central characters, or 'pilgrims of conscience,' undertake a moral pilgrimage of sorts in the course of their story. In order to demonstrate the importance of the moral pilgrim figure in Jenkins's fiction, the first part of the chapter explores in more general terms the function and development of the pilgrim of conscience through the course of Jenkins's work. After this, the essay focuses on how Jenkins's central concerns are revealed through his portrayal of an exemplary type of the moral pilgrim, Bell McShelvie in *Guests of War* (1956).

Keywords

Robin Jenkins – moral quest – conscience – morality – human fallibility – self-knowledge – *Guests of War*

Jenkins's treatment of his central concerns – be it the influence of Calvinism on Scottish society, the question of urban versus rural values, the fragile nature of innocence and the experience of children, the cruelty of war, racial prejudice and cultural conflict, the effects of class division and the injustices of capitalist ideology – is always driven by intense ethical awareness. Jenkins examines the moral inconsistency and hypocrisy of human nature, yet continually throughout his work is concerned with the idea of attainable moral perfection, the elusive possibility that pure goodness can exist in a world of selfishness and greed, where 'goodness' itself can be a highly ambiguous thing. This exploration is conducted through portraying central characters whose experiences bring them towards self-knowledge and/or love for their fellow humans through their own ultimate disillusionment, or acknowledgment of misguided actions and acceptance of their own and others' human fallibility. These central characters are often forced to acknowledge the importance of community, reliance on other human beings, and man's essential loneliness. The fiction of Jenkins argues that we are all flawed as human beings and therefore unable to achieve moral perfection – and that the true wealth of humanity lies in its diversity. Indeed, if moral perfection seems to have been achieved by a character in Jenkins's fiction, this either exists outside reality and beyond the limits of a socially conditioned world (as with Calum in *The Cone-Gatherers* (1955)), or is received with suspicion and scepticism (as with Gavin Hamilton in *A Would-Be Saint* (1978)). Despite all this, Jenkins believes that each individual's effort towards moral perfection is worthwhile, if only to bring him or her face to face with how limited yet precious people really are.

I term such characters 'pilgrims of conscience.'[1] Their moral challenges force them to reach a new understanding of themselves and of human morality. This essay outlines the development of this central figure in Jenkins's work. Most attention is given to one of Jenkins's early manifestations of this character type, Bell McShelvie in *Guests of War*, who, I argue, is a quintessential pilgrim of conscience.

Early Pilgrims of Conscience

Different types of the pilgrim of conscience can be detected in Jenkins's first published novel, *So Gaily Sings the Lark* (1950), a subtle study of character interactions, community, and questions of religion and morality. Its protagonist, David Sutherland, journeys from urban Lanarkshire to Kilcalvonell in the West Highlands (Argyll) to work in forestry, soon falling in love with a local girl, Kirstie Hamilton. At first sight, this might seem to be a simple love story; instead, it is a complex tale of complicated, frustrated, and often cruel love between people who are ill-suited, in terms of their ambitions and expectations, and their attitudes to other people. David's goodness, charity and self-denial is challenged and resented by the materialistically selfish Kirstie.[2] David Sutherland realises this, and he is aware that Kirstie's materialism will in the

---

1   For a full exploration of the pilgrim figure in Jenkins's work, see Ingibjörg Ágústsdóttir, 'Pilgrims of Conscience: Quests for Morality and Self-Knowledge in the Fiction of Robin Jenkins,' Ph.D. Thesis, University of Glasgow, 2001.

2   A similar suggestion is made in the portrayal of another fraught and complicated love affair, that between Hugh Carstares and Constance Kilgour in *Love is a Fervent Fire* (1959), since Constance's uncompromising pride and cruelty is a clear challenge to Carstares's essentially

long run affect his personality: 'she had revealed how serious was her merce-nariness, [and] his own inevitable degeneration was clear to him.'[3] David thus comes up against challenges to his moral integrity; he will be forced to make compromises in order to marry Kirstie. Yet *So Gaily Sings the Lark* is the first of many unresolved novels where Jenkins gives no clear resolution to the central relationship. Contrary to the arguments of Alexander Reid and Francis Hart for a happy ending, there is no clear indication that this is so, as Kirstie's decision on whether to marry David or choose his rival Reverend Kinross, with whom she could move to the city and gain the material comfort she desires, is ulti-mately left unclear.[4]

Two other characters in this first novel can also be read as early types of the moral pilgrim, both of which later grow into a distinctive sub-type, the 'would-be-saint.' First, there is the forestry worker Donald Grant, whose con-cern with moral rightness is later echoed in the more developed character of Gavin Hamilton in *A Would-Be Saint* (1978) (who appears later in Jenkins's last novel, *The Pearl-Fishers* of 2007). Prompted by his Christian awareness to give up his job as ganger, Grant is one of several characters in Jenkins's work who sacrifice their interests in the name of Christian principle. The fact that Grant is later forced to seek employment with the local laird pleases others, because he, 'who had appeared to be walking in the clouds with Christ, had had to do a belly-flop in the dust at the laird's feet and so had regained his humanity.'[5] Grant's asking the laird for a job means that he is no better than others. The uneasiness felt by people at Grant's former sacrifice must therefore spring from their insecurity as to their own spiritual worth. Significantly, the reaction in this novel to a 'would-be-saint' is more or less the same as that of others to the character of Gavin Hamilton. Not knowing how to react to goodness, and not knowing either whether goodness is the real motive behind the character's be-haviour, other people in both narratives welcome any indication that the per-son in question might after all share their common fallibility. This may also be part of the reason why so many dislike Isobel Kinross, the minister's sister, who is seen by most as hiding her 'real' self behind her religion. Presented mainly through other people's biased perspectives, the truth about Isobel's character is

---

kind personality, where Jenkins emphasises, as he recurrently does throughout his work, that love between two people can compromise morality and prove destructive.

3   Robin Jenkins, *So Gaily Sings the Lark* (Glasgow: MacLellan, 1951; repr. Bath: Cedric Chivers, 1971), p. 231.

4   Alexander Reid, 'The Limits of Charity', *Scotland's Magazine* (October 1958), 43–44 (p. 44); Francis Russell Hart, *The Scottish Novel: A Critical Survey* (London: John Murray, 1978), p. 273.

5   Jenkins, *So Gaily Sings the Lark*, p. 253.

made uncertain. She may be a fanatical, sexually starved woman (like the several sexually and psychologically tormented spinsters in Jenkins's subsequent novels) but her charitable deeds and her attempts to gain David's forgiveness for her initial behaviour towards him gradually encourage a positive appreciation of her character. Ultimately, Isobel seems one of few who still retain their faith in a world where old values and ideologies have disintegrated. She is arguably, like Donald Grant, related to the category of 'would-be-saints' in Jenkins's work, as her honesty, faith and personal worth are constantly questioned.

Jenkins's exploration of morality is thus very much focused on different pilgrim types from the outset of his writing career. His early novels set in Scotland, published between 1950 and 1963, albeit often dealing with universal and timeless issues, focus on familiar and home situations. In the semi-autobiographical *Happy for the Child* (1953), the young, hypersensitive, and romantic John Stirling yearns to escape from his unsatisfying and poverty-stricken life, and is painfully aware of his poor background, his own faults, and his cruel ingratitude to his mother.[6] He lacks the courage to defy prejudice against his background, and his moral weakness is emphasised throughout, especially through comparisons with two of his schoolmates: the unfortunate, depraved yet courageous Gourlay, and the cheerful, proud and popular Robert Tull. As noted by Glenda Norquay, the dire circumstances and despair of social misfit Gourlay are set up in sharp contrast to those of Stirling, making Stirling's depression and isolation seem self-inflicted.[7] Ultimately, Stirling may not finally gain greater self-knowledge, or acknowledge his misguided actions, but he reaches a kind of acceptance that his situation must be endured and that his peers do not treat him with such scorn as he had previously imagined.

In *The Thistle and the Grail* (1954), the football club president and factory manager Andrew Rutherford faces a great inner struggle in which he tries to reconcile his own privileged status with his admiration for his father's devotion to the socialist cause, and to the poor. His good job and material comfort are constant reminders of his own compliance with a capitalist society upheld by class division, a system vigorously supported by his wife and his wealthy and ruthless brother-in-law, through whom Rutherford gained his manager's position. Rutherford makes every effort to be a good and charitable Christian, but questions the genuineness of his efforts. This charity is gradually revealed as tainted by selfishness as later with Charlie Forbes in *The Changeling* (1958),

---

6 See Isobel Murray, ed., *Scottish Writers Talking 3* (Edinburgh: John Donald, 2006), pp. 101–146 (p. 104).

7 Glenda Norquay, 'Against Compromise: The Fiction of Robin Jenkins,' *Cencrastus*, 24 (1986), 3–6 (p. 5).

but Rutherford differs from Forbes in that he severely interrogates his own flaws throughout, whereas Forbes's understanding of his own limitations is clouded by self-deception and social ambition. The revelation that his father failed to act according to his own principles signals a change for Rutherford as his expectations of humanity have thus been proven unrealistic. In addition, the final scene in the graveyard, where Rutherford comes to recognise 'the dependence of human beings on one another, living and dead together,' as well as to acknowledge that everyone is finally alone in this world, brings him the ability to love and sympathise with other people and yet expect nothing in return. Rutherford's story constitutes one of the more positive and affirmative endings to be found in Jenkins fiction.[8]

There are many more instances of such self-questioning characters in Jenkins's early Scottish novels, such as Lady Runcie-Campbell in *The Cone-Gatherers* (1955), trapped in a conflict between her Christianity and her rank, and ultimately unable to transcend the limits imposed on her by class. There is the young idealist Andrew Doig in *The Missionaries* (1957), who journeys to the mystical island of Sollas to campaign against the eviction of crofters living there, and who is presented as a modern-day Jason on a quest for the golden fleece of self-knowledge and moral certainty. He gains a humbler recognition of his own failings, and an acceptance of human shortcomings, all of which works to renew his faith in humanity, as he realises that his pity for the crofters has been merely 'academic'.[9] There is Bell McShelvie in *Guests of War* (1956), whose development I will discuss in greater detail below; and there is Charlie Forbes in *The Changeling*, whose goodness proves inadequate when faced with the depth and complexity of Tom Curdie's predicament, and who, like Andrew Doig, realises that 'his compassion was academic, [...] not creative'.[10] And in *A Love of Innocence* (which Francis Hart describes as 'a mature, post-war sequel to *Guests of War*'), Angus McArthur is an aloof, morally dubious but fascinating rogue who gradually comes to realise that his exclusion from ordinary human affairs and his essential loneliness are inescapable due to his own temperament and inability to change, a fact which Jenkins appropriately describes as 'the inescapability from self.'[11] Angus's ambiguous moral worth makes him one

---

8   Robin Jenkins, *The Thistle and The Grail* (London: Macdonald, 1954; repr. Edinburgh: Paul Harris, 1983), pp. 293–294.

9   Robin Jenkins, *The Missionaries* (London: Macdonald, 1957), p. 219.

10   Robin Jenkins, *The Changeling* (London: Macdonald, 1958; repr. Edinburgh: Canongate, 1989), p. 148.

11   Hart, p. 277. Robin Jenkins, *A Love of Innocence* (London: Cape, 1963; repr. Edinburgh: B&W, 1994), p. 314.

of Jenkins's most complex protagonists; although he is in some ways the story's villain, he is also arguably its tragic hero. He may be manipulative, deceitful, conceited, contemptuous, and sexist, but he is finally allowed a more compassionate understanding of the people of Calisay and of his own isolation.

Arguably the quintessential pilgrim of conscience of this first period is Bell McShelvie of *Guests of War*, set in 1939 at the beginning of World War II, with the evacuation of hundreds of women and children from the slums of Gowburgh (Glasgow) to the small, middle-class Borders town of Langrigg. This novel reveals Jenkins's typical concern with class distinction, emphasising the effects of poverty on individuals whose society has left them no choice but to endure conditions that defy human dignity and comfort. Jenkins's central preoccupation with the fallibility of human morality is outstanding in this novel, and in his portrayal of his protagonist Bell McShelvie. The war and the evacuation of Glasgow children will be a crucial turning point in her life. Bell firstly welcomes the war as an opportunity to escape the slums of Gowburgh. In a second sense, however, her desire to leave, when measured against the desperate fight to sustain her family and keep her integrity in the slums, makes for Bell's own personal war, as spelled out in a telling passage early in the novel:

> Here indeed was her battlefield: the enemy she had to fight was despair at the ugliness shutting her in, at the inevitable coarseness and pitiable savagery of many of the people shut in with her, and above all at her inability to keep her own family healthy, sweet, and intact. She was weary of fighting. Even soldiers in war were given relief. But Isaac [her husband, in Glasgow] was not well ... he might soon die, and all the sooner if she forsook him. Flora [her daughter]... might grow up to be little better than a prostitute; she needed, as Meg said, more control now rather than less. The battle was at its height, therefore, and she had made up her mind to desert.[12]

Bell's desire to leave Glasgow and to escape the reality of her circumstance causes her enormous self-criticism, as she sees this as proof that she is traitor to her family and background. She admires and envies her neighbours' preference for the 'grime and racket of the city,' seeing their acceptance of the 'gloomy streets' as their home as the source of their strength and their loyalty to their families.[13] Her sense of disloyalty mixed with a feeling of failure and

---

12   Robin Jenkins, *Guests of War* (London: Macdonald, 1956; repr. Edinburgh: Scottish Academic Press, 1988), pp. 11–12.

13   Ibid., p. 8.

lost opportunities thus adds further to her moral predicament. Her life is very different from what she once dreamt it would be like. She feels that 'young lonely girls dreamed of perfection', and while as adults they should really 'cherish the disappointments,' she does not cherish her own.[14] Her intelligence prevents her; she understands the full scale and consequence of class segregation, and realises the injustice of society through her own suffering as an underprivileged slum-wife. This realisation then forms part of her inner conflict, given her ambitions for personal improvement.

Bell's sense of personal failure is best realised through her relationship with Edgar Roy, the young and handsome teacher from Gowburgh. The romance of Roy and Elizabeth Cargill in many ways emphasises Bell's own underprivileged situation. Parallels and contrasts are made between Bell's own life and the life possibilities of Roy and Elizabeth. Roy's perspective provides a glimpse of Bell's young days, suggesting that she was once 'beautiful and exciting' before she had surrendered to 'voluntary incarceration in the prison-house of poverty-stricken marriage.'[15] Roy is often deeply moved by Bell, and she sometimes reminds him of Elizabeth Cargill; this suggests that, despite Bell and Elizabeth's different stations in life, they share qualities which set them apart from other people. Roy's understanding of Bell, and his comparison of her with Elizabeth, unite with Bell's own reflections on her life to underline her feelings of personal failure. But Roy's admiration of Bell stands in sharp contrast to her envy and resentment towards him. The reason for her spite against the young teacher is simply that she sees in him, and in his relationship with Elizabeth Cargill, a manifestation of what she could wish her own life to be. These feelings of envy add further to her self-accusation. However, it is clear that Bell, like Andrew Rutherford in *The Thistle and the Grail*, is setting impossibly high standards for herself. Isobel Murray argues that any 'moralist less stern than she [Bell] would be unlikely to blame her unkind impulses and be impressed rather by how seldom she yielded to them.'[16] Bell's constant self-questioning is caused by her desire to be a good person, and to be morally fair to other people. Certainly, the reader does not judge Bell as unkindly as she herself does, especially when compared to unpleasant characters like Mrs Aldersyde, Gordon Aldersyde, and Councillor Michaelson, all of whom are devoid of self-reproach.

Bell's development is brought to a resolution through her son's accidental death which, Jenkins suggests, is necessary to Bell's gaining maturity and

14   Ibid., p. 16.
15   Ibid., pp. 81–82.
16   Isobel Murray, 'Introduction,' in *Guests of War*, by Robin Jenkins (Edinburgh: Scottish Academic Press, 1988), p. xvii.

self-knowledge. Bell sees her son's death as just punishment for her desertion of her family, for her condescension towards her neighbours, and for her resentment against Roy. Her unequivocal acceptance is clearly revealed when she first hears of Sammy's accident, as it is clear to her neighbours in Cairnban that 'she had no hope; she was sure the boy was dead.'[17] This 'fatalistic acceptance' of her bereavement is followed by her refusal to accept Langrigg/Gowburgh ideas of 'a splendid and cathartic funeral' for Sammy, choosing instead to bury him without the service of a minister and in the presence of a chosen few.[18] However, Bell's attempt to climb Brack Fell is arguably her real burial of Sammy. But Bell's climbing is also an attempt to overcome her illusions along with the arrogance, resentment, and treachery they have caused, and so achieve the necessary determination to return to Gowburgh 'cleansed and unresentful, prepared to create as much light there as she could, not only for herself and her family, but for her neighbours.'[19] Bell's 'ritual pilgrimage' to Brack Fell fails in the sense that she never reaches the summit, but this seems symbolic of the impossibility of rising above the reality of her Gowburgh existence.[20] This failure emphasises the illusion of her stay in Langrigg, and that she never had a real chance of becoming the mistress of Cairnban or of Mair-Wilson's estate. Her turning back reflects the necessity to recognise the realities of her own life. As a result, Bell has to 'accept an unpretentious, naked, unillusioned existence', as argued by Douglas Gifford.[21] Yet her disappointment at not reaching the summit gives way to a very different moment when she now recognises Langrigg's peace and innocence, but above all its faith, 'simple and courageous as any bird's.'[22] Paradoxically, this is the moment when Bell accepts Gowburgh and decides to return there. She knows that she cannot see Gowburgh, like Langrigg, as peaceful, innocent, and full of faith, but because of this, 'because somehow of its vulnerability, it seemed to her even more dear.'[23] Bell withdraws nothing of her condemnation of Gowburgh and its human greed, brutal indifference to beauty, and 'sordid confinement', but 'over it nevertheless she wished most profoundly to cast whatever protection

---

17   Jenkins, *Guests of War*, p. 255.

18   Ibid., p. 261, p. 265.

19   Ibid., pp. 282–283.

20   Alastair R. Thompson, 'Faith and Love: An examination of some themes in the novels of Robin Jenkins,' *New Saltire*, 3 (1963), 57–64 (p. 64).

21   Douglas Gifford, '"God's Colossal Irony": Robin Jenkins and *Guests of War*,' *Cencrastus*, 24 (1986), 13–17 (p. 16).

22   Jenkins, *Guests of War*, pp. 284–285.

23   Ibid., p. 285.

her blessing offered.'[24] Langrigg's power of transfiguration, may, after all, be illusory; she now sees Gowburgh as her true source of strength: 'The very stones
whose age and grime she had so often condemned would, if she were to touch
them with her hand, prove to have more sustenance for her spirit than these
rocks on the unblemished hill.'[25] Bell's true personal revelation is thereby this
positive acceptance of her life in Gowburgh, a recognition that is imperative to
her survival: 'she no longer saw defeat or disappointment, but only a necessary
resolution.'[26]

The Pilgrim in Jenkins's Foreign Fiction

In the fiction based on Jenkins's years abroad (1960–1974), his interest in questions of morality, the limits of idealism, and social hypocrisy intensifies, especially when viewed in the context of his treatment of racial difference and
colonial subjugation. These issues achieve a more universal resonance in the
fiction focused on settings and characters outside Scotland; indeed, Jenkins
remarked that by travelling he might have been looking for precisely this effect.[27] The theme of moral pilgrimage is still a central one, but now issues of racial and cultural difference and imperialism are the focus. As Gifford suggests:
'[the foreign novels] introduced yet deeper confusions of morality and idealism, in their presentation of central characters whose choices go beyond the
personal to questions of race, culture, and the politics of third world countries
struggling for fairness and identity.'[28] Moreover, the pilgrims of conscience in
these narratives are both British expatriates and natives of countries that are
or have been subjected to British rule, and this often creates further complexity
and ambiguity in the way their development is presented. The most notable
of these stories is perhaps *Dust on the Paw* (1961), in which the marriage of
the secretly racist Harold Moffatt to a Chinese woman, on one hand, and the
engagement of the Afghan Abdul Wahab to a British woman, on the other, are
presented as parallel or mirrored situations. Jenkins emphasises the paradox

---

24   Ibid., p. 285.

25   Ibid., p. 285.

26   Ibid., p. 286.

27   Jenkins stated that when abroad he was possibly 'looking for universal themes not to be
      found [...] in parochial Scotland.' See Robin Jenkins, 'Why I decided Scotland must be
      seen through fresh and truthful eyes,' *Glasgow Herald*, 12 October 1982, p. 11.

28   Douglas Gifford, 'Spring Fiction: Dreams of Love and Justice,' *Books in Scotland*, 57 (Spring
      1996), 8–15 (p. 12).

of idealism and practice through the struggles of conscience of both men. Both are forced to face the pitfalls of their own moral and social idealism and the complications inherent in their inter-racial marriages. Their imperfections betray their ideals. Wahab, the more complex of the two, is both cunning and naively idealistic, manipulating other people to his own ends while longing for a better society where poverty, greed and ignorance do not exist. Yet he experiences intense moments of self-recognition and insight. While he perceives himself as 'an imperfect lover of his fellow men,' he is nevertheless depressed about the essential fallibility of mankind.[29] For Wahab, his own propensity for evil means that evil is part of everyone:

> [...] this spite, selfishness, and treachery which he was displaying were bearable only if he felt that they were restricted to himself; to be reminded that they were probably in every man, and therefore were throughout the world in colossal abundance was terrifying and intolerable [...] Though Wahab nodded and smiled, he not only hated but was afraid of himself. If he was capable of such evil, all those many millions were also.[30]

Wahab's idealism makes him expect much of himself, but when his best intentions fail, his self-awareness gives him insight into the essential imperfections and weaknesses of humanity. Wahab's perspective is therefore central to Jenkins's overall moral vision, where greed, selfishness, spite, and other negative attributes are inseparable from human nature.

A tragic figure from the foreign period is Michael Eking in *The Holy Tree* (1969), a Kalimantan (Sabah/North Borneo) aborigine boy of nineteen whose desperate desire for education leads him to betray political rebels, one of them his brother, to the police, in order to gain a place at Api College. Michael's journey from frustrated and thwarted love of learning, to the hard-bought fulfilment of his ambition, and finally his death by the holy tree, reveals once more Jenkins's preoccupation with human morality and fallibility. Michael is ultimately driven to acknowledge his isolation and to admit the treachery, unfairness, and arrogance that has characterised his treatment of his own people. He realises that he has been unfair to his people in thinking that money and education matter more than self-sufficiency, kinship, faithfulness, and friendship. Formerly contemptuous of their backward stupidity and lack of ambition, seeing them as 'fit only to be the white men's servants,' Michael comes

---

29   Robin Jenkins, *Dust on the Paw* (London: Macdonald, 1961; repr. Glasgow: Richard Drew, 1986), p. 240.

30   Ibid., pp. 358–359.

to recognise the essential wisdom inherent in his people's interdependent self-preservation.[31] Jenkins makes clear that Michael's previous folly has not sprung from material greed, but from the desire to be educated, in his view a necessary step towards becoming 'Westernised.' However, Westernisation, by implication, includes becoming morally corrupt, adding a satiric slant to Jenkins's treatment of colonisation and racial difference, where Western ideology is shown to be guilty of moral decadence despite its positive values of democracy and freedom of speech. Michael can simultaneously equate wealth, influence and power with immorality, yet consider British colonialists as role models, and this suggests that he is simply a victim of Western imperialism, 'caught in a postcolonial social web,' his misguided ideas and actions the result of the imposition of British values on Kalimantan society and character.[32]

The Pilgrim in Later Fiction

The pilgrim of conscience is sustained in the later period of Jenkins's Scottish fiction (1968–2007). His protagonists, however varied their moral perceptions, are either intensely aware of the corrupted morals of their society and haunted by the impossibility of being an example of charity and goodness in a fallen world, or eventually come to see that true human wealth is to be found in what they have hitherto despised and from which they have been excluded: neighbourly good-will and charity, and a sense of community and human kinship. Despite its moral and spiritual degeneration, and recognising that individual isolation may be unavoidable, humanity is made valuable by the virtues of ordinary people.[33]

In Jenkins's later Scottish narratives, his approach to human morality is marked by deeper ambivalences and a more marked irony than before, while some of the texts of this latter period are decidedly innovative, bordering on the surreal, in terms of plot, structure and form. Central figures are also presented in more ambiguous terms. Good examples are Agnes Tolmie in *A Toast to the Lord* (1972), Gavin Hamilton in *A Would-Be Saint*, George Darroch in *The*

---

31   Robin Jenkins, *The Holy Tree* (London: Victor Gollancz, 1969), p. 238.

32   Hart, p. 279.

33   This philosophy is very central to the odd-one-out among Jenkins's foreign novels, *The Sardana Dancers* (1964), which is set in Spain during Franco's dictatorship. Its title refers directly to the novel's concern with human unity, symbolised in the Sardana, a native Catalan dance which celebrates the group, its ring being a symbol of brotherhood, mutual interdependence, and democracy.

Awakening of George Darroch (1985) and Duffy in *Just Duffy* (1988). All are high-ly ambiguous protagonists whose unconventional, extreme behaviour and actions isolate them from their society and render them incomprehensible, even unpleasant, to other characters and the reader. All inhabit an almost mythic realm of extremes: their moral and/or religious stances reject compromise and challenge the mediocre morality of their society, where charity and self-denial are disregarded in favour of material comfort and respectability, and where the majority pay only lip-service to Christianity. Their moral codes stand in sharp contrast with the 'halfway house' ethics of their community; thus Jenkins forces an understanding of the corrupt morals of politicians, the Church, and society in general. And yet, as the stories progress, doubt is cast on each protagonist's moral or spiritual value: are they genuine or false? Are they based on moral and spiritual superiority, or do they originate in pride, stubbornness, and attention-seeking? Are they perhaps insane? As each character is pushed further towards extremes in terms of their behaviour and social interaction, the reader finds it increasingly difficult to identify or sympathise with their actions. Thus, while Jenkins's portrayal of extremes forces a recognition of the moral and spiritual lassitude of our world, his deeply ironic and ambivalent treatment of these protagonists simultaneously questions their moral and/or spiritual value. In this respect, we can detect a deconstructive element in all four texts; they originally appear to establish a system of superior ethical or religious values (the absolutes of goodness and spirituality) which are then undermined, questioned, and deconstructed through narrative ambiguity and irony.

In *A Very Scotch Affair* (1968) and *Fergus Lamont* (1979) (and later *Poor Angus* (2000)), the protagonist is driven by selfish ambition to betray and hurt people who love him, only to reap bitter rewards in the end when it is too late to make amends. These novels emphasise Jenkins's fascination with the moral implications of selfishness, conceit and self-delusion, while his fiction in general indicates that these are moral shortcomings common to all humanity. However, due to their selfish nature and cruelty to those closest to them, Mungo Niven and Fergus Lamont do not easily gain the reader's sympathy. Yet they both understand the repressive nature of their society, and challenge conventionality and uniformity. Neither Mungo nor Fergus is the kind of moral pilgrim most common in Jenkins's fiction. Although Mungo is more aware of his own faults than Fergus, and does experience moments of intense self-awareness and self-blame that invite sympathy, neither of these men actively seeks to transcend his moral limitations, and while they have ideals for improving society, they are far too wrapped up in their self-advancement to be true to these ideals. Ultimately, *A Very Scotch Affair* affirms the centrality of Jenkins's philosophy that there is 'no absolute truth; things do keep shifting.'[34] Yet again, human morality is complex and ambiguous. As Bernard Sellin suggests:

> People are not all of a piece. They are not even made of two parts that can easily interlock, Jenkins seems to suggest. The jigsaw puzzle does not fit. At the core of Jenkins's world then is an immense fracture that runs deep. Reality is always split.[35]

In *Fergus Lamont*, the focus is on Fergus's search for identity, rather than on a personal quest for moral worth. Here Jenkins's treatment of morality is given a peculiarly Scottish emphasis through his examination of Scottish identity, epitomised in the ambiguous protagonist Fergus, who is presented as an ironic parody of the duality of Scottishness and the fragmented Scottish psyche.

These are deeply ambivalent portrayals. There are more straightforward moral protagonists to be found in this last period of Jenkins's writing, characters who are shown truly to struggle with their conscience and whose journey leads to self-confrontation and self-discovery. In *Poverty Castle* (1991), Peggy Gilchrist initially appears to be a secondary character, as the narrative focus of the novel-within-a-novel at first rests on the wealthy, successful, happy, and – by implication and play on words – simple Sempill family. However, when Peggy is introduced, we are soon given insight into her background, views and psychology. A passionate scholar of history, she has developed a shrewd understanding of the political, industrialist, and capitalist forces that have formed her society. She is deeply aware of the unfairness of class division and the hypocrisy of those who uphold the class system. She is a republican, and wants royalty and titled aristocracy to be abolished. Becoming the friend of Diana Sempill, who holds entirely different beliefs regarding the aristocracy (according to her 'it had been the nobility of Scotland who had given the country whatever distinction it had'), Peggy's ideals are in danger of being compromised, especially due to her contradictory emotions of yearning to be one of the Sempills while also feeling guilty at being a traitor to her family and class.[36] Indeed, Peggy's social ideals are in sharp contrast to everything that

---

34   Robin Jenkins, interview, 'Moral Absolutism in the Novels of Robert Louis Stevenson, Robin Jenkins and Muriel Spark: Challenges to Realism,' by Glenda Norquay (unpublished doctoral thesis, University of Edinburgh, 1985), p. 443.

35   Bernard Sellin, 'Commitment and Betrayal: Robin Jenkins' *A Very Scotch Affair*,' in *Studies in Scottish Fiction: 1945 to the Present*, ed. by Susan Hagemann (Frankfurt am Main: Peter Lang, 1996), pp. 97–108 (p. 103).

36   Robin Jenkins, *Poverty Castle* (Nairn: Balnain Books, 1991), p. 174.

the Sempill family stands for. This is what causes her inner conflict of ambition, guilt, and self-reproach. Despite her late entry, Peggy is therefore the one true moral pilgrim of *Poverty Castle*. It is she who brings into the narrative a feeling of balance, sensibility, and genuine insight, both on a universal and personal level. She accepts that the 'contradiction between idealistic intention and pragmatic performance' is part of the human condition, and realises that she is fallible herself and thus liable to fail her social ideals.[37] As Horst Prillinger argues, she 'bases her outlook on life on reality, whereas the Sempills have based their happiness on fictions.'[38]

Finally, one of Jenkins's latest publications, *Childish Things* (2001) confirms once more how important the issues of morality and self-knowledge are to Jenkins's literary vision. The recently widowed, seventy-two-year-old retired schoolteacher Gregor McLeod wavers between self-interested opportunism and self-flagellation and guilt. One minute he questions his own capacity for genuine despair and grief, the next he fantasises about being involved with rich widows for the sake of their possessions. It soon emerges that McLeod has lived his life in disguise, trying to escape memories of his underprivileged and unhappy childhood. He has put on appearances and even lied to his family about aspects of his past, but the truth of his origin has tormented him all his life. As Carl MacDougall comments, these childish things which McLeod 'has tried to outgrow [...] have dominated his life.'[39] When retired Californian filmstar Linda Birkenberger (whom he seeks to impress), distrusting him and his motives, hires Glaswegian private detectives to uncover his lies, McLeod eventually has to face up to his past and acknowledge the callousness and moral cowardice that characterised his treatment of his mother. *Childish Things* yet again highlights the divisions at the heart of Scottish society and character, exploring issues of familial loyalty and moral fallibility, charting McLeod's development from betrayal, selfishness and conceit towards self-knowledge and – perhaps – ultimate redemption.

The development of the pilgrim of conscience in Jenkins's work is central to his exploration of moral issues. Many of Jenkins's pilgrim figures are tormented by a strong sense of moral inadequacy, long for spiritual transcendence, and yearn for a level of goodness that overcomes human frailties. Others are

---

37   Ibid., p. 230.
38   Horst Prillinger, *Family and the Scottish Working Class Novel 1984–1994: A study of novels by Janice Galloway, Alasdair Gray, Robin Jenkins, James Kelman, A.L. Kennedy, William McIlvanney, Agnes Owens, Alan Spence, and George Friel* (Frankfurt am Main: Peter Lang, 2000), p. 153.
39   Carl MacDougall, 'The early years, late woe', review of *Childish Things*, by Robin Jenkins, *The Herald* 5 May 2001, section Weekend Living, p. 13.

isolated and aloof figures who are forced to acknowledge that a sense of community and human kinship should be sought after and cherished when and if achieved. The move towards self-perception among Jenkins's moral pilgrims often depends on the realisation that without accepting the fallible nature of humankind they reject their own place within humanity. Throughout his fiction, and in particular via his deployment of the pilgrim figure, Jenkins highlights the pitfalls of idealism and the discrepancy between principle and practice, suggesting the essentially self-interested motives behind many so-called gestures of charity. His novels emphasise that moral perfection is largely unattainable in a world of economic capitalism, moral selfishness, and spiritual disillusionment, and if true goodness is seemingly achieved, it is never presented straightforwardly or unequivocally. In Jenkins's fictional world, nothing is ever clear-cut or straightforward; characters and story-lines are never presented in black and white, but rather in different shades of grey. Jenkins's central figure, the pilgrim of conscience, is essential to this realistic, if ambiguous, vision of human morality and society.

Works Cited

Ágústsdóttir, Ingibjörg, 'Pilgrims of Conscience: Quests for Morality and Self-Knowledge in the Fiction of Robin Jenkins' (unpublished doctoral thesis, University of Glasgow, 2001).

Gifford, Douglas, '"God's Colossal Irony": Robin Jenkins and *Guests of War,*' *Cencrastus*, 24 (1986), pp. 13–17.

Gifford, Douglas, 'Spring Fiction: Dreams of Love and Justice,' *Books in Scotland*, 57 (Spring 1996), 8–15.

Hart, Francis Russell, *The Scottish Novel: A Critical Survey* (London: John Murray, 1978).

Jenkins, Robin, *The Awakening of George Darroch* (Edinburgh: Harris, 1985; repr. Edinburgh: B&W, 1995).

Jenkins, Robin, *The Changeling* (London: Macdonald, 1958; repr. Edinburgh: Canongate, 1989).

Jenkins, Robin, *Childish Things* (Edinburgh: Canongate, 2001).

Jenkins, Robin, *The Cone-Gatherers* (London: Macdonald, 1955; repr. London: Penguin, 1983).

Jenkins, Robin, *Dust on the Paw* (London: Macdonald, 1961; repr. Glasgow: Richard Drew, 1986).

Jenkins, Robin, *Fergus Lamont* (Edinburgh: Canongate, 1979; repr. 1990).

Jenkins, Robin, *Guests of War* (London: Macdonald, 1956; repr. Edinburgh: Scottish Academic Press, 1988).

Jenkins, Robin, *Happy for the Child* (London: Lehmann, 1953; repr. Nairn: Balnain Books, 1992).

Jenkins, Robin, *The Holy Tree* (London: Victor Gollancz, 1969).

Jenkins, Robin, *Just Duffy* (Edinburgh: Canongate, 1988; repr. 1995).

Jenkins, Robin, *Love is a Fervent Fire* (London: Macdonald, 1959).

Jenkins, Robin, *A Love of Innocence* (London: Cape, 1963; repr. Edinburgh: B&W, 1994).

Jenkins, Robin, *The Missionaries* (London: Macdonald, 1957).

Jenkins, Robin, *Poverty Castle* (Nairn: Balnain Books, 1991).

Jenkins, Robin, *The Sardana Dancers* (London: Jonathan Cape, 1964).

Jenkins, Robin, *So Gaily Sings the Lark* (Glasgow: MacLellan, 1951; repr. Bath: Cedric Chivers, 1971).

Jenkins, Robin, *The Thistle and the Grail* (London: Macdonald, 1954; repr. Edinburgh: Paul Harris, 1983).

Jenkins, Robin, *A Toast to the Lord* (London: Victor Gollancz, 1972).

Jenkins, Robin, *A Very Scotch Affair* (London: Victor Gollancz, 1968).

Jenkins, Robin, 'Why I decided Scotland must be seen through fresh and truthful eyes,' *Glasgow Herald*, 12 October 1982, p. 11.

Jenkins, Robin, *A Would-Be Saint* (Edinburgh: B&W, 1994).

MacDougall, Carl, 'The early years, late woe', review of *Childish Things*, by Robin Jenkins, *The Herald* 5 May 2001, section Weekend Living, p. 13.

Murray, Isobel, 'Introduction,' in *Guests of War*, by Robin Jenkins (Edinburgh: Scottish Academic Press, 1988), pp. vii–xxii.

Murray, Isobel, ed., *Scottish Writers Talking 3* (Edinburgh: John Donald, 2006), pp. 101–146.

Norquay, Glenda, 'Against Compromise: The Fiction of Robin Jenkins,' *Cencrastus*, 24 (1986), pp. 3–6.

Norquay, Glenda, interview with Robin Jenkins, 'Moral Absolutism in the Novels of Robert Louis Stevenson, Robin Jenkins and Muriel Spark: Challenges to Realism,' by Glenda Norquay (unpublished doctoral thesis, University of Edinburgh, 1985), pp. 436–451.

Prillinger, Horst, *Family and the Scottish Working Class Novel 1984–1994: A study of novels by Janice Galloway, Alasdair Gray, Robin Jenkins, James Kelman, A.L. Kennedy, William McIlvanney, Agnes Owens, Alan Spence, and George Friel* (Frankfurt am Main: Peter Lang, 2000).

Reid, Alexander, 'The Limits of Charity', *Scotland's Magazine* (October 1958), pp. 43–44.

Sellin, Bernard, 'Commitment and Betrayal: Robin Jenkins' *A Very Scotch Affair*,' in *Studies in Scottish Fiction: 1945 to the Present*, ed. by Susan Hagemann (Frankfurt am Main: Peter Lang, 1996), pp. 97–108.

Thompson, Alastair R., 'Faith and Love: An examination of some themes in the novels of Robin Jenkins,' *New Saltire*, 3 (1963), pp. 57–64.

What's the Story in *Fergus Lamont*? Or 'Where was Fergus when Kennedy got Shot?'

Michael Lamont and Douglas Gifford

Abstract

In this most complex of all his later 'disruptive' fictions, Jenkins deals with his pro-tagonist Fergus with sly manipulation, confusing the reader with his changing moral perspectives. The chapter discusses these two sides of a character at times surrealistic, at times almost credible, but always leaving the reader with unanswered questions, climactically at the end, when the reader is left to wonder what is the truth of Fergus's autobiography. This novel raises more questions than it answers, to the extent that we wonder whether Fergus (and his author Jenkins) can at any point be fully trusted, Jen-kins anticipating the destabilising postmodernism of later Scottish fiction (especially that of Alasdair Gray). The chapter focuses on Fergus's divided and almost schizo-phrenic personas as the recurrent traits of his life, speculating that Jenkins allows him a tragic and a redeeming ending in a deeply ambivalent conclusion whose ambiguity cannot finally be resolved.

Keywords

dramatic monologue – ambiguity – trauma – divided self – personae – satire – authorial trickery – authorial unreliability – interpolations

Fergus Lamont (1979) is the most complex of Jenkins's later 'disruptive' fictions.[1] The novel is told in first person narrative/monologue, unusual for

---

1   In her study of the later fiction of Robin Jenkins, Glenda Norquay identifies 'disruptive' new elements in Jenkins's later novels (till 1991, therefore comprising *A Would-Be Saint* (1978), *Fergus Lamont* (1979), *The Awakening of George Darroch* (1985), *Just Duffy* (1988), and *Poverty Castle* (1991)). She identifies 'disruption' in these novels as a 'willingness to shock'; in keep-ing the reader 'working at the contradictions rather than expecting answers'; in its denial of stability or security; in the juxtaposition of different forms of writing; and in Jenkins's 'defa-miliarisation'. She finds *Fergus Lamont* 'the most explicit of Jenkins's novels [...] in its linking of moral ambiguity with a specific Scottish context'. Norquay, 'Disruptions: The Later Fiction

Jenkins. (His only other novel in this mode is *Childish Things* of 2001.) Richly and ironically detailed (and often surrealistically hilarious in its tragi-comedy) the reader is left constantly questioning Fergus as unreliable narrator (and ultimately Jenkins as his manipulative author) throughout. The novel poses unanswerable questions – how should we read and respond to his bizarre self-portrait's story of his changing history and identities, as traumatised slum child and adolescent, then soldier, poet, crofter, and recluse, when from damaged childhood on, his story of his actions borders on the schizophrenic (though Fergus rarely admits to suffering psychological damage).[2] Jenkins constantly implies different psychological readings of, and responses to, Fergus's account, in ways which oscillate from sympathetic to condemnatory. He leaves the reader unsure whether his narrative can ever be trusted – especially as Jenkins concludes the novel with a final sleight of hand, in which he leaves the reader with a profoundly unsettling ending. Yet despite the novel's and Jenkins/Fergus's bewildering amount of (deliberately) misleading detail, Jenkins allows the reader to see beyond Fergus's self-centred monologue so as to expose Fergus's psychological deterioration from childhood to his enigmatic end. This chapter focuses on the major stages in this reading, attempting to extrapolate a dominant narrative from Fergus's continual misdirections and self-contradictions.

Jenkins has Fergus begin his autobiography as a sensitive innocent who will be blighted by childhood and lifelong traumas. He presents Fergus's self-portrait in six phases, interwoven confusingly with eight italicised (and undated) time-jumping interpolations.[3] Part One crucially takes Fergus from innocence, to adulthood, and his divided responses to his original trauma.

---

of Robin Jenkins', in *The Scottish Novel Since the Seventies*, ed. by Gavin Wallace and Randall Stevenson (Edinburgh: Edinburgh University Press, 1994), pp. 11–24 (p. 12, p. 17).

2   Fergus does suspect that, after his marriage breakup, he may be approaching breakdown; but he never questions the validity of his two mutually exclusive *personas*. Is he schizophrenic? The Scottish psychiatrist R.D. Laing argued throughout works such as *The Divided Self* (1960) and *Wisdom, Madness and Folly* (1985) that schizophrenia is a strategy that a person invents in order to live in an unbearable period; while *The Oxford Reference Dictionary* sees the condition as marked by coldness, inability to form social relations, breakdown in the relation between thoughts, feelings and actions, delusions, and retreat from social life. All of these descriptions are manifested by Fergus at various stages of his life.

3   The seven italicised interpolations (on pages 48, 78, 107, 168, 199, 237, 270) written during the Glasgow years are not the only disruptive interruptions to the self-portrait; for example, the self-portrait also looks back from Glasgow disillusion at photographs of his fellow officers before going to war, and three years later, his wedding to Betty (with Betty's picture excised). Robin Jenkins, *Fergus Lamont* (Edinburgh: Canongate, 1979), p. 81.

It thus deserves close attention as the first and deepest of Fergus's lifelong traumas. When Fergus's wayward mother returns to Gantock, Fergus (aged seven-and-a-half) is delighted; family, friends, neighbours and others are not. Pregnant with Fergus (by a Scottish nobleman?), forced in Gantock to marry shipyard worker John Lamont for respectability, his mother has abandoned Fergus (at age three) to live with a wealthy businessman for four years. She only returns because her businessman has died and left her penniless. Fergus uncritically adores her. Jenkins means us to sympathise with Fergus's utter confusion as to her hostile reception by the town. Donald, her father (and Fergus's Kirk Elder and Calvinist grandfather), rejects her. She is spat upon by neighbours who call her a 'shameless whure'. She drowns herself. Her father does not come to the funeral but tells the boy his mother is in hell.

The effect of all this on the child, and the idealisation by Fergus of his dead mother in the short time they share before her death, is horrendous in its psychological damage. For the rest of his life, Fergus will wear the kilt bought by his mother to honour her memory, and to establish (as she wished) his difference from Gantock vulgarity.[4] His mother has compared him to a prince, telling him he should be living in a castle. She has thus planted the poisonous seed of aristocratic ambition in him by hinting that he is the bastard son of the son of a Scottish Earl. The novel never resolves this crucial question as to who is Fergus's father. From the moment Fergus chooses to believe in his aristocratic paternity on, it is arguable that nothing Fergus tells us can be taken at face value, since it is the self-contradictory story (or stories) of a perhaps mentally damaged boy and adult. From the moment Fergus puts on his kilt his mother had bought for him, he is arguably creating two opposed *personas* which will damage his entire life. Fergus never stops idolising his mother (though Jenkins implies serious reservations for the reader regarding his mother's wayward selfishness). In one *persona*, following the wishes of his mother, he will assert his aristocratic superiority to Gantock and its working-classes; in the other, he will claim that his deepest loyalties belong with his Gantock and the working class relatives and friends who cared for him after her suicide. On one hand he tells us 'I was the son of an earl's son, but a shipyard's joiner was my father';

---

4   Jenkins never allows the truth of Fergus's paternity to emerge. Gantock gossip seems to favour the earl's son as father, as does Fergus, suggesting that the son was 'packed off' to Australia. We never hear any more about him, though Fergus treasures a photo – which could be of any young man. Another more reliable opinion, that of his sceptical friend Mary Holmscroft, is that his father was an underbutler – 'some kind of flunkey'. *Fergus Lamont*, p. 51. (Mary also says that in his kilt, Fergus looks like Harry Lauder. Arguably, the loss of Mary, his closest friend and critic – contributes to Fergus's final lonely trauma.)

on the other, 'I began to find it difficult to speak to people without making it too plain that I thought they were beneath me'.[5]

Yet Fergus in his school years maintains his friendships with his slum friends, at times telling us that slum Gantock became a playground idyll.[6] At Gantock Academy he is seen as standing up for himself against bullying teachers, with the help of his morally scrupulous slum friend Mary Holmscroft. (Jenkins gives Mary an important role in the novel; very different from him, she, like other un-pretentious supporting characters in Jenkins's fiction, will become the moral yardstick to set against Fergus's increasing egocentric excesses, the realist who cuts down his fantasies.) She understands that Fergus has become mentally damaged, and understands the traumatic effects of his childhood. Part One – and Fergus's late adolescence – ends with an exchange which shows how his mutually exclusive *personas* have damagingly divided him. Mary, now a teacher in Glasgow, and deeply involved in socialist politics, typically exposes what will increasingly be Fergus's unattractive egocentric mental confusions. She meets Fergus in Gantock on the day of a patriotic pre-war service. Arriving are Gantock's wealthy worldly worthies – Kirkhope, the town grocer, Cargill the lawyer, Ettrick, the managing director. Mary, referring to Fergus's earlier confused accusations that they and their like were the 'murderers' of his mother and 'the betrayers of Scotland' asks '"Do you still call them that, now you're on their side?"'. Fergus, in his aristocratic *persona* (and who is going to the church with these 'betrayers'), cannot answer her question, but instead gives the first of a series of a series of contradictory thoughts about his divided loyalties, using what he sees as Scotland's betrayal of itself in 1707 by way of attempted self-justification. (Fergus, in blaming Scotland's bourgeoisie, tellingly avoids the role of Scotland's aristocrats in any 'betrayal' of 1707!)

> I still believed, or rather felt as a poet, that Kirkhope, Cargill and Ettrick, and their kind, had throughout the centuries set up in Scotland a morality that put the ability to pay far in front of the necessity to forgive and love. I also thought that just as the bourgeoisie had sold Scotland to the English for the sake of bigger profits in 1707, so their counterparts still kept up that profitable betrayal [...] I was on the side of aristocracy: it was not corrupted by the urge to make more and more money; and of the

---

5 Jenkins, *Fergus Lamont*, p. 50.
6 Section 8, Part One, has Jenkins show in its two pages how Fergus's Gantock could become almost idyllic for him in summer (an idyll destroyed by Fergus's obsessions regarding his mother and his so-called aristocratic inheritance – and the looming war).

working-class, who had been poor for so long that they had learned how to make life rich with little money. I was aware of course that these attitudes of mine might appear contradictory, especially to a doctrinaire socialist.[7]

Fergus has already become the mentally confused victim of his contradictory loyalties.

In Part Two Fergus claims to be disgusted by the stupidity and hypocrisy of the upper classes – yet he candidly admits that he uses the class system to further his social climb, via the opportunities of war. He creates a totally false story of his to life to further the ends of his aristocratic *persona*, lying repeatedly about his slum origins, pretending to an aristocratic Corse-Lamont background, and developing his elitist persona to impress the OTC Committee.

Fergus becomes an officer, though he continues (unconvincingly) to claim that the snobbery of his elitist *persona* is an act, designed to make him fit in the Officers' Mess. There (for the amusement of his fellow-officers, and to the confusion and disgust of the reader) he mocks his friend Mary Holmscroft's childhood poverty, and her vain attempts to beg credit with shopkeepers for family food. Jenkins implies to the reader that Fergus now enjoys his aristocratic role-playing too much, and suggests a now ominous conflict of *personas*;

> Never was a more despicable act applauded so heartily. My reputation for not caring a damn about anybody or anything was established. [...] It was regarded as the most entertaining night ever in the mess. After it, my lack of sentimentality towards the poor, or rather my courage in expressing it so publicly, was held in awe. That I had once been one of the poor myself, that I considered them to be richer in humanity than lords or lawyers, and that I intended one day to write apocalyptic poetry about them, was not likely now to be suspected. [...] My profounder loyalties, I was glad to see, though of necessity kept secret, were alive and developing.[8]

At the heart of Part Two is Fergus's actual war experience. Jenkins now implies even greater self-delusion in Fergus's reflections on the carnage around him:

---

7 Jenkins, *Fergus Lamont*, p. 77.

8 Ibid., pp. 86–87. On what basis does Fergus claim that his 'profounder loyalties', are developing? Readers are rarely shown anywhere in the self-portrait that these secret loyalties ever come to fruition – unless they are to be found in Fergus's poetry, of which we are never given examples.

> I never thought I might be killed. This conviction did not spring from faith in the God of the Auld Kirk of Gantock: I saw too many men killed with bibles in their pockets and crucifixes round their necks [...] The reason for my confidence was that I felt that I had a greatness in me, too valuable to be lost. I had no idea what supernatural power was interested in preserving me, but all the time, whether in safe billet [...] or on a night raid or going over the top, I was sustained by that strong assurance of deserved immunity.[9]

This uncanny belief in his greatness and self-justification (reminiscent of the delusions of Robert Burns's Holy Willie and Robert Wringhim in Hogg's *Justified Sinner*) gains him the Military Cross and promotion. Does Jenkins now imply that Fergus's self-delusion indicates that he has lost his hold on reality and that his childhood trauma is now exaggerated by war?

In Part Three Jenkins brings his newly-decorated war-hero back to Scotland to promote the war effort with the beautiful but sinister Betty T. Shields. His marriage with Betty (and her humiliating rejection of him) can be read as the latest in the series of lifelong traumatic events for Fergus. As Scotland's most popular wartime novelist, Betty's novels tells of redeeming love through war and tragedy; yet, if we trust Fergus's account, she is the ultimate hypocrite, social climber and arch-Tory. But can we trust Fergus's account, written after his marriage break-up and exile to Gerinish? Their marriage fulfils Fergus's calculating wish for a wealthy spouse. With her come the house and estate of Penvalla. Yet she encourages and pays for his poetry. Both exploit their respective society images. Betty is the pin-up girl of romantic fiction; but behind the image, she cuckolds him – while Fergus threatens to expose that she too is a bastard from a slum background. Additionally, when the goals of his aristocratic *persona* are within his reach as war-hero and wealthy landowner, Fergus makes no attempt to fulfil the idealistic aims of either of his *personas*. He meekly accepts his cuckoldom, even helping his cuckolder. He becomes pathetically acquiescent. Like Waugh's Paul Pennyfeather in *Decline and Fall* (1928), he merely reacts passively to events, content to take Betty's money and live as a landed gentleman – and upper-class drone.

Fergus has in marriage adjusted the opposing positions of his *personas*, subtly introducing a new concept of 'purgation' into his now suspect ideals:

---

9 Ibid., p. 95. The scenes of war and its context in Part Two are impressive (limited to around ten pages), given Jenkins's lack of direct experience, due to his status as a conscientious objector. (Jenkins's own feelings about the stupidity of war surely filter through Fergus's reductive reflections on 'courage', and his contempt for the 'raffle' of life and death for medals.)

> I had promised myself to go back [to Gantock] when I had become famous. Military decorations did not represent the kind of fame I had meant. These would put me at a distance from the folk of the East End, whereas I wanted to be brought as close to them again as I had been long ago as a child of eight. Also, for my mother's sake, I must not go back among her destroyers until I had been acknowledged by the whole world as the grandson of an earl. Only then would I be able to clear my soul of the terror and ignominy of her death. It was not revenge I sought, but purgation; with this would come release of the stores of charity, faith, and hope locked up in me. When I went back to my native town therefore it must be, not just as hero, aristocrat, and poet, but as absolver and redeemer.[10]

Now Jenkins presents Fergus as Messianic as well as delusional. Although Fergus will twice return to Gantock, none of these loftier and secretly held aims, or 'purgation', will be achieved.

Part Four juxtaposes Betty and slum Gantock, with Betty's vengeance, stripping away Fergus's lies, utterly humiliating him amidst the insanitary lavatories of his childhood. This is the end of his fourteen years as married drone. Yet again Jenkins exposes Fergus's opposing *personas*. Fergus has come because his foster father John Lamont is dying. Yet again Fergus's good intentions to visit his childhood family and friends are revealed as superficial – and now as hypocrisy, as he thinks of how they will be flattered by his condescension and his 'landed gentry' manners. They are not, of course. Yet even at this, in Fergus's most unlikeable moments, Jenkins suggests that Fergus, in his secret *persona* of respect and deep loyalty to Gantock's poor, has indeed genuine feelings for them, especially in his uncanny conversation with poor Smout, his simple, decent, uncomplaining childhood friend, and what seems Fergus's genuine honouring of him and the Gantock dead at the war memorial. He claims that he wears his Military Cross not out of conceit, 'but to honour all the Gantock men who had been killed'.[11] Jenkins presents Fergus in this episode at the war memorial as possibly genuinely moving and moved as he weeps for them (despite Jenkins's reductive context as two wee girls giggle at him, seeing him as 'the ghost of a sodger that was killed').[12]

This sympathetic presentation of Fergus is short-lived, as this part of his self-portrait ends in his complete humiliation by Betty, in her ruthless exposure of

---

10   Ibid., p. 116.
11   Ibid., p. 179.
12   Ibid., p. 180.

his wartime pretensions by exposing the sordid realities of his former home in Lomond Street. He is forced to accept her money on condition that he relinquishes marriage and his comfortable occupancy as Laird of Penvalla, accepting exile to Oronsay in the Hebrides.

How does Jenkins mean us to read Part Five, the ten apparently idyllic years in Gerinish with his beloved Kirstie? Predictably, in two opposing ways; in one reading Jenkins tempts us to see Fergus redeeming himself, finding grace, humility and fulfilment in the unaffected simplicity of Hebridean island life and the McLeod family amidst the spare beauty and elemental life of the island, which at times takes on the qualities of myth. (Kirstie will later be likened to a mythic Celtic Goddess or Amazon Queen; wandering her island, at times she seems to be half-woman, half sea or land creature, in strange communion with her landscape.) This idyllic reading comes to a head in the dramatic contrast of the ideal island health and beauty of Kirstie and Fergus, in contrast with the yachting visit of decadent 'kach' [dung] novelist Alastair Donaldson with his superficial aristocratic friends. Jenkins tempts us to see this as the high point of Fergus's island romance, showing up the shallowness of the visitors.[13]

Yet all is seen through Fergus; and is there not a whiff at times of the popular fiction of Betty Shields in Fergus's account, with Fergus hand-in-hand with his 'Celtic Princess', Kirstie at her glorious best? This mythic and romantic reading must be set against another ironic and reductive reading. Fergus, in the stormy sail from Clyde to Lochmaddy and Oronsay, is still the kilted aristocrat, grumbling about the vomiting 'shivering boors' around him. In Oronsay, pipe-smoking Kirstie appears at first to him as a man, then 'a glaikit bitch' and 'hermaphroditish'. Despite telling us that he came to East Gerinish to learn humility, Fergus is still the self-contradictory Fergus of old. He has no sooner told us about this new-found humility when he tells us he plans to leave desolate rainy Gerinish, and to phone Betty to say he will return to Penvalla. Arriving in Gerinish his mental state is clearly unstable, to the point of nervous breakdown. He first sees Gerinish reductively, in terms of rain and abandonment – the sun comes out, and Fergus now thinks of staying to write poetry. Kirstie takes pity on him; she sings, and Fergus, sentimentally moved to tears, thinks he will

---

13   Throughout the Gerinich episodes, Jenkins seems to be more aware of 'Renaissance' fiction than he admits, as the Gerinish years take on Renaissance emphasis on the redemptive relationship of nature and landscape for humanity. There are also Renaissance hints of mythic 'otherness' in the treatment of Kirstie; Fergus likens her to 'one of those creatures in women's shape, that according to Hebridean legend, now and then came from their other world to live among people, nearly always, alas, bringing doom'. Ibid., p. 233.

remain and help her and the McLeod family by buying a much-needed boat, building a jetty and working with his new friends to reclaim the crofting soil. (Later he will speculate that Kirstie's rowing strength could replace a boat's engine!) Tellingly however, and typical of Fergus's constant changes of moral and emotional perspective, Fergus then adds (with a new honesty which might suggest that he is beginning to see himself truly?), 'I knew that as soon as the inspiring song ceased the blaze in my mind would die out, and all the old dull, cautious selfishnesses would revive [...]'.[14] We hear no more of his plans for boat and jetty; and we wonder whether he pulled his weight in island work, or whether he was more often writing poetry instead. Nevertheless, at times it can seem that Fergus is being genuinely changed by the island and its mythic influence:

> No wonder, I thought, this was the land of the second sight. If I stayed here I would be seer as well as poet. There were few places in the world where a man of compassion and intelligence might prepare to take up [...] without sentimentality or vainglory, the burden of all the multitudinous evils and miseries of humanity [...] but if it could be done anywhere it could surely be done here.[15]

This mythic reinvention of himself can be read two ways; the first revealing a new and genuinely sensitive Fergus who, but for Kirstie's death *might* have spent the rest of his life as a fulfilled poet. He genuinely loves her, and is distraught when she dies. Read thus, the Gerinish years can seem filled with grace. Yet we recall previous oscillation in earlier years between sensitive Fergus and self-centred Fergus. Are we wrong to read this as Jenkins slyly reminding us of Fergus's typical self-interest and seeing this as another of his pathetic fallacies, now seeing the island and Kirstie as his selfish mind needs to see them?

Jenkins presents Fergus's relationship with Kirstie with subtle ambiguity. It becomes clear that it is her combination of beauty and child-like simplicity which attracts him. He sees Kirstie as a simple woman who knows her place. 'It pleased her as a woman to serve me as a man', he concludes, leaving her to go out into the storm to get water for his bath.[16] Elsewhere he thinks that her rowing strength will take the place of a boat's engine. Kirstie yearns for a child by Fergus; Fergus (with his traumas of childhood and marriage) is selfishly hostile:

14   Ibid., p. 223.
15   Ibid., p. 234.
16   Ibid., p. 218.

'a child would not add to our happiness, but would destroy it' he tells her, remembering his own alienated children, Dorcas and Torquil.[17] That said, Fergus is genuinely distraught at Kirstie's sudden death (though it comes as news to him that Kirstie had a weak heart). After her death, he knows there is no place for him. The Oronsay mourners make it clear that they come for Kirstie's sake for her funeral, and regard him as irrelevant. He has to leave the island.[18]

In Part Five, Fergus's transition from Gerinish to Gantock reveals that his Gerinish 'humility' is still deeply questionable. Leaving Gerinish via a brief hotel stay in Lochmaddy, he tells us:

> I quickly had it confirmed that to be calmly tolerant of the ill-temper of worldlings not only gave me satisfaction and confidence, it even exhilarated me. In effect and taste it outdid the finest whisky. Was it, in humbler degree, how saints and martyrs felt?[19]

His new 'humility' does not stop him recounting the offences of the hotel 'worldlings' – the boorish handyman who will not shine his shoes, the waitress who attends to others before him, the idle fellows who will not carry his case to the pier, and many others, all of whom he 'forgives' since they have not been 'scoured' of their moral grime. It is as though the years with Kirstie had never happened. He is still the same Messianic self-centred humbug:

> I examined the possibility that I was not really interested in these other people; that I was still, as in the past, interested mainly in myself [...] surely I was entitled to accept, as a possibility at least, that I was returning to Gantock, if not as the saviour I had in my magnanimous and extravagant youth dreamed I might be one day, but as a giver of courage and hope.[20]

---

17   Ibid., pp. 243–244.
18   In typical Jenkins contrast, Fergus's description of Kirstie's simple funeral is reductively tragi-comic, with its endless Gaelic hymns, tipsy old men falling asleep, the Laird (former lover of Kirstie) tormented by clegs, and Fergus probably drunk: 'as chief mourner, I was constantly having bottles pressed upon me. Those offers I could not refuse...'. Fergus is caught between his reductive account of the funeral's grotesque comedy and his genuine tears for Kirstie. Ibid., p. 267. The reader might contrast this reductive funeral with Fergus's later grotesque, bucolic and sentimental envisioning in Glasgow of his own projected funeral. Ibid., pp. 200–204.
19   Ibid., p. 274.
20   Ibid.

Fergus's identity has now become drastically unstable, one moment worrying at his previous faults, the next seeing himself after Gerinish as 'a good man', returning to inspire war-torn Gantock with hope by presenting himself as example (another Messianic intention, of course never fulfilled).

What comes across poignantly in this brief return to Gantock is his sense of alienation. In a sad encounter, Fergus meets his childhood sweetheart, Meg Jeffries. If he had married her, he realises, he might not have become an officer and gentleman, with no Penvalla (or Kirstie). Fergus now begins to see the falsity of his *personas*; with Meg, he might not have been a poet; but 'I would have been happy, my children would have been fond of me, and I would not have been faced with the prospect now before me, of lifelong homelessness.'[21] Facing a long martyrdom of loneliness, he is beginning to see through his own self-deceptions. His kindly relatives, whom he hardly visited in Gantock, are mainly dead or dying – or will die in the imminent bombing.

This final visit to Gantock marks the end of Fergus's self-portrait. His visit to his old teacher Calderwood coincides with the bombing of the town and the Clyde in 1941. War has changed Calderwood from liberal teacher to savage, if realistic cynic. As the bombs destroy Gantock, they finally destroy Fergus's *personas*. Fergus cannot refute Calderwood's ironic nihilism (he sees Calderwood as 'not mad: he was too sane' in his reasoning. '"Explain", murmured Calderwood at my back, "why our airmen are heroes that drop bombs on German towns, and yet German airmen that drop bombs on our town are bastards."')[22] Fergus is reduced to incoherence as he shakes his fist at the bombers. Stripped of egotistical fantasies, he will move to utter loneliness and disillusion in Glasgow. In no other novel (with the exception of *The Changeling*) does Jenkins reveal more existential despair at the human condition. Yet, having utterly reduced Fergus's fantasies, Jenkins has one final dark authorial trick to play.

Fergus will spend his last twenty-odd years as a disillusioned recluse in Glasgow – yet we have only his seven brief interpolated accounts to tell of this, the longest part of his life. He now calls himself William McTavish (yet another identity, this time taken from his slum friend Smout). He lives in a cold tenement flat. He is writing his 'self-portrait' (which ends with the Clydebank blitz of 1941) in a local library. Oddly, his occasional flickers of confidence in his poor fellow men, his lonely stoicism and lack of self-pity begin to earn our sympathy, as do his genuine tears for Kirstie. Yet Jenkins also presents him in these interpolated passages as changed, but still an unreliable egotist, who is

---

21   Ibid., p. 285.
22   Ibid., pp. 292–293.

still tempted to impress with 'my MC, my kinship with the Early of Dardaff, my wife, the once famous Betty T. Shields, my nephew [actually his foster-brother] Samuel Lamont QC, my friend Mary Holmscroft MP [...] and my two volumes of poetry'.[23]

The Fifth and Sixth Interpolations, however, and the novel's final footnote are crucial to the end of Fergus's story – and the answer to the question as to where Fergus was when Kennedy was shot. Fergus has told us several times in these interpolations that his health is failing, as though preparing us for his death. The Footnote on the last page of the novel, purportedly written by Torquil, tells us: 'My father, Fergus Lamont, died on 10th October 1963'.[24] If we have been reading closely, unless Fergus – or Jenkins – is mistaken we can assert that he did not. In the fifth interpolation, the elderly Fergus in his Glasgow library reading room tells us of the two old men poring over a newspaper account of 'what the rest of the world already knew', the assassination of the American President.[25] The only American President to be assassinated at this time in Fergus's life, in a November after the Second World War, was of course John F Kennedy, shot on 22nd November 1963.

So where was Fergus when Kennedy was shot? He certainly was not dead. Fergus is clearly alive in Glasgow on the day of President Kennedy's death – more than one month after the day on which we are told he died. In fact, Fergus tells us he has not been going to the library for some weeks when, in Fergus's sixth and last (undated) interpolation, Torquil (his legal, not actual, son) visits. If Fergus has not been going for some time after JFK's assassination, then Fergus is alive for at least several weeks after Torquil says he died. Unless we accept the discrepancy between the footnote statement of Fergus's death and Fergus telling us that he was alive to hear of it a month later, as a most unlikely authorial mistake by Jenkins, then we have no option but to think that Jenkins is suggesting that the story of Fergus's life – and death – is unresolved for an unspecified period after 23rd of November 1963.

So why the misleading footnote? Why misinform the reader? What does Jenkins want the reader to believe? Did Torquil in fact write it? Did Torquil actually in fact visit? One thing is certain: we are learning all this from a deeply

---

23   Ibid., p. 109.

24   Ibid., p. 293.

25   Ibid., p. 200. At the Association of Scottish Literary Studies Conference, 7 October 1989, Jenkins, in a question and answer session with the audience, described how he had found *Fergus Lamont* the hardest, most complex and most exhausting of his novels to write. (It was six years later that his next novel, *The Awakening of George Darroch*, was published in 1985.) Jenkins urged his readers to be careful regarding Fergus (and himself as author!) regarding their unreliability, since in *Fergus Lamont*, 'the devil is in the detail'.

unreliable author and his central character. Virtually everything Fergus tells us from childhood on is open to question.[26]

It is possible to read the story of Fergus Lamont in very different ways. If we accept that Jenkins has simply erred in his dates, then Fergus's story is the tragic story of a terribly traumatised youngster, whose coping strategies, maintained for the rest of his lonely life, take him close to schizophrenia and total breakdown, victim of his mutually exclusive *personas*. Yet Jenkins has throughout taken great care as to the dating of historical events and matching Fergus's age to them. Why would Jenkins (and Fergus) perpetrate such a fundamental misdating, unless it was meant to leave us to speculate about a very different ending? Fergus has, throughout his life, either caused or endured the closing of doors and relationships, from those of his family, his Gantock relatives and friends to his marriage and those of Gerinish and Glasgow. Indeed, in his hermit-like Glasgow years, he shuts out all who attempt to come close, especially in that last apparent shutting out of his 'son' Torquil in the sixth interpolation. Yet their meeting is subtly different from Fergus's brief and curt meetings with visitors in the Glasgow years. In this meeting with Torquil, Fergus is brought almost to weeping; and Torquil's visit, initially so unpromising, has a surprising new humanity. For Fergus to exclude Torquil 'would break my heart' says Torquil, insisting that Fergus come 'now' to Paris with him.[27] Torquil is persistent and genuinely solicitous towards the man he regards, however mistakenly, as his father. He is himself an artist, and thinks of Fergus as a poet. He is clearly affectionate, where Fergus's snobbish real daughter Dorcas, now Lady Arnisdale, despises her father. Yet Fergus tells us (thinking on his grandfather's shutting out of his mother) that he shuts out Torquil:

> After I had shut the door on him I stood behind it knowing that I had
> been wrong to reject him, as my grandfather had been wrong to reject my

---

26   For all Jenkins repudiates any connection with traditions of Scottish fiction, *Fergus Lamont* does seem to echo a recurrent presentation of unreliable narrators and mutually exclusive interpretations in Scottish fiction from Hogg's *The Justified Sinner* (1824) and Scott's 'Wandering Willie's Tale' (in *Redgauntlet*, 1824) through Stevenson's 'Thrawn Janet' (1881) and *The Master of Ballantrae* (1889) to the short stories of John Buchan and outstandingly in James Barrie's novella *Farewell Miss Julie Logan* (1932). Indeed, *Fergus Lamont* can even be read as anticipating the complex ambiguities of post-modern Scottish writers like Alasdair Gray, Janice Galloway, A.L. Kennedy, and James Robertson, in *Lanark* (1981), *The Trick is to Keep Breathing* (1989), *So I Am Glad* (1995), and *The Testament of Gideon Mack* (2006) respectively.

27   Ibid., pp. 237–238.

mother; but like my grandfather I did not open the door and shout the forgiving words.[28]

Is it possible that this another of Fergus's many misrepresentations of events? No longer seeing himself as one of the elect, unlike his grandfather, does he at last find genuine humanity, and change his mind? Thus Jenkins leaves us, as so often, with so many questions unresolved. Has Fergus's trauma-induced carapace begun finally to crack? Has he come full circle from the traumas which began when he was seven? Torquil, now critical of his own mother and sister, and despite the fact that Fergus is not his father, has come to make this last appeal to the man he thinks of as his father. Given that we now know that the possibility exists that Fergus did not die when the Footnote said, is this the last and most outstanding of Jenkins's and his unreliable narrator's manipulations of the reader? Are we meant to allow the possibility of Fergus and Torquil combining to arrange Fergus's 'death'? Is it conceivable that Jenkins is implying other possibilities – say, that after he slammed the door, Fergus, his trapped loneliness finally becoming unbearable, goes after Torquil? That Fergus then might have left Glasgow with Torquil, reconciled to his 'son', to live thereafter in comfort in France? Has Jenkins allowed Fergus to pull off a final trick of faking his own ending? Arguably, Jenkins wants the reader to experience a similar factual disorientation to that of Fergus.

It cannot be emphasised too often that Fergus's story is being slyly manipulated by Jenkins. The novels of this last period after *George Darroch* and *Fergus Lamont* are especially notable for their disruptive ambiguities. It is as though Jenkins himself is split in this novel (and in many others, especially of this later period) between a pessimistic existentialism (the tragic reading of Fergus's story) and the possibility (if Fergus did not die when Torquil said) that there is a twilight hope of grace for Fergus in the years he may have left (with Torquil in Paris?). Once again it seems possible that Jenkins as author can be seen as moving in his fiction between humane optimism and existential negation.

As with *The Changeling* and so many of Jenkins's novels, Fergus's story is also a story of Scotland. Ultimately Fergus can be read as a device to express Jenkins's ambivalent and oxymoronic views of his loved and deplored country. Fergus's story takes him from working-class poverty through the middle classes to the officers' mess to landed gentry; he then goes to the Hebrides to be a crofter. He takes us from city, to country estate, to island croft; from to Lowlands to Highlands. He is involved on the periphery of both Tory and

---

28   Ibid., p. 241.

Labour politics. He has been street urchin, senior-secondary schoolboy, journalist, soldier and officer, poet, upper class drone, croft worker and old pen-
sioner. Fergus is witness to a vast range of aspects of Scotland, geographical,
historical and cultural. He has been caught in the middle of Scotland's bitter
Catholic-Presbyterian divide, savaging both sides. He has experienced the
good and the bad traditions of Scottish education. He has witnessed bourgeois
and upper class selfishness, and despite his elitist pretensions, he often seems
to be genuinely affected by the plight of the poor. He is deeply sympathetic
to the plight of the private Scottish soldier in war (though sharply critical of
the mindset of their officers). He is critical of both Burns and Scott, as well as
the so-called 'Scottish Renaissance'. Finally – reflecting the fact that this is a
novel which leaves the reader with unanswered questions – does he reflect a
profound ambivalence at the heart of Jenkins's own feelings about Scotland?

Works Cited

Burns, Robert, 'Holy Willie's Prayer', *The Poems and Songs of Robert Burns*, ed. J. Kinsley
    (Oxford: Oxford University Press, 1969), p. 56.
Hogg, James, *The Private Memoirs and Confessions of a Justified Sinner* [1824] (Oxford:
    Oxford University Press, 2010).
Jenkins, Robin, *Childish Things* (Edinburgh: Canongate, 2001).
Jenkins, Robin, *Fergus Lamont* (Edinburgh: Canongate 1979).
Laing, R.D., *The Divided Self: A Study of Sanity and Madness* (London: Tavistock, 1960).
Laing, R.D., *Wisdom, Madness and Folly: The Making of a Psychiatrist, 1927–57* (London:
    Macmillan, 1985).
Norquay, Glenda, 'Disruptions: The Later Fiction of Robin Jenkins', in *The Scottish Novel
    Since the Seventies*, ed. by Gavin Wallace and Randall Stevenson (Edinburgh: Edin-
    burgh University Press, 1994), pp. 11–24.
Waugh, Evelyn, *Decline and Fall* [1928] (London: Penguin Books, 2003).

Confessions of an Unbeliever: Religion in the Novels of Robin Jenkins

Bernard Sellin

Abstract

Of all the themes which run through Robin Jenkins's fiction religion is surely the most dominant, usually a target of criticism in keeping with a Scottish literary tradition of rejection of Calvinism. The permanence of this hostile vein in the second half of the twentieth century is revealing of a long-lasting trauma which has been difficult to overcome. Either in the form of historical recreation, parody or misguided idealism, religion colours Jenkins's work to an unusual degree and also shapes his fiction by giving prominence to the anxieties of conscience and the pressures of the moral quest. Although the verdict is usually negative, rejection does not prevent a certain spiritual longing from finding expression in religious terms.

Keywords

Robin Jenkins – religion – Calvinism – Calvin – Protestantism – Scottish fiction

In one of Robin Jenkins's most striking works, *The Awakening of George Darroch* (1985), one of the characters named Taylor says that 'he has too much respect for God to believe in Him'.[1] A 'self-confessed atheist' and social reformer, Taylor is not Robin Jenkins, though the reader can guess that they have much in common. The statement is probably meant as a joke but also suggests the complex, even paradoxical, relationship between the author and religion, the fundamental theme which runs through his fiction. There is hardly a book in which it does not crop up in one form or another and critics have often underlined this interest, although few detailed studies have appeared so far. For Hart 'Jenkins is nothing if not a religious moralist'.[2] 'The religious preoccupation

---

1   Robin Jenkins, *The Awakening of George Darroch* (Edinburgh: Waterfront Communications Ltd, 1985), p. 229.
2   Francis Russell Hart, *The Scottish Novel: From Smollett to Spark* (Cambridge, Massachussets: Harvard University Press, 1978), p. 285.

is constant' Edwin Morgan adds.[3] Several titles such as *A Would-Be Saint*, *The Holy Tree*, *The Missionaries*, *A Toast to the Lord* or *Some Kind of Grace* already create the expectation of some kind of religious questioning. Two historical novels are set in periods of religious upheaval, *Lady Magdalen* (2003) in Covenanting times and *The Awakening of George Darroch* in the years preceding the Great Disruption in the Scottish Church which led in 1843 to a group of ministers leaving their church in protest against a law which they regarded as a limitation of freedom. The paradox is that we are dealing with an author who is also 'a self-confessed atheist' but who seems unable to escape from his obsessive absorption in religious questioning.

In itself, Jenkins's interest is not unique in the context of Scotland. We know the place religion occupied in the past and the role it played in shaping society. Scottish history is structured, among other factors, along the religious events of the Reformation, the Covenant, and the Disruption of 1843. From the Reformation onwards religion was a major influence in everyday life. Scotland's particular form of Protestantism itself has already received substantial attention. And Scottish literature has returned to the subject again and again, from Burns's satires and the fiction of Scott, Galt and Hogg, outstandingly in *Old Mortality* (*1816*), Galt's *Annals of the Parish* (1821) and *The Entail* (1824) and Hogg's study of fanaticism in *The Private Memoirs and Confessions of a Justified Sinner* (1824). David Craig has underlined that 'Scottish fiction … is concerned with church and religion to a remarkable extent'.[4] Isobel Murray and Bob Tait confirm that the modern Scottish novel is 'very taken up with Calvinism and with attitudes and behaviours springing from the Calvinist tradition'.[5] Indeed, perhaps unexpectedly, in the twentieth century, the decline of religious practice does not moderate this critical view. On the contrary, a new bitterness emerges in the work of prominent Scottish writers like Lewis Grassic Gibbon, Edwin Muir and Fionn MacColla.

Calvinism particularly emphasised the glory and authority of God, and in contrast the depravity of man. More than any religious doctrine, Calvinism is based upon an acute consciousness of Original Sin and consequently of the 'fallen' nature of man. It regards evil as an inevitable part of the human condition. According to its principle of predestination, God separated mankind into

---

3   Edwin Morgan, 'The Novels of Robin Jenkins', in *Essays* (Cheadle: Carcanet Press, 1974), pp. 242–245 (p. 242).

4   David Craig, *Scottish Literature and the Scottish People 1680–1830* (London: Chatto and Windus, 1961), p. 166.

5   Isobel Murray and Bob Tait, *Ten Modern Scottish Novels* (Aberdeen: Aberdeen University Press, 1984), p. 5.

two categories: the elect who would be saved through Christ and the 'repro-bate' marked out as sinners and therefore destined for damnation. Although each individual is encouraged to look for signs of election, there is no certainty as to the final verdict. Not only did this theology encourage self-analysis to an unusual degree, but it also tended to stress obedience, the importance of faith and good works. As it developed over the years Scottish Calvinism has often been regarded as extremely austere, more preoccupied with fearfulness and depravity than with confidence in man. As historians of culture have noted, Calvinism has had a huge impact on literature and arts in general. The conflict between the word of the writer and the Word of creation introduced from the start a tension between the two and led, in the end, to a distrust of literary creation and imagination.

With this context in mind, it is not surprising if Calvinism and its dark angel, John Knox, have become the targets of criticism both in literature and in soci-ety at large. For George Mackay Brown, Scotland is 'the Knox-ruined nation'.[6] Cairns Craig's survey of modern Scottish fiction identifies Calvinism among the main causes of the disaster. In the wake of Edwin Muir he emphasises 'a culture of erasure' in which the national imagination has been maimed.[7] Writ-ers themselves have been active in denouncing the negative influence of the Church (though in recent years more balanced approaches have appeared). As early as 1983 Alan Bold pointed out that Knox has always been an easy scape-goat and that 'the identification of one man with the ills of a nation is symp-tomatic of national uncertainty'.[8] Additionally, although he does not deny the 'troubling legacy' left by Scottish Presbyterianism, Robert Crawford advocates a 'more complex and nuanced' approach which would also recognise the more positive impact which the Scottish religious tradition has promoted in the field of imaginative literature, while Ian Campbell underlines that Calvinism may have been identified as a traumatic experience but it also 'made possible some magnificent literature of protest'.[9]

Robin Jenkins's work should be seen in this context. He is writing within a literary tradition of hostility to the Church but what is striking, and relatively

---

6   George Mackay Brown, *The Collected Poems of George Mackay Brown,* ed. by Archie Bevan and Brian Murray (London: John Murray, 2006), p. 1.

7   Cairns Craig, *The Modern Scottish Novel* (Edinburgh: Edinburgh University Press, 1999), p. 19.

8   Alan Bold, *Modern Scottish Literature* (London: Longman, 1983), p. 8.

9   Robert Crawford, 'Presbyterianism and Imagination in Modern Scotland', in *Scotland's Shame,* ed. by T.M. Devine (Edinburgh and London: Mainstream, 2000), pp. 187–196. Ian Campbell, 'Religious fiction', in *A Companion to Scottish Culture*, ed. by David Daiches (London: Edward Arnold, 1981), p. 310.

unexpected, is the permanence of this religious inspiration in the second half of the twentieth century, at a time when religion was losing its grip on society and most novelists were looking elsewhere for their subject matter or experimenting with form. Jenkins's writings have the same obsessive quality as the novels of his contemporaries Graham Greene and François Mauriac, with one major difference: they were staunch believers and their writings aim, among other things, at expressing their own faith. Robin Jenkins, on the contrary, was born into a family of freethinkers for whom religion was not a priority. He remembers this context in the following words: 'I can't think of any single person in my family who ever went to church, so utterly no religion, although from my books you might think I had a strong religious background'.[10] Church attendance in childhood and adolescence was a part of social norms more than the testimony of any strong commitment. Jenkins tried several denominations in a sort of necessary formation process, starting with the Scottish Episcopal Church and then moving on to the Church of Scotland and the Baptist Church, rejecting each of them in succession.[11] Religion was definitely not part of his philosophical beliefs though he insisted on the inevitable influence of the religious background. In the end, atheism and hostility prevailed. But whereas such positions should have pushed religion to the background of his writings and the margins of futility, the paradox is that this was not the case. Jenkins joined a crusade which, years before, had enlisted Lewis Grassic Gibbon to declare that religion was 'the reign of a cultural aberration'.[12] Far from being a minor theme it is a recurring feature of his novels, with a tenacious permanence which gives them much of their sense of identity. From the novel on the Great Disruption of 1843, *The Awakening of George Darroch*, to the religious sect depicted in *The Missionaries* (1957) or the parodies of *The Thistle and the Grail* (1954), there is hardly a single book that does not examine the theme in one way or another. Jenkins's two historical novels, *Lady Magdalen* and *The Awakening of George Darroch*, deal with two periods in which history, religion and politics are closely associated. *The Thistle and the Grail* considers the decline of faith and Scotland's football craze when football has become the new religion of modern times. *A Would-Be Saint* (1978) depicts a moving personal quest which leads to a rejection of social norms and a spiritual crisis. *A Toast to the Lord* (1972) takes up the issue of election in a modern version of Hogg's *Justified Sinner* and in *The Missionaries* Jenkins depicts a small religious community

---

10   Isobel Murray, *Scottish Writers Talking 3* (Edinburgh: John Donald, 2006), p. 105.

11   Ibid., p. 105.

12   Lewis Grassic Gibbon, 'Religion' in *The Speak of the Mearns: Selected Short Stories and Essays*, ed. by Ian Campbell and J. Idle (Edinburgh: Polygon, 1994), p. 165.

challenging the law on a west coast Scottish island. Although the final verdict is often negative, each examination is carried out in a highly original form. Occasionally, this probing considers new territories such as Catholicism in *The Sardana Dancers* (1964), Islam in *Dust on the Paw* (1961), and even Asian creeds in some of the foreign novels and stories. Within Scotland the opposition between Protestants and Catholics often appears in the background, though no single book is devoted to this situation. In the end, Jenkins's range is large and consistently questions the reader as to any justification of religion.

But we should start at the beginning, with Jenkins's first book entitled *So Gaily Sings the Lark* (1950), not the best known of his twenty-nine novels. What is striking is that the warning is already there in the description of a portrait of John Calvin in the very first pages of the narrative; a portrait which seems to function as a signal of the concerns of the novel: 'On the wall above a bookcase was a portrait of a man, on whose face magnanimity was as meagre as the wispy beard. Going across he found it was a contemporary print of John Calvin.'[13] A first novel is often a tentative attempt to define the new writer's issues, but here Jenkins shows little hesitation in indicating the concerns of his future work. Jenkins also indicates that this haunting presence holds little that is positive.

Jenkins's work is recurrently critical of Scottish Presbyterianism, and there are several ways of assessing this. One indicator is the number of ministers presented sarcastically or negatively. The minister in *So Gaily Sings the Lark* contradicts the values that he is supposed to embody. His behaviour is nothing but hypocrisy, calculation and ambition for social promotion; as the central character, David Sutherland, comments: 'it was odd how those who claimed to serve God always strove to do so as comfortably and lucratively as they could'.[14]

In *A Would-Be Saint* the only person who welcomes the Second World War is the minister.[15] In *Lady Magdalen* one character recalls that 'there had never been a minister in the pulpit at Braco who had taught that God was kind'.[16] Finally in *Fergus Lamont* the minister 'represented that mixture of sanctified lust and hypocrisy which had soiled and stunted the soul of Scotland for centuries'.[17] Throughout the fiction it is difficult to find a minister who offers a charitable and dignified behaviour. One exception is the Reverend McNeil in *A Love of Innocence* (1963), but in this harsh world the good are not rewarded;

---

13   Robin Jenkins, *So Gaily Sings the Lark* (Glasgow: William MacLellan, 1950), p. 23.
14   Ibid., p. 230.
15   Robin Jenkins, *A Would-Be Saint* (London: Victor Gollancz, 1978), p. 100.
16   Robin Jenkins, *Lady Magdalen* (Edinburgh: Canongate, 2003), p. 237.
17   Robin Jenkins, *Fergus Lamont* (Edinburgh: Canongate, 1988), p. 228.

the minister is, as it were, deported to a west coast island, losing in the process much of his income.

Next to the portrait of Calvin in *So Gaily Sings the Lark* is an open Bible from which stands out one sentence from the Book of Proverbs 14. 26: 'in the fear of the Lord is strong confidence'. From the beginning, man's position is defined as subservient to a higher power. The image of God is that of the Old Testament, a vengeful deity who is readier to punish than to forgive.

For this religion fear and therefore obedience are the main motivations, as Cairns Craig has pointed out. For Craig, this trope provides the foundation of Scottish Presbyterianism. 'God-fearing' is the recurrent word, and 'the potency of fear remains central to Scottish culture', recognisable in society but also in many works of fiction, taking the shape of either fearfulness or rebellious fearlessness.[18] First is the fear of God's judgement, a proof of obedience and respect for the Lord, therefore the greatest of virtues for the believer. But this fearfulness, which inevitably has an impact on individual behaviour, often stands in contradiction with its opposite, a fearlessness which rejects the self-repression present in this religious perception and advocates a more confident, even arrogant, approach of community, individual *and* Deity. This latter behaviour is usually deprived of any religious dimension, as it often consists in promoting individual interests with little concern for God although, in some cases, this confidence is presented with God's support. Jenkins's novels include the two extremes of fear and fearlessness, for example in *Fergus Lamont* and *The Cone-Gatherers*. However the opposition between the two notions becomes especially fascinating when they are present within a single character, or in other words when demands for submission to God or a set of moral values close to religious dogma are in conflict with more personal or secular values, for example in *The Awakening of George Darroch*. Exceptionally, fear and fearlessness are present when a character, for example Agnes Tolmie in *A Toast to the Lord*, becomes the embodiment of the contradictions of religious belief and secular interest. (With this novel, Jenkins wrote his own modern ironic version of Hogg's *Justified Sinner*.)

Many novels open on a note of warning which, from the outset, establishes barriers and limits not be trespassed. *Fergus Lamont* is particularly bitter regarding Presbyterianism. The novel covers a lifetime, ostensibly charting a man's painful growth and learning from experience. Yet it opens with a memorable outburst which suggests that the book is not so much a personal memoir as the story of a revenge against society, and particularly, the Church: 'Puritanic

---

18   Cairns Craig, *The Modern Scottish Novel* (Edinburgh: Edinburgh University Press, 1999), p. 37.

and parochial Scots, you murdered my young and beautiful mother' Fergus writes at the very beginning.[19]

Much of the first part is an indictment of Calvinism represented particularly by Fergus's grandfather who, when angry, 'looks like Goad'.[20] He stands for callousness, lack of warmth, moral superiority, and intolerance, while projecting an image of social respectability and integration in the community: he runs the Sunday school, is an elder and a town councillor. By rejecting his daughter, he becomes responsible for her suicide and leaves his grandson a legacy of guilt and inability to forgive which is carried from one generation to the next. Thus Jenkins stresses that not only is religion part of a man's upbringing, it also becomes a burden which can hardly be disposed of. Jenkins himself, though an atheist, must have felt the pressure of this cultural legacy to the point of satirising the inherent characteristics of Calvinist doctrine.

Fear of God entails a behaviour which implies an excessively cautious attention to one's actions and thoughts, a lack of spontaneity and a refusal to take risks for fear of offending. By giving priority to the Kingdom of God, this doctrine regards life as subsidiary, indeed as a negation of life. Human activities, especially those providing pleasure, tend to be condemned. Thus Young Fergus is impressed at the number of things his grand-father disapproves of: 'Catholics, comics, pubs, theatres, high-heeled shoes, cigarettes; and on Sundays everything except going to church and Sunday school.'[21]

Jenkins sees repression of natural instincts at the core of such morality. Stoic endurance often goes with it. Characters who embody this behaviour abound: Miss Kinross, the minister's sister, in *So Gaily Sings the Lark*, Hannah in *The Thistle and the Grail*, Margaret Ormiston in *The Expatriates* (1971). What they have in common is self-righteousness, a repressive timidity in life and a lack of compassion and understanding for those in need of help.

The most detailed analysis of the damage of repression, however, is to be found in *The Cone-Gatherers,* in the portrayal of Duror the gamekeeper. Set in Argyll, the plot seems to dramatise the everlasting struggle between good and evil. The forest which offers the setting is presented at the beginning as an Edenic place from which two 'intruders' are to be expelled. Duror, whose name is clearly associated with hardness and endurance, embodies much Calvinist

---

19   Jenkins, *Fergus Lamont*, p. 1.
20   Ibid., p. 3.
21   Ibid., p. 15. In *A Love of Innocence* on Sunday 'even dogs [...] ought not to be heard expressing their joy.' Robin Jenkins, *A Love of Innocence* (London: Jonathan Cape, 1963), p. 234.

doctrine although he claims he does not believe in God.[22] His knowledge of the Bible dates from childhood, we are told.[23] But Duror's life has become so tense that it is affecting his sanity. His instability is due to several causes: his estrangement from his bed-ridden wife and his sexual frustration, his rejection from conscription, and above all his hatred of the hunchback, Calum. But as the conversation with the doctor testifies, the only remedy perhaps is endurance, acceptance of one's condition, which in the Calvinist doctrine implies a form of acceptance of God's decree.[24] Around him there are even people who consider his burden 'a punishment inflicted by God'.[25] Duror, the gamekeeper, does not claim, like others, to be a pillar of the Church. He does not believe, and yet his personality evokes the Presbyterian when his first reaction is to try to catch the hunchback doing wrong, for example working on Sunday. Duror's hatred of Calum is complex, but it is noticeable that it tends to focus on Calum's physical deformity, a reaction which is not occasional but something ingrained as 'since childhood Duror had been repelled by anything living that had an imperfection or deformity or lack'.[26] Calum identifies with the animal world. To Duror, he is an insult to mankind and to God for being 'not as God meant a man to be'.[27] The hunchback is a challenge to normality so that Duror regards Calum's expulsion as an act of purification.

In this book, as in many of Jenkins's novels, the innocents have to pay a high price. Calum not only is an embodiment of the 'sub-human', an insult to God's creation, but he becomes the unacceptable mirror of Duror's own failings – and therefore to be eradicated.[28] Innocent and different, an outsider to the community and an intruder in the sacred forest, Calum easily becomes the scapegoat or sacrificial victim who, according to René Girard, is at the core of early religious practice, the only way of preventing reciprocal violence from spreading.[29] Calum becomes a victim of Duror's mental disorder; but his is no

---

22   Robin Jenkins, *The Cone-Gatherers* (London: Macdonald, 1955; repr. Edinburgh: Paul Harris, 1980), p. 20.

23   Ibid., p. 20.

24   Ibid., p. 128.

25   Ibid., p. 34.

26   Ibid., p. 19.

27   On the subject see also Gerard Carruthers, 'Creation Festers in Me: Calvinism and Cosmopolitanism in Jenkins, Spark and Gray', in *Beyond Scotland*, ed. by Gerard Carruthers, David Goldie and Alastair Renfrew (Amsterdam and New York: Rodopi, 2004), pp. 167–184.

28   Ibid., p. 22.

29   René Girard, *Violence and the Sacred* (Paris: B. Grasset, 1972; repr. Baltimore: John Hopkins University Press, 1977).

ordinary death. He has been sacrificed like the rabbit caught in a trap earlier in the book.[30] Hanging from a tree, Calum's body evokes a crucifixion, catharsis and the story of another Redeemer. Likewise Gavin Hamilton in *A Would-Be Saint;* Gavin's life becomes a succession of renunciations until the ambiguous end which hints that, unable to live in a world of violence, lies and compromise, he may have chosen death and self-sacrifice.

It is one of the paradoxes of this work that along with a damaging indictment of Calvinism runs a preoccupation which seems to derive from the Calvinist frame of mind itself, an authorial mindset drawn from the cultural sphere that it condemns. And this is first made manifest in Jenkins's constant preoccupation with morality. The moral issues are always there, Jenkins being unrivalled when it comes to presenting moral options in all their baffling complexities in a way reminiscent of one of his characters who is reputed for 'this faculty of being able so early in the morning to engage in comprehensive moralising.'[31] And the remark should probably be taken as self-reflexive, a passing wink at the reader.

To some extent, Jenkins's method consists in exposing the absurdity of the Calvinist rigidity of right and wrong by expanding almost endlessly the exceptions and contradictions inherent in all human situations. In her book *The Puritan-Provincial Vision* Susan Manning explains that, mostly as a result of the Fall, division is at the core of the puritan mind, and that Calvinism developed a conceptual structure of polarities which affected the mental process itself. 'Division becomes the structuring principle of life', she writes.[32] At a human level 'Man is finally divided from and within himself; he becomes a battleground of warring faculties: the intellect against the will, the head against the heart, reason against faith.'[33] One manifestation of this opposition is between fearfulness and fearlessness, but Jenkins's works abound in other examples of similar contrasts. Indeed the torments of conscience find here some of their most remarkable expressions when plots dramatise decisions that have to be taken. Hence a tendency to reason in terms of duality, with two opposite options on offer, each loaded with differing consequences. In *A Very Scotch Affair* (1968) Mungo Niven leaves his dying wife on the pretext of escaping from the vulgarity

---

30   Jenkins writes: 'When he did kneel, on one knee, to break the rabbit's neck with one blow, it was like an act of sacrifice, so swift, so efficient, and somehow so purposeful.' Jenkins, *The Cone-Gatherers*, p. 20.

31   Robin Jenkins, *The Missionaries* (London: Macdonald, 1957), p. 49.

32   Susan Manning, *The Puritan-Provincial Vision. Scottish and American Literature in the Nineteenth Century* (Cambridge: Cambridge University Press, 1990), p. 7.

33   Ibid., p. 7.

of his community. In *The Awakening of George Darroch* the plot focuses on the decision which Darroch is about to take: leaving the Church of Scotland with the risk of endangering his family's material comfort and ruining his career. In *The Thistle and the Grail* there is a scene in which a minor character is faced with the choice of attending a funeral or a football match. The choice may appear trivial but readers are made to understand that the decision affects the whole being, is symptomatic of moral weakness and has, in the end, to be accounted for.

The choice is made all the more difficult by the inner tensions of each character. Seldom do we find one who is all of a piece. Those who belong to this category are also easily rejected. George Darroch, the minister, could be taken for a model of generosity, a man with a conscience caring for the poor and angry at social injustice, but, viewed by others, he is childish, 'a simpleton among theologians' or, worse, 'a lecherous little charlatan'.[34] Jenkins's characters are seldom consistent. They display their contradictions, a fact which explains why it is difficult to speak of absolutes of good and evil. For Jenkins, these absolutes do not exist. More generally, we find heroes who show different facets with many shades in the moral spectrum. Thus it is difficult to find a character who embodies pure evil or pure goodness though some tend towards these extremes, such as Angus McArthur in *A Love of Innocence* and Gavin Hamilton in *A Would-Be Saint,* respectively. To emphasise the complexities of his characters Jenkins is always careful to present them surrounded by opposites who stand for other options and perspectives, while the principle of duality is still maintained. In *Lady Magdalen* man and wife, the soldier and the artist, the soldier and the saint, clash, as do the two sons. Other oppositions recur between religion and art, social rank and justice, Church and King. Elsewhere we find the recurrent opposition between the doctor and the minister, one in charge of the body, the other of the soul (*George Darroch, The Cone-Gatherers*).

This method based on contrasts explains why stylistically, one of Jenkins's favourite words is the conjunction though, as seen in the following description of George Darroch: 'Though he had prayed thousands of times, Darroch still did not find prayer simple; there could be so many complications.'[35] Or also in the opening words of *The Changeling*: 'Though no one would belittle the benevolence of the Good Samaritan, in one respect he was lucky: he was alone with his conscience and his neighbour in trouble.'[36] Such carefully balanced

---

34   Jenkins, *The Awakening of George Darroch*, p. 70, p. 58.

35   Ibid., p. 82.

36   Robin Jenkins, *The Changeling* (London: Macdonald, 1958; repr. Edinburgh: Canongate, 1989), p. 1.

sentences expose the nature of dilemmas or complications. The narrator here
feigns to believe that this is a comfortable position, but Jenkins's work demonstrates that conscience is more likely to engender torment than peace of mind.
Moral man is endowed with a conscience. Here lies both his greatness and his
misery and, in this respect, Jenkins's protagonists tend to belong to two categories. On the one hand there are those who seem to be deprived of a conscience,
acting for their own immediate interests and the satisfaction of their ego, uncaring about the consequences of their actions. Among them would be Mungo
Niven in *A Very Scotch Affair* or Fergus Lamont (for most of the novel). The
second group gathers characters that, on the contrary, have to put up with
their conscience, are often haunted with self-analysis to such an extent that
they make their own lives miserable and become incomprehensible to their
fellow men. The best embodiment is probably Gavin Hamilton in *A Would-Be
Saint* but Charlie Forbes of *The Changeling*, Alistair Campbell in *A Figure of
Fun* (1974) and George Darroch have similar characteristics. Their conscience
leads them to reject the soft options generally acceptable in current morality
in favour of a private quest reminiscent of the Narrow Gate of the Gospels.
Hence the expression 'Holy fools' which has been used to depict these idealists often in contradiction with society's main values. Hamilton, the would-be
saint, becomes more and more isolated within family and community while
his involvement in Church affairs increases. He becomes a Sunday school su-
perintendent and then an elder of the local church.

   In the conclusion of his chapter on religion in Scottish fiction, David Craig
writes: 'We may say that the Scottish novel comes into its own when the domi-
nating religiousness of the culture precipitates in the form of conscience
(whether not specifically theological) – intensely scrupulous conscience whose
demands strain unbearably the individual psyche and the relations of family,
parents and children, persons and community.'[37] Jenkins's work fully embodies
this characteristic. And this form has little to do with stream of consciousness
or psychological fiction in general. It implies intense self-examination with a
view to testing the validity of one's motivations against other people's behaviours, but especially against oneself. Jenkins's characters are thus submitted by
the narrator to a battery of cross-examinations whose purpose is to find the
weak point which will then enable further questioning. In the end few of them
come out without damage. As Alastair R. Thomson mentioned perceptively in
an early essay: 'I think that I am being fair, if I say that in Mr Jenkins' awareness
there is something of the uncompromising, unrelenting moral precision of the

---

37   David Craig, *Scottish Literature and the Scottish People 1680–1830* (London: Chatto and
      Windus, 1961), p. 197.

Presbyterian tradition. No sound Presbyterian is ever guilty of intellectual or spiritual vagueness or untested benevolence. [...] I feel that many of Mr Jenkins' characters are perpetually involved in a rigorous, not lightly forgiving self-examination. They sense that we must not only know the enemy in our hearts before we face the enemy in the hearts of others but we must learn to forgive ourselves before we dare to forgive others.'[38]

A useful example is the opening of chapter seventeen of *The Awakening of George Darroch*. Darroch is praying, or rather trying to pray. Darroch agonises regarding the pitfalls – 'whether to speak aloud or inwardly', selfishness, self-pity, the nature of God and how he should be addressed. The narrative then moves on to another point, namely whether it is better to give God a human face or not, before Darroch considers family worries, social injustice, and running away to Italy with a woman he hopes to marry. The episode ends with the following: 'Out of this turmoil of soul-searching, he thought, I shall emerge a better and braver man, and a more resourceful minister.'[39] The conclusion is of course another form of self-delusion. So at the end of this humorous inner debate nothing has really been achieved; prayer becomes impossible.

Fergus Lamont opens with an angry outburst against 'Puritanic and parochial Scots' blamed for having led his mother to suicide. Coming as it does on the very first page, the accusation is a powerful criticism of the nation but it is also remarkable that the next sentence immediately introduces a degree of personal responsibility and self-blame: 'As one of you, I must share the blame.'[40] Elsewhere, at the end of *The Missionaries*, Andrew Doig finds himself unable to condemn the religious community he wanted to support on arrival on the island. Although he now sees them as mere humbugs deprived of any religious dignity, he finds himself unable to despise the members of the community on the ground that, to some extent he is one of them, 'members of the same species'.[41] Jenkins even suggests that it is foolish to try to define degrees of responsibility. Once we start doing so we must be ready to accept compromise and, inevitably, dishonesty.

Religion shares many characteristics with myth. Both take us outside the realm of ordinary reality into a world pregnant with supernatural beings and events. Both are also associated with the sacred. According to Eliade and Malinowski myth meets the demands of religion. It provides a framework,

38   Alastair R. Thomson, 'Faith and Love: An examination of some themes in the novels of Robin Jenkins', *New Saltire* 3 (Spring 1962), p. 59.
39   Jenkins, *The Awakening of George Darroch*, p. 83.
40   Jenkins, *Fergus Lamont*, p. 1.
41   Jenkins, *The Missionaries*, p. 234.

safeguards moral principles and, in the end, offers man a set of practical rules.[42] For the novelist myth also offers a symbolic structure which runs through the plot. For Cairns Craig Jenkins's characters 'regularly find themselves entrapped in a world shaped according to the demands of ancient myth'.[43]

Nowhere is the intrusion of myth more evident than in *The Missionaries*, a novel which inextricably mixes the mythical and the religious to such an extent that it raises the subject on the very first page in a debate which tries to assess the compatibility of each field. Is religion likely to be contaminated by myth or can the latter be helpful in the quest for truth? Religion is at the core of the plot since it revolves around an expedition by a local Sheriff and his staff in order to dislodge a small community of religious sectarians who have illegally taken possession of a plot of land on a west coast island. Taking part in the adventure is the Sheriff's nephew, an idealistic young man who is determined to defend religious belief in an age of growing materialism. These are, once more, some of the author's favourite themes, but what is striking is the intrusion of myth in the shape of the Greek legend of Jason and the Argonauts in search of the Golden Fleece. The boat used by the party is called the Argo. Andrew has founded a University society called The Argonauts and whose badge represents the Argo.[44] And if Andrew Doig prides himself on playing the role of a 'twentieth century Jason' the girl he meets turns into a modern Medea.[45]

The warning expressed at the beginning against 'contaminating religion with mythology' proves relevant and by the end of the book Andrew, the text's 'Jason', has learnt a lesson.[46] But *The Missionaries* also underlines Jenkins's use of mythology. Mythology puts forward, like religion, irrational elements, thus raising immediate suspicion in an uncompromising writer such as Robin Jenkins. The examples of Andrew Doig in *The Missionaries* and Charlie Forbes in *The Changeling* tend to confirm that heroic, mythical associations belong to the past, indeed to myth, or falsehood. The 'missionaries' of the novel make a pitiful crew with nothing in common with the original Argonauts, Hercules, Orpheus and Theseus, among others. Far from using myth in order to enhance the spiritual values contained in the quest, it serves as an ironic double for the futility of the attempt. As in Joyce's *Ulysses*, mythical parallels do not

---

42   Mircea Eliade, *Aspects du mythe* (Paris: Gallimard, 1963), p. 33. Originally published in English as *Myth and Reality* (New York: Harper and Row, 1963).

43   Cairns Craig, *The Modern Scottish Novel* (Edinburgh: Edinburgh University Press, 1999), p. 146.

44   Jenkins, *The Missionaries*, p. 8.

45   Ibid., p. 227.

46   Ibid., p. 7.

contribute to making the main character more heroic, but just more human, more fallible.

If myth fails, it does not mean that religion succeeds. By the end of *The Missionaries*, religion has been stripped of its possible appeal. The religious community presented at the beginning as a model of resistance to materialism and an example of spiritual purity loses its glamour when members finally reveal their true nature of 'small-minded, crafty, grasping, lecherous bigots'.[47]

This being said, the rejection of religion in its social and institutional forms does not preclude the expression of spiritual needs in an age of growing materialism and cynicism. Robin Jenkins may have claimed he was an atheist but he also confessed that he had 'a certain mystic longing which is in no way satisfied' since 'Scottish Presbyterianism blights it completely.'[48] Repeatedly, his novels stress the decline of true religious faith but also the necessity of maintaining some moral and spiritual values. The latter are not necessarily dependent on religion but they tend to be presented in a network of religious references which, though hostile to Calvinism, maintain a definitely Christian message originating in the New Testament and highlighting the necessity of love, social justice, compassion and humility. Consequently it is not surprising if references to Christ's example run through his novels, from the crucifixion scene at the end of *The Cone-Gatherers* to the would-be saint, Gavin Hamilton. Magdalene was indeed the name of Montrose's wife but, when reading *Lady Magdalen* (2003) it is difficult to avoid the connection with the biblical figure of Mary Magdalene, one of Christ's closest followers, present at the Crucifixion. Numerous other examples could be given of a discourse which, while rejecting Calvinism, introduces ambiguity into the narrative in a way which is fairly characteristic of the author's general method, as if two contradictory messages were fighting for supremacy, one hostile to religion and the other more open to some form of religious understanding. As demonstrated by Glenda Norquay in her study of the later fiction of Robin Jenkins, it is often very difficult to come to any definite conclusion since the reader is faced with a number of opposite strategies and statements which contradict one another. Thus Jenkins often creates characters who believe in God in order to test the solidity of their religious positions. The fact that most of them fail is not a surprise. Yet at the same time the reader feels some admiration for those, who, like Gavin Hamilton, succeed in maintaining their faith though, in his case, the price to pay is high.

Religion is a fundamental subject of Jenkins's fiction. It runs through most of his novels, though each work has its own specificity and there are later novels

---

47   Ibid., p. 234.
48   Douglas Eadie, 'The Wanderer in Search of Scotland', *Weekend Scotsman*, 12 June 1971, p. 2.

which develop new themes, such as *Poverty Castle* (1991), *Poor Angus* (2000) or *Childish Things* (2001). As far as Scottish Calvinism is concerned, however, the perspective is invariably critical, in keeping with traditions of Scottish fiction. Jenkins once said 'I am left today wondering if religion does more harm than good'.[49] The paradox is that while blaming Calvinist theology he uses a method which, in its intense moral probing and opposition of polarities, seems derived from the very mode of thought that he rejects. Yet, in contrast to this dark view of human relationships is a more positive attempt at restoring spiritual values which, though not necessarily religious, often finds expression in religious references, symbolism and language. This leaves the impression of an author with pressing spiritual demands but who finds his quest thwarted both by the nature of Scottish Calvinism and the materialistic evolution of the modern world.

Works Cited

Bold, Alan, *Modern Scottish Literature* (London: Longman, 1983).

Campbell, Ian, 'Religious fiction', in *A Companion to Scottish Culture*, ed. by David Daiches (London: Edward Arnold, 1981), p. 310.

Carruthers, Gerard, 'Creation Festers in Me: Calvinism and Cosmopolitanism in Jenkins, Spark and Gray', in *Beyond Scotland*, ed. by Gerard Carruthers, David Goldie and Alastair Renfrew (Amsterdam and New York: Rodopi, 2004), pp. 167–184.

Craig, Cairns, *The Modern Scottish Novel* (Edinburgh: Edinburgh University Press, 1999).

Craig, David, *Scottish Literature and the Scottish People 1680–1830* (London: Chatto and Windus, 1961).

Crawford, Robert, 'Presbyterianism and Imagination in Modern Scotland', in *Scotland's Shame*, ed. by T.M. Devine (Edinburgh and London: Mainstream, 2000), pp. 187–196.

Eadie, Douglas, 'The Wanderer in Search of Scotland', *Weekend Scotsman*, 12 June 1971, p. 2.

Eagleton, Terry, *On Evil* (New Haven: Yale University Press, 2010).

Eliade, Mircea, *Aspects du mythe* (Paris: Gallimard, 1963). Originally published in English as *Myth and Reality* (New York: Harper and Row, 1963).

Gibbon, Lewis Grassic. 'Religion' in *The Speak of the Mearns: Selected Short Stories and Essays*, ed. by Ian Campbell and J. Idle (Edinburgh: Polygon, 1994).

Gifford, Douglas, Alan MacGillivray, and Sarah Dunnigan, eds., 'Postwar scepticism 2: Robin Jenkins', *Scottish Literature* (Edinburgh: Edinburgh University Press, 2002), pp. 847–860.

49   Robin Jenkins, 'Why I decided Scotland must be seen through fresh and truthful eyes', *Glasgow Herald*, 12 October 1982, p. 11.

Gifford, Douglas, '"God's colossal irony": Robin Jenkins and *Guests of War*', *Cencrastus* 24, (1986), 13–17.

Girard, René, *Violence and the Sacred* (Paris: B. Grasset, 1972; repr. Baltimore: John Hopkins University Press, 1977).

Hart, Francis Russell, *The Scottish Novel: From Smollett to Spark* (Cambridge, Massachusetts: Harvard University Press, 1978).

Jenkins, Robin, *The Changeling* (London: Macdonald, 1958; repr. Edinburgh: Canongate, 1989).

Jenkins, Robin, *The Cone-Gatherers* (London: Macdonald, 1955; repr. Edinburgh: Paul Harris, 1980).

Jenkins, Robin, *Fergus Lamont* (Edinburgh: Canongate, 1988).

Jenkins, Robin, *Lady Magdalen* (Edinburgh: Canongate, 2003).

Jenkins, Robin, *A Love of Innocence* (London: Jonathan Cape, 1963).

Jenkins, Robin, *The Missionaries* (London: Macdonald,1957).

Jenkins, Robin, *So Gaily Sings the Lark* (Glasgow: William MacLellan, 1950).

Jenkins, Robin, *The Thistle and the Grail* (London: Macdonald, 1954).

Jenkins, Robin, *A Very Scotch Affair* (London: Gollancz, 1968).

Jenkins, Robin, 'Why I decided Scotland must be seen through fresh and truthful eyes', *Glasgow Herald*, 12 October 1982, p. 11.

Jenkins, Robin, *A Would-Be Saint* (London: Victor Gollancz, 1978).

Manning, Susan, *The Puritan-Provincial Vision. Scottish and American Literature in the Nineteenth Century* (Cambridge: Cambridge University Press, 1990).

Morgan, Edwin, 'The Novels of Robin Jenkins', in *Essays* (Cheadle: Carcanet Press, 1974), pp. 242–245.

Murray, Isobel, 'Robin Jenkins', *Scottish Writers Talking 3* (Edinburgh: John Donald, 2006), pp. 101–146.

Murray, Isobel and Bob Tait, *Ten Modern Scottish Novels* (Aberdeen; Aberdeen University Press, 1984).

Norquay, Glenda, 'Disruptions: The Later Fiction of Robin Jenkins', in *The Scottish Novel since the Seventies*, ed. by Gavin Wallace and Randall Stevenson (Edinburgh: Edinburgh University Press, 1993), pp. 11–24.

Thomson, Alastair R, 'Faith and Love. An examination of some themes in the novels of Robin Jenkins', *New Saltire* 3 (Spring 1962), pp. 57–74.

'A Kind of Truth': Innocence and Corruption in *Lady Magdalen* and *Just Duffy*

Margery Palmer McCulloch

Abstract

Robin Jenkins's novels offer ironical narratives of ambivalence and equivocation, of apparent hypocrisy, of lives and motivations being other than what they seem. This chapter will explore contrasts in Jenkins's depiction of innocence and corruption with brief reference to a range of his fiction but with more extended discussion of these contrasting but equivocal qualities in the contemporary urban setting of *Just Duffy*, published in 1988, and the historical setting of *Lady Magdalen*, a late novel set in the early seventeenth century in the context of the conflict between Charles I and the Covenanters over the introduction of bishops into the Scottish Presbyterian Kirk. Although relationships with specific fiction by Muriel Spark will not be directly addressed, the discussion of Jenkins's exploration of false consciousness and self-delusion will implicitly bring together their shared interest in 'a kind of truth' in regard to human life.

Keywords

absolute truth – Calvinism – Covenanters – female subordination – false consciousness – innocence – *Justified Sinner* – morality – narrative irony

In an article in the June 1990 issue of *Lines* magazine, the critic Philip Hobsbaum pointed to what he called the 'second revival of Scottish literature this century, that which took place in Glasgow.' For Hobsbaum, this 'second revival' was characterised by a 'nakedness of demotic speech', by the ability of writers such as poet Tom Leonard and prose-writers Alasdair Gray and James Kelman 'to use speech as it is and not as it might be', and by doing so 'to give voice to the inarticulate, the uneducated, the dispossessed'. He continued: 'It is an extraordinary achievement to bring the voices of the people into literature, and it has not happened as often as one might suppose.'[1]

---

1   Philip Hobsbaum, 'Speech rather than Lallans: West of Scotland Poetry', *Lines Review*, 113 (1990), 5–10 (p. 7).

Hobsbaum was right to notice a distinctively different approach in Glasgow poetry and fiction in the 1960s and later decades. However, I would suggest that also important to this new phase of the fiction revival are immediate predecessors of Kelman and Gray such as George Friel with his *Mr Alfred M.A.*, and especially Robin Jenkins with thirty-two books of fiction from *So Gaily Sings the Lark* of 1951 to *Lady Magdalen* of 2003 and the posthumous *Pearl Fishers*, published in 2007. In a different but equally important way from Kelman, Gray and their followers, Robin Jenkins brought the voices and everyday preoccupations of ordinary people into literature. And what is especially significant about Jenkins is that through his particular way of democratising fiction, his novels provide a bridge between the new social, secular and ideologically-motivated ethics of later twentieth-century fiction and the earlier nineteenth-century philosophical or religious tradition of Hogg and Stevenson.

Jenkins shares with Muriel Spark this literary bridging space between centuries; and as in Spark's fiction his novels open up not the 'absolute truth' that was an ideal aim for both writers but a more enigmatic 'kind of truth' about the lives of their characters.[2] Jenkins differs from Spark, on the other hand, in that while Spark's interests would appear to be primarily philosophical and psychological in relation to the operation of determinism and choice in human life, Jenkins's preoccupation is more closely related to ethical issues involving innocence and corruption, false consciousness, and the question of how we live with one another in our mundane lives. In pursuit of these related, although differentiated objectives, both novelists offer scenarios involving role-playing and self-delusion with, in Spark's case in particular, a witty, dramatic, comedic or satiric input. While Jenkins's novels are not devoid of humour (especially in works of elderly self-delusion such as *Childish Things* of 2001), what one finds more generally in his fiction are ironical narratives of ambivalence and equivocation, of hypocrisy, of lives and motivations being 'other' than what they seem; scenarios in which the religious election of Calvinism is replaced by a more materialistic election – or in the case of *Fergus Lamont* an imagined aristocratic election. As in *The Cone-Gatherers*, innocence and evil-doing are sometimes placed in a more direct opposition to each other; other narratives show how childhood innocence can be destroyed by the motivations of the adult world; and in works such as *The Changeling* and *Just Duffy* the concept of innocence or goodness is itself put under scrutiny and found to be an ambivalent quality. This present essay will explore Jenkins's treatment of innocence and corruption in two novels: in the contemporary urban setting of *Just Duffy*,

2   Muriel Spark in interview with Frank Kermode, *Critical Essays on Muriel Spark* ed. by Joseph Hynes (New York and Oxford: Maxwell Macmillan International, 1992), p. 30.

first published in 1988; and in his less usual deeply historical setting of *Lady Magdalen*, a late novel set in the early seventeenth century in the context of the conflict between Charles I and the Covenanters over the introduction of bishops into the Scottish Presbyterian Kirk. The discussion will begin chronologically, in terms of historical time as opposed to publication date, with *Lady Magdalen* in which the Calvinist religion which featured prominently in Scottish writing of an earlier period is itself overtly among the categories of false consciousness examined by the happenings in the text.

Lady Magdalen's historical setting and the placing of a woman at the centre of its narrative initially set it apart from Jenkins's more familiar scenarios – although it is important to recognise that in Jenkins's fiction, as in the fiction of Neil M. Gunn, Lewis Grassic Gibbon and the contemporary James Kelman, the positives of human existence are more generally to be found in female characters as opposed to their male protagonists, even if these female characters are not at the centre of a novel's plot. On the other hand, as the story of the young wife of James Graham, Marquis of Montrose, unfolds, so too does Jenkins's characteristic fictional preoccupation with false consciousness and innocence betrayed. At the age of fourteen, Magdalen Carnegie is betrothed to the sixteen-year-old James Graham, Earl of Montrose who – or more accurately his advisers – had decided that, being an only son, he should marry and have heirs as soon as possible. The safety of the earldom will depend upon him having male heirs to succeed him, especially in turbulent times. Magdalen's marriage engagement is made also for her father's political convenience which, we are told, 'mattered more than her personal happiness'.[3] In the girl's protests that she is too young for marriage, Lord Carnegie perceives 'a virginal dread that did her credit; after all she was just 14; her breasts were scarcely formed'.[4] Others, more concerned for Magdalen's welfare, recognise that if her future husband's main motive is to beget male heirs to secure his family succession, then this frail child, whose mother had herself died in giving birth to her, is a cruel choice of partner. Jenkins's stage seems set for tragedy.

Magdalen, however, turns out to be no victim heroine, and Jenkins's plot does not offer an explicit critique of the subordination of women, although it does point to the absence of women from recorded history as well as to the injustices and sufferings which arise from their lack of control over their own lives. Instead, Magdalen is that singular kind of character which is so difficult to portray successfully in fiction, a heroine who keeps her essential innocence and goodness in the midst of corruption and in a situation where events and

---

3   Robin Jenkins, *Lady Magdalen* (Edinburgh: Canongate, 2003), p. 9.
4   Ibid., p. 9.

authority are beyond her control. Her father at times wonders if it is 'retarded development or godliness' which is the source of a questioning that penetrates disconcertingly to the moral core of a situation. We are told that he 'and others less percipient, were often left with the feeling that there was a part of Magdalen difficult to convince. Only the absolute truth could do it, and that was as rare as swallows in winter.'[5]

As a character, therefore, Magdalen to some extent stands alongside the child Maisie in Henry James's *What Maisie Knew*, especially in the earlier stages of her representation; and perhaps more closely, as the narrative develops, alongside Jane Austen's Fanny in *Mansfield Park* – characters who maintain a childhood innocence or goodness, a truthfulness, in a context of equivocation and political manoeuvring: domestic and social manoeuvring in the fiction of Austen and James; domestic, national, and religious manoeuvring in Jenkins's plot. It is not an easy task to convince readers of the authenticity of 'good' characters. Austen's Fanny is not the most popular of her heroines. Jenkins, however, does succeed with Magdalen, and his success derives partly from a narrative method which employs direct speech, an unobtrusive flexibility in focalisation, and a modified form of interior monologue as well as narrative irony. Readers are therefore led to experience *with* Magdalen as her story unfolds in the snapshots of her life in her father's home of Kinnaird and later at Montrose's Kincardine Castle, where the battles and betrayals of the Covenanting period are brought to us through their effect on the lives of the villagers around her. Most importantly, Magdalen's goodness and innocence are not dependent on her status as a child, as we find in James' narrative of Maisie, or upon her situation as a disabled character, as in Jenkins's own earlier novel *The Cone-Gatherers* (1955). What we have in *Lady Magdalen* is the story of a child bride, married for her apparent docility, inexperience, and good family political and religious connections, growing to maturity and learning to trust her own judgements, and to act upon them in the domestic areas where she can exercise control. She learns also to question her husband's actions in relation to the wars. She asks him on his return from negotiations with the King at Berwick, 'curiously confident' despite their apparent failure: 'Did you not tell me once that honour is more important to you than life?'[6] And when he answers: 'That is what I believe. What are you imputing?', she continues, with hesitation, but feeling that she has to speak what she thinks:

---

5   Ibid., p. 102, p. 5.
6   Ibid., p. 158.

Is it honourable to let men like Lord Rothes keep on regarding you as their friend and ally when you are all the time waiting for a suitable opportunity to join their enemies?[7]

Despite James's anger and her father's earlier advice that on such matters she should keep her opinions to herself, she continues:

You think, James, you and the Earl of Argyll and the Earl of Rothes and the King and my father and Mr Henderson [the minister] and all the rest of you, that you are making the history of our country with your arguments in Parliament and your wars but it is not so. What you are doing is wasteful. It benefits no one. You do not build up, you break down, you destroy. Scotland is a poor country, but it is you, all of you, with your quarrels and wars, who have made it poor and who keep it poor.[8]

Astonished as well as angry at his wife's criticism – 'Who have you been talking to? Who has given you these ideas?' – James nevertheless decides to be 'tolerant. After all, she was young and knew nothing of the world.'[9] Magdalen's words, however, have their substantiation in the wounded conscripted men who return injured to their homes, unable any longer to contribute to the work of the community or to support their large families; substantiation too in the depiction of the suffering of the women who lose sons and husbands. James's tolerant, half-serious warning: 'Just so long as you do not pervert my sons' is answered by his wife's: 'You have already done that, James. They think that war, that killing people, is glorious.'[10] The reader is not given James' response to this final chiding, if he even recognises it as such; but listening in imagination to Magdalen's castigation of her imperious husband, with his mistaken certainty that he fighting for God as well as for the King, one remembers the words of Edwin Muir in his poem 'Scotland 1941' which looks back on the tragedies of Scottish history: 'Montrose, Mackail, Argyle, perverse and brave [...] such thriftless honour in a grave/Such wasted bravery [...] Such hard-won ill'.[11] And this 'hard-won ill' is suffered not only by Montrose in his later defeats and final hanging in Edinburgh, but, as Magdalen charges, by ordinary men

---

7   Ibid., p. 161.
8   Ibid.
9   Ibid., p. 162.
10   Ibid.
11   Edwin Muir, *Complete Poems of Edwin Muir* (Aberdeen: Association for Scottish Literary Studies, 1991), pp. 100–101.

and women all over Scotland, whose lives are destroyed by the effects of a religious war which becomes a civil war in which families and communities are set up against each other, all claiming to be fighting for the defence of the law of God.

It is also this 'wasted bravery' and 'hard-won ill' which provide the counterpoint to the integrity of Magdalen and which link this historical novel with the themes of false consciousness and betrayal in Jenkins's fictions of the contemporary world. In addition to Montrose's self-regard and self-deception in relation to the decisions he makes, there is his willingness to sacrifice his young sons to his cause, and his refusal to acknowledge the part his own worldly ambitions have played in the destruction arising from the supposedly religious wars. Self-regard and a lack of consideration for others is also dominant in the behaviour of the Calvinist minister Mr Henderson who in the early stages of the action had no protest to make in relation to Magdalen's childlike physical unreadiness for marriage, but was all too prepared to stress the importance of the union of the families as 'stalwart champions of Christ's Reformed Kirk [...] in the troubled times ahead' as he carried out the ceremony of 'holy wedlock'.[12] Angrily referred to by Montrose's unhappy sister Katherine as 'that stinking hypocrite', he shows a similar lack of compassion during the wars to villagers around the castle who are suffering as a consequence of the fighting.[13] Magdalen's father is throughout the plot portrayed as devious and cynical, willing to sacrifice others in order to maintain his own social and political status. Even Francis Gowrie, who, in his youth, had protested in church at the burning of an old woman as a witch, eventually loses his idealism in the face of the corruption he sees around him and retreats from his concern with humanity into an obsession with art, especially Italian art – a papist abomination in the eyes of his Calvinist compatriots. Francis himself would in time have been a more suitable husband for Magdalen, for both young people had been strongly attracted to each other and had shared many interests and opinions, but her father's insistence on the early union with James Graham prevented any development of their relationship.

As is shown through the portrayal of the minister Mr Henderson in the family and community sphere, religion is also more widely portrayed as a constant source of strife, corruption, and oppression as in the Covenanters' familiar perverse battle-cry 'Christ and no quarter'. Jenkins does not lead his readers into the battle-fields themselves, but their consequences are portrayed in the devastated countryside and broken communities through which various characters

---

12   Jenkins, *Lady Magdalen*, p. 27.
13   Ibid., p. 23.

have to travel on foot or horseback when attempting to communicate with Montrose; and on one occasion to deliver his sons to him as he had commanded. Magdalen's part in this religious civil war is confined to the domestic arena, and in this sphere her actions follow what she thinks of as the teachings of 'gentle Christ, source of all love' as opposed to Mr Henderson's 'angry Jehovah'.[14] In Kincardine she gives refuge and medical help if possible to those fleeing wounded from the battles, from whatever side they appear to come; she helps where she can the shattered families around the castle; and she stands alone on the ramparts in the later stages of the warfare, facing the troops sent to destroy it. Worn out by childbearing and by her essentially delicate physical constitution, she dies at an early age with the knowledge of one son dead in battle, but without knowing the fate of her favourite second, unwarlike, son who was forced to join his brother in his father's war camp. Her death comes also before the end of the action of the novel as a whole, which itself comes to a close inconclusively with Montrose in his war camp finishing off a letter to the King, having previously written letters of condolence to relatives of some of those killed in battle. As readers, we are not taken into his state of mind at this point and his future final defeat and execution in Edinburgh is not foretold.

Lady Magdalen was published in 2003. This was a period when, after the hopefulness of the breaking down of the Berlin Wall in 1989 and the subsequent improvement in relations between the West and the former Soviet Union, Britain and the USA had become involved in a war in Afghanistan. This war was supposedly to hunt down Osama bin Laden and his followers, held responsible for the attacks on New York on 11 September 2001, and it was followed in March 2003 by the bombing and invasion of Iraq and the removal of Saddam Hussein: actions defended by the perceived need to destroy weapons of mass destruction (which proved to be non-existent) and to expel bin Laden's al Qaeda followers (who had never had any significant presence in Iraq). The invasion itself was carried out on the basis of an equivocal interpretation of United Nations resolutions. As a child and young man Robin Jenkins had experienced the consequences of World War One, and he had been a conscientious objector in World War Two, planting trees for the Forestry Commission in the West Loch Tarbert area (like the two brothers in his later novel *The Cone-Gatherers*). When the war ended, he worked as a teacher in Afghanistan and Borneo as well as in Europe and finally Dunoon on the Clyde. It may be, therefore, that it was this dubious outbreak of international warfare at the beginning of a new century which led Jenkins to explore in one of his last novels an historical situation where thoughtless 'heroism' and self-aggrandisement and self-deception, as well as duplicity towards others, led to the marginalisation

---

14   Ibid., p. 30.

of sane voices in society and ultimately to indiscriminate destruction. Earlier, in 1978, Jenkins's *A Would-Be Saint* had taken its theme from the nuclear submarines coming and going in the waters of the Firth of Clyde, a stretch of water overlooked by his home on the hillside above Toward Point, near Dunoon. He has been quoted as saying that despite the détente which arose after 1989, he saw 'no reason to be hopeful that the human race won't wipe itself out with these weapons, maybe not next year, not the next 50 years. Unless more people take up the "wrong-headed" position I did.'[15] In the context of such a comment, *Lady Magdalen*, and its convincing seventeenth-century setting, may have been consciously designed to send a topical warning to our present-day warring world.

In *Just Duffy*, in contrast to the historical *Lady Magdalen*, Jenkins's preoccupation with the ethics of how we live with one another is played out in the modern secular world of run-down inner cities and soulless housing schemes; of an alienated teenage culture and shifting moral and social values. In this book, ambiguity of character and moral ambivalence prevail throughout the text. The initial – and the final – ambiguity lies in the character of Duffy himself, Jenkins's eponymous anti-hero; and as the story unfolds, his name and the title of the book take on additional resonances. 'Just Duffy', the teenager replies to a police patrol which stops him for questioning and asks for his name. And initially, to the book's readers and to his fictional neighbours and most of his acquaintances, he is just that – an inconsequential, not over-intelligent but polite youth; the kind of lad one does not need to approach warily. He is 'just Duffy'. However, as the narrative unfolds, the reader begins to suspect that this is perhaps not his whole story. Duffy may appear simple, but he has his own code of morality and a judgemental attitude towards his fellow – and in his eyes fallen – human beings. These include his own mother, who certainly does not provide a reasonable or reasoning role model for her son. As she prepares to set off for a 'trial honeymoon' on the Costa del Sol with her current male companion, she rages at Duffy in her frustration over his inscrutability:

> You think we're all hypocrites, don't you? But you're the worst hypocrite yourself. Duffy, that wouldn't hurt a fly. Duffy, that all the little kids like and the old women. Always a helping hand. Always a nice smile. The wee girls are safe with Duffy, though he is a bit simple. They don't know, do they, that you despise them all?[16]

---

15   Robin Jenkins, quoted by Lorn MacIntyre in Obituary article, 'Weekend Review', *The Herald* 26 February 2005, p. 16 (no primary source for Jenkins quotation given in the article).

16   Robin Jenkins, *Just Duffy* (Edinburgh: Canongate, 1988; repr. Edinburgh: Canongate, 1995), p. 3.

Insignificant 'just Duffy' is therefore also *just* Duffy, who looks on the conduct of human affairs with moral severity. He had asked his history teacher 'what gave nations the right to declare war and thereafter claim that the killing of their enemies was permissible and legal'; and when Mr Flockhart answered, somewhat cynically, 'Most of them would say God', Duffy was certain that if he were ever to employ God as his excuse in a battle, 'his purpose would be to save and not to destroy'.[17] Duffy believed also that 'truth, at its core, was simple' and that 'the greatest favour you can do people is to force them to face the truth about themselves'.[18] Both Mr Flockhart and his mother try to instil some everyday common sense into him, the history teacher with his emphasis on perspective: truth 'looks different according to the angle you view it from'; and his mother with her: 'You're looking for perfection, Duffy, and it doesn't exist [...] You've got to make allowances. We're only human'.[19] Yet, for Duffy, this excuse is the most inexcusable of all:

> That was the excuse they fell back on: they were only human. Yet they took it for granted that they were so favoured by God that He had made the whole universe for their benefit.
>
> His mother had said that he preferred animals to people. If he did, their lack of presumption was one of the reasons.[20]

In this way, *just* Duffy, with his perception of human inadequacy, becomes ultimately translated into *justified* Duffy who determines to wage war on 'Defilers of truth and abusers of authority', in order to bring them to a realisation of their sins, then to repentance, and finally to a re-ordering of their ways.[21] Having painted his declaration of war on the walls of the Town Hall, then, like the warring nations about which he had questioned his history teacher Mr Flockhart, like God in the Old Testament stories about His making the rivers of Egypt run with blood (and like Robert Wringhim in Hogg's *Justified Sinner* (1824)), Duffy feels *justified* in 'using evil to bring about good'.[22] His first action is a symbolical tearing of pages from books in the public library, for books, he has found, are economical with the truth. Then he progresses to depositing small amounts

---

17   Ibid., p. 2.
18   Ibid., p. 27.
19   Ibid., p. 10, p. 11.
20   Ibid., p. 11.
21   Ibid., p. 25.
22   Ibid., p. 30.

of human excrement inside the hymn books of the important members of St Stephens Church in the west end of the town. St Stephens, appropriately in relation to Duffy's activities, is a church built by nineteenth-century dissenters who seceded from the established Church of Scotland at the time of the Disruption, and it is now the keeper of the town of Lightburn's middle class morality. Unfortunately, in his need for accomplices in this spreading of excrement task, Duffy employs three acquaintances, one of whom, Crosbie, is unreliable as well as vicious. In an attempt to prevent his own discovery when Crosbie begins the unravelling of the excrement mystery by returning to the scene of the crime, and by his deliberate taunting of the police, Duffy passes over the final line of evil by murdering his untrustworthy companion. Yet even at this point he appears able to persuade himself that his actions have been justified: if Crosbie betrays him to the police, then the whole cause will be lost. Duffy reasons:

> In a nuclear war many millions of people, most of them innocent, would be killed. Everybody knew that, most were reconciled to it, a few protested, and nobody was sure whom to blame. Surely therefore it would be the blackest hypocrisy for anyone to pretend to be shocked by his killing of one person, who was evil, and if allowed to live, would do great harm.[23]

In addition, when he eventually tracks Crosbie down to his old tenement home, now about to be demolished, Duffy discovers that Crosbie suffers from severe headaches, diagnosed as relating to a brain tumour which will one day kill him. As he strikes the first blow at Crosbie's head for the sake of preserving his own security, Duffy tells himself that he is also 'doing Crosbie a good turn in making sure that this headache would be his last. He was not an assassin or executioner but a deliverer'. Yet, no sooner has he struck the final blow, when he feels 'dimly as yet, that he had done something so infinitely wrong that everybody in the world was diminished by it'.[24]

Throughout this novel there is a convincing depiction of shifting values in the late twentieth century, communicated through an unobtrusive third person narrative which takes the reader into the mind of the main character and into his social context, and which is accompanied by lively, often dramatic, direct speech from individual characters or between characters. The narrative is also at times rich in comedy (even although dark comedy) in addition to the horror of the scene of the killing of Crosbie. Perhaps most surprising of all is

---

23   Ibid., p. 150.
24   Ibid., p. 155, p. 156.

the confidence with which this author, himself born in 1912, communicates convincingly the late twentieth-century sexual contexts of his adult and teen-age characters. Traditionally, Scottish fiction by male authors in particular has been characterised by its awkwardness or avoidance in relation to the depiction of sexual relations. Jenkins, in contrast, appears at ease with sexuality. In *Lady Magdalen*, his approach is, on the one hand, economic but entirely convincing in relation to his principal character's youth and simplicity. As Magdalen's arranged wedding day approaches, the reader is told, without specific details, how her senior relatives make her aware of the procreative purpose of marriage, and how this is to be carried out between her and her new husband. Similarly, Magdalen's thoughts and behaviour as she waits for, then receives her new husband in their cold winter bedroom, are communicated with sensitivity towards both characters. This is in contrast to the irony with which Jenkins depicts members of the household – male and female – who hope to use their generous sexual favours for their own ends. Sexuality itself is therefore never the negative target in Jenkins. In contrast, the character to be wary of in his fictional scenarios is the one who has a repressed or warped attitude to human sexuality. In *Just Duffy*, therefore, it is Duffy himself, who cannot bear to be physically touched and who avoids sexual contact, who is the danger to society, not the physically generously endowed but educationally backward Molly who delights in giving sexual pleasure, but whose sexual relations with Duffy in the aftermath of his murder of his mate Crosbie have the effect of pushing him further along the road to a possible insanity.

One of the most disturbing aspects of this urban novel with its deprived social setting and largely teenage cast of characters is therefore the way in which it unsettles our social and moral judgements. Is Duffy actually simple-minded, as neighbours and acquaintances tend to believe, able to understand only partially, and lacking the street-wise qualities which enable most of us to survive in difficult situations? Is he a hypocrite, as his mother believes, or – something not dissimilar – an astute teenager who keeps his actual intelligence to himself for his own as yet unknown reasons and purposes, as the teacher Flockhart suspects? And how should we judge Flockhart, introduced to us initially as 'the kind of teacher who not only asked questions, he answered them too, as honestly as he could'?[25] Was it honest or responsible to give the kind of worldly-wise answers to his low-grade 4x class which they did not have either the living experience or intelligence to put into perspective? Flockhart's 'people have gone mad because they expected too much' may well have been unwittingly a tragic comment on Duffy's ultimate situation.[26] The character of Duffy remains

25   Ibid., p. 2.
26   Ibid., p. 238.

an enigma to the end, as he leaves St Stephens' churchyard having rejected his initial intention to commit suicide by burning as had done Savonarola, who also 'had wanted to make people better than they wanted to be'.[27] Instead, realising that he has made himself an outcast, he makes his decision: 'He would go to the coup and wait. If they came in time he would say nothing. For the rest of his life he would have nothing to say'.[28]

In the process and ending of both the historical *Lady Magdalen* and contemporary *Just Duffy* there is to be found a moral and philosophical link with Neil M. Gunn's novel *The Green Isle of the Great Deep*, published in 1944 during World War Two, which explores how 'at the core of a theory or a plan, *in addition to the highest intention there can abide self-delusion and the last refinement of cruelty*'.[29] This insight is particularly relevant to the large-scale warring events and personal betrayals in *Lady Magdalen* but it is also disturbingly relevant to the obsession of the deprived teenager Duffy with 'truth' and 'justice' in a fictional society which appears to the reader as well as to Duffy to be lacking in these attributes; and it is especially disturbing in a situation where, unlike the characterisations of the main players in *Lady Magdalen*, the nature of Duffy's character and mental stability are in question from the outset of the plot, and remain uncertain at its ending. In correspondence with Robin Jenkins about *Just Duffy* in 1992, after the initial hardback copy had been remaindered by its publisher, and before its reissue as a Canongate Classic in 1995, he added another layer of perplexity in relation to the interpretation of the book and its ending. Jenkins wrote:

> *Just Duffy* was described by one reviewer as a 'bleak masterpiece'. Of course I accepted one word but not the other. I would even claim that it is one of my most hopeful books. Duffy in the end sees the quiet everyday friendliness towards one another of the churchgoers as beautiful. You have to be an outcast like him to see it.[30]

This suggests, perhaps, that the author himself did not believe Duffy had become insane, but that in the end he acknowledged his own act of evil and so was prepared to wait for whatever retribution would come, including death if he remained undiscovered at the coup. Yet enigmatic endings in relation to immoral, evil, even more everyday self-deluded actions are a repeated feature in

---

27   Ibid., p. 243.
28   Ibid., p. 244.
29   Neil M. Gunn, *The Green Isle of the Great Deep* (London: Faber and Faber, 1944), p. 218. Emphasis present in Gunn's text.
30   Robin Jenkins, letter to Margery Palmer McCulloch, 28 October 1993.

Jenkins's works. Despite Iain Crichton Smith's attempt to give a Christian sacrificial redemption interpretation to the events which bring *The Cone-Gatherers* to a close, while stressing also Lady Runcie-Campbell's repentance of her earlier rejection of Calum, such an interpretation does not sit easily with the way in which this ending is brought to us through the patterning and sequence of the descriptive elements of the text where Neil's 'moans and yelps of lamentation like an animal' as he struggles to reach his dead brother prevail over Lady Runcie-Campbell's 'purified hope, and joy' as she discovers her son is safe. Similarly, it is not quite certain that Fergus Lamont has truly accepted the error of his self-deluded 'election' as he writes the autobiographical account of his life that will be his memorial after death. And once again, the seeming redemptive final words 'I felt only pity and love' as Fergus watches the German-raids over his town during World War Two are unsettlingly enigmatic.

Lady Magdalen also, to a certain extent, relates to this question of characteristic ambiguity in the endings of Jenkins's fiction, despite the fact that as readers of Scottish history we are aware of Montrose's duplicity in his dealing with King and supposed comrades on the Covenanting side which lead eventually to his death on the gallows in Edinburgh. In Jenkins's fictional account, however, we are left without any knowledge of whether, as he sits at the end of the novel's action writing to both King and relatives of his dead men, he understands and accepts responsibility for the disaster he has brought about, on the national and personal level. On the other hand, this minor element of ambiguity in the ending is counterpointed strongly by the lack of ambiguity in characterisation throughout *Lady Magdalen*'s fictive account of this historical period. Such characterisation, together with the factual historical accounts which have come down to us over the centuries, make this final Jenkins novel published before his death a particularly unequivocal exploration of innocence and corruption in human affairs. *Just Duffy*, as previously argued, is different in the sense that we are never quite certain as to whether Duffy is pretending to be simple-minded for his own reasons, or whether he genuinely does not have the intellectual capacity to realise that he is on the wrong road. Yet, leaving Duffy himself aside, this book with its late twentieth-century setting also exposes, as does *Lady Magdalen* in its different context, the inequalities and injustices in society, including the betrayal of young people by society's exploitative sexual mores and class segregation. It is not, however, as Jenkins himself insisted, and like *Lady Magdalen* also, an entirely bleak book. One of Duffy's initial accomplices, Helen Cooley with her irregular life-style and previous reform school background, is found in the course of the action to have a greater clarity of judgement and understanding of her fellow human beings than the retributive children's panel who had sentenced her. However misguided the under-educated and sexually-exploited Molly might be, there is within her a capacity for love and understanding towards others which could in different social circumstances have developed in directions more positive for her own sake as well as society's. The exploitative Mick, well-known to the local police, is the only one who weeps for his mate Crosbie.

As with Jenkins's fiction writing as a whole, both books considered in detail here – *Just Duffy* set in the contemporary world, and *Lady Magdalen* recounting a story of historical social and national destruction through false consciousness and double-dealing, speak to us with a 'kind of truth' about the nature and needs of our own unsettled social and political times.

Works Cited

Gunn, Neil M., *The Green Isle of the Great Deep* (London: Faber and Faber, 1944).

Hobsbaum, Philip, 'Speech rather than Lallans: West of Scotland Poetry', *Lines Review*, 113 (1990), 5–10.

Hynes, Joseph, ed., *Critical Essays on Muriel Spark* (New York and Oxford: Maxwell Macmillan International, 1992).

Jenkins, Robin, *Just Duffy* (Edinburgh: Canongate, 1988; repr. Edinburgh: Canongate, 1995).

Jenkins, Robin, *Lady Magdalen* (Edinburgh: Canongate, 2003).

Jenkins, Robin, letter to Margery Palmer McCulloch, 28 October 1993.

MacIntyre, Lorn, Obituary in 'Weekend Review', *The Herald*, 26 February 2005, p. 16.

Muir, Edwin, *Complete Poems of Edwin Muir* (Aberdeen: Association for Scottish Literary Studies, 1991), pp. 100–101.

The Past is Not a Foreign Country: Jenkins, Scotland and History

David S. Robb

Abstract

Jenkins's approach to history is his own, as a discussion of his two historical novels, *The Awakening of George Darroch* (1985) and *Lady Magdalen* (2003) reveals. They are set in periods of Scottish history during which Scotland was deeply riven, ideologically and politically, and clearly reflect Jenkins's concern with Scotland as a whole. In them he confronts some deep-seated myths and preconceptions about Scotland and the Scots. They illuminate many things elsewhere in his fiction; conversely, our understanding of his two historical novels is deepened when they are placed in the larger context.

The main emphasis of the chapter, however, is a discussion of the two novels as individual creations: their 'worlds' are distinct from each other, and each stands on its own as a notable modern example of the Scottish historical novel.

Keywords

Scotland – history – values – idealism – innocence – national crisis – family life – pacifism – religion – life choices

Of Robin Jenkins's almost three dozen works of fiction, only two are what readers would immediately describe as historical novels. Jenkins was not essentially a historical novelist: he was not habitually interested in stories set in periods distinct from the present or very recent past for the sort of purposes that we can see in the work of writers for whom the historical mode is central to their creativity and thinking. He has none of Walter Scott's concern with historical change – with, that is, the political or cultural tensions which fuel the emergence of a future out of a past. He is not setting out to explore the relationship between past and present, or to tell a nation's story. Equally, he does not turn to history for escapist ends, as Scott did in part, and as countless of Scott's successors have done from that time to this. There is no sign in Jenkins's two historical novels that he would wish to see them grouped with the 'romantic' fiction on bookshop shelves. They must be seen, rather, as taking their place within the larger tendencies and concerns of his fiction as a whole. The fact that they are 'historical' does not mean that either their methods or their concerns are markedly different from those we find elsewhere in his work. Indeed, they share a very great deal with his other novels.

That said, it has to be acknowledged that a number of Jenkins's other novels might be loosely termed 'historical', in that they are set in periods somewhat previous to the date of publication: they take their readers back in time at least by a few decades. (In much the same way, *Sunset Song*, published in 1932, is 'historical' in that it is set before, during and immediately after the First World War.) Thus, *Guests of War* (1956) is set early in the Second World War; *The Cone-Gatherers* (1955) is also set during that conflict. Other novels look backwards over longer periods: *A Would-Be Saint* (1978) and *Fergus Lamont* (1980), for example, tell of lives lived through several decades of Scotland's twentieth century. There is a sense of a historical turning-point, too, in *Dust on the Paw* (1961), a novel about the twentieth century changes in Afghanistan and its people. Nevertheless, his many novels set in a recent past – a past which does not greatly draw attention to itself and which seems to be little more than part of the furniture of a thoughtful mind – do not prevent his two full-scale historical novels from standing out clearly as such. On the other hand, the fact that his various near-historical novels do not place their 'historical' dimensions in the forefront of their interest for the reader carries over, to some extent, to those two which he sets in markedly distant periods. Even so, in them Jenkins is concerned, in part, to challenge common assumptions about their historical moments.

The concern with a nation and a people in *Dust on the Paw* can be found in the large number of novels he set in Scotland of whatever period. Readers can be forgiven for assuming that much of the time Jenkins wrote a lot about Scotland simply because he was Scottish born and bred. It was the country he knew best of all. One does not have to read much of him, however, to realise that he was deeply concerned with the country and its people as such – he would turn to Scotland as more than just the handiest repository of potential tales. Some of his novels appear to set out to be statements, about Scotland, or to explore what he saw as general features of Scottish life or general Scottish attitudes and characteristics. Thus, *Fergus Lamont*, with its tale of an ambiguous hero and his fraught relationship with the land and people who bore him, hints that Fergus, however caricatured, is a deeply serious comment on Scotland. The title of *A Very Scotch Affair* (1968) seems, similarly, to be a giveaway, and so it proves, despite its being an intensely focused account of the experiences of a small handful of characters in a very short space of time. Mungo Niven's story is offered as an expression of national tendencies, with a typicality underlined by the explicit Glaswegian overtones of his name. Jenkins clearly wrote and thought much about his native land and was prepared to use his fiction as a way of illuminating, criticising and appreciating the country and community from which he sprang.

His two explicitly historical novels were *The Awakening of George Darroch* (1984) and *Lady Magdalen* (2003). They both appear to belong to the second half of Jenkins's career as a novelist, although (as is the case with his other writings) it is not clear when precisely they were written. *George Darroch* is set in 1843, during the Disruption, the high point of a long-running Scottish national religious controversy. Its central figure is a fictional Scottish minister who emerges from obscurity to precipitate and lead the mass exodus of ministers who followed the Evangelical leaders out from the General Assembly and thus from the Established Church of Scotland itself. *Lady Magdalen* is set in the first half of the seventeenth century, at the time of the signing of the National Covenant in 1638, and the Bishops' Wars and the Wars of the Three Kingdoms during the 1640s. Lady Magdalen is the wife (of whom history tells us next to nothing) of James Graham, Marquess of Montrose (of whom history tells us a great deal). Both novels are set at moments of crisis and division within Scotland. The choices and allegiances of the key figures are central concerns and the historical contexts are very important: the reader must thoroughly appreciate the historical moments in order to understand what is going on. They would thus appear to be, in their very nature, novels fundamentally concerned with Scotland and its history.

In each case, the reader is provided with an explanatory introduction. That for *George Darroch* is notably long and detailed; that for *Lady Magdalen* is notably brief and laconic. Both are revealing. For *George Darroch*, Jenkins rightly assumes that late twentieth-century knowledge of the Disruption is likely to be minimal or non-existent, so he provides several paragraphs of succinct explanation of the issues and progress of the Ten Year Conflict, bringing out the seriousness with which the dispute was regarded in the Church and nation, and also the seriousness of the practical consequences for ministers and their families of relinquishing the state connection. Hardship, poverty and uncertainty were the likely outcomes for any minister who 'walked out'. Those involved in 1843 regarded the controversy, and the heroic departure of around a third of the ministers of the national church, as a matter of huge weight and historical significance. Jenkins notes, with apparent surprise and disapproval, how modern awareness of this event has dwindled to next to nothing. His novel, then, appears to have sprung from a desire to rectify this situation, and to take advantage of the high drama inherent in what is sometimes still thought of as the most momentous happening in Scotland in the whole of the nineteenth century. This is arguably the only modern novel centred on this event, and its two nineteenth-century predecessors, *The Disruption* (1847) by William Cross and *Johnny Gibb of Gushetneuk* (1871) by William Alexander, languish in obscurity, the one so weak as a novel that it is rightly forgotten, the other so challenging in the vigour of its dialect that it has remained mainly a mere local enthusiasm, despite its imaginative strengths. Jenkins's three introductory paragraphs lead one to expect that his novel will be centrally concerned with the Disruption itself, which turns out not to be the case, however.

Lady Magdalen, on the other hand, could scarcely have had a briefer intro-duction: 'In the opinion of many Scots the most charismatic character in their history was James Graham, Marquess of Montrose. Lady Magdalen Carnegie was his wife.'[1] At first glance, this is no more than a basic explanation of the title. The book which follows does indeed make of this forgotten historical fig-ure a moving and memorable character. However, as one reads, one realises that Jenkins is as concerned with the first sentence as he is with the second. This is a novel which is primarily concerned to challenge the perception of Montrose as a heroic figure whose charisma enabled him to achieve astonish-ing success in his dashing campaign of 1644–45, and whose continuing cha-risma has seduced succeeding generations right up till the present day. The power of his glamour emerged in his own lifetime and his military successes, as sensational as they were ultimately fruitless, continued to form prominent and admired parts of eighteenth-century re-tellings of the seventeenth cen-tury's civil upheavals. When Scott took him up in two accounts, in *A Legend of Montrose* (1819) and *Tales of a Grandfather* (1828–29) the scene was set for Montrose's embedding in the pantheon of romantic Victorian Scottish heroes, amongst historians and the wider population alike. The trend continued into the twentieth century, in such accounts as H.E. Marshall's Scott-inspired his-tory book for children, *Scotland's Story* (1906), John Buchan's *The Marquis of Montrose* (his biography of 1913), and Nigel Tranter's two volume fictional ac-count of 1972–73.[2] (The more academic historians among today's writers take a similarly respectful, indeed enthusiastic, view of James Graham.) Whether it was Tranter's paean of praise for his vision of the ultra-loyal, ultra-principled, selflessly dutiful, merciful, home-loving, war-hating warrior which prompted

1 Robin Jenkins, *Lady Magdalen* (Edinburgh: Canongate, 2003), p. vi.
2 H. E Marshall, *Scotland's Story: A History of Scotland for Boys and Girls* (London, Edinburgh, Paris, Melbourne, Toronto, New York: Thomas Nelson and Sons, 1906). Nigel Tranter, *The Young Montrose* (London, Sydney, Auckland, Toronto: Hodder & Stoughton, 1972). Nigel Tranter, *Montrose: The Captain General* (London, Sydney, Auckland, Toronto: Hodder and Stoughton, 1973). John Buchan, *The Marquis of Montrose* (London, Edinburgh: Thomas Nelson & Sons, 1913).

Jenkins to a totally revisionist account cannot be determined. The fact remains that he offers us a Montrose who never appreciates his home or his wife, abandoning her company at every opportunity, a man driven by the ambition to rise to the top in the political and ideological upheavals of the time and who instinctively plunges into war's extension of politics by other means as the readiest way to attain his destiny.

Jenkins is thoroughly conversant with the outline and details of Montrose's career, though it is not clear how far he assumes that his reader is similarly knowledgeable. That career takes place off-stage, as the story is told largely from the domestic point of view of Magdalen herself. She is, like her author, an instinctive pacifist in an age of apparently inescapable warfare. (Jenkins had been a conscientious objector during the Second World War, and the novel appeared in 2003, the year of the British and American invasion of Iraq.) Jenkins expresses his own hatred of warfare through that of his character, and a constant theme of the book is the ruining of lives as a result of armed conflict. The underlying rhythm of the book derives from the counterpointing of home and domesticity against the threatening violence of the outer world. Magdalen's own home circumstances carry the main burden of this theme, but it is confirmed in such stories as that of the happy, peace-loving marriage of the schoolmaster Blair with the servant-girl Cissie (quietly courageous when their little Perth home has to give shelter to non-Covenanting travellers). Other humble households are trashed by war, as in the case of the tragic loss of the nephews of George Graham of Braco, seduced by their youthful belief in the glamour and honour of war into joining Montrose's cause, thus devastating their widowed mother. Similarly, we hear of the local blacksmith dragged to war from his family and his essential occupation and returning to them maimed, disfigured and useless. The motif recurs of war and the ideological conflicts of the age pulling young men from their homes, whether from their ignorant enthusiasm and masculine codes of honour, or from the near-impossibility of escaping the depredations of a civil conflict. Montrose's own family (and thus Magdalen) are the most prominent victims: her would-be warrior son John dies from the hardships of his father's Highland campaigning, while the younger and more sensitive James is removed from his parents and imprisoned as a hostage in Edinburgh Castle. Nor does the war merely drag men, willingly or unwillingly, away from their homes to a distant disaster; periodically, it also arrives to threaten or destroy those homes itself. Thus the domestic sanctuary of the art-loving Francis Gowrie and his wife is devastated, Gowrie himself being killed as he tries to stop the barbarity. Most prominently of all, Magdalen has to face down her husband's opponents as they are about to destroy the family castle by cannon fire: her heroic confrontation on the battlements is the supreme outward manifestation of the quiet courage she shows throughout.

Jenkins has no patience with centuries of enthusiastic veneration for Montrose's striking series of victories against the odds: *Lady Magdalen* is one of the most revisionist treatments of history one is likely to meet in the realm of fiction. He chooses, of course, to ignore the oft-told details of James Graham's capture, summary trial and execution, the part of his story which conclusively gilds his charismatic military reputation. His legendary courage and grace at the end has no place here, although the book offers regular reminders that the result of his ambition will be the noose. The narrative ends as Braco, having risked his life to inform Montrose of Magdalen's death, parts in something like hopeless disgust at the incorrigible coolness of the great general, even in the aftermath of his disastrous defeat at Philiphaugh. The destroyer will clearly continue on his disastrous path to the end.

Jenkins is an author who continually judges people and behaviour with a subtlety, tolerance and charity which can verge on ambiguity, but his vision of Montrose is startlingly clear, decisive and explicit and his novel an arrestingly direct anti-war statement. And it confronts and quarrels with the words which the reader first encounters on the reverse of the dedication page: 'In the opinion of many Scots the most charismatic character in their history was James Graham ...'[3] Jenkins is not merely concerned with offering his own interpretation of a famous figure from the past: he is challenging and condemning the whole militaristic strand in Scotland's sense of itself, a feature which twentieth century history has only intensified.

The Awakening of George Darroch takes an equally subversive approach to history, vigorously undermining some settled assumptions. In this case, however, the object of Jenkins's challenge to our preconceptions is not an individual reputation, but a movement and an age. The standard view of the Disruption amongst historians is that of the Evangelicals themselves, namely that it was a strikingly heroic manifestation of principle in an age which had apparently been sapped by the pragmatism and materialism of a no-longer-fanatical religious outlook. Jenkins does not take sides in the great conflict, unlike his predecessor William Alexander. Admittedly, the seriousness of the threat of poverty and hardship to the families of those ministers who quit the Establishment is fully conveyed so that their courage and firmness of belief is clearly acknowledged. The Moderate mind-set is shown as being much taken up with creature comforts and social status, religious zeal being less in evidence. Nor did Moderatism, on the evidence of the book, do much to discourage crude jokes and thoughts or excessive drinking among its clergy. On the other hand, the novel gives sympathetic voice to the oft-repeated view amongst its characters that the Evangelical insistence on the headship of Christ is really little

---

3 Jenkins, *Lady Magdalen*, p. vi.

more than a high-flown piece of specialised theology, far down the path which leads to assessing the scope for angelic dancing offered by pinheads. At the heart of the book is the juxtaposition of the religious dispute, fundamental in its way as it may have been, with the appalling social conditions and brutal lack of charitable instinct in Jenkins's portrayal of Scotland in the 1840s. Darroch finds himself briefly involved with Taylor, a leading agitator who is striving to bring about the political and social changes which modern readers now regard as basic, and is immediately sympathetic to him. Similarly, he is the only character who is truly charitable towards, and supportive of, the desperate Mrs Cooper, a prostitute facing execution for the murder of her own prostitute daughter: she had herself attempted suicide and is being nursed back to health only so that she can be subjected to the full rigour of the law. Jenkins portrays a society crying out for a spiritual revolution of a kind totally different from that with which the Evangelicals are concerned – the Moderates, of course, are entirely accepting of the way things are, as their discussion with Darroch on the evening before the Disruption reveals.

Jenkins seems intent on undermining other historical pre-conceptions, all in the spirit of making us think and judge afresh. Our sense of the Victorian age as one of sexual repression and embarrassment is likely to be totally upset by his insistence that sexual thoughts and behaviour were as prevalent then as they are in our own lives, or in the world around us. Indeed, there is a dimension of sex-comedy about the book which is very deliberate. Jenkins creates a series of surprises for his reader, apparently delighting in a very unorthodox depiction of Victorian life. Thus, we are as startled as George himself to be suddenly confronted by the splendidly nude body of his colleague's unabashed wife. Nor do we expect a Victorian minister's son to be in the habit of climbing trees so as to spy on the undressed body of a young widow – any more than we expect a young Victorian widow not only to be aware of the fact but to take mischievous delight in completely exposing herself to his youthful gaze. It is equally unexpected, at least in the standard vision largely derived from the classics of Victorian fiction, when a dying wife persuades her housekeeper to seduce her husband by way of entrapment. By the time we encounter a newly married couple interrupted while on the floor in the throes of some enthusiastic naked love-making, we are perhaps a little less surprised. Jenkins's Victorian world seems far less Victorian than we expect: it is merely a comic version of the world so often portrayed in the fiction of our own day, and the implication is that human behaviour is timeless. Once again, the differences we expect history to deal with are drastically played down; indeed, to a surprising extent, this historical novel seems to invoke history only to deny its significance. Jenkins is striving to free us from the confines of history, just as he portrays his central character escaping from the vision and priorities of his own time.

The revolution, the discovery of a social Christianity, which George Darroch brings about in himself, is the book's riposte to the upheaval which history tells us occurred in May 1843. This is Darroch's awakening, and the goodness which marks him out from most of the other characters consists of his ability to respond to the human needs of his time with a mind liberated from all the orthodoxies in the air he breathes and with a moral courage focused on (we conclude) far more important matters than those which exercise the Evangelicals as a whole. As in *Lady Magdalen*, Jenkins challenges the dire failings of a society, and of a moment in history, through the spectacle of an inexplicably right-minded individual who finds the courage to stand out against the evils of the time. Jenkins's own lonely fight, of course, had taken the form of his registering as a conscientious objector during the war, an experience which gave rise directly to at least two further novels. It would be easy simply to say that in the two historical novels with which we are concerned here, Jenkins was just giving his oft-told story new guises as a change from his more frequent settings amongst the hardships of life for working-class people in the mid-twentieth century. And so, to some extent, he is, although it is also tempting to see in them the glimmerings of a further dimension pointing to a wider view of Scotland and its past. Between them, *Lady Magdalen* and *The Awakening of George Darroch* confront two of the most widely accepted components of the image of Scotland and its history, an image held both by native Scots and by the rest of the world: Scotland as a nation of soldiers, and Scotland as a nation of marked religious piety and individualism. Two novels are perhaps insufficient to establish a trend, but there is enough evidence across the total range of his fiction to indicate that it was habitual with Jenkins to be thinking about the general characteristics of the country and the people from whom he sprang. Passages like the following from A *Very Scotch Affair* can frequently be encountered:

> By the time Andrew's letter arrived, seven weeks after their arrival in Barcelona, the affair was over. Mungo had been installed in a bedroom of his own, breakfast was eaten together, respect was pretended, endearments were omitted, money was seldom mentioned though often thought about, acquaintances were told the little they needed to know, and the ultimate disruption was waited for, as if predestined. It was a very Scotch dissolution to a very Scotch affair.[4]

This summary of the ending of Mungo Niven's squalid little, though life-changing, escapade is striking. It feels central to that novel, of course, in the

---

4   Robin Jenkins, *A Very Scotch Affair* (London: Gollancz, 1968), p. 137.

way that it echoes and apparently illuminates the book's title. We can feel the duality in Jenkins's choice of words: the 'affair' is both the sexual fling in which Mungo was indulging even while his wife was dying of cancer back home in Glasgow, and it is also the more general story of his family's destruction as a group as a result of the double blows of his desertion and his wife's death. In what sense, one wonders, has all this been 'very Scotch'? Mungo Niven has been driven in part (he believes) by the desire to better himself, not in an economic sense but in terms of achieving a social and cultural potential of which he feels denied by his life in the 'ghetto' of his working-class, near-slum environment. He is seduced by the desire to be, and to participate in, something 'higher' than the condition to which he had been born; he cannot accept the commonness and the limitations of his Scottish post-war world. Consequently, he is blind to its virtues, and to the value of the people who live in it. He is also kidding himself: he lacks the capacity to exercise properly the intellectual and cultural tastes to which he aspires, and in any case what is really driving him, as much as anything else, is the combination of sexual dissatisfaction with a wife who (through age and child-bearing) no longer attracts him, and the sudden opportunity of taking up with a younger model. What seems to be 'very Scotch' about this? Jenkins seems to be suspicious of what is often lauded as a particular Scottish form of ambition, and of that style of 'getting on' which involves cutting oneself off from one's roots. Earlier writers may also have been troubled by their observation of Scotland's 'lads o' pairts': 'Ian Maclaren' (in *Beside the Bonny Briar Bush*) and George MacDonald (in *Robert Falconer*), for example, both indulge the sentimentality of showing characters with spectacular promise and academic achievement, or who make their way professionally in the wider world, returning instinctively to their humblest roots as they approach the end of their lives. Furthermore, Mungo's idealistic vision of a life of cultural and sexual self-fulfilment entails a naivety which shows up his provincialism, a provincialism which is in itself enough to permanently debar him from the gloriously transcendent life-style to which he aspires. In other words, the big fool is forever stuck in the ghetto simply because of who he is: he should have known that his affair was never going to last (Jenkins's sad summary quoted above beautifully conveys the speedy inevitability of the outcome) and that he himself was never really cut out for better things. Jenkins seems to have surprisingly little respect for the mere aspirational impulse itself. Nor does he seem to have much patience for people who try to dress up lust as something more idealistic: the honest valuing of sex and the body is one of his characteristics and if he is seeing in the story of poor Mungo's naivety and hypocrisy a representation of the way Scottish men have often been clumsy and graceless in their sex-lives, who is to say he is wrong?

It is a further unexpected collocation of words, however, which leads us from the above passage back to the two historical novels. Taken in isolation, the close juxtaposition of 'disruption' and 'predestined' might be dismissed as without significance, despite the fleeting possibility of a religious reference to be detected in the charge which sparks between them. When one remembers, however, that Jenkins would publish, seventeen years later, a novel focused squarely on Scotland's great religious Disruption, one begins to suspect that he had long been aware of, and interested in, that portion of Scotland's history and that, furthermore, he saw it as having a significance for Scotland well beyond the fact that those involved felt it as 'soul-shaking'. Was Jenkins writing a novel about it merely because it seemed a shame that it is now forgotten (as his foreword seems to imply)? Is it not more likely that, once again, he had long regarded the Disruption as 'a very Scotch affair', as this temptingly significant use of the word 'disruption' in the novel of that title might suggest? Its use, after all, seems far from inevitable in the context of the sentence itself.

George Darroch, at first glance, seems a very different character from Mungo Niven. He is far more sensitive and concerned with the woes of others, and capable of change where Mungo's self-deceptive posturing will clearly continue long after his story ends. Nevertheless both characters are portrayed with complexity and ambiguity, so that we might have some difficulty in deciding how, finally, their author wishes us to respond to them. Mungo's desire for better things, to be unconfined by the material and cultural impoverishments of life in the 'ghetto', can spark some sympathy in us, just as it does, briefly, in his daughter Peggy. Where Mungo's selfish folly is flecked with faint hints of justification, however, George's undoubted fundamental goodness is flecked by quite serious flaws. His moral contradictions arise less from his lustfulness in itself, though his selfishness in making his wife pregnant yet again after he has been warned of the danger to her life does not endear him to the reader. However, there is a strong suspicion held both by the characters who understand him and eventually also by the reader that there is an element of the calculated, the staged, the self-glorifying in some of his moments of moral triumph. His son James, in despair at witnessing his father's perfectly judged act of apparent leadership in instantly following the Evangelical leaders out of St Andrew's church, 'knew what had happened: given the best opportunity of his life to show off his father had not been able to resist it. For the sake of a moment's vanity he had sentenced his family to years of hardship.'[5] The novel's brief fourth and last part, describing the scene in and around St Andrew's church on the day of the Disruption itself, studiously avoids offering any insight into what

---

5   Robin Jenkins, *The Awakening of George Darroch* (Edinburgh: Waterfront, 1985), p. 266.

may be inwardly driving George Darroch at the moment of final choice. The end of the previous part had indicated, somewhat obscurely, that he had now reached a stage of inner awakening which had left him without fear or 'vulnerability'. This is sufficiently reticent to leave the reader still wondering what his eventual choice will be, thereby re-enacting the tension felt by all concerned as the moment of commitment approaches for Darroch and for all the other heads of ministerial households. What would George do, and how many would rise from their seats? The question introduces, appropriately, some real tension as the end of the book nears, just as it created the high drama of the moment in historical reality. But Jenkins's insistence, at this point, on the outsider's view – that is, the reader's, the narrator's and that of the observing characters in the public gallery – means that Darroch cannot finally be cleared of James's suspicion. Throughout the novel, he has been capable of various inner failings and contradictions. Indeed, at that moment of choice, the reader cannot know whether George's action is the result of a settled decision, perhaps taken before, or during, or soon after his encounter with the Moderate faction the night before, a meeting which had faint echoes of Christ's verbal escape from the attempt of the Pharisees to entrap him over the matter of the lawfulness of paying taxes to Caesar (Matthew 22. 15–22 and Mark 12. 13–17). Or is George's rising from his seat a purely spontaneous action?

Even if we decide that James is wrong, however, and that Darroch plays his part in the theatricality of the moment (the whole event has been thoroughly stage-managed, we realise by this point in the book) with the purity of mind and spirit implied by the outward nobility of his choice, he seems to me to be still blameworthy in terms of Jenkins's values as expressed both within the book and throughout so much of his writing. Indeed, it is at this moment of decisive and outwardly selfless public action that he is most similar to Mungo Niven. Darroch shares a surprising amount with the Glaswegian Lothario, notably a dying wife for whom he is insufficiently concerned as he makes his own private journey towards a perfection of life which, even without the complication of a fatal illness, she would not share. Both men are concerned with ideals which are for themselves alone. And the single-minded pursuit of those ideals, in each case, is in fundamental conflict with the unity and well-being of their families. Mungo's story, at its deepest, is that of the destruction of his family: his wife's death, of course, would have been a moment of crisis in any case, and the three children have each of them strong leanings towards a selfish individuality which would have strained the family's cohesion. But it is the astonishing selfishness of Mungo's behaviour which is decisive, in the event: he has put himself in the position of being unable to sustain the family's identity and security to prevent its fragmentation at the point of crisis. It had been his wife, however transformed from the desirable nymph he had first married, who had performed the humanly essential task of making the family a coherent whole.

George's children are also seen as strongly individualistic and distinct from each other, though the danger of their splitting apart is less immediate. What danger there may be lies in the over-riding threat to family life which has always formed part of the story of the Disruption, and which Jenkins keeps at the forefront of our attention, from the foreword of the novel onwards. The probable consequence for Darroch's family of his quitting the Establishment is a fundamental concern of the book and its characters, as it is for the other Evangelical clergymen we encounter in it. History tells us, at least in the conventional reading, that the willingness of the Evangelicals to accept the loss of family comfort and security (especially in a Victorian world as brutal as the one Jenkins depicts) was one of the most noble and praiseworthy aspects of the whole affair. Then and since, the willingness of the departing ministers to give up all material advantages for the sake of a spiritual ideal has been seen as marking their particular distinction. And not theirs alone – it has sometimes been a point of national self-glorification that only in Scotland (it is suggested) could this sacrifice have been made on such a scale.[6]

Does Jenkins fall in with this view? If we have doubts that he does so, they arise only in part from the possibility that Darroch's departure from the church involved his love for the grand gesture. It is noteworthy that the novel's final focus is not on the father, but on James. Throughout, he has not been an entirely sympathetic character, but his hard realism in demanding that his father treat his ministerial calling as a career to be pursued on behalf of his large family has not been rejected outright. The moment of drama over, his father having marched off to Tanfield in the wake of Chalmers and his fellow church leaders, James watches his other immediate family members taking their first steps into their future separate lives: the Darroch family will no doubt eventually suffer something of the same fate as the Nivens. But not yet: '[Annabel] had reminded him how he might after all find a fruitful purpose at Cadzow, or even at Craignethan. He could keep his promise to his mother to look after his sisters.'[7] These final words of the novel assert the crucial obligation of family life and its supportive function. George is not the only Darroch who grows and changes. Arthur and James are moving from their particular immaturities

---

6 For example, see Henry Cockburn, *Journal of Henry Cockburn, Being a Continuation of the Memorials of His Time: 1831–1854*, II (Edinburgh: Edmonston & Douglas, 1874), p. 32.

7 Jenkins, *The Awakening of George Darroch*, p. 269.

to embrace healthy and fruitful ways of life, Arthur with the possibility of a 'proper' girl-friend and James shouldering the burden of caring for his family – unlike his father, who seems content to leave such responsibilities to the Lord.

The socially committed Christianity which George Darroch discovers is clearly praiseworthy and a harbinger of a future which this Scotland of 1843 desperately needs. If he has gone out with the Evangelicals, it is no longer because of any narrow concern with the tussle between Church and State, but because a new future must emerge in opposition to the Moderates' satisfaction with their present condition. His awakening to the nation's true needs stands in judgement on the conventional heroes of the Disruption also, their theological concerns ultimately of little moment in the far wider demands of the world they are living in. But his willingness to destroy his own family's life limits his credibility with Jenkins and the reader. As an individual, he has to make difficult choices within a deeply divided nation, just as (in his different way) Mungo feels he must between the diverse life-styles of Scotland as it enters that decade of social transition and fluidity, the 1960s. George Darroch's awakening is another very Scotch affair.

So too, however, is James Graham's chosen path, which also involves the crushing destruction of family life. He also, of course, has his ideals just as Mungo and George have, and Jenkins gives us even less encouragement to regard them as totally worthy. For royalty and the divine right of kings, Montrose sacrifices his family and, in particular, the wife he had never properly appreciated. Indeed, James Graham is like the other two husbands: they are all in some sense implicated in their wives' deaths, not directly as physical killers (though George Darroch's libido takes him very close) but as husbands whose personalities and behaviour towards their women are life-denying, and whose carelessness of their wives' emotional needs seems to contribute to their passing away. And just like Mungo and George, Montrose deceives both others and himself into thinking that he is not, ultimately, driven by merely selfish instincts. In reality, he seeks glory, power and distinction. Magdalen in dying resembles the other two wives but she is, of course, far more our concern as an individual character than either Bess Niven or Margaret Darroch. We care for the latter two primarily because of their sad fates and their selfish treatment at the hands of their husbands. Magdalen Carnegie utterly dominates her novel, however, as a positive embodiment of all the goodness, strength and value which Jenkins associates with healthy family life; she shows the universal goodness to which we should all aspire, and (ultimately) embodies the value Jenkins places upon the female sex as a whole. James Graham's historically conditioned ideals, both of loyalty to the king and of warlike masculinity, pale to worthlessness in comparison with Jenkins's version of the Eternal Feminine.

What, then, does the historical dimension add to these two novels by Robin Jenkins? Do they finally boil down to little more than inventive further treatments of some of his perennial themes? We can say, I think, that Scottish history contains popular myths which, in Jenkins's view, demand to be challenged. And it reveals a frequently divided nation in which temporary ideals and loyalties endanger the values upon which human life permanently depends. In sum, history adds the long view. Distance makes it easy for us to view Montrose's goals, and his efforts, merely as part of the awfulness of life in seventeenth century Scotland with its religious and constitutional conflicts mercifully far behind us. History has washed Montrose away, except in the memories of those who choose to regard him as charismatic; the personality and instincts of his wife, as imagined by Jenkins, continue to appeal to us. Equally completely, as Jenkins's foreword reminds us, the Ten Year Conflict and the Disruption have also been washed from the national recollection. The modern consciousness of Scotland no longer particularly venerates the participants and their concerns. But George Darroch's instinct for good amidst all the bad around him shares a little of Magdalen Carnegie's idealism, and we welcome the strong hints, in the novel's final pages, that in the Disruption nothing terribly important has occurred after all, either to the nation or in the lives of the main characters. Even George is likely to be given a new living, and the others parting from each other on the Edinburgh street as the excitement subsides have pleasant, very normal futures to look forward to. Jenkins's foreword, after all, is more neutral than we perhaps first thought: it does not castigate the present for forgetting and undervaluing the Disruption, but merely records the fact that what had seemed to some as of the utmost importance emerges from history as nothing of the sort, and that moral choices of the present are as complex as those of the past.

Works Cited

Buchan, John, *The Marquis of Montrose* (London & Edinburgh: Thomas Nelson & Sons, 1913).

Cockburn, Henry, *Journal of Henry Cockburn, Being a Continuation of the Memorials of His Time: 1831–1854*, II (Edinburgh: Edmonston & Douglas, 1874).

Jenkins, Robin, *The Awakening of George Darroch* (Edinburgh: Waterfront, 1985).

Jenkins, Robin, *Lady Magdalen* (Edinburgh: Canongate, 2003).

Jenkins, Robin, *A Very Scotch Affair* (London: Gollancz, 1968).

Marshall, H.E., *Scotland's Story: A History of Scotland for Boys and Girls* (London & Edinburgh: Thomas Nelson & Sons, 1906).

Tranter, Nigel, *Montrose: The Captain General* (London: Hodder & Stoughton, 1973).

Tranter, Nigel, *The Young Montrose* (London: Hodder & Stoughton, 1972).

Reprise or Resolution? *A Would-be Saint* and Robin Jenkins's Final Novel, *The Pearl Fishers*

Linden Bicket

Abstract

Robin Jenkins has been read by critics primarily as a social realist, who departs from the mysticism of his Scottish Literary Renaissance forebears most obviously in his urban depictions of contemporary working-class Lanarkshire life. A new reading of *A Would-Be Saint* (1978) and this novel's relationship with Jenkins's later *The Pearl Fishers* (2007) recoups an understanding of this novelist as deeply influenced by both the religious environment of his youth, and by eighteenth-century Romanticism. This new reading suggests that Jenkins's work can be opened to wider theological and literary horizons than previously thought.

Keywords

realism – romance – morality – sainthood – Christianity – Scott

Soon after he died in 2005, Robin Jenkins's daughter discovered the manuscript for what was to become his final, posthumously-published novel, *The Pearl Fishers*. This undated manuscript – originally titled *The Tinker Girl* – is now held in the National Library of Scotland's archives.[1] It is unclear whether Jenkins had intended this remaining work to be published or not. But though it remained unpublished during the author's lifetime, and was found – perhaps abandoned – in a drawer, *The Pearl Fishers* is no strange or isolated text within Jenkins's overall corpus. It is a response, or coda, to the story of Gavin Hamilton, the conscientious objector and main protagonist of Jenkins's earlier novel, *A Would-Be Saint* (1978).

In fact, *The Pearl Fishers* alludes in several ways to some of the key fictions created by Jenkins during his long literary career, and responds subtly to these

---

[1] See Rosemary Goring, 'Introduction', *The Pearl Fishers* (Edinburgh: Polygon, 2007), p. v. *The Tinker Girl* (undated ms and two tss), National Library of Scotland Acc. 12645. Kind permission to quote from this manuscript has been granted by Robin Jenkins's Literary Executor.

in terms of moral concerns and major themes. The title is not accidentally similar to *The Cone Gatherers* (1955), as *The Pearl Fishers* also deals with outcasts who reap the fruits of the natural world, and focuses on an innocent who faces potential destruction. As with Jenkins's earlier novel *The Changeling* (1958), this final novel is concerned with diagnosing hypocritical and self-serving attempts at social justice, the character of Gavin Hamilton realising, unlike *The Changeling*'s Charlie Forbes, that 'there was no virtue in being kind to people if in doing so you humiliated them.'[2] And, like *Matthew and Sheila* (1998), *The Pearl Fishers* represents a profound meditation on the nature of true goodness, and the difficulty of maintaining this in a fallen and corrupt world. However, *The Pearl Fishers* does not merely gather together the old threads of Jenkins's previous, carefully-woven moral tapestries. This chapter will argue that although Jenkins's typically non-committal 'kind of grace' is finally granted in this, his last work, its manuscript reveals much about the author's creative process, and particularly his salvaging, recycling and updating of various fictions, including works by that most Romantic of novelists, Sir Walter Scott. *A Would-Be Saint*, and the later *The Pearl Fishers* are also ideal novels to explore when considering the history of Jenkins's critical reception, which has seen him only as a proponent of social realism. This critical view is challenged by these two novels, which follow the journey of a deeply religious main protagonist who eventually meets a socially marginalised (and romantically imagined) heroine.

In his review of *A Would-Be Saint*, Christopher Nouryeh identifies that this text contains many of the recurrent, distinguishing tropes of Jenkins's fiction. He writes that this is a novel 'in the tradition of modern realism' and argues that '[w]hat is truthfully told is real everyday life – its trivialities, practical preoccupations, ugliness and vulgarity. To put it another way, real everyday occurrences in a low social stratum'.[3] Critics have long noted that Jenkins's concern with everyday life in the Central Belt of Lanarkshire has focussed almost obsessively on post-war poverty, lack of communication and spiritual emptiness. Roderick Watson argues that Jenkins's novels, first appearing in the 1950s, 'set the scene for much of the realistic fiction of the next two decades'. His writing is 'much gloomier' than his contemporary Muriel Spark's, and indeed it is arguably much less formally experimental.[4] Jenkins does not possess Spark's postmodern playfulness, manifested in mapping disrupted teleology against the failed attempts at predestination or authorial control by various characters,

---

2 Jenkins, *The Pearl Fishers*, p. 63.

3 Christopher Nouryeh, Review of *A Would-Be Saint*, *World Literature Today*, 55:2 (1981), 317.

4 Roderick Watson, *The Literature of Scotland: The Twentieth Century* (New York, N.Y.: Palgrave Macmillan, 2007), p. 160, p. 161.

nor does he display Spark's curiosity about and rejoicing in new forms – most obviously the *nouveau roman* – and gleeful disruption of literary genre. Instead, in his work we read 'moral realism', and, in Brian Morton's summation, 'sheer old-fashionedness [...] Robin Jenkins's fate was to write at a time when the proper matter of fiction was supposed to be psychology, history and its illusions, or the nature of fiction itself, anything but questions of good and evil.'[5]

However, some critics have identified that Jenkins does not present a wholly quotidian fictional universe. Glenda Norquay claims that Jenkins often creates 'fantastic and grotesque personalities', which link him to his eighteenth-century literary ancestors Hogg and Scott, and she maintains that 'his novels initially appeared to offer social realism but they were concerned with much wider metaphysical explorations'.[6] In his assessment of Jenkins, Jeffrey Hill argues that he differs to his Scottish Literary Renaissance forebears because they offered a 'more truthful perspective on the Scottish predicament', whereas Jenkins's work contains echoes of late nineteenth-century Kailyard fiction.[7] Hill compares Jenkins unfavourably to his grittier English counterparts, Braine, Sillitoe and Storey, and concludes that he 'turned his back on the present and, without ever becoming a historical novelist in the conventional sense of the term, recreated a recent past in which to explore Scotland's spiritual malaise.'[8] So, as Norquay and Hill suggest, the critical near-consensus that Jenkins rejects the mysticism of his Renaissance forebears in favour of 'gritty' modern realism is worth questioning.

A Would-Be Saint, like many of Jenkins's works, draws heavily from his own experiences. The novel traces the life of Gavin Hamilton from boyhood – during which his father is killed in the First World War and the boy earns a scholarship to study at a prestigious fee-paying school – to early manhood. Hamilton becomes a conscientious objector, and he is consequently sent to work for the forestry commission in Argyll for the duration of the War. So far, all of this is in line with Jenkins's own biography, and in this novel – as in *The Changeling* – the poverty of grey, working class industrial Lanarkshire is pitted against the Highlands, a locus that Watson identifies as 'a place of remote

---

5   Brian Morton, 'Goodness in a Fallen World: The Fate of Robin Jenkins', *Scottish Review of Books*, 1:3 (2005), 8–9.

6   Glenda Norquay, 'Jenkins, (John) Robin (1912–2005)', *Oxford Dictionary of National Biography*, Oxford University Press, Jan 2009. http://www.oxforddnb.com/view/article/94884 [accessed 30 Aug 2015].

7   Jeffrey Hill, *Sport and the Literary Imagination: Essays in History, Literature, and Sport* (Bern: Peter Lang, 2006), p. 36.

8   Ibid., p. 37.

beauty, old estates or isolated forests'.[9] Ardmore forest in Argyll, where Hamilton is a forestry worker, also provides the setting for *The Pearl Fishers*, and in this text the woodland setting delivers the 'seemingly edenic backdrop [that] offers Jenkins' characters space for spiritual clarity, a timeless, unworldly environment where the essentials of life can be calmly examined.'[10] A major departure from Jenkins's own biography in these two novels is that his protagonist Hamilton is a sincere and zealous Christian, who wishes eventually to study for ministry in the Church of Scotland. The second notable departure from the re-telling of Jenkins's own life experience in *The Pearl Fishers* is that Hamilton meets and falls in love with Effie Williamson – a young woman who travels with her family, fishing for freshwater Scottish pearls.

Hamilton is something of a puzzle in *A Would-Be Saint*, and not simply to the other characters in his fictional world, but also for Jenkins's readership. From childhood, he is sombre and slightly withdrawn, feeling a degree of affection towards two school friends but rarely showing it. He is a skilful footballer and it is on the pitch that he seems most in communion with others, but Hamilton's seriousness continues into adulthood, and his attempts at charity seem intended mostly 'to test his fitness to call himself a Christian'.[11] Rather than revealing any genuine altruism, Hamilton's behaviour appears to display only his desire to 'practise his Christianity' on the needy.[12] Even the local minister finds him 'too virtuous by half'; such is his joyless, even priggishly-lived faith.[13] In her interview with Jenkins, Isobel Murray neatly sums up the experience of many critics and readers where she says 'Gavin seems to me to be a misanthrope'.[14] Of Hamilton's drawing away from human community in order not to feel any degree of indebtedness, and thus collusion with the Second World War and the war effort, Murray notes: 'I don't find the turning away very sympathetic.'[15] This has been a problem for Jenkins's readers, too. Jenkins notes in his interview with Murray that 'somebody in the *Times Literary Supplement* said of Gavin that he was the most obnoxious hero she had read in modern fiction [...] I meant him to be a would-be saint'.[16]

---

9   Watson, p. 161.

10   Rosemary Goring, Introduction to *The Pearl Fishers*, p. vii.

11   Robin Jenkins, *A Would-Be Saint* (London: Gollancz, 1978; repr. Edinburgh: B&W, 1994), p. 75.

12   Ibid., p. 80.

13   Ibid., p. 83.

14   Isobel Murray, ed., 'Robin Jenkins', in *Scottish Writers Talking 3* (Edinburgh: John Donald, 2006), pp. 101–146 (p. 119).

15   Ibid.

16   Ibid., p. 117.

The divergence between Jenkins's intentions for Hamilton and this character's reception tells us much about Jenkins's own religious imagination –
despite the fact that he is usually received as, and proclaimed himself to be an
atheist writer not prone to discussing spiritual matters. Perhaps the unpopular-
ity of Gavin Hamilton in both his fictional world and within Jenkins's readership is due to his unknowability. As readers, we never gain a clear understanding of Hamilton's religious formation (we see no-one in his family speaking
to him about faith), nor are we allowed access to his own understanding of the
universe as divinely created. Instead, what we are presented with is a character
who is strongly morally opposed to war (as was his author), and we only view
his religious belief through the perspective of other characters. There is no opportunity for us to really understand this belief, nor Hamilton's individual motivations and complexities.

In a discussion about his own largely nonreligious childhood with Isobel
Murray, Jenkins claims that as far as religion went, there was

> Absolutely none! Not a scrap! [...] And I can't think of any single person
> in my family who ever went to church, so utterly no religion, although
> certainly from my books you might think I had a strong religious back-
> ground. Although *myself*, as a boy, I used to go to the Scottish Episcopal
> Church [...] And then I went to the Church of Scotland, and then I went
> to the Baptist Church. I was trying them all out! I must have been at this
> time about fourteen, fifteen.[17]

Despite his assertion that there was absolutely no religious devotion or Church
attendance in his boyhood, Jenkins clearly demonstrates his early interest in
religious practice here. He also identifies his grandfather as 'a Protestant freethinker', and, later, he calls his family 'pagans', before qualifying this by stating:
'Oh yes, we were Protestants! And I'm telling you they would have fought bitterly to get Protestant in front of that word pagan, which is astonishing.'[18]

Gavin Hamilton also seems to be a product of 'Protestant pagans', in that
his hometown of Auchengillan, a small mining village in Lanarkshire, appears largely non-religious but generally Presbyterian in character. Hamilton
laments that 'Football had taken the place of religion in Scotland. Christ the
Redeemer was of less consequence than the scorer of the winning goal.'[19] But
Hamilton is no mystic; he is identified in the later *Pearl Fishers* as

---

17   Ibid., p. 105.
18   Ibid., p. 105, p. 140.
19   Jenkins, *A Would-Be Saint*, p. 70.

a Christian, an over-zealous one at that, but like other ambitious young men entering the Church of Scotland ministry nowadays he had no patience with impossibilities like the Resurrection, the Virgin Birth, and other miracles. He saw Jesus Christ as a Great Example, which seemed to Mr Rutherford as rational an attitude as any.[20]

Gavin Hamilton conforms nicely to the 'lad o' pairts' archetype of nineteenth-century (often Kailyard) Scottish fiction. He is a Protestant success who, though of humble origins, is able to achieve social mobility and deliver much back to the community after receiving a University education. But of course, Hamilton is much more than this; he is 'a would-be saint', and in his conception of saint-hood in this novel, Jenkins reveals his Protestant understanding of the term. Jenkins admits to Murray: 'I think [Hamilton] believed in God, which I don't, and therefore it's a wee bit difficult for me just to see what the fellow was after', but nonetheless he paints Hamilton as 'rational' and 'ambitious', and notes:

> I think St Teresa had a tremendous amount of pride. I don't think you could be a saint without a tremendous amount of pride. No use saying to me, a saint is full of humility, not true! You cannot stand up against the whole of mankind and say, God loves me, without having tremen-dous pride. It would be a very meek thing to say: I am humble in God's eyes: God doesn't love me any more than he loves anybody else, but these saints don't think that. If they thought that, nobody would pay them the slightest attention. A saint has got to have arrogance: I do feel that. [...] Only saints are truly adult; they have put away childish things, the rest of us have not. [...] After all I think I show in him one or two little things like his kindness to other people. He is kinder to other people than most of the others.[21]

Jenkins's reading of sainthood is coloured by his post-Reformation under-standing of the saint as, primarily, a good example to the faithful. Hamilton is a would-be saint in Jenkins's eyes because his especially good deeds encour-age the growth of his spiritual arrogance. He is nothing like the holy men and women of Jenkins's Catholic contemporary George Mackay Brown, who imag-ines the saint as a holy intercessor – one who will provide supernatural assis-tance after death. In fact, Hamilton sounds rather like the kind of minister that Brown often lampoons in his short fiction; he is an unimaginative do-gooder

---

20   Jenkins, *The Pearl Fishers*, p. 159.
21   Murray, ed., *Scottish Writers Talking*, pp. 120–121.

who does not believe in miracles, and who mostly sees ministry as a kind of practical social work. Hamilton, fervent and sincere though he is, is very much a product of the author's own, down to earth view of sanctity. It is entirely fitting that he appears in one of Jenkins's most realist novels, one depicting a small community in the grip of Depression in the 1930s. Hamilton is no *deus ex machina*; he is the creation of a 'Protestant pagan' whose literary influence can be traced in the work of the later James Kelman, the self-confessed 'Protestant atheist' who has inherited much of Jenkins's worldview.

So far, so realist. We are only offered the most fleeting glimpses of Hamilton's inner life, and perhaps the reason that Jenkins focuses so intensely on unemployment, poverty and lack of opportunity in *A Would-Be Saint* is because he is familiar with this milieu. He does not place Gavin in Church at any point in his novel (though we know he attends and worships regularly), nor does he offer a glimpse into Hamilton's prayer life. Perhaps this is simply too alien for an author who stated that 'God has shown great signs to me that he doesn't give one damn about fellow man.'[22]

However, Jenkins's would-be saint is also part of a universe that is not as Godless as Jenkins (nor many of his critics) would have us believe. Jenkins is often read as highly critical of Scottish Calvinism, but in fact, his depiction of the world as a vale of tears, populated by highly moral (and immoral) characters does reflect something of a Scottish Calvinistic imagination. We might read these characters as the elect and the damned, desperately seeking salvation or 'some kind of grace' in a world abandoned by an authoritarian God. In his interview with Murray, Jenkins adds:

> If you're going to exasperate me, you'll bring forward some instance where God has involved people in some dreadful predicament, and then has released them from it. I immediately say, who the hell put them into it in the first place? Therefore I think God has got nothing whatsoever to do with love of humanity, and we are on our own as regards that, and we have to look at humanity's manifold crimes, which are far greater, as far as I can see, than its manifold kindnesses, and are far more dangerous. We are now in a situation where we can and I do think that we will destroy ourselves. I do think that deeply.[23]

The deity that Jenkins imagines, and yet insists that he does not believe in, is a world away from the immanent God of Brown, Spark, or George Friel

---

22   Ibid., p. 120.
23   Ibid., p. 120.

(another proponent of social realism, but one whose works are shot through with hopeful religious invocations). This deity is at best remote and at worst malign, and his fallen creations' sinfulness (Jenkins secularises this by using the term 'crimes') outweighs their capacity for good. There is something almost gnostic about Jenkins's conception of a false God, or demiurge, who creates a flawed world and then abandons it. Reading Jenkins's work under this kind of lens opens it up to wider spiritual dimensions than previous studies have shown. The apocalyptic and scriptural language used by Jenkins in his interview with Murray, the narrative point of view in *A Would-Be Saint*, and the submerged religious imagery and language of *The Cone-Gatherers* (and elsewhere in his corpus) shows that Jenkins's work is more inflected by religious belief than is often thought. Therefore, the picture of Jenkins as a straightforward socialist realist is more complicated than critics thus far have suggested. There are certainly elements of the Kailyard built into his small-town setting and religious main protagonist. Perhaps more importantly, the construction of this character and Jenkins's conception of his sanctity reveal that the author cannot help but disclose something of his own religious formation, however much he denies that this was a factor in his upbringing.

However, Hamilton's rather dour, serious (and unknowable) faith is not the only one presented in the novel. The pedestrian world of Jenkins's would-be saint is illuminated by the glamour of a person of a different faith in this text. When the young Hamilton meets Jewish Rachel Hallad, 'the girl with dark skin', who speaks in an accent 'too refined to be Scottish', he is struck by her apparent exoticism.[24] Rachel lives in neighbouring middle-class Lendrick, in a 'large grey stone house with its two ornamental turrets that gave it the appearance of a small castle.'[25] The house is named 'Ivanhoe', and Rachel is so informed by Walter Scott's literary heroine Rebecca, daughter of Isaac, that Hamilton is 'reminded of Rebecca the beautiful Jewess' from *Ivanhoe* itself.[26] Jenkins weaves the threads of eighteenth-century romance into the text so finely that he has Hamilton and Rachel's father, a writer, discuss Scott's novels in his study. This is not the first instance of Jenkins using Scott's heroines as the template for his own, of course. In *Poverty Castle* (1991) the five Sempill sisters (Diana, Rebecca, Rowena, Jeanie and Effie) are all named after characters from Scott's novels.

Rachel Hallad seems at first to be a promising romantic interest for Hamilton, but after she moves away from Lendrick he communicates with her only by letter, and eventually he terminates their correspondence entirely, as he believes

24   Jenkins, *A Would-Be Saint*, p. 31.
25   Ibid., pp. 39–40.
26   Ibid., p. 41.

that appreciating her letters means that he is in danger of enjoying his time as a forestry worker. (This would mean that he is in some way implicated in the war effort and is indebted to a system he regards as morally abhorrent.) Rachel does not fulfil her early promise as a major presence and love interest in the text. She does not help progress the plot in a significant way, and, like Hamilton's childhood friend McIntyre, she inhabits only a small portion of the novel's first fifty pages. In the middle of Hamilton's adolescence, the text tells us that she 'had gone to live in London a year or so ago'.[27] Hamilton's later girlfriend, the rich but cruel Julia Bannatyne, is 'the best catch in town', and offers Hamilton a far better opportunity to 'practise his Christianity'. When he offers shelter to a pregnant prostitute called Jessie, Hamilton realises that if she were to help him, Julia could have 'joined in what was after all an act of Christian redemption'. Ultimately, though, 'what he could not accept in [Julia] was her callousness'.[28] None of these women provide Hamilton with what he really craves – a highly moral (yet deeply desirable) Christian woman in difficult circumstances, whom he can help.

Nonetheless, Rachel Hallad does pave the way for the definitive and still-more 'exotic' romantic attachment of Hamilton's life (and one who is again named after a heroine of Scott's) – Effie Williamson of *The Pearl Fishers*. In his interview with Isobel Murray (conducted in 1985, seven years after the publication of *A Would-Be Saint*), Jenkins hints that he is tempted to begin work on this companion novel. He notes that he has 'left an avenue for Gavin. You remember the minister's sister?' and adds:

> I had thought that I could write one day a sequel to *A Would-Be Saint* where he marries this woman. Because I always like to think of stories with such a background. I like that kind of thing! It seems to inspire me. And to bring Gavin back into the fold – to see if he *could* come into the fold, with her help. Not so much her help but through helping *her*.[29]

As Murray notes, his last, posthumously-published novel directly echoes Jenkins's very first novel, *So Gaily Sings the Lark* (1951). In this text, an unemployed miner plants trees in the Highlands of Scotland and has to choose between two women. One is the repressed sister of the local minister, while the other looks 'as beautiful as [David] could have wished', the living personification of

---

27　Ibid., p. 46.
28　Ibid., p. 65.
29　Murray, ed., *Scottish Writers Talking*, p. 123.

the 'exaltation and the tantalising unattainableness of that lucid land.'[30] This first storyline is directly mapped onto the plot of Jenkins's final novel. When we meet Hamilton in *The Pearl Fishers*, the war has ended. He is still working in the forest and is readying himself to study for ministry. He is now a firmly established member of the Highland community through his work with the other foresters (though 'he was seldom invited to their homes. Their wives were never quite at ease in his company').[31] At the beginning of the novel, Jenkins makes it clear that Hamilton 'would have to have a wife.' The natural choice appears to be Miss Fiona, the Kilcalmonell minister's sister, who 'was at least ten years older and very plain, with no figure to speak of.' She is 'entirely suitable, being pious, prudish and virginal.'[32] However, Miss Fiona's prospects are ultimately dashed by the arrival of beautiful young Effie, who arrives at the beginning of the novel's second chapter amid blazing sun and wild roses in full bloom. Jenkins's frequently-used – and not unproblematic – trope of contrasting one (as he sees it) unfeminine, virginal spinster with a curvaceous, young beauty is in evidence here as it is also in *So Gaily Sings the Lark*, *The Expatriates*, and *Dust on the Paw*. This is a plot device that he recycles frequently. Effie, then, ticks all the boxes on Jenkins's list and allows him to recycle one of his favourite storylines. She is the beautiful young foil to the spinsterish Miss Fiona, but her poverty and vulnerability will allow Hamilton to shed his former diffidence and fully 'come into the fold' of the community in his attempts to help her.

But why is intelligent, glamorous, wealthy Rachel Hallad the early template for Effie, the humble, itinerant pearl fisher? Scott's heroines are a persuasive connection here again, as is his treatment of religion. In *Ivanhoe*, Scott makes the Jewish Rebecca (who Hamilton associates so clearly with Rachel) unquestionably heroic, as he simultaneously critiques anti-Semitism and denigrates the treatment of Isaac. Scott writes:

> [...] there was no race existing on the earth, in the air, or the waters, who were the object of such an unintermitting, general, and relentless persecution as the Jews of this period. Upon the slightest and most unreasonable pretences, as well as upon accusations the most absurd and groundless, their persons and property were exposed to every turn of popular fury; for Norman, Saxon, Dane, and Briton, however adverse

---

30   Robin Jenkins, *So Gaily Sings the Lark* (Glasgow: MacLellan, 1951; repr. Bath: Cedric Chivers, 1971), p. 21, p. 111.

31   Jenkins, *The Pearl Fishers*, p. 2.

32   Ibid., p. 3.

these races were to each other, contended which should look with greatest detestation upon a people, whom it was accounted a point of religion
to hate, to revile, to despise, to plunder, and to persecute.[33]

Effie and her family of 'tinkers' are subject to local prejudice, ridicule, and
distrust throughout *The Pearl Fishers* in just this way. Anti-Semitism is clearly
not the root of this treatment of the Williamson family (though there may be
a sectarian motivation for some of this behaviour, as we will see), but deep-
rooted suspicion and dislike – even ethno-religious bigotry – is at the heart
of the community's dislike of the travellers. Effie approaches Hamilton and
the other foresters at the beginning of Chapter 2. Her family's two 'creaky de-
crepit carts drawn by small shilpit horses' interrupt their day's work, and Angus the foreman sneers that she and the others are '[h]uman trash, and not so
human at that'.[34] The immediate dehumanisation of the family sets the tone
for the abuse they will suffer throughout the novel. 'Weeping hysterically' at
the thought of Hamilton and Effie's burgeoning romance, even the utterly respectable Miss Fiona calls Effie a 'tinker bitch', before screaming 'words that as
a minister's sister and a minister's daughter she out not to have known, far less
used.'[35]

Scott's treatment of travellers in his novel *Guy Mannering* (1815) is another
persuasive source for this tale, set by Jenkins in Scotland's romantic Highland
heartland. Deborah Epstein Nord argues that Scott's novel was 'the single most
important literary influence on the nineteenth-century fascination with Gypsies', that its heroine Meg Merrilies was 'one of Scott's most charismatic and
celebrated characters', and that this novel offered readers 'a version of the
history of the Gypsies that emphasises their deep and mystical presence in
the Scottish past.'[36] Jenkins draws on all of these ideas in his creation of the
heroine Effie Williamson and her traveller family. Unlike Scott's Rebecca, Effie
is not Jewish; it is probable that Jenkins bases the Williamsons on the family of Duncan Williamson, the traveller whom the folklorist and poet Hamish
Henderson interviewed, and whose family were steeped in traveller mythology, lore, and storytelling. However, like Rebecca and Scott's heroine Meg Merrilies, there are repeated references to Effie throughout *The Pearl Fishers* as

---

33   Walter Scott, *Ivanhoe* [1819] (Edinburgh: Archibald Constable and Co., 1820), p. 120.

34   Jenkins, *The Pearl Fishers*, p. 4.

35   Ibid., p. 163.

36   Deborah Epstein Nord, *Gypsies and the British Imagination, 1807–1930* (New York; Chiches-
      ter; West Sussex: Columbia University Press, 2006), p. 25.

'a member of an outcast tribe'.[37] Moreover, there is deep ambiguity over her religious belief in the text. Characters frequently speculate with a marked degree of suspicion on this subject. Mr Rutherford the jeweller 'had no idea what the religious beliefs of travellers or tinkers were', while Gavin Hamilton reminds himself that '[h]e should remember that these people, Effie among them, were pagans.'[38] However, Effie is no 'Protestant pagan' in the style of the author's own lowland Scots family. When Hamilton tells her that a pagan is 'a person of no religion', Effie replies 'I'm not a pagan. I have a religion. I'll tell you about it when I know you better.'[39]

It may be that Jenkins is simply keen to borrow a number of romantic tropes from Scott, including the names and attributes of female heroines. However, it is these heroines' cultural and specifically religious 'glamour' that Jenkins borrows most obviously from his romantic forebear. Rachel's Jewishness is contemplated often by Hamilton, and in its unfamiliarity, it contrasts excitingly with his own cradle Scottish Presbyterianism. Rachel seems 'more French than Scottish' in her expensive clothes and lipstick. When he first meets her, Hamilton thinks that she had 'such dark skin that he wondered if she was an Indian.' And when she speaks to him matter-of-factly about her lack of faith in the human race, Hamilton ruminates: 'These seemed strange things for a girl dressed so richly to be saying. Was it because she was Jewish?'[40]

Effie's cultural and religious difference is borrowed from Scott too (as we will see) but in her case it is the cultural markers of Catholicism which set her apart and intrigue Hamilton. There are a number of areas where Effie's conception as a Catholic (or at a least Catholic-sounding) heroine are instanced in *The Pearl Fishers* and in its early manuscript draft, *The Tinker Girl*. This handwritten manuscript differs in some significant details to the posthumously-published novel, and in fact the published novel omits some key features that explain the development of Hamilton and Effie's accelerated – some might argue absurdly rapid – relationship. In the manuscript, Jenkins sets out passages of dialogue between the two characters, which help to flesh out their mutual attraction. This is not the case in the published novel. Though they only meet at the beginning of Chapter 2, by the beginning of Chapter 3, Hamilton makes sure to pick Effie 'the most beautiful rose in the garden', his hands trembling with nervousness. Jenkins notes: '[i]t was much too simple to say that he had fallen in love with her', but nonetheless Effie has quickly cast a powerful spell

---

37   Jenkins, *The Pearl Fishers*, p. 136.

38   Ibid., p. 159, p. 92.

39   Ibid., p. 132.

40   Jenkins, *A Would-Be Saint*, p. 39.

on the dour, devout, Presbyterian Hamilton.[41] This may be due in part to her amped-up sexuality and femininity: there are several references in the novel to Effie's breasts and general attractiveness, as well as to her purity and virginity, an apparently winning combination which make her an enchanting prospect to Hamilton. But a large part of Effie's allure also has to do with her cultural difference. Notably, when Murray questions Jenkins on whether he had investigated Catholicism along with other Christian denominations in his boyhood, he says, 'I never tried the Catholics. No, I did not! Because the Catholics were a breed apart…'.[42]

Effie is of course short for Euphemia, the name of the third-century martyr. In *The Tinker Girl*, Effie's sister and mother – Morag and Nellie – are given the names Margaret and Agnes, both of them saints' names, which reflect the Catholic culture of Scots and Irish travelling families. Hamilton the Good Samaritan has found in Effie a pearl of great price, and a 'treasure' whose 'remarkable grace' is commented on so frequently that it becomes almost monotonous in the text. Like the man who sells everything he has for the pearl (or, Kingdom of Heaven) in the Gospel of Matthew, Hamilton is willing to open his home and adopt Effie's pearl-fishing family within days of meeting them, much against local, largely bigoted, opinion. This is a world away from 1930s industrial Auchengillan, as seen in *A Would-Be Saint*. With his Highland locus and his romantic heroine, Jenkins appears to find new opportunities to embed religious imagery and intertextual reference into *The Pearl Fishers*, and to delve deep into the resources of eighteenth and nineteenth-century romance.

The resource of romance by way of Scott is exploited even more powerfully in depictions of Effie as a kind of Highland 'noble savage'. When we first encounter Effie in *The Pearl Fishers* she is focalised through Hamilton's perspective, and his conflicting feelings of prejudice and desire are emphasised:

> With increasing astonishment he saw that she was very good-looking. No, that was too tame a word; beautiful was more like it, ridiculous though it seemed. Her eyes were an unusual shade of brown and, in spite of her tiredness, were eager and alert. He was reminded of a deer. She had the same grace, the same air of wildness, as if she was poised to flee, into the forest and up onto the tops of the hills. As brown as a Native American, she was wearing a necklace of blue stones and pinned to her jumper between her breasts was a single white wild rose.[43]

---

41 Jenkins, *The Pearl Fishers*, p. 18.
42 Murray, ed., *Scottish Writers Talking*, p. 105.
43 Jenkins, *The Pearl Fishers*, p. 6.

This description taps knowingly into nineteenth-century ideas of the primitive other; indeed the manuscript for *The Tinker Girl* emphasises race much more keenly than the later novel, noting that Effie's face 'was tanned as dark as a Red Indian's or Egyptian's' (and in this sense the focus on race makes her description similar to that of Rachel, who Hamilton initially thinks may be Indian).[44] Here and elsewhere, Effie is depicted in the same anthropological terms as the Highlander in Scott's work; she is viewed as the product of an older culture – one shrouded in folklore and mysticism – and is compared to other indigenous peoples.[45] The words 'savage' and 'primitive' are often used to describe Effie, even (ironically) by Effie herself as she determines to go to the local kirk, to show 'all the people in the church that a tinker girl was not the pitiful savage they were convinced she must be.'[46]

However, this description of Effie also draws very consciously on Scott's depiction of the Highland Jacobite Flora McIvor, the heroine of *Waverley* (1814). Like Flora, who wears the Jacobite white cockade, bilingual Effie wears the 'single white wild rose'.[47] Both heroines seduce their lowland admirers in the same way, by exploiting sublime landscape and placing themselves in the role of Celtic bard. Famously, Flora guides the naïve Waverley to a scenic spot and sings 'a Highland song', accompanied by a harp. '"To speak in the poetical language of my country"', Flora begins beguilingly, '"the seat of the Celtic Muse is in the mist of the secret and solitary hill, and her voice is in the murmur of the mountain stream. He who woos her must love the barren rock more than the fertile valley, and the solitude of the desert better than the festivity of the hall."'[48] This of course produces in the young English soldier Waverley a 'wild feeling of romantic delight', and Flora's 'few irregular strains introduced a prelude of a wild and peculiar tone, which, harmonised well with the distant waterfall, and the soft sigh of the evening breeze in the rustling leaves of an aspen which overhung the seat of the fair harpress.'[49] In this way, argues Jennifer Camden, 'Scott connects Flora to both the Jacobite and bardic traditions of the

44   Jenkins, *The Tinker Girl*, National Library of Scotland Acc. 12645, manuscript p. 2.
45   And as with the description of Effie above, that narrator of Scott's 'The Two Drovers' also taps into ideas of pre-Celtic deer cults when he notes that Robin Oig M'Combich is 'as light and alert as one of the deer of his mountains'. Walter Scott, 'The Two Drovers', in *The Oxford Book of Scottish Short Stories*, ed. by Douglas Dunn (Oxford: Oxford University Press, 1995), p. 32.
46   Jenkins, *The Tinker Girl*, National Library of Scotland Acc. 12645.
47   Jenkins, *The Pearl Fishers*, p. 6.
48   Walter Scott, *Waverley: Or, 'Tis Sixty Years Since, Volume 1* [1814] (Boston: Wells and Lilly, 1915), p. 192.
49   Ibid.

Scottish Highlands: sister of a chieftain and pupil of the last harpers and bards of the Highlands, Flora represents the last gasp of an independent Scottish identity.'[50] This is easily compared with the scene in Jenkins's *The Pearl Fishers* where Hamilton listens to Effie sing 'a lament, in Gaelic. He stood at the foot of the stairs, listening, moved to tears'.[51] The moment in *The Tinker Girl* where Hamilton approaches Effie, the beautiful young apprentice to her Grandfather's bardic traditions, is an even more pointed comparison. Effie stands in the evening twilight, stroking one of the horses which pull the family's carts:

> What he had previously seen as coarseness in her he now saw as wildness.
>   'Grandfather wants to speak to you,' she said.
>   He had forgotten grandfather. In any case, he would have nothing to say to a stupid old man who had tried to marry off his fifteen-year-old daughter to a drunkard of fifty. Was that why she had tried to drown herself?
>   'I think he wants you to listen to one of his poems.'
>   He wondered what kind of poet could a 75 year-old traveller be? A sort of Highland McGonigall?
>   'What are his poems about?'
>   'Lots of things. Mountains. Lochs. Camping sites. War. Love.'
>   'Love?'
>   'Why not love? Don't all poets write about love?'
>   'Are they all in Gaelic?'
>   'Of course'
>   'Have any of them ever been written down?'
>   'No, but men from universities have said they should be. I know lots of them by heart.'
>   'Recite one to me.'
>   Not to him, it seemed but to the horse. She spoke into its ear.
>   It sounded like a poem all right.
>   'Very sad,' he said. 'What's it about?'[52]

Effie is not only the image of Scott's Flora in this scene; she also echoes Wordsworth's 'solitary Highland Lass!' gazed at by a speaker who imagines that she

---

50   Jennifer Camden, *Secondary Heroines in Nineteenth-Century British and American Novels* (Surrey: Ashgate, 2010), p. 64.
51   Jenkins, *The Pearl Fishers*, p. 52.
52   Jenkins, *The Tinker Girl*, National Library of Scotland Acc. 12645, manuscript pp. 16–17.

'sings a melancholy strain'.[53] Hamilton's gaze and his subsequent foolishness are highlighted clearly in this passage; he is shown to be intellectually snobbish (contemptuously assuming the old Bard to be 'a Highland McGonigall') and ignorant of Gaelic culture – imagining it only as one of lament and loss, where in fact Effie explains later that she has sung him quite a happy song.

Hamilton is certainly less passive and swooning that the captivated Waverley in this poetic scene, but Effie's charms have begun to work on him, and undoubtedly his perception of her 'wildness' contributes to the rather dull Hamilton's burgeoning imagination. He even begins to regard her as something close to magical, when he asks later, '"Tell me, Effie, in traveller mythology, is there a story about a roe deer being turned into a beautiful girl?"'[54] There are hints throughout that Effie is something like the fairy women of Scottish Gaelic mythology, who turned themselves into red deer. It is not for nothing that for Rosemary Goring, The Pearl Fishers has a 'fairy-tale quality', and that '[t]here is something fable-like about Effie, too, so out of kilter with the rest of her family that she might almost be a creature from another element or world, a selkie, sprite, or the heroine of a Border Ballad rather than a twentieth-century novel.'[55]

Goring's identification of this fantastical, supernatural timbre in Jenkins's novel is significant. It is unthinkable that Effie would appear in one of Jenkins's novels set in industrial Lanarkshire. She is entirely moulded from myth and Scottish romance. Steeped in the oral song culture of Gaelic Scotland, with her dark eyes and hair, she could also quite easily be the passionate heroine of one of Scott's novels. In The Tinker Girl, Jenkins even provides Effie with a fair-haired doppelgänger typical of Scott's fictions.[56] But the strong influence of romance and the identification of a fantastical, supernatural element are

---

53   William Wordsworth, 'The Solitary Reaper', in The Complete Poetical Works of William Wordsworth ed. by Henry Reed (Philadelphia: J. Kay, Jun., and Brother / Boston: J. Munroe, 1837), p. 200.

54   Jenkins, The Pearl Fishers, p. 95.

55   Rosemary Goring, Introduction to The Pearl Fishers, p. vi.

56   Mary McGilp appears in a photograph shown to Effie by Mrs McTeague, a local woman who wishes to save Hamilton from what she assumes are Effie's clutches. Effie gazes at Mary: 'There she was, tall, fair-haired, beautifully dressed, an eminently suitable wife for Gavin. She could hardly have been a greater contrast to the tinker girl.' Mary is the blonde, 'eminently beautiful, and eminently prudent' foil to Effie, in the same way that gentile Rose Bradwardine is the foil to Jacobite Flora Mac-Ivor of Waverley. Jenkins, The Tinker Girl, National Library of Scotland Acc. 12645, manuscript p. 50. Alexander Welsh, The Hero of the Waverley Novels, With New Essays on Scott (Princeton, New Jersey: Princeton University Press, 1992), p. 49.

surely highly unusual elements for Jenkins to build into this text. Goring notes that Jenkins 'was not a fanciful novelist' and that 'For all his imaginative verve, his eye was firmly fixed on the moral universe than on any invisible faerie kingdom.'[57] Ultimately, Effie, like Gavin, is rather unknowable. In *A Would-Be Saint* Jenkins sews the seeds of romance, which come to full fruition in his later *The Pearl Fishers*. The novel ends with a strong hint that the besotted Hamilton and Effie will marry – providing her with the safety, security and love that she has always craved. Perhaps its debt to Scott and its far more overt mythological, fairy tale leanings are the cause of (what might have been) Jenkins's reticence to publish this novel in his lifetime. *The Pearl Fishers* is not the best of Jenkins's novels. Its plot seems a little flimsy in places – Goring recognises that 'it is a less sophisticated novel than many of his others' – and the almost fanatical preoccupation with detailing the beauty of Effie's body means that she is given very little in the way of a fully fleshed-out psychology.[58] While Gavin is 'lightly sketched' in the novel, Effie is, by the end, a beautiful, sensual emblem of romance with an alluring whiff of religious glamour. We are never given a window into Gavin's inner religious life, and Effie offers us only the most tiny, tantalising hint at her own.

There are, then, a number of conclusions to be drawn from the interaction between Jenkins's apparently unusual preoccupation with religion and romance in *A Would-Be Saint* and *The Pearl Fishers*. First of all, these two novels complicate the picture of Jenkins as a straightforward social realist. Jenkins may often be read as vastly different in outlook to his immediate 'Scottish Literary Renaissance' forerunners because of his oft-noted gritty realism, but as these novels show, this is not entirely the case. Jenkins's attraction to religious mystery, embedded parable, and biblical echo are often critically ignored in favour of focus on his quest for an ethical, secular way of life, but these two novels reveal that he still works with an existing stock of religious language and imagery – even if his narratives of religious belief are not wholly convincing. The connection between Scott and Jenkins has been discussed meagrely so far in critical studies of the latter author, but, clearly, the influence of Jenkins's Romantic precursor is not slight. Jenkins may have felt that *The Pearl Fishers* owed too much to Scott, and that it was perhaps even derivative, revealing too obviously the author's admiration for the Wizard of the North. It may be, too, that Jenkins felt that the relationship between Effie Williamson and Gavin Hamilton was not yet fully developed. He admits in his interview with Isobel Murray:

---

57   Rosemary Goring, Introduction to *The Pearl Fishers*, p. vi.
58   Ibid., p. xi.

I wasn't any good at describing love affairs. To hark back to *Guests of War*, the love affair between the hero and the girl is so perfunctorily done, my heart was never in it. [...] In fact my son-in-law, a diplomat, accused me of never being able to describe love in my books. He probably meant love with sexuality in it, thought I was too much of a Calvinist. I've often wondered if that is the case, because I don't see why I should be a Calvinist.[59]

But, as the love relationships (whether divine or secular) of *A Would-Be Saint* and *The Pearl Fishers* reveal, Jenkins's creative process is shaped and moulded by a Calvinistic imagination – one attracted to, and perhaps fearful of romance.

Works Cited

Camden, Jennifer, *Secondary Heroines in Nineteenth-Century British and American Novels* (Surrey: Ashgate, 2010).

Dunn, Douglas, ed., *The Oxford Book of Scottish Short Stories* (Oxford: Oxford University Press, 1995).

Hill, Jeffrey, *Sport and the Literary Imagination: Essays in History, Literature, and Sport* (Bern: Peter Lang, 2006).

Jenkins, Robin, *The Pearl Fishers* (Edinburgh: Polygon, 2007).

Jenkins, Robin, *So Gaily Sings the Lark* (Glasgow: MacLellan, 1951; repr. Bath: Cedric Chivers, 1971).

Jenkins, Robin, *The Tinker Girl*, undated manuscript and two typescripts, National Library of Scotland Acc. 12645.

Jenkins, Robin, *A Would-Be Saint* (London: Gollancz, 1978; repr. Edinburgh: B&W, 1994).

Morton, Brian, 'Goodness in a Fallen World: The Fate of Robin Jenkins', *Scottish Review of Books*, 1:3 (2005), 8–9.

Murray, Isobel, ed., 'Robin Jenkins', in *Scottish Writers Talking 3* (Edinburgh: John Donald, 2006), pp. 101–146.

Nord, Deborah Epstein, *Gypsies and the British Imagination, 1807–1930* (New York; Chichester; West Sussex: Columbia University Press, 2006).

Norquay, Glenda, 'Jenkins, (John) Robin (1912–2005)', *Oxford Dictionary of National Biography*, Oxford University Press, Jan 2009.

Nouryeh, Christopher, Review of *A Would-Be Saint*, *World Literature Today*, 55:2 (1981), 317.

Scott, Walter, *Ivanhoe* [1819] (Edinburgh: Archibald Constable and Co., 1820).

---

59   Murray, ed., *Scottish Writers Talking*, p. 140.

Scott, Walter, *Waverley: Or, 'Tis Sixty Years Since, Volume 1* [1814] (Boston: Wells and Lilly, 1915),

Watson, Roderick, *The Literature of Scotland: The Twentieth Century* (New York, N.Y.: Palgrave Macmillan, 2007).

Welsh, Alexander, *The Hero of the Waverley Novels, With New Essays on Scott* (Princeton, New Jersey: Princeton University Press, 1992).

Wordsworth, William, *The Complete Poetical Works of William Wordsworth* ed. by Henry Reed (Philadelphia: J. Kay, Jun., and Brother / Boston: J. Munroe, 1837).

Old Themes and Self-Reflection in Jenkins's Later Novels

Ingibjörg Ágústsdóttir

Abstract

Robin Jenkins considers and questions his own achievements and the role of the artist in the novels *Poverty Castle* (1991), *Willie Hogg* (1993), *Poor Angus* (2000) and *Childish Things* (2001). In *Leila* (1995) Jenkins reworks old themes and plot elements. This later text can partly be seen as a 'rewriting' of the earlier *A Figure of Fun* (1974). This essay details how Jenkins's writing becomes increasingly self-reflective during the last decade of his writing career. Some texts can be seen as partly autobiographical in the way they present characters' attributes and experiences that are comparable with elements of Jenkins's own life experience and opinions, as well as narrative details which refer directly to Jenkins himself and his circumstances. As a result, all the narratives in question arguably reflect Jenkins's need to re-examine and reflect back on his central fictional concerns, his literary achievement, and the role of the artist in Scotland.

Keywords

Robin Jenkins – old themes – self-reflection – rewritings – role of the artist – semi-autobiography – author achievement – metafiction

In her 1993 essay on the 'disruptive' element of Robin Jenkins's fiction, Glenda Norquay argues that his 'recent writing can be seen as both a continuation and a development of his previous work, but in both respects maintaining a disruptive character which is distinctively his own'.[1] Norquay's estimate is that the challenges in Jenkins's work, which operate as a force for disruption, 'emerge more sharply in the period since 1979' and that since then Jenkins has 'both built upon and diverged from his early works'.[2]

---

1   Glenda Norquay, 'Disruptions: The Later Fiction of Robin Jenkins', in *The Scottish Novel Since the Seventies: New Visions, Old Dreams*, ed. by Gavin Wallace and Randall Stevenson (Edinburgh: Edinburgh University Press, 1993), pp. 11–24 (p. 22).

2   Ibid., pp. 11–12.

Fergus Lamont (1979), one of Jenkins's finest novels, continues the ruthless social analysis that characterises much of his earlier fiction, emphasising the essentially fragmented nature of Scottish society and the great divergence between social classes in Scotland. Further, *Fergus Lamont* continues the novelist's interrogation of Calvinist morality. It is strongly focused on individual self-deception and self-justification, and on the confrontation of idealism and human self-interest. The novel therefore represents an obvious continuation of Jenkins's earlier concerns. Yet *Fergus Lamont* also diverges from the earlier fiction in terms of both narrative technique and narrative approach to these concerns. The first person narrative perspective means that our interpretation of events is entirely dependent upon Fergus's biased vision, so that we are forced to identify with a character we are often inclined to dislike. At the same time, Jenkins approaches Fergus and the novel's main issues with an even greater degree of irony and ambivalence than in his earlier work. Likewise *Poverty Castle* (1991), which, while typically Jenkinsian in its concern with moral binaries and social justice, also presents a significant break from Jenkins's former narrative methods by its implicitly metafictional nature and double frame of reference, rendered via its juxtaposition of the story of a dying novelist, who wants his last novel to be a 'celebration of goodness,' with the actual novel he is writing.[3]

While this combination of continuation and disruption is apparent in Jenkins's later Scottish narratives, the novels of this period, in particular from 1990 onwards, are also increasingly self-reflective on Jenkins's part. *Poverty Castle*, *Willie Hogg* (1993), *Poor Angus* (2000) and *Childish Things* (2001) can also be seen as partly autobiographical in the way they present characters' attributes and experiences that are comparable with elements of Jenkins's own life and opinions, as well as narrative details or descriptions which refer to Jenkins and his circumstances. Often Jenkins seems to be questioning his achievements and the role of the novelist/artist. At the same time, one text from this last period of Jenkins's writing, *Leila* (1995), very blatantly revisits and reworks old themes and plot elements, so much so that it becomes a rewriting of Jenkins's earlier novel *A Figure of Fun* (1974). These texts arguably reflect Jenkins's need to reconsider his central fictional concerns, his literary achievement, and the role of the artist in Scotland.

Poverty Castle, *Willie Hogg*, *Poor Angus* and *Childish Things* are in many ways dissimilar, set in different locations (Argyll, Glasgow/Arizona, Islay, Lunderston /California, respectively), and with different types of characters from mixed social backgrounds. Nevertheless, the four narratives continue Jenkins's exploration of the ambiguous nature of goodness and moral fallibility,

---

3   Robin Jenkins, *Poverty Castle* (Nairn: Balnain Books, 1991), p. 7.

the conjunction of social idealism and human self-interest, and the limits of self-knowledge, while the narrative developments of *Willie Hogg* highlight Jenkins's interest in religion and the elusive possibility of spiritual affirmation. That said, the four novels reveal how Jenkins's writing becomes increasingly self-reflective during the last decade of his career. The old novelist in *Poverty Castle*, the eponymous protagonists of *Willie Hogg* and *Poor Angus*, and the retired school-master Gregor McLeod in *Childish Things* can all be read as in some ways related to the author himself. The first is a novelist trying to write a novel that can celebrate goodness without irony, and yet be truthful about the world's morally degenerate state. In the second, Willie Hogg is an atheist searching for spiritual affirmation, whose grief for his wife is portrayed in a highly intimate manner. In *Poor Angus* an artist returns to Scotland from the Far East, determined to find artistic inspiration in his native land. *Childish Things* has Gregor McLeod as a formerly brilliant bursary-winning pupil from a Lanarkshire mining village whose mother was left on her own to support her children after her husband died during World War I, and who suffers guilt over the betrayal of his family and background. The novels' function and development arguably reflect Jenkins's need to re-examine and reflect his fictional (and personal?) concerns and achievements. In these novels, Jenkins also slips in narrative details or descriptions which slyly refer to himself and his life.

Poverty Castle appears at first to be the almost surreal story of an attractive family, the Sempills, who are creating their dream home ('Poverty Castle') in Argyll. What makes this novel surreal (and metafictional) is the fact that the cantankerous novelist (simply called Donald) is part of the narrative, along with his long suffering wife Jessie. Donald's attempt to celebrate goodness, and yet to be truthful regarding the morally degenerate state of the world, mirrors the yearning present throughout Jenkins's fiction for an attainable level of goodness that transcends human frailties. Donald's self-conscious quest for moral perfection in fiction correlates to the numerous characters in Jenkins's fiction who long to be an example of charity and selflessness in an otherwise selfish and corrupt world. The revelation that Donald's novel fails to portray morality in such straightforward, binary terms corresponds with Jenkins's overall presentation of human morality in his fiction, and with the fact that the apparently well-meaning idealism of Jenkins's protagonists usually proves fallible, limited, even false, and their charity devalued through their implicitly selfish motives.

Through the story of Donald and his novel, Jenkins comments on the nature of fiction-making and emphasises the problems of portraying reality through literature. For a long time, Donald has hoped to write a novel that will celebrate goodness, but without irony. In opposition to this goal is his angry awareness that the evils and injustices of the world have proliferated in the twentieth century:

> Fear of nuclear holocausts increased. Millions guzzled while millions starved. Everywhere truth was defiled, authority abused. Those shadows darkened every thinking person's mind: he could not escape them. They would make it hard for his novel to succeed.[4]

Donald's wife Jessie argues that the world's condition, combined with Donald's pessimistic vision of humanity, make his aim practically inconceivable. As the novel-within-a-novel progresses, the validity of Jessie's critical view becomes apparent. She notices how Donald has 'cheated' by making the Sempill family wealthy, and thus made things easy for them, and she perceives the name Poverty Castle as 'blatant irony'.[5] Importantly, Jessie's comments highlight the ambiguous quality of the Sempills' goodness, as well as demonstrating that Donald is unable to write a story without irony. His essentially reductive view of human morality prevents him. The meta-novel thus questions the ability of literature to do justice to the complexities and paradoxes of humanity.

This metafictional quality of *Poverty Castle* and the efforts of Donald the novelist have an obvious relevance to Jenkins himself. Norquay touches on this idea when suggesting that *Poverty Castle* 'may be read as a form of retrospective analysis of the writer's work,' and that it serves as an 'ironic comment' on Jenkins's own 'inability to settle for the comfortable and comforting.'[6] I would go further. There are obvious parallels between Jenkins himself and Donald the fictional novelist. Jenkins expressed a similar desire (and recognition of its unlikely fulfilment) in an interview with Norquay: 'I thought in my mellow old age I would write novels to reconcile myself to humanity; the sun shining, everyone laughing merrily, the gates of heaven opening, but, alas, no.'[7] The initial portrayal of the Sempills and their world corresponds with Jenkins's desire, and its failure. There are other obvious affinities between Jenkins and his fictitious writer: Jessie's comment that Donald has always been 'severe' on his characters echoes Jenkins's admission that he is 'severe' on his characters.[8] Like

---

4   Jenkins, *Poverty Castle*, p. 7.
5   Ibid., p. 54, p. 55.
6   Norquay, 'Disruptions,' p. 16, p. 12.
7   Robin Jenkins, interview, 'Moral Absolutism in the Novels of Robert Louis Stevenson, Robin Jenkins and Muriel Spark: Challenges to Realism,' by Glenda Norquay (unpublished doctoral thesis, University of Edinburgh, 1985), p. 448.
8   Jenkins, *Poverty Castle*, pp. 7–8. Jenkins, interview, 'Moral Absolutism,' by Norquay, p. 448.

Jenkins, Donald feels that 'because he had been born and brought up amongst them the Scots were the only people he felt competent to portray'.[9] Donald and Jenkins share the view that Scotland is 'The only country in history that, offered a modest degree of self-government, refused it'; and like Jenkins himself, Donald has written many novels but has not enjoyed wide recognition.[10] There are more trivial similarities: like Jenkins's own house, Donald's overlooks the Firth of Clyde and is situated not far from the Holy Loch; the name *Poverty Castle* is based on the old name of Jenkins's house, which used to be 'Poverty Hall' and even Harvey the white cat seems based on Jenkins's own domestic pet.[11] Douglas Gifford argues that there is 'a feel of something deeply personal' in Jenkins's portrayal of Donald.[12] *Poverty Castle* can be read as metafiction, but also as a highly idiosyncratic *Künstlerroman*.

There are likewise self-reflective references in *Willie Hogg*, published two years after *Poverty Castle*. The eponymous protagonist travels with his seemingly simple wife Maggie to Arizona to visit Maggie's dying sister. This journey marks a major change, as the formerly bewildered Maggie is transformed into a sensible and confident woman, thus forcing Willie to reassess her abilities, his feelings for her, and his own views on humanity and religion. As so often, *Willie Hogg* is haunted throughout by the elusive possibility of spiritual affirmation, and this echoes clearly the dichotomous nature of Jenkins's overall approach to religion and spirituality in his work. Further, able neither to accept nor repudiate God, Willie's confusion over the possibility of God and spirituality seems to agree with Jenkins's own ambivalent and paradoxical outlook on religion. Like Jenkins himself, Willie got married by declaration.[13] There is even the fact that Willie and Jenkins share *Riders of the Purple Sage* by Zane Gray as a favourite boyhood story.[14] More importantly, Jenkins experienced deep

---

9   Ibid., p. 9.

10   Ibid., p. 9.

11   See Robin Jenkins, interview, 'The Symbolism of Good and Evil: Studies in the Novels of Robin Jenkins', by Winifride Logan (unpublished dissertation, University of Glasgow, 1991), p. 44; and Jenkins, interview, 'Moral Absolutism,' by Glenda Norquay, p. 448. Jenkins says: 'Harvey, our white cat, is the most dignified creature under the sun, harms nothing except the odd fieldmouse'.

12   Douglas Gifford, 'Scottish Fiction: Old and New Masters,' *Books in Scotland*, 39 (Autumn 1991), 5–13 (p. 6).

13   Jenkins, *Willie Hogg*, p. 64. Details on Jenkins's own marriage by declaration can be seen in his poem 'Cardwell Bay 1937,' published in *Fallen Angels: Paintings by Jack Vettriano*, ed. by W. Gordon Smith (London: Pavilion, 1994), p. 92.

14   Jenkins, *Willie Hogg*, p. 70. Jenkins, interview, 'A Truthful Scot,' by Ágústsdóttir, p. 13. Gray's novel is one of Jenkins's own favourite boyhood stories.

personal loss at the death of his own wife, which is clearly reflected in his compassionate and entirely convincing portrayal of Willie's grief for Maggie. This, however, is typically never sentimental or melodramatic; Jenkins's sharp ironic wit counterbalances the tragedy.

There is another interesting twist to the narrative which emphasises its self-reflective quality. *Willie Hogg* is comparable to *Poverty Castle* in seemingly presenting a character that directly represents Jenkins himself. The character is minor, introduced through Willie as he tells his friends about the poem he is going to read at Maggie's graveside. This poem was written by a man whom Willie heard read in Paisley, and whom Willie describes as being recently widowed, old, and with white hair, a description that fits Jenkins himself in the years preceding the publication of *Willie Hogg*.[15] Moreover, the poem that is read by Willie at Maggie's funeral and in the novel's final scene, called 'What has she lost?', is part of the novel and therefore written by Jenkins himself, and accordingly it seems that Jenkins has slipped himself (the poet with the white hair) into his own plot, as being a character that has some influence on events.[16] In light of this, it seems likely that the poem was actually written by Jenkins after his own wife died. The poem thus adds to the self-reflective quality of the novel while also strengthening the comparison between Jenkins and Willie Hogg as united by their loss.

Although *Poor Angus* contains no such subtle insertion of the author himself into the narrative, there are details here that could be interpreted as partly autobiographical.[17] *Poor Angus* tells the story of Angus McAllister, a painter who has returned to Scotland from Basah in the Far East to find inspiration in his native Hebridean Island, Flodday.[18] He is befriended by Janet Maxwell, a woman with second sight who plans to use a potential romantic attachment with Angus as a means of revenge against her unfaithful husband. However, she is only the beginning of Angus's troubles, as two former mistresses from his years in Basah, Nell Ballantyne and Fidelia Gomez, suddenly appear at his

---

15   Jenkins, *Willie Hogg*, p. 157.

16   Ibid., p. 166.

17   A detailed analysis of the issues of art and identity in *Poor Angus* can be found here: Ingibjörg Ágústsdóttir, '"In my own country, where I most desire": Art and Identity in Robin Jenkins's *Poor Angus,' Latitude 63°North: Proceedings of the 8th International Region and Nation Literature Conference, Östersund, Sweden 2–6 August 2000*, ed. by David Bell (Östersund: Mid-Sweden University College, 2002), pp. 129–139.

18   *Basah* is clearly an anagram of *Sabah*, but Jenkins himself lived and taught in Sabah for several years. There is no island called Flodday in Scotland, but it is most likely based on Islay, as Jenkins mentioned Islay when discussing the plot of *Poor Angus* with me. See Jenkins, interview, 'A Truthful Scot,' by Ágústsdóttir, p. 18.

doorstep; subsequently the husbands of Janet, Nell and Fidelia also arrive on Flodday. The novel is a tragi-comedy, focusing on Angus's rejection of Fidelia and his failure to support her in her fight to keep her daughter from her powerful Manila racketeer husband Gomez. Reminiscent of the fate of Andrew McAndrick in 'Imelda and the Miserly Scot', the selfish Angus ultimately gets his comeuppance as Fidelia murders him with a primitive blowpipe he had kept as souvenir from his life in the Far East. *Poor Angus* is a cross-over between Jenkins's Scottish and foreign fiction; it is demonstrative of Jenkins's stated passion to write about his native country (emphasised in the prescript to the novel), while the foreign element is also of major importance. Both Angus's past life in Basah (provided through narrative flashbacks) and Fidelia's arrival constitute an exotic element that intrudes on the more homely Scottish setting and has a significant bearing on plot developments.

Angus's fate, as well as the fact that he is in many ways comparable to several other characters in Jenkins's fiction, such as Alastair Campbell in *A Figure of Fun*, Fergus Lamont, and Mungo Niven in *A Very Scotch Affair*, strongly echoes plot elements and character portrayal in some of Jenkins's earlier fiction. Angus shares many traits with figures such as Mungo, Fergus and Alastair. While idealistic, he is nevertheless full of vanity, arrogance and selfishness. He is a male chauvinist as well as being racially and socially prejudiced, and he does not have genuine compassion for others. Other characters also echo figures from Jenkins's other stories. For instance, both Nell and Fidelia are portrayed similarly to the former mistresses of the Scottish protagonists in *The Expatriates* and 'Imelda and the Miserly Scot'. Gifford remarks on this similarity between *Poor Angus* and Jenkins's other fiction, stating that it is 'as though Jenkins wants to make a parodic comedy of his various kinds of fiction, with tragedy sneaking in in absurd fashion to undercut all expectations'.[19] The difference, however, lies in the fact that Angus is an artist, and his outlook on art and artistic merit are important to Jenkins's presentation of human moral behaviour as well as in relation to his portrayal of Scotland and Scottish culture.[20] As with Lynedoch in *The Sardana Dancers*, Jenkins explores the role of the artist and his place inside and outside of Scotland through his portrayal of Angus. *Poor Angus* is however different from the earlier novel in showing a Scottish artist seeking inspiration in Scotland instead of somewhere else, reversing the

---

19   Douglas Gifford, 'Second sight of the first order', *The Scotsman* 10 June 2000, Section S2 Weekend, p. 9.

20   Only two other characters in Jenkins's fiction are artists: Lynedoch in *The Sardana Dancers* and the eponymous hero of *Fergus Lamont*.

earlier presentation of a Scottish artist seeking artistic shelter and inspiration abroad due to feeling that his native country is hostile to his art.

The prescript to the novel (Milton's 'In my own country where I most desire') is very appropriate to both Angus's situation and to Jenkins's own writing career.[21] Several aspects of Angus's life are comparable to Jenkins's own, which perhaps causes Manfred Malzahn to term Angus an 'author surrogate'.[22] We are told of Angus's return to Scotland as inspiration for his art, that while he has 'painted scenes more exotic than these', portraying the landscapes, flora and fauna of his native island is an expression of 'his love and loyalty, as well as the [...] longings of his soul'. Despite this, his fellow islanders dismiss his work as 'gaudy smudges' and him as 'an eccentric fraud', a fact Angus is sorry about though not surprised.[23] Angus's experience here reflects Jenkins's own, having returned after a period of years residing in far-away countries, during which he portrayed scenes 'more exotic' than those of Scotland in his fiction, and feeling that his fiction was under-estimated by the Scottish readership. Jenkins's approach to the islanders' dismissal of Angus and his art is clearly ironic, and while Flodday is here arguably presented as an ironic symbol of Scotland, it seems likely that Jenkins is comparing the lack of respect for Angus's art, on one hand, to the limited recognition of his own art as a Scottish writer, on the other. Such a reading conveys a subtle comment on how Jenkins may have seen his own career as an artist and his place as such within Scotland. The Scottish artist returned home feels let down by the lack of enthusiasm shown for his art in Scotland, but perseveres despite this in portraying his country in his own highly reductive and idiosyncratic manner. Angus is further comparable to Jenkins in having received some recognition from the critics, and this is described in terms easily applicable to Jenkins's writing: 'He had been mentioned in a *Herald* review as an interesting new painter. The boldness of his colours, "the influence of the tropics" particularly in his portraits of women, had been noticed'.[24] Finally, the fact that Angus and Jenkins share the experience of

---

21   From John Milton's 'Samson Agonistes', line 980. When Samson has been cast into prison in Gaza because of his wife's treachery, Dalila pays him a visit and pleads with her blind husband for forgiveness and reconciliation. Rejected by Samson, she leaves saying that she will become famous among the Philistines for delivering Samson to them: 'But in my countrey where I most desire, / In *Ecron, Gaza, Asdod* and in *Gath* / I shall be nam'd among the famousest / Of Women, sung at solemn festivals, / Living and dead recorded ...' (Milton, 'Samson Agonistes', ll. 980–984).

22   Manfred Malzahn, 'Where Extremes Meet in Midfield: The Aesthetics of Robin Jenkins', *Edinburgh Review*, 106 (Spring 2001), 39–46 (p. 44).

23   Robin Jenkins, *Poor Angus* (Edinburgh: Canongate, 2000), pp. 3–4.

24   Ibid., p. 4.

having worked as teachers in Sabah for a number of years provides a clear link between the author and his creation.

Childish Things continues this self-reflective fiction. There are too many obvious parallels between Jenkins himself and Gregor McLeod not to see this novel as being partly autobiographical. The summary of McLeod's early life given in the detective's report corresponds closely with Jenkins's own experience.[25] Like Jenkins, McLeod was born in a Lanarkshire mining village, and his father died of rheumatic fever shortly after returning from the Great War. McLeod's mother was left to support her children and, like Jenkins, McLeod was a brilliant student and won a bursary to a fee-paying Academy. There are numerous other details that are autobiographical, but the most striking is that McLeod's birthdate is that of Jenkins himself, 11 September 1912.[26] The novel is dedicated to the memory of Jenkins's mother. Arguably, Jenkins is himself a quintessential pilgrim of conscience, whose philosophy on the elusive nature of self-knowledge, the fallibility of humanity, and moral ambiguity is derived from the keen interrogation of his own morality. Jenkins's comment that 'Novelists who seek to study the virtues and vices of humanity find them all most readily in themselves' accords with the view of Bernard Sellin;

> ...if you consider the entire work there is such consistency that one can detect the author's involvement in most of his books in one form or another, as if Jenkins' moral questioning also applied to himself. It is undeniable that many of the tensions found in the books originate in the author's own doubts or rather honesty.[27]

Childish Things can be read as the culmination of such authorial honesty, an uncompromising self-analysis which simultaneously extends to the universal nature of human morality.

Jenkins's one explicitly 'foreign' narrative published during this period, *Leila* (1995), clearly reworks old themes and plot elements, even representing a rewriting, of one of Jenkins's earlier 'foreign' novels, *A Figure of Fun*, published in 1974. Twenty-one years after the publication of *A Figure of Fun*, Jenkins produced *Leila*, a novel that is set in Savu (Brunei) and, like *Dust on the Paw*, *The*

---

25   Robin Jenkins, *Childish Things* (Edinburgh: Canongate, 2001), pp. 242–247.

26   Ibid., p. 243.

27   Robin Jenkins, 'The writer on writing,' in *The Cone-Gatherers*, by Robin Jenkins (Harlow: Longman, 1991), p. viii. Bernard Sellin, 'Commitment and Betrayal: Robin Jenkins' *A Very Scotch Affair*', in *Studies in Scottish Fiction: 1945 to the Present*, ed. by Susanne Hagemann (Frankfurt am Main: Peter Lang, 1996), pp. 97–108 (p. 99).

Holy Tree, and *A Figure of Fun*, centres on the workings of idealism and morality in a world of cultural difference, racial prejudice, inter-racial relationships, and political revolution. Compared to *A Figure of Fun*, *Leila* attracted some critical attention.[28] With the exception of Douglas Gifford, however, critics failed to see how heavily it draws on the earlier novel. Both novels are set in a former British colony, Brunei, and both are concerned with the limits of idealism, racial and cultural difference, and local politics.[29] Like Alistair Campbell in *A Figure of Fun*, the protagonist of *Leila*, Andrew Sandilands, is Scottish and works in the field of education (as a teacher and vice principal).[30] While Campbell hopes to be appointed as Minister of Education, Sandilands is also expecting a promotion, to become Principal at the Training College where he works. Like Campbell, Sandilands plays golf with the Sultan, despotic ruler of Savu, and is similarly presented as aloof, prudish, awkward, and dour, though liked and respected by his compatriots, especially for his skills at golf and sailing. Sandilands is a complicated and paradoxical character. Like Campbell, he is idealistic but beset by self-interrogation, painfully aware of his own inadequacy, opposed to racism yet inherently prejudiced towards colour, unimaginative and ordinary yet longing to transcend the conventional and comfortable limits of his existence. Further, both Campbell and Sandilands face a challenge and a choice, encapsulated in their relationships with two very different women. A nurse like Fiona Kemp of *A Figure of Fun*, Jean Hislop is practical, efficient, robust, and sexy, her crassness and vulgarity hiding her essential sensitivity and her genuine love for Sandilands. By contrast, the half Scottish, half Malaysian Leila Azaharri, like Anna Imrie of the earlier novel, is unconventional, remote, fiercely idealistic, courageous, committed, and devotes her profession

---

28   See: Paul Binding, 'A Calvinist out east', review of *Leila*, by Robin Jenkins, *Times Literary Supplement* 1 March 1996, p. 25; Suhayl Saadi, 'Infinite Diversity in New Scottish Writing', *The Association for Scottish Literary Studies* (23 August 2010), <http://www.arts.gla.ac.uk/scotlit/asls/SSaadi.html> [accessed 26 August 2014]; Gifford, 'Spring Fiction: Dreams of Love and Justice,' *Books in Scotland*, 57 (Spring 1996), 8–15 (p. 13); Carl MacDougall, 'Condemned to be an outsider,' review of *Leila*, by Robin Jenkins, *The Herald*, 3 February 1996, p. 14; Isobel Murray, review of *Leila*, by Robin Jenkins, *Scottish Literary Journal*, Supplement 45 (Winter 1996), 58–60 (p. 60).

29   Gifford, 'Spring Fiction.' (see note 27 above).

30   A character named Andrew Sandilands is also the central figure in an unpublished novel by Jenkins, called *A Prayer Before Killing*, the manuscript of which passed to the National Library of Scotland after Jenkins's death. This novel also has a foreign setting. It revolves around conflict in which Sandilands has to fight the Japanese and kill people in a brutal manner. Like in *Leila*, there is also a local woman with whom Sandilands is involved, but who dies tragically.

as a lawyer to championing the poor and victimised. In choosing between the two women, Sandilands faces a similar choice to that of Campbell: marriage to the Scottish nurse means predictable safety and comfort as well as conventionality, mediocrity and compromise; marrying Leila means stepping into dangerous waters and beyond his limitations, as well as being a defiance of prejudice, and a challenge to his moral inadequacy. Finally, as in *A Figure of Fun*, the narrative focus of *Leila* stays mostly with the protagonist throughout, until the final passages when narrative access is transferred onto the Scottish nurse, through whose perspective the remainder of the story is presented.

Has Jenkins simply rewritten *A Figure of Fun* through choosing to 'go back' to the 'same essential divisions of loyalty' that Gifford describes?[31] There are some differences; the novels differ in their resolutions, while the political focus of *Leila*, its democratic elections and the subsequent uprising, are based on real events in Brunei history.[32] In *Leila*, Jenkins's critique of British policy in the East becomes stronger, since in *Leila*, the survival of a traditional, autocratic government is necessary for the continuation of the British presence in Savu, thus determining British reaction to the protests of Leila's democratic party. As Jenkins has suggested, the double standards of the British, champions of democracy and freedom of speech, were made evident: 'As a British officer confessed to me we were on the wrong side in that nasty little war: British soldiers, Scottish soldiers, sent to crush by force an elected democracy. It was kept well hidden from the British people.'[33] Jenkins's exposure of the imperial legacy emerges more clearly and more effectively than in the earlier novel.

In terms of fictional characters, Andrew Sandilands differs from that of Campbell. Whereas in *A Figure of Fun*, Campbell shirks away from the challenge represented by Anna Imrie, Sandilands brushes aside all his reservations, even his own colour prejudice, and marries Leila (although a part of his reason seems to be his sudden need to gain the love and trust of Leila's daughter, Christina). From the outset of their relationship, however, 'there is a feeling of impending doom', as MacDougall comments, and the tragic death of Christina

---

31   Gifford, 'Spring Fiction,' p. 12.

32   Jenkins has commented that the events of *Leila* are based on a revolution in Brunei (see Eleanor Morton, 'Easily led by his creations', *The Herald,* 12 February 1999, p. 24). This refers to the armed uprising of Brunei in December 1962, and which also forms the background to the events of *The Holy Tree*. The name of Leila's party (The People's Party) echoes the name of PRB (Brunei People's Party), and, exactly like Leila's party, the PRB had won an overwhelming victory (all seats except one) in the elections to the Legislative Council in 1962. Even Leila's surname, Azaharri, is the same as that of PRB's leader, Sheikh Ahmad M. Azahari.

33   Robin Jenkins, letter to Ingibjörg Ágústsdóttir, 14 December 2000.

then sets the tone for subsequent turn of events.[34] As Murray suggests, Sandilands and Leila are 'strikingly mismatched'.[35] While Leila has courage, genuine compassion for the poor, and a 'passion for justice,' Sandilands is 'conventional and cautious' and his sympathy for the poor has always been 'theoretical and distant.'[36] He is not interested in politics, whereas Leila is fiercely, even fanatically, committed to her party's fight for democracy. She eventually rejects her husband in favour of martyrdom. And even though he outwardly condemns colour prejudice, Sandilands suffers from it because of his upbringing by a 'bigoted, embittered, vindictive, and unloving' mother.[37] As a result, his love for Leila, though genuine, is laced with shame; he sees Leila's beauty as 'tainted', and finds that 'deep within him aversion lurked', as he thinks of her colour.[38] And yet, although Sandilands and Leila are not well suited and their relationship ends tragically, Sandilands' marriage to Leila represents a break from convention that Campbell is incapable of; after all, Campbell would never have considered marrying a woman of colour. More importantly, after overcoming his initial reservations about adopting the daughter of one of Leila's clients, a native woman charged with murder, the persistent determination of Sandilands to keep the girl indicates that he is finally able to overcome his weaknesses. Thus, even if his marriage to Leila has suffered because of his timorousness and inadequacy, his refusal to abandon the plan of taking little Mary to Scotland ultimately manifests his integrity and dedication. As suggested by Binding, therefore, Sandilands' love for both Christina and Mary constitutes his ultimate moral transcendence:

> In many ways an unsatisfactory man, Andrew Sandilands, by his love for his stepdaughter (who dies young) and for his adopted daughter from Savu's slums, gives meaning – and a kind of redemption – to ugly times in an ugly world.[39]

Both men are weak; but unlike Campbell in *A Figure of Fun*, who is not fond of native children, Jenkins shows Sandilands as genuinely attached to both Christina and Mary. Jenkins now suggests through Sandilands that it is indeed possible to overcome the limitations imposed on us by our nature and environment.

---

34 MacDougall, 'Condemned to be an outsider,' p. 14.

35 Murray, rev. of *Leila*, p. 59.

36 Robin Jenkins, *Leila* (Edinburgh: Polygon, 1995), p. 48, p. 14, p. 58.

37 Ibid., p. 98.

38 Ibid., p. 11, p. 46.

39 Binding, 'Calvinist out east,' p. 25.

As often in Jenkins's fiction, children are a new beginning in the protagonist's life.

The four novels *Poverty Castle*, *Willie Hogg*, *Poor Angus*, and *Childish Things* all include elements that refer to Jenkins himself, his life experiences, opinions and his own writing of fiction. The central characters are all somehow comparable to Jenkins, and we see subtle details and descriptions that are implicitly self-revealing on his part. This arguably reflects Jenkins's need to re-examine and reflect back on the central concerns of his work, his own achievement as a writer, and his role as a Scottish artist. Thus there is a movement towards the metafictional, especially in *Poverty Castle*. Another type of self-reflective movement manifests in the way Jenkins reworks the earlier *A Figure of Fun* in his last novel set abroad, *Leila*. Here Jenkins's approach proves in some ways bolder than before: he is more directly critical of British policy in the East, and his portrayal of Andrew Sandilands suggests that it is possible, though not easy, to overcome the limitations imposed by human nature and environment.

Works Cited

Ágústsdóttir, Ingibjörg, "'In my own country, where I most desire": Art and Identity in Robin Jenkins's *Poor Angus*,' in *Latitude 63°North: Proceedings of the 8th International Region and Nation Literature Conference, Östersund, Sweden 2–6 August 2000*, ed. by David Bell (Östersund: Mid-Sweden University College, 2002), pp. 129–139.

Ágústsdóttir, Ingibjörg, 'A Truthful Scot,' *In Scotland*, 1 (Autumn 1999), pp. 13–22.

Binding, Paul, 'A Calvinist out east,' review of *Leila*, by Robin Jenkins, *Times Literary Supplement*, 1 March 1996, p. 25.

Gifford, Douglas, 'Scottish Fiction: Old and New Masters,' *Books in Scotland*, 39 (Autumn 1991), pp. 5–13.

Gifford, Douglas, 'Second sight of the first order,' *The Scotsman*, 10 June 2000, Section S2 Weekend, p. 9.

Gifford, Douglas, 'Spring Fiction: Dreams of Love and Justice,' *Books in Scotland*, 57 (Spring 1996), pp. 8–15.

Jenkins, Robin, 'Cardwell Bay 1937,' in *Fallen Angels: Paintings by Jack Vettriano*, ed. by W. Gordon Smith (London: Pavilion, 1994), p. 92.

Jenkins, Robin, *Childish Things* (Edinburgh: Canongate, 2001).

Jenkins, Robin, *Leila* (Edinburgh: Polygon, 1995).

Jenkins, Robin, letter to Ingibjörg Ágústsdóttir, 14 December 2000.

Jenkins, Robin, 'Novelist in Scotland,' *Saltire Review*, 5 (1955), pp. 7–10.

Jenkins, Robin, *Poor Angus* (Edinburgh: Canongate, 2000).

Jenkins, Robin, *Poverty Castle* (Nairn: Balnain Books, 1991).

Jenkins, Robin, *Willie Hogg* (Edinburgh: Polygon, 1996).

Jenkins, Robin, 'Why I decided Scotland must be seen through fresh and truthful eyes,' *Glasgow Herald*, 12 October 1982, p. 11.

Jenkins, Robin, 'The writer on writing,' in *The Cone-Gatherers*, by Robin Jenkins (Harlow: Longman, 1991), pp. v–viii.

Logan, Winifride, interview with Robin Jenkins, 'The Symbolism of Good and Evil: Studies in the Novels of Robin Jenkins,' by Winifride Logan (unpublished dissertation, University of Glasgow, 1991), pp. 42–48.

MacDougall, Carl, 'Condemned to be an outsider,' review of *Leila*, by Robin Jenkins, *The Herald*, 3 February 1996, p. 14.

Malzahn, Manfred, 'Where Extremes Meet in Midfield: The Aesthetics of Robin Jenkins,' *Edinburgh Review*, 106 (Spring 2001), 39–46.

Morton, Eleanor, 'Easily led by his creations,' *The Herald*, 12 February 1999, p. 24.

Murray, Isobel, review of *Leila*, by Robin Jenkins, *Scottish Literary Journal*, Supplement 45 (Winter 1996), pp. 58–60.

Norquay, Glenda, 'Disruptions: The Later Fiction of Robin Jenkins,' in *The Scottish Novel Since the Seventies: New Visions, Old Dreams*, ed. by Gavin Wallace and Randall Stevenson (Edinburgh: Edinburgh University Press, 1993), pp. 11–24.

Norquay, Glenda, interview with Robin Jenkins, 'Moral Absolutism in the Novels of Robert Louis Stevenson, Robin Jenkins and Muriel Spark: Challenges to Realism,' (unpublished doctoral thesis, University of Edinburgh, 1985), pp. 436–451.

Saadi, Suhayl, 'Infinite Diversity in New Scottish Writing', *The Association for Scottish Literary Studies* (23 August 2010), <http://www.arts.gla.ac.uk/scotlit/asls/SSaadi.html> [accessed 26 August 2014].

Sellin, Bernard, 'Commitment and Betrayal: Robin Jenkins' *A Very Scotch Affair*,' in *Studies in Scottish Fiction: 1945 to the Present*, ed. by Susan Hagemann (Frankfurt am Main: Peter Lang, 1996), pp. 97–108.

Robin Jenkins: Further Reading

Stewart Sanderson

Jenkins's Fiction and Poetry

So Gaily Sings the Lark (Glasgow: Maclellan, 1950; Bath: Cedric Chivers, 1971).

Happy for the Child (London: J. Lehmann, 1953; Nairn: Balnain Books, 1992).

The Thistle and the Grail (London: Macdonald & Co., 1954, 1984; Edinburgh, Polygon, 1994).

The Cone Gatherers (London: Macdonald & Co., 1955; Edinburgh: Canongate, 2012).

Guests of War (London: Macdonald & Co., 1956; Edinburgh: Scottish Academic Press with The Association for Scottish Literary Studies, 1988).

The Missionaries (London: Macdonald & Co., 1957; Edinburgh: Birlinn, Polygon 2005).

The Changeling (London: Macdonald & Co., 1958; Edinburgh: Canongate, 1989, 1995, 1997, 2000, 2002, 2008).

Love is a Fervent Fire (London: Macdonald & Co., 1959; Edinburgh: Birlinn, Polygon, 2005).

Some Kind of Grace (London: Macdonald & Co., 1960; Edinburgh: Birlinn, Polygon, 2004).

Dust on the Paw (London: Macdonald & Co., 1961; New York: Putnam, 1961; Glasgow: Richard Drew, 1986).

The Tiger of Gold (London: Macdonald & Co., 1962).

A Love of Innocence (London: Jonathan Cape, 1963; Edinburgh: B&W Publishing, 1994).

The Sardana Dancers (London: Jonathan Cape, 1964; Edinburgh: Birlinn, Polygon, 2006).

A Very Scotch Affair (London: Gollancz, 1968; Edinburgh: Birlinn, Polygon, 2005).

The Holy Tree (London: Gollancz, 1969).

The Expatriates (London: Gollancz, 1971).

A Toast to the Lord (London: Gollancz, 1972).

A Far Cry from Bowmore and Other Stories (London: Gollancz, 1973).

A Figure of Fun (London: Gollancz, 1974).

A Would Be Saint (London: Gollancz, 1978; New York: Taplinger, 1980; Edinburgh: B&W Publishing, 1994).

Fergus Lamont (Edinburgh: Canongate, 1979, 1997; New York: Taplinger, 1979).

The Awakening of George Darroch (Edinburgh: Paul Harris, 1985; Edinburgh: B&W Publishing, 1995).

Just Duffy (Edinburgh: Canongate, 1988, 1995).

Poverty Castle (Nairn: Balnain Books, 1991; Edinburgh: Birlinn, Polygon, 2007).

Willie Hogg: a novel (Edinburgh: Birlinn, Polygon, 1993).

Leila (Edinburgh: Birlinn, Polygon, 1995, 2007).
Lunderston Tales (Edinburgh: Birlinn, Polygon, 1996).
Matthew and Sheila (Edinburgh: Birlinn, Polygon, 1998).
Poor Angus (Edinburgh: Canongate, 2000).
Childish Things (Edinburgh: Canongate, 2001).
Lady Magdalen (Edinburgh: Canongate, 2007).
The Pearl Fishers (Edinburgh: Birlinn, Polygon, 2007).

Poems

'Homemaker', *Chapman* 71 (Winter 1992–1993), 72.
'Tavira', *Chapman* 71 (Winter 1992–1993), 72–73.
'Waiting', *Chapman* 71 (Winter 1992–1993), 73–74.
'Desolation', *Chapman* 71 (Winter 1992–1993), 74.
'Next Morning', *Chapman* 71 (Winter 1992–1993), 74–75.
'Cardwell Bay 1937', in *Fallen Angels: Paintings by Jack Vettriano*, ed. by W. Gordon Smith
(London: Pavilion Books, 1994), p. 92.

Jenkins's Essays, Journalism, Interviews

Ágústsdóttir, Ingibjörg, 'A Truthful Scot: Inga Ágústsdóttir talks to Robin Jenkins',
In Scotland 1 (Autumn 1999), 13–22.
Jenkins, Robin, 'Novelist in Scotland', *Saltire Review* 5 (1955), pp. 7–10.
Jenkins, Robin, 'Why I decided Scotland must be seen through fresh and truthful eyes',
Glasgow Herald, 12 October 1982, p. 11.
Murray, Isobel, 'Robin Jenkins', in *Scottish Writers Talking 3* (Edinburgh: John Donald,
2006), pp. 101–146.

Selected Literary Criticism of Robin Jenkins

Ágústsdóttir, Ingibjörg, 'Chaos and Dissolution: Deconstruction and Scotland in the
Later Fiction of Robin Jenkins', *Revista Canaria de Estudios Ingleses*, 41 (2000),
103–116.
Ágústsdóttir, Ingibjörg, 'The Forgotten Novels of Robin Jenkins: A Thematic Survey',
Edinburgh Review, 106 (Spring 2001), 23–32.
Ágústsdóttir, Ingibjörg, 'Full Circle: The Function of Place in the Fiction of Robin Jen-
kins', in Susanne Hagemann, ed., *Terranglian Territories: Proceedings of the Seventh
International Conference on the Literature of Region and Nation* (Frankfurt am Main:
Peter Lang, 2000), pp. 179–186.

Ágústsdóttir, Ingibjörg, '"In my own country, where I most desire": Art and Identity in Robin Jenkins's *Poor Angus*,' in *Latitude 63°North: Proceedings of the 8th International Region and Nation Literature Conference, Östersund, Sweden 2–6 August 2000*, ed. by David Bell (Östersund: Mid-Sweden University College, 2002), pp. 129–139.

Binding, Paul, 'Ambivalent Patriot: The Fiction of Robin Jenkins', *New Edinburgh Review*, 53 (1981), 20–22.

Binding, Paul, 'A Calvinist out east,' review of *Leila*, by Robin Jenkins, *Times Literary Supplement*, 1 March 1996, p. 25.

Burgess, Moira, 'Robin Jenkins: A Novelist of Scotland', *Library Review*, 22 (1970), 409–412.

Craig, Cairns, 'Introduction' to *The Thistle and the Grail* (Edinburgh, Paul Harris, 1983), pp. 1–5.

Craig, Cairns, 'Robin Jenkins – A Would-Be Realist?', *Edinburgh Review*, 106 (2001), 12–22.

Gardiner, Michael, Graham Macdonald and Niall O'Gallagher, eds., *Scottish literature and postcolonial literature: comparative texts and critical perspectives* (Edinburgh: Edinburgh University Press, 2011).

Giammetti, Paul, 'Introduction' to *The Cone Gatherers* (Edinburgh: Canongate, 2012), pp. i–x.

Gifford, Douglas, 'Breaking Boundaries: From Modern to Contemporary in Scottish Fiction', in Brown, I., Clancy, T., Manning, S. and Pittock, M., eds., *The Edinburgh History of Scottish Literature: Modern Transformations: New Identities (from 1918)* (Edinburgh, Edinburgh University Press, 2006), pp. 237–253.

Gifford, Douglas, '"God's Colossal Irony": Robin Jenkins and *Guests of War*', *Cencrastus* 24 (1986), pp. 13–17.

Gifford, Douglas, 'Imagining Scotlands: The Return to Mythology in Scottish Fiction', in *Studies in Scottish Fiction: 1945 to the Present*, ed. by Susanne Hagemann (Frankfurt am Main: Peter Lang, 1996), pp. 17–49.

Hart, Francis Russell, 'Novelists of Survival: Linklater and Jenkins', in *The Scottish Novel: From Smollett to Spark* (Cambridge, Mass.: Harvard University Press, 1978), pp. 246–287.

Mackay, Marina, 'Rewriting and the Politics of Inheritance in Robin Jenkins and Jean Rhys', in Michael Gardiner, Graham Macdonald and Niall O'Gallagher, eds., *Scottish literature and postcolonial literature: comparative texts and critical perspectives* (Edinburgh: Edinburgh University Press, 2011), pp. 158–169.

Malzahn, Manfred, *Aspects of Identity: The Contemporary Scottish Novel (1978–1981) as National Self-Expression* (Frankfurt am Main: Peter Lang, 1984).

Malzahn, Manfred, 'Where Extremes Meet in Midfield: The Aesthetics of Robin Jenkins', *Edinburgh Review* 106 (Spring 2001), 39–46.

Marr, Andrew, 'Afterword' to *The Changeling* (Edinburgh: Canongate, 2008), pp. 225–232.

McCulloch, Margery Palmer, 'Introduction' to *Just Duffy* (Edinburgh: Canongate, 1995), pp. v–xi.

McCulloch, Margery Palmer, 'What Crisis in Scottish Fiction? Creative Courage and Continuity in Novels by Friel, Jenkins and Kelman', *Cencrastus* 48 (Summer 1994), pp. 15–18.

McCulloch, Margery Palmer, 'Hogg's *Justified Sinner* and Robin Jenkins's *Just Duffy*' in *Studies in Hogg and His World* 6 (1995), 12–21.

Miller, Gavin, 'Sympathy as Cognitive Impairment in Robin Jenkins's *The Cone-Gatherers*: The Limits of Homo Sacer', *Journal of Literary Disability*, 2:1 (2008), 22–31.

Milton, Colin, review of '*Just Duffy*, by Robin Jenkins', *Scottish Literary Journal Supplement* 29 (Winter 1988), 27–29.

Morgan, Edwin, 'The Novels of Robin Jenkins', in *Essays* (Cheadle: Carcanet Press, 1974), pp. 242–245.

Morton, Brian, 'Goodness in a Fallen World: The Fate of Robin Jenkins', *Scottish Review of Books*, 1:3 (2005), 8–9.

Murray, Isobel, 'Introduction' to *Guests of War* (Edinburgh: Scottish Academic Press with Association for Scottish Literary Studies, 1988), pp. vii–xxii.

Murray, Isobel, '"Not So Simple Annals of the Poor": Robin Jenkins's Early Fiction', *Ideas and Production*, IX & X (1989), pp. 70–84.

Murray, Isobel, 'One Toe in Eden Still: Robin Jenkins's Fiction', *Scottish Review* 38 (1985), 88–95.

Murray, Isobel, 'Robin Jenkins' Fiction', *Laverock* (1996), pp. 33–36.

Murray, Isobel and Bob Tait, 'Fergus Lamont', in *Ten Modern Scottish Novels* (Aberdeen: Aberdeen University Press, 1984), pp. 194–218.

Norquay, Glenda, 'Against Compromise: The Fiction of Robin Jenkins', *Cencrastus* 24 (1986), pp. 3–6.

Norquay, Glenda, 'Disruptions: The Later Fiction of Robin Jenkins', in *The Scottish Novel Since the Seventies*, ed. by Gavin Wallace and Randall Stevenson (Edinburgh: Edinburgh University Press, 1994), pp. 11–24.

Norquay, Glenda, 'Four Novelists of the 1950s and 1960s', in *The History of Scottish Literature, Volume 4: Twentieth Century*, ed. by Cairns Craig (Aberdeen: Aberdeen University Press, 1988), pp. 259–275.

Norquay, Glenda, 'Moral Absolutism in the Novels of Robert Louis Stevenson, Robin Jenkins and Moral Spark' (PhD thesis, University of Edinburgh, 1985).

Norquay, Glenda, 'Robin Jenkins', *British Novelists Since 1960*, in *Dictionary of Literary Biography* XIV, ed. by Jay L. Halio (Detroit: Gale Research, 1983), pp. 433–438.

Prillinger, Horst, *Family and the Scottish Working Class Novel 1984–1994: A study of novels by Janice Galloway, Alasdair Gray, Robin Jenkins, James Kelman, A.L. Kennedy,*

William McIlvanney, Agnes Owens, Alan Spence, and George Friel (Frankfurt am Main: Peter Lang, 2000).

Sellin, Bernard, 'Commitment and Betrayal: Robin Jenkins' *A Very Scotch Affair*', in *Studies in Scottish Fiction*, ed. by Susanne Hagemann (Frankfurt am Main: Peter Lang, 1996), pp. 97–108.

Sellin, Bernard, 'Robin Jenkins: The Making of the Novelist', *Cencrastus* 24 (1986), pp. 7–9.

Sellin, Bernard, 'Varieties of Voice and Changing Contexts: Robin Jenkins and Janice Galloway', in Brown, I., Clancy, T., Manning, S. and Pittock, M., eds., *The Edinburgh History of Scottish Literature: Modern Transformations: New Identities (from 1918)* (Edinburgh, Edinburgh University Press, 2006), pp. 231–236.

Smith, Iain Crichton, 'Introduction' to *The Cone Gatherers* (Edinburgh, Paul Harris, 1980), pp. 1–5.

Smith, Iain Crichton, *Robin Jenkins: The Cone-Gatherers* (Scotnote) (Aberdeen: The Association for Scottish Literary Studies, 1995).

Spence, Alan, 'Introduction' to *The Changeling* (Edinburgh, Canongate Classics, 1989), pp. v–xii.

Tait, Bob, 'Introduction' to *Fergus Lamont* (Edinburgh: Canongate, 1997), pp. v–ix.

Thompson, Alistair R, 'Faith and Love: An Examination of Some Themes in the Novels of Robin Jenkins', *New Saltire* 3 (1963), pp. 57–64.

General Secondary Material

Bold, Alan, *Modern Scottish Literature* (New York: Longman, 1983).

Brown, Ian and Alan Riach, eds., *The Edinburgh Companion to Twentieth-Century Scottish Literature* (Edinburgh: Edinburgh University Press, 2009).

Burgess, Moira, *The Glasgow Novel* (Glasgow: The Scottish Library Association, Glasgow City Council, The Mitchell Library, 1999).

Burgess, Moira, *Imagine a City: Glasgow in Fiction* (Glendaruel: Argyll Publishing, 1997).

Carruthers, Gerard, *Scottish Literature* (Edinburgh: Edinburgh University Press, 2009).

Carruthers, Gerard, David Goldie and Alastair Renfrew, eds., *Beyond Scotland: New Contexts for Twentieth-Century Scottish Literature* (Amsterdam and New York: Rodopi, 2004).

Carruthers, Gerard, and Liam McIlvanney, eds., *The Cambridge Companion to Scottish Literature* (Cambridge: Cambridge University Press, 2012).

Craig, Cairns, *The History of Scottish Literature: Twentieth Century*, IV (Aberdeen: Aberdeen University Press, 1988).

Craig, Cairns, *The Modern Scottish Novel: Narrative and the National Imagination* (Edinburgh, Edinburgh University Press, 1999).

Craig, Cairns, *Out of History: Narrative Paradigms in Scottish and English Culture* (Edinburgh: Polygon, 1996).

Crawford, Robert, *Scotland's Books: The Penguin History of Scottish Literature* (London: Penguin, 2007).

Gifford, Douglas, Sarah Dunnigan and Alan MacGillivray, *Scottish Literature in English and Scots* (Edinburgh, Edinburgh University Press, 2002).

Hart, Francis Russell, *The Scottish Novel: A Critical Survey* (London: John Murray, 1978).

Lindsay, Maurice, *History of Scottish Literature* (London: Robert Hale, 1977).

Murray, Isobel and Tait, *Ten Modern Scottish Novels* (Aberdeen: Aberdeen University Press, 1984).

Murray, Isobel and Tait, *Scottish Novels of the Second World War* (Edinburgh: WP Books, 2011).

Schoene, Berthold, 'A Passage to Scotland: Scottish Literature and the British Postcolonial Condition', *Scotlands* 2.1 (1995), 107–122.

Walker, Marshall, *Scottish Literature Since 1707* (New York: Longman, 1996).

Wallace, Gavin and Randall Stevenson, eds., *The Scottish Novel Since the Seventies* (Edinburgh: Edinburgh University Press, 1994).

Watson, Roderick, *The Literature of Scotland: The Twentieth Century* (Basingstoke: Palgrave MacMillan, 1984, 2007).

Index